BERLIN COQUETTE

signale
modern german letters, cultures, and thought

Series editor: Peter Uwe Hohendahl, Cornell University

Signale: Modern German Letters, Cultures, and Thought publishes new English-language books in literary studies, criticism, cultural studies, and intellectual history pertaining to the German-speaking world, as well as translations of important German-language works. *Signale* construes "modern" in the broadest terms: the series covers topics ranging from the early modern period to the present. *Signale* books are published under a joint imprint of Cornell University Press and Cornell University Library in electronic and print formats. Please see http://signale.cornell.edu/.

BERLIN COQUETTE

Prostitution and the New German Woman, 1890–1933

JILL SUZANNE SMITH

A Signale Book

CORNELL UNIVERSITY PRESS AND CORNELL UNIVERSITY LIBRARY
ITHACA, NEW YORK

Cornell University Press and Cornell University Library gratefully acknowledge
The Andrew W. Mellon Foundation and the College of Arts & Sciences, Cornell
University, for support of the Signale series.

First published 2013 by Cornell University Press and Cornell University Library

Printed in the United States of America

Library of Congress Cataloging-in-Publication Data

Smith, Jill Suzanne, 1972– author.
    Berlin coquette : prostitution and the new German woman, 1890/1933 / Jill
Suzanne Smith.
        pages cm. — (Signale : modern German letters, cultures, and thought)
    Includes bibliographical references and index.
    ISBN 978-0-8014-5267-3 (cloth : alk. paper) — ISBN 978-0-8014-7834-5
(pbk. : alk. paper)
    1. Prostitution—Germany—Berlin—History—19th century.
2. Prostitution—Germany—Berlin—History—20th century. I. Title.
    HQ200.B4S65   2013
    306.74094309'034—dc23   2013036665

Cornell University Press strives to use environmentally responsible suppliers
and materials to the fullest extent possible in the publishing of its books. Such
materials include vegetable-based, low-VOC inks and acid-free papers that are
recycled, totally chlorine-free, or partly composed of nonwood fibers. For further
information, visit our website at www.cornellpress.cornell.edu.

Cloth printing   10 9 8 7 6 5 4 3 2 1
Paperback printing   10 9 8 7 6 5 4 3 2 1

For Fabian, my favorite Berliner

Contents

Illustrations

ACKNOWLEDGMENTS

It is my great fortune to have an exceptional network of colleagues, mentors, friends, and family members who supported this project over the years. The research and writing of this book was made possible through the generous support of a Bowdoin College Faculty Research Fellowship and Fulbright Junior Research Grant, both of which allowed me to spend the 2009–10 academic year in Berlin, the city that continues to inspire me as a teacher and a scholar. I thank the librarians and archivists at the Bundesarchiv-Filmarchiv, the Geheimes Staatsarchiv and the Staatsbibliothek zu Berlin Preussischer Kulturbesitz, the Landesarchiv Berlin, and the Stiftung Deutsche Kinemathek for granting me access to their rich collections and answering my inquiries with patience and generosity. Cornelia Pastelak-Price of the Jeanne-Mammen-Stiftung and Rainer Herrn of the Magnus-Hirschfeld-Gesellschaft have my gratitude for their sincere interest in my work; they have become trusted friends and colleagues. The Humboldt University's Center for Transdisciplinary Gender Studies (ZtG) was my host institution while in Berlin, and its managing director at the time, Christina von Braun, made me feel most welcome.

I am lucky to be a part of the dynamic and collegial Department of German at Bowdoin College. The sound advice, encouragement, and feedback I received from Helen Cafferty, Steve Cerf, and Birgit Tautz were invaluable to this project. Colleagues and friends from the broader Bowdoin community also read and commented on various portions of the manuscript, fellowship applications, or publishing materials, and I am especially grateful to Barbara Weiden Boyd, Aviva Briefel, Meggan Gould, Mark Foster, Aaron Kitch, Matt Klingle, Steve Perkinson, Arielle Saiber, and Marilyn Reizbaum. My former students Sally Hudson, Julia Littlefield, and Rebecca Silva asked probing questions about Weimar Berlin that helped me to express my own ideas with greater clarity.

Beyond Bowdoin, my colleagues in German studies offered insight and references that were vital to the revision of this book. Special thanks go to Jaimey Fisher, Veronika Fuechtner, Malte Hagener, Hope Harrison, Andrew Hewitt, Jennifer Hosek, Peter Jelavich, Erik Jensen, Barbara Mennel, Christian Rogowski, Julia Roos, Suzanne Royal, Don White, and Bethany Wiggin. The 2005 DAAD Summer Seminar at Cornell University, expertly directed by Leslie Adelson, provided me with an important opportunity to share my work with a group of wonderful scholars. Now that the book has found a home at Cornell University Press, I thank Peter Uwe Hohendahl, Kizer Walker, Marian Rogers, the *Signale* editorial board, and my anonymous readers for helping me to make this a better book and for seeing the manuscript through the publication process. Above all, I thank my mentors, Fritz Breithaupt and Katrin Sieg, whose unflagging confidence in me and in my work remains a great source of motivation, and whose own work enriches and enlivens the field of German studies.

My friends and family were tireless cheerleaders, and their love and support kept me going. I warmly thank my sister Ellen and her family, as well as my German in-laws Chris, Sebastian, Jürgen, and Carola. Dear friends Janet Lassan and Johannes Elwardt, Elliott Schreiber, and Mihaela Petrescu never failed to boost my spirits, and my best friend, Carol Newell, came through in a pinch as a perceptive, critical reader. My parents taught me the importance of hard work and dedication, balanced with creativity and curiosity. They also believed in the value of asking questions for which there is no clear-cut answer. My father, Lowell, did not live to see this book in print, but his memory sustained me through the entire process, as did the love and encouragement of my mother, Judy. No one supported me more than my husband, Fabian Rueger, who read every word of every version of this manuscript with his skillful historian's eye, endured my moods, cheered me on, and made me laugh when I needed it most. I dedicate this book to him, with love and gratitude.

An earlier version of chapter 4, "Working Girls: White-Collar Workers and Prostitutes in Late Weimar Fiction," appeared in *German Quarterly* 81, no. 4 (Fall 2008): 449–70. Material from chapter 3 was published in two separate essays: "Richard Oswald and the Social Hygiene Film: Promoting Public Health or Promiscuity?," in *The Many Faces of Weimar Cinema*, ed. Christian Rogowski (Rochester, NY: Camden House, 2010), 13–30; and "Just How Naughty *Was* Berlin? The Geography of Prostitution and Female Sexuality in Curt Moreck's Erotic Travel Guide," in *Spatial Turns: Space, Place, and Mobility in German Literary and Visual Culture*, ed. Barbara Mennel and Jaimey Fisher (Amsterdam: Rodopi, 2010), 53–77. Finally, portions of the introduction and chapter 3 were published in my essay "Prostitutes in Weimar Berlin: Moving beyond the Victim-Whore Dichotomy," in *Beyond Glitter and Doom: The Contingency of the Weimar Republic*, ed. Godela Weiss-Sussex, Jochen Hung, and Geoff Wilkes (Munich: Iudicium, 2012), 135–47. I am grateful to the respective presses for their permission to reprint this material.

Berlin Coquette

INTRODUCTION: BERLIN'S BOURGEOIS WHORES

In the winter of 1988, the women of Hydra organized a "Whores' Ball" (*Hurenball*) in West Berlin. Hydra, a support organization founded in 1980 by prostitutes and their advocates, actively lobbies for sex workers' civil rights and the elimination of the social and moral stigma attached to prostitution. The 1988 ball raised funds for Hydra's social initiatives, including extensive outreach to economically disadvantaged prostitutes and heightened awareness of HIV/AIDS, but it also celebrated nearly a decade of the organization's advocacy work in Berlin. Hydra's organizing team envisioned "an intoxicating nighttime ball" in Berlin's International Conference Center, featuring performances by the transvestite diva Georgette Dee and other renowned musical acts. Their twin goals of charity fundraising and lavish celebration resulted in a high ticket price for the event, and one of Berlin's left-liberal daily newspapers, the *tageszeitung* (*taz*), complained that the cost of admission to the ball automatically excluded the majority of "poor whores" from attending. Despite their misgivings, a slew of Berlin journalists attended the ball, among them some from the *taz*. In their report on the ball, the *taz* writers expressed their disappointment with the disparity between what they had imagined the ball would be and what they actually observed: "A whores' ball, that sounds like lace panties, like immorality, like sin, like scandal, brothel, and *Irma la Douce*." But the ball they attended was, instead, "a proper event through and through" with "few garter belts, no naked body parts, the majority of men in suits or tuxedos. Not a real whore to be found." The women of Hydra, many of them self-identified "whores," saw the *taz* article as a clear example of how, even in left-liberal circles, dominant clichés of prostitutes persist. If the journalists at the *taz* could not find poor, downtrodden victims at the whores' ball, then they at least expected to see glamorous femmes fatales parading around in risqué lingerie. They wanted to experience Berlin's famed sexual decadence for themselves, and instead they found proper women and articulate, "well-behaved intellectuals," like the former prostitute turned detective novelist Pieke Biermann. In short, they found bourgeois whores. In their written reaction to the article in the *taz,* the women of Hydra, mimicking the shocked tone of the press and adding more than a hint of sarcasm, asked: "What will the world come to, if we can no longer tell who's a whore and who isn't?"[1]

This book is much like the whores' ball, for it presents its readers with images of prostitutes in Berlin that defy common stereotypes of deviance and destitution. It does so, however, by examining debates on prostitution that took place up to a century before the women of Hydra organized their first ball. During the post-Bismarckian *Kaiserreich* (1890–1918) and the Weimar Republic (1918–33), prostitution became a central vehicle through which social activists, artists, and cultural critics negotiated gender and labor divisions in the modern metropolis. The diverse range of responses to prostitution that emerged from Wilhelmine and Weimar Berlin led to productive discussions about extramarital sexuality, women's financial autonomy, and respectability. Some artists and writers who lived and worked in the German capital at the time were able to see beyond dichotomized images of prostitutes and envision them as something other than victims or villains. Granted, some of Berlin's most iconic cultural texts serve up visions of female monstrosity and victimization that are impossible to erase from our index of images of prostitutes in the German capital; Alfred Döblin's modernist masterpiece *Berlin Alexanderplatz* (1929) and George Grosz's scathing visual portraits of metropolitan decadence and sexual murder spring immediately to mind. Without ignoring these images, this book shows that the ideas of prostitutes as rational workers and as elegant bourgeois "cocottes" (*Kokotten*) also surfaced and took hold during this period and give us a far more complex, differentiated picture of gender and sexuality in modern Berlin. My work disrupts the dichotomized reading of prostitutes as either victims or agents of destruction reproduced in existing scholarship, which, much like the *taz*'s article about the Whores' Ball, perpetuates stereotypes of prostitutes and produces narratives laden with judgments that do an injustice to the very context they

---

1. The episode of the whores' ball is described and documented by the Prostituierten-Projekt Hydra (Prostitute Project Hydra) in *Beruf: Hure* [Occupation: Whore] (Hamburg: Galgenberg, 1988), 180–83. All translations from the German, unless otherwise stated, are mine. The *taz* article references the 1963 film *Irma la Douce,* a romantic comedy about a policeman who falls in love with a Parisian prostitute. Billy Wilder directed and Shirley MacLaine and Jack Lemmon starred in the film.

are describing. Analyses that view prostitution only through the restrictive, dual lens of destitution and sexual deviance lead to less nuanced readings of primary sources and hence to a larger-scale misreading of the intricacies of gender relations, sexuality, and desire in the specific urban context of Berlin and their representation in imaginative texts.

There is no doubt that prostitutes are paradoxical figures, for they can represent both the affirmation and the subversion of social structures. An institution that promotes sexual relations without emotional attachment, prostitution detaches love from sex. As public women who sell their bodies in a market dominated by male buyers, prostitutes seem to reinforce patriarchal capitalism, yet they can also be seen as exploited workers and potential revolutionaries. It is perhaps no surprise that Berlin, as one of the quintessential modern cities in early twentieth-century Europe, inspired incredibly rich discourses on prostitution—discourses that reflected the paradox inherent in prostitution but also discourses that transcended the usual clichés about prostitutes. Whereas certain authors treat prostitution as a symptom of a corrupt bourgeois economic order and exploitative gender relations, others use the discussion of prostitution to explore visions of alternative moralities or sexual countercultures, such as the free-love relationship, the "New Morality" articulated by feminist radicals, lesbian love, or various incarnations of the "New Woman." Identifying cliché-defying figures such as the plucky working-class prostitute or the fashionable *Kokotte,* however, raises the same question posed—albeit tongue in cheek—by the women of Hydra: What happens when we can no longer distinguish between prostitutes and nonprostitutes? This is an issue raised repeatedly by the cultural texts and social phenomena I explore here. Without question, the proliferation of discourses on prostitution between 1890 and 1933 was inextricably linked to both the controversy surrounding, and the gradual acceptance of, the growing number of single working women living in Berlin. Most of the texts I examine blur the boundaries between prostitutes and other women in a way that challenges readers to interrogate existing structures of female sexuality, work, morality, and desire.

Berlin, Berlin

Around the turn of the century and certainly during the Weimar years, the city of Berlin had a reputation for lawlessness and sexual licentiousness. Readers of this book will likely be familiar with the oft-cited depiction of Berlin as the "Whore of Babylon," which gained cultural currency during this time and has proven its staying power. The aim of this book, however, is to call this seemingly neat analogy between the feminized and debauched German capital and a biblical whore into question and to explore instead the myriad meanings attributed to prostitutes and prostitution in the social debates and cultural texts of this specific time and place. As Judith R. Walkowitz has shown in her work on prostitution, female sexuality, and moral panic in late Victorian London, cities in upheaval are, all too often, portrayed simply as sites of sexual danger and despair. In *City of Dreadful Delight*, Walkowitz "maps out a dense cultural grid" of "conflicting and overlapping representations of sexual danger" in London at the height of the panic surrounding the Whitechapel murders, and in the process, she uncovers "contiguous stories of sexual possibility and urban adventure" created by a new and "different set of social actors."[2] Drawing inspiration from Walkowitz's scholarship on London, I argue that similar dynamics of social tumult and possibility were at work in Berlin at the close of the nineteenth century—complex dynamics that are obscured by the apocalyptic image of Berlin as the "Whore of Babylon." In order to challenge this particularly tenacious depiction of Berlin, it is important to consider what socioeconomic, political, demographic, and cultural factors combined to make Berlin a unique focal point of the modern urban discourse on prostitution within Germany.

Named as the capital of the unified German nation in 1871, Berlin made a rapid transition from Prussian backwater to major industrial and cultural center. Between 1871 and 1905 Berlin's population surged from 826,000 to over two million people in the city proper, making it the largest city in Germany and the fourth largest in Europe.[3] Its new status as a "world city" (*Weltstadt*) was based primarily on the industrial strength and technological innovation of companies like Borsig, Siemens, AEG, and AGFA. Large-scale factories employed many of the new immigrants from the eastern provinces of Pomerania and Silesia, who lived in overcrowded tenements in Berlin's northern and eastern districts and who, because of rising disillusionment about their work and housing conditions, became a radicalized and politicized urban proletariat. Although their public political activity was significantly hampered by the antisocialist legislation pushed through the German parliament by Otto von Bismarck in 1878, the repeal of the law in 1890 saw them emerge with increased numbers and electoral support. In so-called Red Berlin, the workers' protests found a sympathetic ear among the educated urban bourgeoisie, some of whom held prestigious academic positions at the Friedrich-Wilhelm University (today the Humboldt University), while others produced naturalist plays and novels that exposed the travails of the urban poor. As a site of sociopolitical organization and agitation, Berlin became the center of the "reform milieu," consisting of men and women who cast a critical eye on the modern present and sought alternatives that they hoped would subsume modernity's

---

2. Judith R. Walkowitz, *City of Dreadful Delight: Narratives of Sexual Danger in Late-Victorian London* (Chicago: University of Chicago Press, 1992), 5, 18.

3. The population statistics given do not count the suburbs that would become part of "Groß-Berlin" in 1920. With those suburbs included, the population of greater Berlin in 1905 was nearly three million. See David Clay Large, *Berlin* (New York: Basic Books, 2000), 9, 48; Andrew Lees, *Cities, Sin, and Social Reform in Imperial Germany* (Ann Arbor: University of Michigan Press, 2002), 2; see also Peter Jelavich, *Berlin Cabaret* (Cambridge, MA: Harvard University Press, 1993), 12.

oppressive elements—capitalist exploitation, socioeconomic inequality, increasing alienation—under its emancipatory ones.[4]

In addition to being a city of immigrants and workers, Berlin was also a "city of women." Lured by the possibility of greater financial and social autonomy, single women flocked to the capital by the thousands. Those from more humble backgrounds generally found work in the textile industry or domestic service, while bourgeois women pursued careers as teachers, social workers, and journalists. Women from a variety of class backgrounds took positions in Berlin's burgeoning service industry, working as clerks in shops and offices throughout the city. In many cases, work brought with it increased mobility and a sense of financial independence that allowed women to take advantage of metropolitan consumer culture and mass entertainment. Berlin-based women writers became some of the bestselling authors of their time, female architects planned and built housing and training facilities for single working women, and female artists gained access to Berlin's renowned Academy of Arts. Across the socioeconomic spectrum, however, women workers received less professional training, fewer opportunities for advancement, and significantly lower pay than their male counterparts.[5] Distressed by these inequities, women banded together and rallied support for increased educational and occupational opportunities, making Berlin the seat of the German women's movement and its diverse factions. Tied as it was to concerns about both women's labor and sexual morality, prostitution became a point of heated controversy within the early feminist movement.

Indeed it is no exaggeration to state that prostitution was one of the most discussed issues in late nineteenth- and early twentieth-century Germany. Despite the adage that defines prostitution as the "world's oldest profession," the rapid industrialization, the rise of modern capitalism, and the severing of traditional kinship ties that accompanied the growth of urban centers in western Europe and the United States during the nineteenth century resulted in a particularly modern

---

4. On the urban reform milieu, see Lees, *Cities, Sin, and Social Reform;* and Kevin Repp, *Reformers, Critics, and the Paths of German Modernity: Anti-Politics and the Search for Alternatives, 1890–1914* (Cambridge, MA: Harvard University Press, 2000). For a discussion of working-class influence on the urban progressivism of the bourgeoisie, see David Blackbourn and Geoff Eley, eds., *The Peculiarities of German History: Bourgeois Society and Politics in Nineteenth-Century Germany* (Oxford: Oxford University Press, 1984), especially 15–19, 148–49. On Berlin as a "red city," see Large, *Berlin,* 40–45, 99–107; and Alexandra Richie, *Faust's Metropolis: A History of Berlin* (New York: Carroll & Graf, 1998), 153–87.

5. This sketch of women in imperial Berlin is drawn from a myriad of sources, including Carol Elizabeth Adams, *Women Clerks in Wilhelmine Germany* (Cambridge: Cambridge University Press, 1988); Ute Frevert, *Women in German History: From Bourgeois Emancipation to Sexual Liberation,* trans. Stuart McKinnon-Evans (Oxford: Berg, 1989); Stephanie Günther, *Weiblichkeitsentwürfe des Fin de Siècle* (Bonn: Bouvier, 2007); Despina Stratigakos, *A Women's Berlin: Building the Modern City* (Minneapolis: University of Minnesota Press, 2008). The label "city of women" is still used today by broad-based organizations such as the Überparteiliche Fraueninitiative (Multi-partisan Women's Initiative; ÜPFI) to portray Berlin's vibrant and diverse feminist culture.

form of "large-scale, commercialized prostitution."[6] As Germany's largest metropolitan center, Berlin experienced the shift to modern prostitution most acutely, and by the close of the nineteenth century, the number of prostitutes working in the capital was estimated to be between 20,000 and 50,000.[7] The lack of precision in these statistics betrays the difficulty that Berlin authorities had enforcing the system of regulation officially instituted by the German state in 1871, a system that had been in effect in most cities and territories decades before unification but was implemented differently by each locality. Clause 361/6 of the Imperial Criminal Code provided the legal basis for regulationism and stated: "Any woman shall be punished with imprisonment who, having been placed under police control on account of professional prostitution, violates regulations adopted by the police for the protection of health, order, and decency, or any woman who engages in prostitution for pay without having been placed under such control."[8]

Clause 361/6 criminalized only those women who engaged in prostitution without being registered with a branch of the local police known as the *Sittenpolizei* (morals police or vice squad). Once registered, they were subject to regular compulsory medical exams, and their domiciles, clothing, and public actions were placed under surveillance by the vice squad. The regulation system, however, could not successfully prevent clandestine or "occasional prostitution" (*Gelegenheitsprostitution*), and each city took its own approach to the enforcement of regulations, with Berlin being notoriously lax. In her recent study of German prostitution regulation and its reform during the Weimar years, Julia Roos emphasizes the vast differences

---

6. Elizabeth Bernstein, *Temporarily Yours: Intimacy, Authenticity, and the Commerce of Sex* (Chicago: University of Chicago Press, 2007), 23. See also Timothy J. Gilfoyle, "Prostitutes in History: From Parables of Pornography to Metaphors of Modernity," *American Historical Review* 104 (February 1999): 119; Victoria Harris, *Selling Sex in the Reich: Prostitutes in German Society, 1914–1945* (Oxford: Oxford University Press, 2010), 9–11.

7. See Richard J. Evans, *Tales from the German Underworld* (New Haven, CT: Yale University Press, 1998), 198; Abraham Flexner, *Prostitution in Europe* (New York: Century, 1914), 143; Robert Hessen, *Die Prostitution in Deutschland* (Munich: Albert Langen, 1910), 27.

8. On Clause 361/6 see Flexner, *Prostitution in Europe*, 113. See also Julia Bruggemann, "Prostitution, Sexuality, and Gender Roles in Imperial Germany: Hamburg, A Case Study," in *Genealogies of Identity: Interdisciplinary Readings on Sex and Sexuality*, ed. Margaret Sönser Breen and Fiona Peters (Amsterdam: Rodopi, 2005), 22–23; Harris, *Selling Sex in the Reich*, 10; and Julia Roos, *Weimar through the Lens of Gender: Prostitution Reform, Women's Emancipation, and German Democracy, 1919–33* (Ann Arbor: University of Michigan Press, 2010), 22. I use Roos's translation of the law.

Prostitution during this period was defined exclusively as female prostitution; male prostitution was criminalized under §175 of the penal code, which declared male homosexuality to be an illegal act. Male prostitutes do not fit within the scope of my book, for the discourses of gender, sexuality, and criminality that apply to them are decidedly different from those involving female prostitutes, especially during the periods in history that I analyze. For recent work on male prostitution and its tenuous relationship with male homosexuality, see Martin Lücke, "Beschmutzte Utopien: Subkulturelle Räume, begehrte Körper und sexuelle Identitäten in belletristischen Texten über männliche Prostitution 1900–1933," in *Verhandlungen im Zwielicht: Momente der Prostitution in Geschichte und Gegenwart*, ed. Sabine Grenz and Martin Lücke (Bielefeld: Transcript, 2006), 301–18; and David James Prickett, "Defining Identity via Homosexual Spaces: Locating the Male Homosexual in Weimar Berlin," *Women in German Yearbook* 21 (2005): 134–61. For a perspective that compares the regulation of male prostitution in post–World War II Berlin with that in the Weimar years, see Jennifer Evans, "Bahnhof Boys: Policing Male Prostitution in Post-Nazi Berlin," *Journal of the History of Sexuality* 12 (October 2003): 605–36.

in local policies regarding prostitution and notes the degree of autonomy that Berlin authorities granted prostitutes. Unlike Hamburg, which established an extensive network of police-monitored brothels and sought to isolate prostitution within specific streets and districts, Berlin allowed prostitutes to choose where to live and ply their trade. In spite of efforts by the municipal authorities to designate urban spaces that were legally off-limits to prostitutes, including schools, zoos, museums, churches, theaters, and sixty-three of Berlin's streets and squares, the majority of prostitutes circulated freely, turning supposedly restricted areas such as the Tiergarten, Potsdamer Platz, and Friedrichstrasse into some of the best-known areas of sex commerce in the city. At the beginning of the twentieth century, and most markedly in the 1920s, commercial entertainment venues such as vaudeville or variety theaters, dance halls, and *Nachtcafés* (night cafés) provided both career and occasional prostitutes with alternatives to the *Pension* (a type of brothel) or street, making it even more difficult for the vice squad to determine which female patrons of such venues were prostitutes and which were not. This constant evasion revealed just how untenable regulation was, and critics of the system repeatedly claimed that only about 10 percent of all prostitutes working in the city were actually registered. Roos's archival research, which documents 3,500 prostitutes registered in Berlin on the eve of the First World War, supports the claims of inefficacy leveled against the regulatory system by social reformers of the time.[9]

The city's critics—many of them non-Berliners—saw the pervasive presence of prostitutes on the streets and in the nighttime hot spots of Berlin as a clear sign of urban alienation and decline. In their eyes, modern Berlin became the mythical "Whore of Babylon," a harbinger of impending doom whose erotic allure could only be read as destructive. As modernist art historians Hanne Bergius and Dorothy Rowe and literary scholars such as Isabelle Siemes and Nicola Behrmann have argued, the prostitute became a visual and poetic allegory for Berlin itself, used by artists and writers to express their discontent with metropolitan modernity.[10] This urban discontent is often described in strictly gendered terms. "In the works

---

9. Roos, *Weimar through the Lens of Gender,* 16–17, 63; statistics on the number of regulated prostitutes in Berlin appear on p. 17. On the case of Hamburg, see Bruggemann, "Prostitution, Sexuality, and Gender Roles"; and Harris, *Selling Sex in the Reich,* 30–34, 98–101. For the regulations placed on registered prostitutes in Berlin, see *Polizeiliche Vorschriften zur Sicherung der Gesundheit, der öffentlichen Ordnung und des öffentlichen Anstandes* (1913), Landesarchiv Berlin (LAB), HLA, B. Rep. 235–13 (Nachlaß Anna Pappritz). The same regulations are reprinted in Flexner, *Prostitution in Europe,* 415–18. On the small percentage of registered prostitutes, see, for example, Anna Pappritz, ed., *Einführung in das Studium der Prostitutionsfrage* (Leipzig: Johann Ambrosius Barth, 1919), 144–45.

10. Hanne Bergius, "Berlin als Hure Babylon," in *Die Metropole: Industriekultur in Berlin im 20. Jahrhundert,* ed. Jochen Boberg, Tilman Fichter, and Eckhart Gillen (Berlin: Beck, 1986), 102–19; Dorothy Rowe, *Representing Berlin: Sexuality and the City in Imperial and Weimar Germany* (Aldershot, UK: Ashgate, 2003); Nicola Behrmann, "Sucht: Abgründiger Körper; Die Prostituierte als Medium der literarischen Moderne," in Grenz and Lücke, *Verhandlungen im Zwielicht,* 223–35; Isabelle Siemes, *Die Prostituierte in der literarischen Moderne 1890–1933* (Düsseldorf: Hagemann, 2000), 285–93, 302–3. See also Beth Irwin Lewis, "*Lustmord:* Inside the Windows of the Metropolis," in *Women in the Metropolis,* ed. Katharina von Ankum (Berkeley: University of California Press, 1997), 202–32; and Maria Tatar, *Lustmord: Sexual Murder in Weimar Germany* (Princeton, NJ: Princeton University Press, 1995).

of male modernists," the art historian Marsha Meskimmon claims, "images and descriptions of prostitutes...signified the fears and desires of the male subject faced with the commodification, urbanization and alienation of modernity."[11] An aspect of modernity most often maligned through the artistic employment of the prostitute, scholars like Bergius, Meskimmon, and Rowe contend, was the rise of the "New Woman." Practical, career-oriented and in no great rush to get married, the New Woman was blamed by progressive sex reformers and conservative nationalists alike for the breakdown of the family and the moral weakening of the German state. In the wake of the First World War, emancipated women appeared in public in even greater numbers, and their behavior and appearance caused a good deal of confusion. As Atina Grossmann describes the New Woman, she "bobbed her hair, smoked in public, shaved her legs, used makeup, indeed, presented herself in such a manner that it sometimes became difficult to distinguish the 'honest women' from the 'whores.'"[12] Such confusion was particularly acute in the urban environment of Berlin, where women on their way to or from work walked the city streets unescorted, and where they also took advantage of metropolitan nightlife, frequenting spaces that were acknowledged markets for clandestine prostitution. Bergius, Meskimmon, and Rowe, among others, read texts or works of art that depict this confusion between "honest women" and "whores" as a deliberate conflation carried out to misogynist ends by men who fear and revile women's emancipation. But such a reading, while convincing in some cases, relies on both a simplified interpretation of the prostitute as "a sexually voracious and devouring female," to cite a common phrase from Rowe's book, and a dichotomized view of gender.[13] It assumes that if men draw, paint, or write about prostitutes, they automatically do so with chauvinistic motives—with the intention of portraying female sexual deviance. By failing to closely examine how, by whom, and to what end images of prostitutes are conflated with those of other women, such an analysis ignores the richness of social and cultural discourses on prostitution and new womanhood produced in Berlin between 1890 and 1933.

Urban Street Scenes and the Rise of the Cocotte

The realm of visual arts offers a stunning array of portraits of prostitutes walking the streets of turn-of-the-century and Weimar Berlin, and yet the attention of art scholars and museum curators tends to focus on the works of only a handful of male artists, most notably on the expressionist artists of the Brücke and on Otto Dix

---

11. Marsha Meskimmon, *We Weren't Modern Enough: Woman Artists and the Limits of German Modernism* (Berkeley: University of California Press, 1999), 27.

12. Atina Grossmann, "The New Woman and the Rationalization of Sexuality in Weimar Germany," in *Powers of Desire: The Politics of Sexuality,* ed. Ann Snitow, Christine Stansell, and Sharon Thompson (New York: Monthly Review Press, 1983), 156.

13. Rowe, *Representing Berlin,* 91.

and George Grosz. Until recently, the works of woman artists like Jeanne Mammen and of popular artists such as Heinrich Zille have been given short shrift, especially outside of Berlin, despite the fact that, at the time of their creation, these artists' works were widely distributed and viewed by their contemporaries.[14] In contrast to artists like Dix and Grosz, who created haunting and even horrifying portraits of prostitutes, displaying them as victims of grinding poverty or as diseased deviants, Mammen and Zille produced images of prostitutes that captured the rebellious and irreverent spirit of the capital city.

Heinrich Zille, Berlin's "one-of-a-kind chronicler" of the urban working-class *Milljöh* (Berlin dialect for "milieu"), drew a plump and defiant prostitute raising her fist in the air and struggling to wrestle free from the clutches of two Prussian vice squad officers for the cover of his 1908 collection *Kinder der Strasse: 100 Berliner Bilder* (Children of the Street: 100 Berlin Pictures).[15] Accompanied by cynically witty captions written in Berlin dialect, Zille's drawings were widely published in the satirical periodicals *Simplicissimus, Ulk,* and the *Lustige Blätter* and made him one of the most adored and admired artists of his time. In 1925, just one year after Zille's induction into the Prussian Academy of Arts, the satirist Kurt Tucholsky wrote of him: "Zille's soul is Berlin through and through: soft, sharp tongued, possibly with warm feet, and: everything's only half as bad as it seems.... Zille is amoral to the core. He doesn't judge, he draws. He doesn't condemn, he feels."[16] This nonjudgmental perspective is evident in Zille's 1902 rendition of *Zwei Strassenmädchen* (Two Girls of the Street), which shows a pair of corpulent prostitutes strutting confidently along the city street. One of them reminisces about how she "used to run around with high-ranking politicians and barristers" (fig. 1). By portraying its subjects as mature women rather than "girls" and by dressing them in the humble clothing of the working class—not quite fitting the company of lawyers and

14. Museum culture in the United States is particularly fixated on the works of Dix, Grosz, and the artists of the Brücke. Consider the exhibitions that have been organized in New York City alone within recent years: *Glitter and Doom: German Portraits from the 1920s* (Metropolitan Museum of Art, 2006), which featured works by Otto Dix, George Grosz, and Christian Schad most prominently; *Kirchner and the Berlin Streets* (Museum of Modern Art, 2008); *Brücke: The Birth of Expressionism in Dresden and Berlin, 1905–1913* (Neue Galerie for German and Austrian Art, 2009); the Otto Dix retrospective (Neue Galerie, 2010); and *German Expressionism: The Graphic Impulse* (Museum of Modern Art, 2011), which is rife with images of prostitutes. To my knowledge, the only work by an art historian that analyzes representations of prostitutes by Mammen and Zille alongside those of Dix and Grosz is Rita Täuber, *Der häßliche Eros: Darstellungen zur Prostitution in der Malerei und Grafik 1855–1930* (Berlin: Mann, 1997). Meskimmon's study of women modernist artists and their depictions of prostitutes is also a valuable contribution to the field; see Meskimmon, *We Weren't Modern Enough,* 22–72. For a more extensive discussion of visual culture in Weimar Berlin and the works of Jeanne Mammen in particular, see chapter 3.

15. Heinrich Zille, *Kinder der Strasse: 100 Berliner Bilder* (1908; repr., Hannover: Fackelträger-Verlag, 1997). The quote is from Matthias Flügge, *H. Zille, Berliner Leben: Zeichnungen, Photographien und Druckgraphiken 1890–1914* (Berlin: Akademie der Künste; Munich: Schirmer/Mosel, 2008), 1.

16. Kurt Tucholsky [Peter Panther], "Berlins Bester," in *Gesamtausgabe,* ed. Antje Bonitz, Dirk Grathoff, Michael Hepp, and Gerhard Kraiker, vol. 7, *Texte 1925,* ed. Bärbel Boldt and Andrea Spingler (Reinbek bei Hamburg: Rowohlt, 2002), 42–43.

Figure 1. Heinrich Zille, *Zwei Strassenmädchen* (Two Girls of the Street), 1902. Courtesy of Staatliche Kunsthalle Karlsruhe Kupferstichkabinett.

politicians—Zille's etching creates the type of tension between image and written text that provokes a chuckle without a trace of ridicule. What Zille and his work exemplified for Tucholsky and for most of his admirers was the Berlin personality: a curious mixture of rebellion and compassion, of biting wit (the legendary Berliner

Schnauze) and gumption. The artist's matter-of-factness, coupled with skepticism of authority and traditional morals, allowed him to portray the urban street milieu without making prostitutes into poor, helpless victims or dangerous scoundrels.[17]

Although Zille was best known for his vibrant depictions of Berlin's working class, he captured the gamut of urban characters in his drawings and photographs, among them the fashionable cocottes that graced the busy promenades of the city center (fig. 2). The women's feather-plumed hats, elaborate fur-lined collars, and the cinched-in waists of their dresses—meant to accentuate their curves—offer visual clues about the meaning of *cocotte*. The term is derived from the French colloquial diminutive "little hen" and shares its root, *coq*, with the word *coquette* (literally, "little she-cock"), which was used already in seventeenth-century France to conjure images of pride, vanity, and lust but was not yet used as an explicit reference to prostitutes. Originally a term of endearment for children, *cocotte* became a word for "prostitute" only in the late 1860s, when it was used to identify the elegant prostitutes who strutted the streets of French cities. By blending the outward appearance and mannerisms of "respectable" womanhood with implicit sexual availability for a price, cocottes marketed themselves to a discerning bourgeois clientele eager to purchase "the illusion of seduction."[18] The verbal play of *coquette* and *cocotte* is evident in the images of urban cocottes, images that blurred the lines between flirtatious, fashionable women and women for hire.

Particularly in Paris, cocottes were thought to be so ubiquitous that they became key tropes of late nineteenth-century urban modernity. In his book on artistic representations of Parisian social life and sexual mores in the works of French impressionists, T. J. Clark claims: "Modernity *was* made of dandies and *cocottes*, especially the latter."[19] As Alain Corbin documents in his analysis of prostitution in France, the bourgeois demand for prostitutes increased significantly between the latter half of the nineteenth century and the First World War. Corbin attributes this increased demand to several factors, the first being the state of bourgeois marriage and its built-in sexual "double standard." The double standard granted bourgeois men sexual license while it perpetuated a "cult of purity" for bourgeois women that made them sexually inaccessible before marriage and accessible primarily for reproductive purposes thereafter. Bourgeois men, who were marrying later in life in order to ensure financial security before marriage, were encouraged to seek satisfaction of their sexual desires elsewhere, ostensibly with prostitutes.

---

17. On the distinctive Berlin character, see Jelavich, *Berlin Cabaret,* 30–33; Large, *Berlin,* xxvii; Richie, *Faust's Metropolis,* 157, 184–85.

18. T. J. Clark, *The Painting of Modern Life: Paris in the Art of Manet and His Followers,* rev. ed. (Princeton, NJ: Princeton University Press, 1999), 107.

19. Clark, *The Painting of Modern Life,* 103, emphasis in original. For another analysis of prostitution in French impressionist paintings that pays close attention to changing social and sexual relations in late nineteenth-century Paris, albeit through the theoretical lens of psychoanalysis, see Charles Bernheimer, *Figures of Ill Repute: Representing Prostitution in Nineteenth-Century France* (Cambridge, MA: Harvard University Press, 1989), 89–128, 157–99.

Figure 2. Heinrich Zille, *Zwei Kokotten* (Two Cocottes), n.d. Reprinted from Matthias Flügge, *H. Zille, Berliner Leben: Zeichnungen, Photographien und Druckgraphiken 1890–1914* (Berlin: Akademie der Künste; Munich: Schirmer/Mosel, 2008).

Out of the perceived importance of men's work within bourgeois culture came the need for "more conspicuous forms of consumption" and the growing impetus for bourgeois men to purchase luxury wares with their earnings, even if those wares were women.[20]

Social and sexual dynamics comparable to those described by Clark and Corbin in reference to Paris were at work in late nineteenth- and early twentieth-century Berlin, and the elegant cocottes allowed their clients to maintain the facade of respectability while satisfying their physical desires. The urban chronicler Hans Ostwald, who made a lucrative writing career out of revealing every detail of Berlin's varied prostitution markets to his readers, stated that "the rise of the bourgeoisie gave birth to a commensurate form of prostitution," namely, one that would fulfill "the needs of a refined and bored, unsatisfied class."[21] A delicate balance was being struck in urban bourgeois culture between the urge for sexual adventure and the need to remain respectable, and this tenuous balance between titillation and restraint revealed a concomitant eroticization of the bourgeoisie and an "embourgeoisement" of prostitutes that was embodied by the figure of the cocotte. It is, therefore, not surprising that the French term *cocotte* was imported into German parlance around the turn of the century. Although the term *Kokette* was used already in eighteenth-century German literature to refer to a prostitute-like or "loose" and lustful woman, *Kokotte* was a virtually unused term in nineteenth-century Germany. However, the word *Kokotte*—and with it, the particular image of commodified sexuality it conjured—quite literally exploded onto the cultural scene in the first three decades of the twentieth century, particularly in the popular

---

20. Alain Corbin, *Women for Hire: Prostitution and Sexuality in France after 1850,* trans. Alan Sheridan (Cambridge, MA: Harvard University Press, 1990), 193–206. Timothy J. Gilfoyle makes a similar argument about the culture of bourgeois "sporting men" and the growing market for elegant prostitutes in nineteenth-century Manhattan in his book *City of Eros: New York City, Prostitution, and the Commercialization of Sex, 1790–1920* (New York: W. W. Norton, 1992), 92–116, 157.

21. Hans Ostwald, *Das Berliner Dirnentum* (Leipzig: Fiedler, 1905–7), 2:73. Ostwald (1873–1940) is to Berlin's print culture what Zille is to the visual realm. His first book, the autobiographical novel *Vagabunden* (1900; repr., Frankfurt am Main: Campus, 1980), established him as one of the first German writers to document sympathetically the lives of vagabonds, beggars, and prostitutes. His multivolume studies of prostitution, the sexual underworld, and the demimonde (*Halbwelt*) in Berlin include the *Großstadt-Dokumente* (Berlin: Seeman, 1904–8), which he edited and partially authored; *Das Berliner Dirnentum*; and several versions of his *Kultur- und Sittengeschichte Berlins* (Berlin: Klemm, 1911, 1924, 1926). These studies tell of hierarchies among prostitutes, of secret terms and nicknames, and describe in great detail the many districts and locales in which readers could experience this world for themselves. Ostwald's books literally map out the world of Berlin prostitution by examining the history and demise of the brothel system, listing the streets and squares traversed by unregistered prostitutes, and providing narrative accounts of men's visits—including his own—to various dance halls and cafés, at which prostitutes were either employed or conspicuously present. Virtually forgotten until the 1990s, Ostwald's works are now enjoying a resurgence of popularity in the scholarly community and beyond, with reprints of his 1926 *Berliner Kultur- und Sittengeschichte* (Paderborn: Voltmedia, 2006) available in Berlin bookstores. See Evans, *Tales from the German Underworld,* 171–93; Peter Fritzsche, "Vagabond in the Fugitive City: Hans Ostwald, Imperial Berlin, and the *Großstadtdokumente*," *Journal of Contemporary History* 29 (1994): 385–402; Rowe, *Representing Berlin,* 90–122; Ralf Thies, *Ethnograph des dunklen Berlins: Hans Ostwald und die Großstadtdokumente 1904–1908* (Cologne: Böhlau, 2006).

print media.[22] Despite the prevalence of *Kokotten* in novels, magazines, and news-papers, as well as in emerging art forms such as cabaret songs, some of which I will document in the pages of this book, scholarly analyses of the cocotte in the modern German context have, until now, focused exclusively on the realm of visual arts. In fact the most heated debate about cocottes in German visual culture has revolved around a small set of iconic images: Ernst Ludwig Kirchner's Berlin street scenes from 1913–14.

This group of Kirchner's paintings, which were praised by Weimar-era art critics for their portrayal of the "modish elegance" and the dynamism of the city street, have in more recent scholarship been erroneously compared to the apocalyp-tic metropolitan visions of Ludwig Meidner, George Grosz, and Otto Dix. Doro-thy Rowe, for example, claims that Kirchner's street scenes "betray the obvious agenda of sexual anxiety so prevalent" in works by Grosz and Dix.[23] Critics like Charles Haxthausen, Ian Buruma, and Suzanne Royal, however, have countered Rowe's view by arguing that neither the paintings nor the primary source material on Kirchner provide evidence of sexual anxiety toward or moral judgment of pros-titutes or women in general. Instead, these art historians view Kirchner's works in the context of Berlin's fashion industry and its entertainment culture, areas of urban life that the artist also studied and depicted while living in the German capi-tal. In so doing, these scholars point to the less overt forms of commodified female sexuality connected to the spheres of fashion and entertainment and direct viewers' attention to the "pervasive erotic ambiguity" of the street scenes and the cocottes at their center.[24]

---

22. According to Jacob and Wilhelm Grimm's *Deutsches Wörterbuch,* (Leipzig: S. Hirzel, 1854–1960), s.vv. "kokett" and "Kokette," a *Kokette* was not just lustful and vain; she could also be inten-tionally deceitful. The definitions of *Kokotte,* its French roots, and statistics on the usage of the word in German come from the *Digitales Wörterbuch der Deutschen Sprache,* a research initiative run by the Berlin-Brandenburgische Akademie der Wissenschaften, http://www.dwds.de. A Google word search for the terms *kokett* and *Kokotte* in German print media also shows a clear spike in usage of these words between 1900 and 1930. For the definition of *embourgeoisement* as a process by which respectability "spread to all classes of the population," see George Mosse, *Nationalism and Sexuality: Respectability and Abnormal Sexuality in Modern Europe* (1985; repr., New York: Fertig, 1997), 182.

23. Curt Glaser, *Die Graphik der Neuzeit: Vom Anfang des XIX. Jahrhunderts bis zur Gegenwart* (Ber-lin, 1923), 540; trans. and quoted in Charles W. Haxthausen, "'A New Beauty': Ernst Ludwig Kirch-ner's Images of Berlin," in *Berlin: Culture and Metropolis,* ed. Charles W. Haxthausen and Heidrun Suhr (Minneapolis: University of Minnesota Press, 1990), 61. Glaser was one of the preeminent art histori-ans and critics of his time. For Rowe's readings of Kirchner's paintings, see *Representing Berlin,* 149–54, here 149.

24. Haxthausen, "A New Beauty," 80. See also Ian Buruma, "Desire in Berlin," review of *Kirchner and the Berlin Street,* by Deborah Wye, *New York Review of Books,* December 4, 2008, 19–20; and Suzanne Royal, "Fashion and Conflict: Kirchner's Representations of the Fashionably Dressed Woman in Ber-lin," in *Fashion and Transgression,* ed. Nancy J. Troy (Los Angeles: USC Fischer Gallery, 2003), 32–37. In her catalog for the recent exhibition of Kirchner's street scenes at the Museum of Modern Art (MoMA) in New York City, Deborah Wye suggests that Kirchner was intimately acquainted with the world of occasional or covert prostitution through his close relationship with Erna and Gerda Schilling, both of

Figure 3. Ernst Ludwig Kirchner, *Potsdamer Platz*, 1914. Courtesy of Bildarchiv Preussischer Kulturbesitz Berlin. Photograph from Art Resource, New York.

Indeed the cocottes' elegant appearance and subtle gestures of sexual availability manipulate and confound traditional notions of respectability by making it difficult for men on the street, be they potential clients or vice squad officers, to distinguish between "upstanding" women and prostitutes. What keeps Kirchner's paintings so controversial among art historians is how they provoke viewers not merely to recognize these blurred boundaries between types of women but to contemplate the myriad social meanings of such a blurring. In his modern masterpiece *Potsdamer Platz* from 1914, the greenish, masklike faces of two slender cocottes and the geometric composition of the metropolitan backdrop turn the city square into a stage on which both grief and desire are performed (fig. 3). The cocotte in profile wears the black veil of a war widow, while her forward-facing companion unsettles viewers with her determined stance and direct gaze. In this painting, prostitutes are barometers of their social climate, adapting to the somber atmosphere of a nation newly at war and hinting at the existential precariousness that the First World War brought with it. As Rita Täuber notes, dressing as war widows was a clever strategy used by actual prostitutes in wartime Berlin "to conform to the changed face of the street but, at the same time, to attract more attention through the appealing combination of mourning clothes and makeup." On the other hand, Ian Buruma argues, the violence of war also produced real widows who turned to prostitution just to get by.[25] The blurring of lines between widows and cocottes, in the case of Kirchner's *Potsdamer Platz*, inspires critical contemplation of how desire and gender roles were altered by war and what strategies women used to survive it. As the Weimar social commentator Curt Moreck observed, the war caused a sharp rise in occasional prostitution, and "the female body became ... an asset, from which women of all levels of society knew how to draw interest."[26]

The commodification of the female body is depicted in more explicit terms in Kirchner's street scene *Friedrichstrasse, Berlin,* also from 1914 (fig. 4). Named after the main shopping and entertainment thoroughfare in the Wilhelmine capital, the work presents the street itself as a destination and the cocottes as its main attraction. Kirchner's depiction of the cocottes is rife with "narrative complexity" that mixes danger with playfulness, and urban coolness with the heat of desire.[27] Like the images of the cocottes in *Potsdamer Platz,* the women's pallid skin and hollow eyes could be read as signs of illness, marking them as potential spreaders of venereal disease, yet their painted faces—red lips, rouged cheeks—could also be interpreted as signs of their strategic self-fashioning. Deborah Wye reads the cocottes' "strikingly assertive poses" as evocative of "a store window display" or "a fashion show

whom were cabaret dancers in Berlin. Erna Schilling became Kirchner's lifelong companion. See Wye, *Kirchner and the Berlin Street,* exhibition catalog (New York: Museum of Modern Art, 2008), 36, 43.

25. Täuber, *Der häßliche Eros,* 98. On the war widows, see Buruma, "Desire in Berlin," 20.

26. Curt Moreck [Konrad Haemmerling], "Die Erotik des Hinterlandes," in *Sittengeschichte des Weltkrieges,* ed. Magnus Hirschfeld (Leipzig: Verlag für Sexualwissenschaft Schneider & Co., 1930), 2:26.

27. Wye, *Kirchner and the Berlin Street,* 74.

Figure 4. Ernst Ludwig Kirchner, *Friedrichstrasse, Berlin,* 1914. Courtesy of Staatsgalerie Stuttgart. Photograph from Staatsgalerie Stuttgart.

runway," and the seemingly endless string of male admirers stretching out behind them underscores their desirability.[28] Täuber likens the cocottes to "pied pipers" and thereby implies that their charms are impossible to resist. The men who are drawn to them are portrayed as a mass of consumers lacking subjectivity, a clear reversal of gender norms of the time, which tended to define the mass as feminine and the individual as masculine.[29] The phalanx of faceless men in bowler hats and black suits that stretches out behind the well-dressed cocottes in Kirchner's *Friedrichstrasse* insinuates that there was a growing market for upscale prostitution in Berlin. Similar to works by French impressionist painters like Edgar Degas, Édouard Manet, and Henri Toulouse-Lautrec that depict coded gestures and erotically laden interactions between bourgeois gentlemen and the women who work in Parisian bars and entertainment venues, Kirchner's street scenes reveal the connections between consumer culture, urban nightlife, and the eroticization of the bourgeoisie without the lurid revulsion that emanates from the postwar works of Dix and Grosz.[30] In the presence of so many potential customers, lined up as if in a crowded store, the elegant prostitutes' commodity status is emphasized, but it is not condemned. Kirchner's cocottes exemplify what I will refer to throughout this book as "self-conscious commodities," women who accurately gauge men's desires and project an image that appeals to those desires in order to reap financial benefits.[31]

Following Kirchner's departure from the capital city in 1917, perhaps no other Berlin artist captured the "pervasive erotic ambiguity" that radiated through the city streets better than Jeanne Mammen. Mammen was a prolific and well-known artist who sketched and painted women in various scenes of metropolitan nightlife, the sexual underworld, and lesbian subcultures. Much like Zille, Mammen made a living by publishing her work in some of the era's most popular illustrated magazines, including *Ulk, Uhu, Jugend,* and *Simplicissimus.* Her *Berlin Street Scene* (fig. 5), published in the October 1929 issue of *Ulk,* exemplifies the "unnerving multiplicity of meaning" that viewers can discover in Mammen's work.[32] The

---

28. Wye, *Kirchner and the Berlin Street,* 75, 69. The same interpretation could be applied to Kirchner's painting *Rote Kokotte* (1914).

29. Täuber, *Der häßliche Eros,* 97–98. On the gendering of mass culture as feminine, see Andreas Huyssen, "Mass Culture as Woman: Modernism's Other," in *After the Great Divide: Modernism, Mass Culture, Postmodernism* (Bloomington: Indiana University Press, 1986), 44–64.

30. On the comparison of Kirchner with the French impressionists, see Haxthausen, "A New Beauty," 73.

31. Although my work focuses on the "self-conscious commodity" (my term) as a model for women's sexual and social behavior, I do not see it as a necessarily gender-specific term. In John Henry Mackay's novel *Der Puppenjunge* (The Hustler, 1926), which also takes place in Berlin and features the shopping arcades of the Friedrichstrasse as a market for male prostitution, the young protagonist must recognize himself as a commodity and embrace that status before he can gain a position of power over his male customers.

32. Eva Züchner, "Langweilige Puppen: Jeanne Mammens Großstadt-Frauen," in *Jeanne Mammen 1890–1976: Gemälde, Aquarelle, Zeichnungen* (Cologne: Wienand, 1997), 54.

Figure 5. Jeanne Mammen, *Berliner Strassenszene* (Berlin Street Scene), ca. 1929. Courtesy of Jeanne-Mammen-Stiftung. Copyright 2012 Artists Rights Society (ARS), New York / VG Bild-Kunst, Bonn.

watercolor's composition, with its multiple focal points and diagonal axes, portrays both the dynamism of the streets and the distracted, splintered vision of the modern urban spectator. The first axis comes from the top left corner in the form of a beam of light cast from an open-air café, while the double-decker bus zooming across the right center of the artwork constitutes another axis. The third axis is the diagonal line of a low wall in the bottom center of the piece that separates the café patrons from the busy sidewalk. At the intersection of these three axes, standing still among the hustle and bustle of the street scene, are two men and two women who seem to be striking a deal. Whereas one of the women stands in hunched resignation, looking apathetic at best, the other holds her head high, casting a haughty, cool gaze in the men's direction. If she is a prostitute, then she is certainly a self-conscious commodity. Aligned as it is with the top of the stouter man's hat, the axis created by the light from the café emphasizes the direction of the man's gaze and hence of his studied appraisal of the women's bodies. This could be a spontaneous flirtation between four strangers, it could be an arranged meeting between acquaintances, but it could also be the negotiation of a price for an evening of pleasure. The meaning of this encounter is left open to the viewer.

Although the linear flow of the painting's axes draws the viewer's eye to the center of the street scene, the sides of Mammen's composition offer more compelling imagery. A large, buxom woman seated at a café table dominates the lower left portion of the street scene and dwarfs her petite, bobbed-haired companion. The two women stare in opposite directions—one absentmindedly sips her drink while the other scrutinizes the many passersby, but their hands and knees touch, and the smaller woman's wispy fingers graze the corpulent woman's knee. There is some sort of intimacy between these two women, yet the nature of that intimacy remains unclear. Like the street scene itself, in which physical proximity does not necessarily translate into emotional connection, this coupling represents a curious tug-of-war between distance and closeness. Perhaps the most eye-catching figure in the entire street scene, however, is the coquettish woman at the far right. With her hand on her outthrust hip in a pose that emphasizes her posterior curves, she casts an almost taunting, jeering glance over her fur-bedecked shoulder. The pose, like the ruffled hem of her dress, is flirtatious, yet her eyes remain blank and narrow, and her lips are either slightly puckered or drawn into a sneer. Because she is simultaneously aggressive and coy, because she draws attention without conveying genuine affection, she is the visual embodiment of what I mean by "Berlin coquette." She is irreverent, urbane, and although there is clearly coldness in her gaze, there is also a sense of playfulness to this figure. Mammen's street scene presents viewers with the myriad forms that women's sexuality might take—heterosexual, lesbian, commodified—and leaves them open to interpretation and free of judgment.

On Context and Complexity: Critical Approach and Structure

In *Berlin Coquette,* the prostitute functions as the starting point rather than the end point for critical readings of social phenomena and cultural texts. Rather than interpreting prostitution as a dead end within narratives of women's emancipation, as some scholars have, this book challenges assumptions that the prostitute's meaning is fixed and negatively encoded. The act of challenging entrenched assumptions about prostitutes within current scholarship is a key step toward formulating what Gayle Rubin calls a "radical theory of sex." Rubin's essay "Thinking Sex," which takes the historical long view in order to identify important similarities and differences between the sexual debates of the late nineteenth century and those of the final decades of the twentieth century, provides a fitting theoretical frame for my discussion of prostitution and its connection to the broader discourse on non-normative sexuality.[33] A radical theory of sex, according to Rubin, "must build rich descriptions of sexuality as it exists in society and history." To do so, it must free itself from "persistent features of thought about sex," prejudices that condemn certain sexual acts and thereby prevent the articulation of a critical, contextualized study of sexuality. The condemned acts are those that fall outside of what Rubin

---

33. Gayle Rubin, "Thinking Sex: Notes for a Radical Theory of the Politics of Sexuality," in *Pleasure and Danger: Exploring Female Sexuality,* ed. Carole S. Vance (Boston: Routledge & Kegan Paul, 1984), 267–319.

calls "the charmed circle" of acceptable sexual behavior, which is defined as heterosexual, marital, monogamous, procreative, and confined to the private sphere. Rel-
egated to the "outer limits" of sexual activity, prostitution is laden with negative
value in a hierarchical approach to sex that is "less a sexology than a demonology."[34]
Only once we disentangle ourselves from this "demonology" of sex can we formu-
late a description of sexual behavior that reveals the various meanings ascribed to it
in specific local and temporal contexts. Like Judith Walkowitz, Rubin argues that
times of great anxiety surrounding sexuality are precisely the contexts in which
"the domain of erotic life is, in effect, renegotiated."[35] In imperial and Weimar Berlin, there was certainly no shortage of panic over the reported rise in rates of venereal infection, the "moral decline" of the city's youth, the social mixing of classes
in public spaces, and falling birth and marriage rates, and all of these things were,
in the discourse of the time, connected to discussions of prostitution and its regulation.
And yet, as I will show, prostitution was not simply defined by the oppressive regulatory measures or discourses of moral panic that sought to contain and control it.
One of the primary aims of this study is to show how, in Wilhelmine and Weimar
Berlin, discourses surrounding prostitution, its causes, and its possible alternatives
led to frank, productive discussions about sexuality, ones that defied the double
standard in order to contemplate potential nonmarital outlets for women's desire.
Such discussions allowed reformers and writers to envision new social and sexual
identities for women, such as the flirtatious single woman, the unwed mother, the
divorcee, the widow, and the lesbian. Put simply, prostitution played a central role
in the renegotiation of erotic life.

To use Rubin's work as a theoretical frame for this book entails a conscious (and
cautious) application of what has been mistakenly called "prosex feminism" to the
study of prostitution. I leave "prosex feminism" in quotation marks because this
is a label that has been placed on Rubin's work and does not properly capture the
delicate balance that she and her other "prosex" colleagues strike between a critique of sexual oppression and an acknowledgment of desire. Finding space for
pleasure, play, and desire within the discussion of commodified sexuality, and of
women's sexuality more broadly, does not ignore the existence of danger and violence within patriarchal heterosexual relations. This may be a difficult balance to
strike, but to deny one side or the other is perilous.[36] For Rubin, prostitutes are both
victims of moral stigmatization *and* "erotic dissidents" whose sale of sex for money
reveals the gendered power dynamics of commercial sex and, at the same time,
calls traditional structures of intimacy into question, thereby creating room for less

---

34. Rubin, "Thinking Sex," 275, 281, 301.

35. In "Thinking Sex," 267, Rubin cites Walkowitz's work as a laudable example of "sex radical"
scholarship. On the importance of local and temporal context, see Rubin, 277, 288.

36. This argument is made most convincingly by Carole S. Vance in her essay "Pleasure and Danger: Towards a Politics of Sexuality," in Vance, *Pleasure and Danger,* 1–27. See also Rubin, "Thinking
Sex," 275.

traditional (extramarital, nonprocreative) expressions of desire.[37] While "prosex feminism" insists on attributing agency to prostitutes, it is a form of agency that is nuanced and problematized, much like my concept of the "self-conscious commodity." Agency is, without a doubt, a crucial element in the recognition of prostitutes' dignity as human beings and of their roles as social actors rather than victims. But as a term that has become ubiquitous within feminist scholarship in the last two decades, *agency* can also be applied too broadly or recklessly to the study of prostitution, as evidenced by Victoria Harris's recent book, *Selling Sex in the Reich*. Although she presents compelling archival material, including police records on and interviews with prostitutes in Leipzig and Hamburg, Harris insists on a simplified form of agency that manifests itself as belligerence or lawlessness. She then goes on to perpetuate a dichotomized image of prostitutes as agents or victims. Based on relatively scant historical evidence, Harris makes sweeping claims about the antagonisms expressed toward prostitutes by feminists and sex reformers. By erroneously establishing direct ties between Weimar-era social reform programs and Nazi concentration camps, Harris ultimately attributes prostitutes' victimization to those who first sought to help them and then, she claims, violently oppressed them.[38] In contrast, the following analysis sets itself apart from Harris's study of prostitution in the German context in its exercise of restraint in regard to the attribution of agency to prostitutes, in its differentiated view of the social reform milieu, and in its temporal and localized focus on Berlin in the late imperial period and the Weimar Republic.

Berlin Coquette embeds close readings of literary and cultural texts within their sociohistorical context. Centrally informed by literary scholarship on the prostitute as a recurring motif in German and Austrian modernist drama, poetry, and prose, and by the work of historians on political debates concerning the legal and medical regulation of prostitution and the central role that regulation played in the German nation's effort to promote public health and battle venereal disease, it draws the disciplines of social history and cultural studies more closely together than existing studies have done.[39] It does so by showing that cultural texts did not merely

---

37. Rubin, "Thinking Sex," 287, 306. I use the term *extramarital* to mean "outside of marriage" and not as a synonym for *adulterous*, as most dictionaries define it. This is consistent with other scholarship on prostitution and sexuality; for example, see Gilfoyle, "Prostitutes in History," 138.

38. Note one of the most egregious examples of Harris's forced claims of historical continuity: "The social worker bent on 'emancipating' the prostitute from regulation in the early 1920s became the *same individual* responsible for sending her to a concentration camp." Harris, *Selling Sex in the Reich*, 175, emphasis added. Harris offers only one historical example to support this sweeping claim.

39. For literary analyses of prostitution, see Eva Borst, *Über jede Scham erhaben: Das Problem der Prostitution im literarischen Werk von Else Jerusalem, Margarete Böhme und Ilse Frapan* (Frankfurt am Main: Lang, 1993); Dietmar Schmidt, *Geschlecht unter Kontrolle: Prostitution und moderne Literatur* (Freiburg im Breisgau: Rombach, 1998); Christiane Schönfeld, ed., *Commodities of Desire: The Prostitute in Modern German Literature* (Columbia, SC: Camden House, 2000); Siemes, *Die Prostituierte in der literarischen Moderne*. For historical work on prostitution in imperial and Weimar Germany, see Lynn Abrams, "Prostitutes in Imperial Germany, 1870–1918: Working Girls or Social Outcasts?," in *The*

reflect the social circumstances in which they were created; rather, they also often helped to shape popular opinion and influence social behavior. My interdisciplinary configuration of sources—archival documents, sociopolitical essays, popular novels, satirical plays, an erotic travel guide, moral histories (*Sittengeschichten*), visual images, and social hygiene films—makes it possible to chart changing attitudes toward prostitution and to show how they were connected to social shifts in the embattled areas of marriage, sexuality, work, and morality. Because of the range of texts and discourses this book explores, it calls for a heterogeneous theoretical approach, drawing from theories of sexuality and social power, respectability, space, gendered spectatorship, and feminist dramaturgy. This approach once again takes cues from Rubin, who cautions against applying a singular universalizing theory—Marxism, psychoanalysis, or feminism—to the analysis of sex and instead advocates an openness to "theoretical as well as sexual pluralism."[40]

By examining the interconnectedness of the social and cultural realms as they relate to prostitution specifically and, more broadly construed, to issues of gender and sexuality, my book also draws methodological inspiration from what Kathleen Canning calls "relentless relationality." A productive approach to gender history, Canning argues, is one that studies "both the social and the symbolic relations between the sexes, conjoining them where possible," and highlights "a reciprocal relationship between ideologies and experiences of gender that were lived and assigned meaning differently by male and female actors."[41] Plainly stated, this book explores two types of relationality: gender relations and the relationship between social reality and its representation in imaginative texts. Because of its focus on female prostitution, my analysis admittedly has more to say about women's sexuality and gender roles than men's, but it is built on the premise that men's and women's roles are mutually constitutive and that masculinity and femininity cannot be studied in isolation.[42] As I have argued above, gender alone did not necessarily dictate the shape or tone of the discourse on prostitution, and in social reform circles and urban spaces, there was just as much cross-gender collaboration as there was antagonism.

The discussion of prostitution in Wilhelmine and Weimar Berlin crossed disciplinary lines, just as it defied traditional boundaries drawn by class, gender, and confessional and political affiliation. The reform milieu, as Kevin Repp describes it,

---

German Underworld: Deviants and Outcasts in German History, ed. Richard J. Evans (London: Routledge, 1988), 189–209; Bruggemann, "Prostitution, Sexuality, and Gender Roles"; Richard J. Evans, "Prostitution, State, and Society in Imperial Germany," *Past and Present* 70 (February 1976): 106–29; Harris, *Selling Sex in the Reich;* and Roos, *Weimar through the Lens of Gender.*

40. Rubin, "Thinking Sex," 309.

41. Kathleen Canning, *Gender History in Practice: Historical Perspectives on Bodies, Class, and Citizenship* (Ithaca, NY: Cornell University Press, 2006), 62.

42. For recent examples of a relational approach to gender beyond Canning's work, see Annette F. Timm and Joshua A. Sanborn, eds., *Gender, Sex, and the Shaping of Modern Europe: A History from the French Revolution to the Present Day* (Oxford: Berg, 2007), ix; and Erik N. Jensen, *Body by Weimar: Athletes, Gender, and German Modernity* (Oxford: Oxford University Press, 2010), 9–10.

was a "tangled web of crisscrossing paths meeting at odd junctures in unexpected antagonisms and alliances." With Berlin as the site of their web, the writers, artists, and reformers whose works I analyze forged various "intertwining relationships" in the city's many periodicals, reform organizations, and social circles, ones that demonstrate the cross-fertilization between the social and cultural realms.[43] To give a few examples of the interconnections between the authors, thinkers, and artists whose works are featured in the coming chapters: both Georg Simmel and Helene Stöcker were regular contributors to the journal *Freie Bühne,* where Otto Erich Hartleben's plays were reviewed and discussed; Hartleben was a member of the social reform group known as the Friedrichshagen Circle, as were Hans Ostwald and Magnus Hirschfeld; in the early Weimar Republic, Hirschfeld worked as a consultant and coauthor on Richard Oswald's popular social hygiene films; Oswald's films were critically reviewed by Kurt Tucholsky and Siegfried Kracauer; Kracauer was a former student of Simmel, as was Anna Pappritz. Pappritz and Hirschfeld worked, albeit in different organizations, directly with prostitutes and rallied for the deregulation and decriminalization of prostitution.

In addition to the cultural players, some of the women who appear in the pages of this book are prostitutes. Although they are admittedly few and far between, they are prostitutes who confounded abolitionist reformers like Pappritz with their unrepentant attitudes and self-definition as civil servants, prostitutes who banded together in the days of revolution that followed World War I to publish their own newspapers and form organizations like the Hilfsbund der Berliner Prostituierten (Auxiliary Club of Berlin Prostitutes), and prostitutes who petitioned the municipal government for protection against police harassment once prostitution was officially decriminalized under the Law to Combat Venereal Diseases (Reichsgesetz zur Bekämpfung der Geschlechtskrankheiten, or RGBG) of 1927.[44] The social implications of the RGBG for both Weimar gender roles and prostitutes' increased self-awareness and agency have been investigated with considerable acumen by Julia Roos, but what is missing from her excellent study is how these social changes were both reflected and expanded on in the cultural texts of their time. Without considering the sassy prostitutes' songs (*Dirnenlieder*) that were performed on stages throughout Berlin, without contemplating the various forms of urban womanhood and the economies of desire at work in Jeanne Mammen's watercolors, and without examining how popular novels by women authors gave legitimacy and agency to women who engage in various forms of commodified sexuality—from high-price

---

43. Repp, *Reformers, Critics,* 229, 260. For the cross-gender initiatives and the vast network of reform organizations in Berlin, see also Lees, *Cities, Sin, and Social Reform,* 300, 321.

44. See Roos, *Weimar through the Lens of Gender,* for an in-depth analysis of the RGBG, the debates leading up to its passage, the law's repercussions, and the Nazi backlash against it. Roos also conducts a valuable scholarly analysis of the short-lived newspaper founded by prostitutes and their communist advocates in Hamburg, *Der Pranger* (The Pillory), a paper that was also widely distributed and read in Berlin (Roos, 79–84). On *Der Pranger,* see also Harris, *Selling Sex in the Reich,* 64–68.

prostitution to posing for nude advertisements—the complex interweaving of prostitution, new womanhood, and desire that took place in the German capital between 1890 and 1933 cannot be fully grasped.

This book begins by showing how the discussion of prostitution was mobilized to criticize bourgeois conjugality. Chapter 1 examines turn-of-the-century texts written by the socialist politician August Bebel, the urban sociologist Georg Simmel, and the bohemian playwright Otto Erich Hartleben that describe marriage and prostitution as mutually reinforcing institutions entrenched in a male-dominated capitalist economy. Although Bebel was confident that the triumph of socialism over bourgeois capitalism would automatically eradicate prostitution and revolutionize marriage, Hartleben and Simmel hesitated to predict the demise of either institution. The authors' occasional recourse to chauvinist or essentialist descriptions of women, descriptions that were integral parts of the very social and moral structures they were criticizing, reveals just how difficult it was to envision alternative structures of intimacy in Wilhelmine society. And yet, upon close reading, these texts pose subtle, tentative alternatives to marriage and prostitution, including the free-love relationship (Bebel, Hartleben), flirtation, and lesbianism (Simmel).

Chapter 2 looks at the role that debates on prostitution played in the formation of various radical bourgeois feminist camps at the turn of the century, from the abolitionist movement led by Anna Pappritz to the League for the Protection of Mothers headed by Helene Stöcker. In their campaigns to abolish the state regulation of prostitution, feminists such as Pappritz called attention to the dangers that men's rampant sexual desire posed to *all* women, and presented themselves as beacons of moral authority and as those most fit to "rescue" and "reeducate" prostitutes. The limits to Pappritz's charitable perspective, however, are revealed when she confronts registered prostitutes who describe themselves as workers providing a valuable service to the state. This chapter focuses on such confrontations—both real and imagined—between bourgeois feminists and prostitutes.

In both chapters 1 and 2, the varying perspectives on prostitution articulated by prominent figures in Berlin's reform milieu, most of them members of the left-liberal bourgeois intelligentsia, are brought to light in a way that reveals both their progressivism and its limits. During the Wilhelmine period, leftist political figures like Bebel and feminists such as Pappritz and Stöcker used prostitution as a polemic device to interrogate capitalism and patriarchy. Their initial interest in prostitutes did not signify a concern for the individual women's choices or motivations but rather relied on their categorization as "exploited" persons, as social victims of a corrupt socioeconomic order. Any sympathy for prostitutes themselves was thwarted by the reformers' utter contempt for prostitution as an institution. In its inability to distinguish between the individual and the institution, the turn-of-the-century social critique of prostitution was, more often than not, collapsed with a moral condemnation of prostitutes. Hence as much as they claimed to distance themselves from pseudoscientific theories that defined prostitution in physiological or pathological terms, exemplified by Cesare Lombroso and Guglielmo Ferrero's theory of the "born prostitute," Richard von Krafft-Ebing's classification of prostitutes as nymphomaniacs, and Otto Weininger's outrageous assertion that all women were either mothers or prostitutes driven by an inherent urge to copulate, many of the writers I investigate slipped from a sociocritical into a pathological discussion of prostitution.[45] The very definition of female sexuality within German culture was heavily influenced by sexological texts like Krafft-Ebing's, which presented sexual passivity as "normal" and active expressions of desire as "abnormal" for women. With this context in mind, especially in the case of bourgeois feminists, the struggle for women's increased financial autonomy and social mobility often meant the denial of sexual desire.

To emphasize only the oppressive elements of social reform discourses on prostitution, however, would be to deny their complexity and their modernity. Respectability, a "distinct set of attitudes, discursive practices, moral assumptions" that had, since the advent of the nineteenth century, been based on proper manners, moral (i.e., sexual) virtue, and the strict demarcation of gender roles, remained "a central...part of the bourgeoisie's formation as a cultural as well as a social entity."[46] However, as the century drew to a close, the meaning of respectability became increasingly diffuse, and its association with a particular social class became less fixed. As the lines of propriety were drawn and redrawn by socialists, feminists, sexologists, cultural critics, artists, and writers in Wilhelmine and Weimar Berlin, the discussion of prostitution played a crucial role in the reconfiguration of respectability, just as the changing meanings of respectability helped, albeit slowly and gradually, to remove the moral stigma from prostitution. And where the texts of social reformers and intellectuals sometimes fell short, I show, literary and artistic works pushed the boundaries of what readers could envision in terms of social change. Chapter 2, for example, culminates in an analysis of Margarete Böhme's 1905 best-selling novel *Tagebuch einer Verlorenen* (Diary of a Lost Girl). Whereas the feminist writings I analyze use prostitution in their critical essays as a social irritant and an impetus for change, Böhme offers an individual portrait of a fallen daughter turned prostitute who is not simply a victim but an agent as well. The novel cleverly challenges the very definition of respectability by offering up the

45. Cesare Lombroso and Guglielmo Ferrero, *The Female Offender*, 1894, trans. William Ferrero (New York: D. Appleton, 1899); Richard von Krafft-Ebing, *Psychopathia sexualis*, 1886, trans. Franklin S. Klaf (New York: Stein and Day, 1965); Otto Weininger, *Geschlecht und Character: Eine prinzipielle Untersuchung* (Vienna: Braumüller, 1903); *Sex and Character: An Investigation of Fundamental Principles*, ed. Daniel Steuer, trans. Ladislaus Löb (Bloomington: Indiana University Press, 2005).

46. Woodruff D. Smith, "Colonialism and the Culture of Respectability," in *Germany's Colonial Pasts*, ed. Eric Ames, Marcia Klotz, and Lora Wildenthal (Lincoln: University of Nebraska Press, 2005), 5, 10. See also Smith's book-length study, *Consumption and the Making of Respectability, 1600–1800* (London: Routledge, 2002). Naturally, my discussion of respectability is also centrally informed by George Mosse's seminal study, *Nationalism and Sexuality*.

image of a sexual underworld that has a greater sense of kindness, charity, and community than polite, bourgeois society. The attribution of agency to a prostitute and the blurring of lines between prostitutes and respectable women are subtle gestures in Böhme's book that become more clearly expressed in works created in Weimar Berlin.

Images of prostitutes pervaded visual and popular culture in Weimar Berlin, and alongside the increased cultural currency of the prostitute came the ever-more-public presence of the post–World War I generation of bourgeois and petit bourgeois women. In their critical exploration of the blurred lines between prostitutes and New Women, chapters 3 and 4 show how the topic of prostitution provided a discursive space for certain artists and authors—many of whom were women—to contemplate various economies of desire, as well as the advantages and limitations of women's work. Chapter 3 delves into Weimar Berlin's legendary nightlife, but not in order to feed the popular myth of the city's sexual decadence. It explores instead the possible effects of increased public contact between men and women, as well as between young, single, working women and prostitutes, in various urban spaces—cinemas, cafés, cabarets, and streets. Chapter 4 looks more closely at the world of women's work, in particular white-collar jobs, in the social context of the late Weimar Republic. Just as they were linked to a critical contemplation of sexual power dynamics and desire, debates on prostitution provoked a closer examination of women's work, drawing attention to gendered pay inequities and to the social value—or lack thereof—placed on types of women's labor. By examining the conflation of white-collar women and prostitutes in two contemporary best sellers, Vicki Baum's *Menschen im Hotel* (Grand Hotel, 1929) and Irmgard Keun's *Das kunstseidene Mädchen* (The Artificial Silk Girl, 1932), I take issue with scholars who read prostitution in these novels as a simple trope for gendered exploitation. Throughout the book, my less polarized approach to gender, bolstered by readings of cultural criticism, popular films, cabaret songs, visual artworks, and mixed-media texts, helps me to distinguish between cultural works or social discourses that collapse prostitutes with other urban women to misogynist ends, those that emphasize the democratization of gender and the growing social acceptance of women's sexual desire and financial independence, and those that do a bit of both.

Erasing the Stigma: A Brief Glance Ahead

In October 2001, the women of Hydra had a good reason to celebrate. The German federal parliament passed a petition supported by the Social Democratic Party (SPD) and the Green Party/Coalition 90 that effectively decriminalized prostitution and obliterated Paragraph 138 of German Civil Law Code (Bürgerliches Gesetzbuch, BGB), which, since 1901, had defined prostitution as a violation of public morality. The petition, which became law in January 2002, made prostitutes eligible for social welfare benefits such as health insurance, retirement funds, unemployment benefits, and occupational retraining if they wish to leave the sex industry. It also declared the financial agreement between the prostitute and client to be a binding contract, subject to legal recourse if not fulfilled by the client. By officially removing the moral stigma (*Sittenwidrigkeit*) from prostitution, this law was the culmination of years of tireless lobbying on the part of prostitutes' rights groups like Berlin's Hydra. What rarely gets acknowledged in contemporary discussions of the law, however, is that it was nothing new for Berliners. In fact, the federal law is almost identical to a Berlin city ordinance passed in December 2000 by the Administrative Court (Verwaltungsgericht), and the court's decision was based on a series of surveys indicating that the majority of citizens polled supported both the social recognition and legal support of prostitutes.[47] Even in the 1980s, when other German cities like Munich and Hamburg were tightening controls on red-light districts and creating restricted zones (*Sperrbezirke*) that were off-limits to prostitutes, the West Berlin government refused to set such restrictions, and Berliners were also much less apt to vote for the forced registration and medical examination of prostitutes by health authorities than were other West Germans. As the women of Hydra proclaim, "We Berliners can count ourselves lucky."[48]

The passage of the Prostitutes' Law (Prostituiertengesetz, or ProstG) of 2002 has been accompanied by a vibrant discourse on prostitutes and prostitution in the mainstream media, feminist publications, contemporary art exhibits, and novels. Feminist scholars writing in a special issue of the journal *beiträge zur feministischen theorie und praxis* devoted to prostitution decried the law's passage and contended that prostitution's legalization would result in greater incidences of sexual abuse of women by men. The liberal mainstream magazine *Der Spiegel* published an article entitled "Die bürgerlichen Huren" (The Bourgeois Whores) featuring interviews with several women from Hydra. A multimedia art exhibit *Sexwork: Art Myth Reality,* in the words of one of its organizers and contributing artists, challenged "the diminution of prostitutes to extreme typecasts" by offering differentiated artistic perspectives on sex work. And Sonia Rossi, a mathematics student from a "typical bourgeois family" in western Europe, hit the best-seller list with *Fucking Berlin* (2008), an autobiographical account of how she financed her university education by working in various clubs, massage parlors, and brothels throughout the city.[49]

47. For a summary of the legal debates and decisions that led up to the passage of the Law Regulating the Rights of Prostitutes, known by the federal government and discussed in the media in short as the Prostitutes' Law (ProstG), and in particular of the role played by the Administrative Court in Berlin, see Lorenz Böllinger and Gaby Temme, "Prostitution und Strafrecht—Bewegt sich doch etwas?," *Zeitschrift für Sexualforschung* 14 (December 2001): 336–48.

48. Hydra, *Beruf: Hure,* 175. See pp. 172, 210, and 213 for a comparison of prostitutes' rights in Berlin, Munich, and Hamburg.

49. "Prostitution," special issue, *Beiträge zur feministischen Theorie und Praxis* 58 (2001); see especially the opening editorial, pp. 5–10. Ralf Hoppe, "Die bürgerlichen Huren," *Der Spiegel,* August 27, 2001, 84–90. Judith Siegmund, "Prostitution—Was macht hier die Kunst?" / "Prostitution—Which Role Can Art Play?," in the exhibition catalog *Sexwork: Kunst Mythos Realität* (Heidelberg: Kehrer,

Loaded as it still may be with narratives of victimization and debauchery, the contemporary German debate centers on "professional prostitutes who are described as emancipated women, as independent mercantilists, or self-confident employees who constitute a representative average of the population, who are in control of their own decisions."[50] The twenty-first-century discourse on prostitution clearly recalls the debates that took place in Wilhelmine and Weimar Berlin, but it still pales in comparison to the vibrancy of those earlier debates. Yet current scholarly discussion proceeds as if these historical antecedents did not exist. By tracing the origins of the "bourgeois whore" and other cliché-defying images of prostitutes back to these early debates, this book tells a story of prostitution in Berlin that might just be more "modern" than our own contemporary discussions of commodified sexuality.

2007), 10; the exhibition ran from December 2006 through February 2007 at three different locations in Berlin. Sonia Rossi, *Fucking Berlin* (Berlin: Ullstein, 2008), 15.

50. Susanne Dodillet, "Cultural Clash on Prostitution: Debates on Prostitution in Germany and Sweden in the 1990s," in Sönser Breen and Peters, *Genealogies of Identity*, 41–42.

1

Sex, Money, and Marriage: Prostitution as an Instrument of Conjugal Critique

"As long as marriage exists, so will prostitution," wrote Georg Simmel in an essay published in the Social Democratic weekly *Die Neue Zeit* in 1892.[1] As Simmel's proclamation suggests, turn-of-the-century debates surrounding prostitution were inextricably linked to discussions of the current state of marriage and its possible reform. Although on the surface bourgeois morality dictated that prostitution remain outside the boundaries of respectable society, it was often understood by mainstream society to be a "necessary evil" essential to the maintenance of bourgeois women's premarital chastity and the guarantee of men's sexual freedom.[2] The institution of the bourgeois family was considered by critics to be protected by prostitution, which offered bourgeois men an outlet for their sexual desires—desires that, if not transferred to the prostitute, could devastate the sanctity of the family.[3] Bourgeois men's patronage of prostitutes was treated with discretion within the

---

1. "Solange die Ehe existiert, solange wird es Prostitution geben." Georg Simmel, "Einiges über die Prostitution in Gegenwart und Zukunft," *Die Neue Zeit,* January 13, 1892, 517–25; reprinted in *Schriften zur Philosophie und Soziologie der Geschlechter,* ed. Heinz-Jürgen Dahme and Klaus Christian Köhnke (Frankfurt am Main: Suhrkamp, 1985), 60–71, here 66.

2. F. J. Behrend, *Die Prostitution in Berlin* (Erlangen: Palm & Enke, 1850), 8, 11, 20; Julius Kühn, *Die Prostitution im 19. Jahrhundert* (Leipzig: Barsdorf, 1871), 71. These are just a few examples; the phrase "necessary evil" is ubiquitous in the discussion of prostitution during this era.

3. Behrend, *Die Prostitution in Berlin,* 39, 75, 155. See also Hessen, *Die Prostitution in Deutschland,* 52–54.

middle classes but was publicly aired by various critics of bourgeois culture. Leaders of the burgeoning socialist movement such as August Bebel used prostitution as a polemic device, arguing that it was an integral part of the bourgeois capitalist economy. Portraying prostitutes as victims of a corrupt socioeconomic order on the one hand and as markers of bourgeois perversion and degeneration on the other, socialist and leftist-progressive writers attempted to show that the bourgeoisie had compromised its own doctrine of respectability and should therefore be denied a position of moral, social, and economic power. The image of the working class as unruly and sexually permissive and the bourgeoisie as beacons of respectability was turned upside down, and as the nineteenth century drew to a close, "it was...the bourgeoisie who embodied vice."[4]

With the establishment of a unified German nation in 1871, the state regulation of prostitution was codified under Clause 361/6, and registered prostitutes, while legally sanctioned to ply their trade, were subject to police surveillance and control. The state's regulation of prostitution was intimately connected to the maintenance of nineteenth-century bourgeois respectability, and yet this connection was supposed to remain a secret. In his examination of respectability and its formative role in the creation of German national identity, George Mosse defines one of the central tenets of respectability as "the proper attitude toward sexuality." What constituted this "proper attitude toward sexuality" was an emphasis on restraint and moderation over excess, and on strict gender demarcations, which portrayed women as sexually passive and men as active. Manliness and virility went hand in hand, and active sexual desire was a defining characteristic of the male citizen who could create and sustain a strong and healthy nation.[5] As the newly formed German state took an ever more active "regulative interest in the family as the vital site for the health of the national body," an almost obsessive focus was placed on conjugality and reproduction.[6] The bourgeois conjugal model dictated that women remain chaste until marriage, after which they were to fulfill their domestic roles as wives and mothers. Male sexuality was, in theory, also contained within marriage, but in practice, men's pre- and extramarital dalliances were tolerated and even regarded as natural. Prostitutes, although outwardly shunned as immoral by most members of bourgeois society, were, by means of the regulatory system, made available to male citizens for discreet and allegedly disease-free sexual encounters. Defenders of regulated prostitution argued vehemently that the existence of prostitution prevented men from seducing and thereby sullying the reputations of their would-be wives. Prostitution's existence, therefore, was crucial to maintaining bourgeois respectability, one of the pillars of late nineteenth-century civil society.

---

4. Corbin, *Women for Hire*, 190.
5. Mosse, *Nationalism and Sexuality*, 1, 13.
6. Geoff Eley, "Is There a History of the *Kaiserreich?*," in *Society, Culture, and the State in Germany, 1870–1930*, ed. Geoff Eley (Ann Arbor: University of Michigan Press, 1996), 41.

When studying nineteenth-century gender roles, one of the central paradigms that emerges is the public/private split, commonly understood to refer to men's access to the public sphere of work, politics, and organized leisure activities, on the one hand, and women's relegation to the private, or domestic, sphere of home and family, on the other. In regard to sexual self-determination, however, Isabel Hull draws our attention to a different, yet equally gendered, type of public/private split that developed gradually over the course of the eighteenth century and became one of the defining characteristics of the nineteenth-century "sexual system." Tracking the evolution of German civil society with a male citizen at its center, Hull argues that active, autonomous sexual desire was increasingly gendered as masculine and that men's sexual transgressions became shrouded in secrecy. The sexual behavior of the male citizen was private; the sexual behavior of women was not, especially if it transgressed the boundaries of marital, procreative sex. Women who "were not circumscribed within an easily recognizable domestic environment," who "did not keep the secret of their sexual intimacy," and who were also "economically independent" were defined as "public" women and were often labeled and treated as prostitutes. Their sexual actions were therefore open to public scrutiny, strict moral judgment, and legal penalties.[7]

How did prostitution, which was not a contested topic during the eighteenth century, become, alongside male homosexuality and venereal disease, one of "the classic themes of nineteenth-century sexual discourse"? If Enlightenment thinkers and lawmakers were, as Hull contends, "preoccupied with laying down the principles of 'normality'" within the sexual discourse of their time, then those who sought to define the social and sexual parameters of nineteenth-century Germany often did so through a discourse of abnormality or deviance.[8] If the new nation was to be a robust and powerful one, then those groups that were deemed to put the national health at risk were viewed with suspicion, if not treated with disdain. The most tangible indicator of the health of the nation was its birthrate, and, much like the birthrate of its European neighbors, Germany's was steadily declining in the final decades of the nineteenth century. "Abnormal" groups were comprised of individuals whose sexual behavior inhibited their ability to produce healthy offspring; in other words, these were nonprocreative people—homosexuals, prostitutes, single women, and persons with venereal diseases. Their behavior was studied, classified, and publicized by the fledgling discipline of sexual science, and in the case of prostitutes and male homosexuals, it was subject to legal discipline.[9] Although the

---

7. Isabel V. Hull, *Sexuality, State, and Civil Society in Germany, 1700–1815* (Ithaca, NY: Cornell University Press, 1996), 391–92, 405–6. Hull defines the "sexual system" as "the patterned ways in which sexual behavior is shaped and given meaning" by social and legal institutions and by thinkers who shape civil society (1).

8. Hull, *Sexuality, State, and Civil Society*, 258.

9. On the declining birthrate and the formulation of a discourse of *Bevölkerungspolitik* (population policy) that centered on venereal disease prevention and eventually eugenic screening, see Annette

fear of the growing numbers of unmarried women was based less on reality than on "imagined demography," Catherine Dollard argues in her study of "the surplus woman" in Wilhelmine Germany, the notable public presence of single women was an urban, middle-class phenomenon most easily observed and documented in Berlin.[10] The upstart German capital was the center of debates on public health issues and became the first city in imperial Germany to open a treatment clinic for venereal disease.[11] As public women who were particularly visible in Berlin and who were assumed to be the primary culprits in the spread of venereal infection, prostitutes were associated both with the perceived increase in numbers of unwed women and with the rise in VDs, making prostitution part and parcel of the anxious discussions about public health and especially about women's economic and sexual independence.

By the early 1890s, the public outcry over prostitution in Berlin reached a fever pitch. The widespread willingness to speak so openly about prostitution was sparked by the 1891 murder trial involving the pimp Hermann Heinze and his prostitute wife Anna, who were charged with murdering a night watchman while attempting to rob a Berlin church of its silver. The extensive coverage of the trial in the urban press and the decision of the judge to open the trial to the public attracted a large crowd of spectators, a gathering that caused well-dressed bourgeois ladies to literally rub elbows with thieves and prostitutes from Berlin's impoverished north end. The trial even captured the attention of Kaiser Wilhelm II and inspired the parliament's passage of a slate of restrictive laws—dubbed the *lex Heinze*—meant to curb pimping activities and to censor "pornographic" literature, theater, and visual media. As a result of the myriad social, sexual, and moral issues it raised and the national publicity it received, the Heinze trial "was the most important legal event since the lapse of the Anti-Socialist Law" in 1890, legislation that had banned all public political activity by socialists for more than a decade.[12] In fact, these two legal events—the murder trial of a Berlin pimp and his prostitute wife

Timm, *The Politics of Fertility in Twentieth-Century Berlin* (Cambridge: Cambridge University Press, 2010), here 5–8. On the identification of "abnormal" or "deviant" groups and the growing public interest in sexual deviance in late nineteenth-century Germany and Austria, see Harry Oosterhuis, *Stepchildren of Nature: Krafft-Ebing, Psychiatry, and the Making of Sexual Identity* (Chicago: University of Chicago Press, 2000), 28–29.

10. Catherine L. Dollard, *The Surplus Woman: Unmarried in Imperial Germany, 1871–1918* (New York: Berghahn, 2009), 71, 80–82.

11. The clinic opened in 1904 in Berlin-Lichtenberg. Timm, *The Politics of Fertility,* 54.

12. There is a growing body of scholarship on the *lex Heinze*. My information on the trial comes primarily from Benjamin Carter Hett, *Death in the Tiergarten: Murder and Criminal Justice in the Kaiser's Berlin* (Cambridge, MA: Harvard University Press, 2004), 55–103, here 100. See also Evans, *Tales from the German Underworld,* 188–89, 192–93. On the censorship laws, see Wolfgang Hütt, *Hintergrund: Mit den Unzüchtigkeits- Gotteslästerungsparagraphen des Strafgesetzbuches gegen Kunst und Künstler 1900–1933* (Berlin: Henschel, 1990), 9–25, 81–103; R. J. V. Lenman, "Art, Society, and the Law in Wilhelmine Germany: The Lex Heinze," *Oxford German Studies* 8 (1973): 86–113; Peter Mast, *Künstlerische und wissenschaftliche Freiheit im Deutschen Reich 1890–1901* (Munich: Schäuble, 1980), 139–90. The antisocialist legislation went into effect under Bismarck in 1878 and was allowed to lapse in 1890.

and the lapse of antisocialist legislation—are connected by more than the "moral panic of considerable proportions" they allegedly unleashed.[13] Both events signified a growing preoccupation with the social effects of industrialization and the travails of the urban poor. Kaiser Wilhelm II charted a "new course" to improve industrial working conditions, calling for an International Conference on Labor Protection to be held in Berlin in March 1890. In its focus on working women and on issues such as maternity leave, the Kaiser's "new course" offered state protection from exploitative working conditions by shortening the workday, yet it also expanded the state's intervention into the familial realm. At the same time, with the resignation of Otto von Bismarck from his post as German chancellor and the contiguous repeal of the Anti-Socialist Law in 1890, new social actors became a vocal and visible part of German civil society, including Social Democrats, members of the women's movement, social scientists, and naturalist writers, allowing for a multiplication of critical perspectives on social issues, including bourgeois marriage, gender roles, and economic equality.[14]

Both the *lex Heinze* and the renewed political activity of socialists also significantly affected the dissemination of print and visual media. The censorship laws passed as a result of the Heinze trial represented a tightening of state control within the cultural realm, and yet, as I will show in the case of Otto Erich Hartleben, Berlin theaters devised creative strategies to get around restrictive measures. With the lapse of Bismarck's Anti-Socialist Law, the publication and distribution of socialist writings was no longer forbidden. This allowed for the broader dissemination of ideas, such as those articulated by August Bebel in *Women and Socialism,* a book that he had written in 1879 but that did not become available outside underground socialist circles until 1891. Both Bebel's book and the Heinze trial, in quite different ways, broke the silence surrounding men's sexual behavior and the role that men might play in prostitution, be it as pimps in the case of Hermann Heinze or as clients in the case of the bourgeois men that Bebel would take to task. By contemplating the class and gender dynamics that allowed prostitution to flourish in the capital city, critics like Bebel broke through the protective seal that had ensured men's sexual privacy for most of the nineteenth century.

Challenging bourgeois norms both from the outside and from within, three men helped to shape the turn-of-the-century discourse on prostitution in Berlin: August Bebel, one of the early figureheads of the socialist movement; Georg Simmel, one of the founders of modern sociology; and the bohemian playwright and satirist Otto Erich Hartleben. Their motivations for taking on the topic of prostitution and using it to critique bourgeois mores likely reflected their different sociopolitical

---

13. Evans, *Tales from the German Underworld,* 189.

14. On the growing "vitality of civil society" in the 1890s, see Kathleen Canning, *Languages of Labor and Gender: Female Factory Work in Germany, 1850–1914* (1996; repr., Ann Arbor: University of Michigan Press, 2002), 130–49, here 144; on "the generation of 1890," see Repp, *Reformers, Critics,* 25–26.

perspectives. To assert the social and political power of the proletariat, Bebel had to discredit the bourgeoisie, and as Hull has so persuasively shown in her work on the early modern period, "sexual argumentation" was "very useful in redrawing social lines."[15] Bebel's method of redrawing the social lines of his time was to demonstrate bourgeois culpability in regard to prostitution and the decline of the family. The public intellectual and social philosopher Simmel's writings on prostitution read like thought experiments inspired by his observations of social and sexual behavior within urban capitalist modernity. Hartleben's involvement in the reformist debates of the Friedrichshagen Circle and in bohemian café culture, combined with his early enthusiasm for social democracy, caused him to look at proper society and its moral philistinism with an especially critical eye. However diverse these writers' perspectives might have been, the approach they took to prostitution is significant for several reasons. In their attempts to explain prostitution's existence, they diverged from the late nineteenth-century pseudoscientific discourse on prostitution and women's sexual behavior exemplified by Richard von Krafft-Ebing's *Psychopathia sexualis* (1886) and Cesare Lombroso and Guglielmo Ferrero's study *The Female Offender* (1894). While the pseudoscientific discourse portrayed prostitution as a physiological or pathological phenomenon inherent to some women, Bebel, Simmel, and Hartleben treated it primarily as a socioeconomic issue. Instead of arguing that women were driven to prostitution by inner psychoses such as nymphomania or "moral insanity," they located the cause of prostitution in outside forces like poverty, social injustice, and moral hypocrisy.[16] The purveyors of hypocrisy were located in a bourgeois culture that insisted on morally condemning prostitutes while concurrently using them to preserve the purity of future bourgeois wives. Most markedly, Bebel, Simmel, and Hartleben used prostitution to criticize the institution of bourgeois marriage, arguing that it was based not on love but rather, similar to prostitution, on money.

The idea that bourgeois marriage could or should be based on love began to take root during the German Enlightenment and can be seen as a result of the increased emphasis placed on the individual. Individuation and subjectivity, characterized by a search for happiness and self-fulfillment, introduced an element of personal choice that stood at odds with the "arranged" marriage based on a private, primarily financial, agreement between two families. In early discussions of love-based marriages, love was defined not as a prerequisite for but rather as a result of marriage. It was an emotion defined by the mutual support, affection, and even friendship required for a lasting union; it was rarely equated with sexual attraction between spouses. The primary purpose of conjugal sex was reproduction, not

---

15. Hull, *Sexuality, State, and Civil Society*, 2.

16. For Krafft-Ebing's classification of prostitutes as nymphomaniacs, see *Psychopathia sexualis*, 323. In *The Female Offender*, 154, 310–11, Lombroso and Ferrero define "moral insanity" as an inherent coldness or dulled sense of emotion that is characteristic of prostitutes.

pleasure, especially for the bourgeois wife.[17] The clearest visions of romantic love, which did offer some space for sexual desire, were the products of literary fantasy, and one of the most marked examples was Friedrich Schlegel's novel *Lucinde* (1799). In Schlegel's work romantic love was defined by its exclusivity. Based on the principle that there is only *one* perfect partner for each individual, romantic love's fulfillment, and hence the individual's, was contingent on finding and remaining with that one particular person. In contrast to marital unions formed through interfamilial contracts, in which the married couple defined itself through class and familial allegiance, the romantic pair was defined by each partner's exclusive identification with the other.[18] Was romantic love, however, to be found only in literature? Schlegel may have described true love as an eternal bond that transcended social reality, but by the late nineteenth century, the institution of civil, state-sanctioned marriage made love all the more beholden to social approval. The codification of civil marriage in 1875 under Bismarck further exacerbated the inherent tension between romantic love as a private bond between two individuals and the concept of marriage as a social institution requiring legal validation.[19] In this tug-of-war between emotion and institution, at least in bourgeois circles, it seemed the institution had won.

Those who sought to challenge the socioeconomic power and moral authority of the bourgeoisie did so by striking at one of the main sources of that power: the family. The family was "an institution which displayed the wealth and cultural capital of the bourgeois" and "provided the means through which dynastic ambitions were realized." Marriage was thus not only the necessary step toward founding a family but also "the center point around which all discussion of sexual behavior revolved."[20] As staunch critics of bourgeois society, Karl Marx and Friedrich Engels bemoaned women's enslavement within monogamous marriage, which dictated their financial dependence on their husbands and required them to perform an exclusively reproductive role. Using anthropological texts by Johann Jakob Bachofen and Lewis Henry Morgan to bolster their socioeconomic critique, Marx

---

17. Sources that inform my discussion of the eighteenth- and nineteenth-century bourgeois marriage and the concept of the love match include Lynn Abrams, "Companionship and Conflict: The Negotiation of Marriage Relations in the Nineteenth Century," in *Gender Relations in German History: Power, Agency, and Experience from the Sixteenth to the Twentieth Century,* ed. Lynn Abrams and Elizabeth Harvey (Durham, NC: Duke University Press, 1997), 101–20; Frevert, *Women in German History,* 31–72, 130–37; Hull, *Sexuality, State, and Civil Society,* 5, 285–98, 409–10; Günther Saße, *Die Ordnung der Gefühle: Das Drama der Liebesheirat im 18. Jahrhundert* (Darmstadt: Wissenschaftliche Buchgesellschaft, 1996), 18–49.

18. Saße, *Die Ordnung der Gefühle,* 48–49.

19. The 1875 institution of civil marriage was one of Bismarck's calculated strikes against the authority of the church, particularly the Catholic Church. The law asserted the power of the nation-state over that of the pope by requiring the state's approval of all marriages but making church weddings optional.

20. The first two quotes come from David Blackbourn, "The German Bourgeoisie: An Introduction," in *The German Bourgeoisie,* ed. David Blackbourn and Richard J. Evans (London: Routledge, 1990), 10; the third quotation is from Hull, *Sexuality, State, and Civil Society,* 285.

and Engels argued that, with the advent of patriarchy, women became the first exploited class.[21] This collapsing of gender with class had lasting effects on modern discourses on marriage and prostitution: Bebel, Simmel, and Hartleben, to varying degrees, reflected the influence of Marx's and Engels's writings in their works, for they saw prostitution and marriage as mutually reinforcing institutions. All three authors criticized the marriage of convenience (*Kaufehe*) as a form of prostitution, all agreed that women's economic dependence on men was detrimental, and all three raised the possibility of "free love" as an alternative to prostitution and marriage. Like Engels, Bebel envisioned a postbourgeois society in which gender equality would be demonstrated by women's freedom to choose their own partners and also to separate from them as they please.[22] While Bebel prophesied free love, Hartleben and Simmel treated it with skepticism. In his early essay on prostitution and marriage, "Einiges über die Prostitution in Gegenwart und Zukunft" (Thoughts on Prostitution in the Present and Future), Simmel claimed that "truly free love" can exist only in a social utopia—not necessarily Bebel's socialist utopia—that no longer judges the moral legitimacy of sexual relations so stringently.[23] Nearly a decade later, in his *Philosophie des Geldes* (The Philosophy of Money, 1900), he implicitly presented free love as an oxymoron and thereby questioned its very viability. Indeed a close reading of the latter text shows that if Simmel acknowledged the existence of free love at all, he equated it not with a freely chosen romantic bond but with the most fleeting of relationships—prostitution.

This chapter analyzes the affinities and divergences between the bohemian playwright, the urban sociologist, and the socialist politician in their assessments of prostitution, gender relations, sexuality, and respectability. While Bebel was certain that a socialist revolution would bring an end to prostitution and give new life to marriage, Hartleben and Simmel were wary of such radical change. All three men expressed sympathy for the prostitute, but it is in this sympathy that the ambivalence of their writings resides. Particularly in the cases of Bebel and Simmel, repeated references to prostitutes as victims of social ills (*Mißstände*) deny prostitutes

---

21. These ideas find their clearest articulation in Friedrich Engels, *The Origin of the Family, Private Property, and the State,* trans. Alec West (1942; rev. and repr., New York: International, 1972). Although the first edition of Engels's book first appeared in 1884, one year after Marx's death, it was based on collaborative work between Marx and Engels that dated back to the middle of the century. See Engels, *Der Ursprung der Familie, des Privateigentums und des Staats* (Zurich: Druck der Schweizerischen Genossenschaftsbuchdruckerei, 1884); reprinted in Karl Marx and Friedrich Engels, *Gesamtausgabe*, vol. 29 (Berlin: Dietz, 1990). West's translation is based on the book's fourth edition, which appeared in 1891, and shows Bebel's influence. For an overview of turn-of-the-century patriarchal critiques written by both men and women, see Ann Taylor Allen, "Patriarchy and Its Discontents: The Debate on the Origins of the Family in the German-Speaking World, 1860–1930," in *Germany at the Fin de Siècle: Culture, Politics, and Ideas,* ed. Suzanne Marchand and David Lindenfeld (Baton Rouge: University of Louisiana Press, 2004), 81–101.

22. Bebel, *Die Frau und der Sozialismus* (Stuttgart: Dietz, 1891), 337–38; Engels, *The Origin of the Family,* 135, 144–45.

23. Simmel, "Einiges über die Prostitution," 66.

the possibility of agency. The depiction of women as passive objects in the "social causes" discourse shows that it is actually not completely separate from the sexological writings of Krafft-Ebing, who argued that women consistently play a "passive *rôle*" in "sexual relations...and long-existent social conditions."[24] Hartleben's plays, in contrast, portray female characters who struggle to achieve sexual and financial autonomy. With numerous obstacles to this autonomy placed before them, these characters contemplate choosing prostitution or other forms of commodified sexuality—such as the role of the kept woman—over other seemingly less desirable options. Hence these women take on an active, albeit limited, role in deciding their own fates. Even Hartleben's texts, however, contain a general ambivalence concerning women's sexuality. While all three writers delivered a scathing critique of bourgeois marriage and pondered alternatives to it, none of them explicitly or unequivocally advocated women's sexual freedom. True, Bebel's text clearly portrays sexual liberation as available to all in the wake of revolution, but his plea for moderation in all areas of life—particularly in the sexual realm—and his definition of prostitution as a form of sexual depravity show how much he clings to a discourse of respectability. Simmel and Hartleben, on the other hand, have difficulty imagining a form of women's sexuality that is not channeled into marriage, motherhood, or prostitution. Their inability to depart completely from essentialist descriptions of "womanhood," descriptions that were an integral part of the rigid system of gender roles criticized by their works, reveals just how entrenched traditional ideas of femininity and female sexuality were in Wilhelmine society.

Prostitution as Bourgeois Institution: August Bebel's *Women and Socialism*

August Bebel's highly influential treatise *Die Frau und der Sozialismus* (Women and Socialism) was one of the first books of its time to critically address the Woman Question (*Frauenfrage*), concerning what role the growing number of young, single women were to play in modern German society.[25] However, the book, which

---

24. Krafft-Ebing, *Psychopathia sexualis*, 130. On Krafft-Ebing's gendered concept of desire, see Oosterhuis, *Stepchildren of Nature*, 57.

25. August Bebel (1840–1913) was, along with Wilhelm Liebknecht, one of the founding members of the Social Democratic Party (SPD) in 1869. Before the SPD's founding, Bebel was elected president of the League of German Workers Associations, a post that also led to his first election to the German Reichstag in 1867. Between the SPD's founding in 1869 and the repeal of the antisocialist legislation in 1890, he was imprisoned six times for leftist political agitation, once for nearly three years (1872–75). Before and after serving time in prison, he served as an SPD representative in the federal parliament from German unification until his death in 1913, with only one loss in the early 1880s. Bebel's text has a complex publication history. The first edition, entitled *Die Frau und der Sozialismus*, was published in Zurich in 1879 and banned in Germany because of the 1878 antisocialist laws. Although Bebel sought to publish the second edition under a less explicitly political title in 1883, *Die Frau in der Vergangenheit, Gegenwart und Zukunft*, this version was banned as well. Still, even before the ban on socialist literature was lifted in 1890, more than 20,000 copies were printed and circulated among readers in Germany, and

reached a wide audience both in Germany and abroad, was just as concerned with married women.[26] It delivered a damning critique of the current state of marriage, arguing that the division of labor within bourgeois marriage, which defined the man's role as that of sole breadwinner and the woman's as dutiful wife and mother, encouraged the spread of prostitution. Although recent studies of prostitution and female sexuality in the German context all cite Bebel's work, none conduct a close reading of it.[27]

In one of the most widely quoted passages from his book, Bebel writes: "Marriage represents one side of sexual life of the bourgeois world, and prostitution represents the other. Marriage is the front, and prostitution the back of the medal."[28] The "medal" (*Medaille*) is also meant to evoke the image of a coin, for Bebel views both bourgeois marriage and prostitution as business transactions. Marriage guarantees the man a certain social standing, and prostitution caters to his sexual desires. As the legitimate side of bourgeois intimate life, marriage is the visible side of the medal, while prostitution is hidden on its reverse side as the dirty secret that everyone knows. The widespread expectation that bourgeois men accumulate wealth sufficient to support a wife and children prevented them from marrying until quite late in life, at least into their thirties. Potential bourgeois wives were expected to remain virgins until marriage and to become pregnant soon thereafter, yet men's recreational sex was subtly encouraged and was often undertaken with a prostitute. This double standard that allowed men unlimited access to sex and

---

once it was no longer banned, the book saw 60,000 new copies before 1900 and the same number before Bebel's death. The book went through a total of fifty-three printings in Bebel's lifetime and had broad popular appeal. For a clear account of the book's publication history and a critical view of existing English translations, see Anne Lopes and Gary Roth, *Men's Feminism: August Bebel and the German Socialist Movement* (Amherst, NY: Humanity Books, 2000), 22, 29, 32, 35–37. For my analysis, I used the ninth edition of the German text published by Dietz in 1891, the year that the ban on the text was lifted, and the book was therefore available on the open market. The ninth edition constitutes the first complete revised version by Bebel and marks the beginning of its widespread impact outside underground socialist circles. English quotations come from a revised reprint of Hope Adams Walther's translation, which uses the 1883 title, *Women in the Past, Present, and Future* (Oxford: Zwan, 1988). Because there is no authoritative translation of the work into English, I cite the German version when paraphrasing Bebel's ideas and give the pages for both the German and the English versions when quoting directly from the text. In order to avoid awkward or antiquated wording, which often does not capture the vivid language of Bebel's own text, I have, in many cases, modified the translation. Within the body of my text, I always refer to the book as *Women and Socialism*, since this remains truest to the original title.

26. As Lopes and Roth contend, Bebel's work was read more widely than Marx and Engels's writings, including Engels's *The Origin of the Family*. See Lopes and Roth, *Men's Feminism*, 29, 61, 73–74. The text also had an immense international impact; for example, Corbin, *Women for Hire*, 235, documents how it shaped the socialist discourse on prostitution in France.

27. For works that cite Bebel as a key figure in the late nineteenth-century discourse on prostitution in Germany, see Roos, *Weimar through the Lens of Gender*, 137, 139–40; Bruggemann, "Prostitution, Sexuality, and Gender Roles," 31–32; Evans, *Tales from the German Underworld*, 170; Schönfeld, *Commodities of Desire*, 14. Even Lopes and Roth focus more on the reception of *Women and Socialism* and on Bebel's public and private life than on an in-depth reading of the text itself. For their brief discussion of the book's analysis of prostitution, see Lopes and Roth, *Men's Feminism*, 72–73.

28. Bebel, *Die Frau und der Sozialismus*, 140; *Women in the Past, Present, and Future*, 91.

barred bourgeois women from sexual knowledge and experience actually cor-
rupted, even destroyed marriage, according to Bebel. Led to believe that marriage
would fulfill their romantic fantasies of love, bourgeois women were often gravely
unprepared for and disappointed by the realities of sexual intercourse. Once the
marriage bond was sealed, women found that their role was mainly reproductive,
and yet, as Bebel points out, they were often kept from fulfilling this role by their
husbands' pre- and extramarital affairs, which had as their possible consequences
venereal disease and infertility. This exposure of bourgeois men's sexual transgressions is one of *Women and Socialism*'s major critical interventions in the sexual discourse of the late nineteenth century. Bebel's book presents both prostitutes and
wives as economically and sexually bound to bourgeois men, wives even more so
than prostitutes. The wife is treated like a material possession, a piece of property
(*Privateigentum*) over which the husband has exclusive and lasting control.[29] The
prostitute, Bebel contends, enjoys a higher degree of autonomy than the wife, and
he asks his readers to ponder this comparison: "Now I ask, is not such a marriage—
and the number is great—worse than prostitution? The prostitute is at least to a
certain extent free to withdraw from her shameful trade; she has, at least if she is
not the inmate of a brothel, the right of refusing to do business with a man whose
personality repels her. But a wife is sold into the hands of her husband and must
endure his embraces, though she may have a hundred causes to hate and abominate
him."[30] This passage is certainly noteworthy in its attribution of rights and free-
doms to the prostitute and its description of prostitution as a relatively pliant trade
that women can withdraw from if they please. Still, the main point is not to laud
prostitutes but to emphasize the dire situation of the wife. Prostitution is used as
a polemic device to show that *even* a prostitute can reject both the sexual advances
of the bourgeois man and his money, but a wife suffers doubly in her sexual and
economic dependence on her husband, making her little more than his slave.[31]

Despite the hint of freedom and agency lent to prostitutes in the above passage,
more often than not Bebel portrays them as victims of poverty and capitalist exploitation. He clearly connects prostitutes with working-class women when he argues
that female factory workers, seamstresses, waitresses, and domestic servants making mere subsistence wages sometimes turn to prostitution to make ends meet.[32]
This connection between prostitutes and women workers, however, has its limits. While both underpaid factory work and prostitution are dire consequences of
bourgeois capitalism, prostitution is, for the author, a dishonest or dirty trade that

---

29. The ideas expressed in this paragraph can all be found in Bebel, *Die Frau und der Sozialismus*,
94–148, especially 94–95, 103, 118, 135–36, 139–40, 148.

30. Bebel, *Die Frau und der Sozialismus*, 93; *Women in the Past, Present, and Future*, 55–56.

31. Bebel uses the terms *Sklaverei* and *Geschlechtssklaverei* to describe bourgeois marriage, in *Die
Frau und der Sozialismus*, 2, 4.

32. See Bebel, *Die Frau und der Sozialismus*, 98, 101, 148, 154–55.

sullies those who engage in it.[33] Try as he might to separate the women (prostitutes) from the institution (prostitution), Bebel's rhetoric of enslavement, oppression, and victimization excludes prostitutes from one of the main objectives of his book: to mobilize women workers to overthrow the bourgeois order. His hesitance to mobilize prostitutes could be explained by the Marxist classification of prostitutes as belonging to the *Lumpenproletariat,* a group of disparate "underworld figures" including vagabonds, thieves, ragpickers, and procurers. Socialists tended to regard these figures as "politically pliant and volatile" and therefore viewed them with skepticism and even trepidation.[34] Deemed incapable of stable political allegiance, the *Lumpenproletariat* was seen to be difficult if not impossible to mobilize for revolution.

Bebel's ambivalence toward prostitutes was also an effect of his implicit association of prostitution with sexual excess, even deviance. Just as the text expresses sympathy with the prostitute as a social victim, it also defines prostitution as a clear sign of bourgeois degeneration. Indeed the author repeatedly cites prostitution, homosexuality, and pederasty as examples of an "unnatural satisfaction of sexual desire." Bebel's criticism of homosexuality may seem odd considering his later political support of Magnus Hirschfeld's campaign to repeal §175, the law that declared homosexuality a criminal act. However, he sympathized only with "born homosexuals"—a concept central to Hirschfeld's campaign as well—and not with those who chose to experiment with what he called "the abnormalities of the ancient Greeks." Following the logic and terms of Bebel's text, if men who consciously engage in homosexual activity are "unnatural" or "abnormal," then a woman who chooses to sell her body also commits a "crime against morality."[35] This makes the prostitute sound more like a culprit than a victim. Indeed if she is an integral part of bourgeois sexual life, and that life is deemed to be harmful, then she, too, might signify danger and disease. Bebel's copious statistics documenting the high rates of syphilis and gonorrhea among bourgeois men support his diagnosis of bourgeois society as sick, even degenerate.[36] Health, after all, was a central component of respectability, particularly in late nineteenth-century Germany. As Mosse shows, "Vice and virtue became a matter of health and sickness. To remain healthy entailed a willingness to follow the dictates of nature, which supported the new respectability."[37] Bebel's rhetoric of natural versus unnatural or healthy versus unhealthy behavior bears a striking resemblance to bourgeois respectability.

33. Bebel describes prostitution as "dieses schmachvolle Handwerk" (this shameful trade) and laments that the prostitute "geht...elend zu Grunde" (meets a dreadful demise) (*Die Frau und der Sozialismus,* 146–48).

34. Evans, *Tales from the German Underworld,* 215, 220.

35. All quotations in this paragraph appear in Bebel, *Die Frau und der Sozialismus,* 158; see also *Women in the Past, Present, and Future,* 104. The translations, in this case, are mine.

36. Bebel, *Die Frau und der Sozialismus,* 147–49, 158–59.

37. Mosse, *Nationalism and Sexuality,* 13.

An adherence to respectable norms represented the right to power, and according to Bebel's text a healthy body politic could be achieved only by socialist revolution. In the future social democratic society, all individuals would be able to develop naturally within healthy conditions, eating a proper diet and living in homes complete with adequate space, heat, and light. The erasure of class difference would end patriarchal rule, making gender equality possible. Marriage would cease to be an institution and would constitute instead a private bond between equals with no need for legal or religious legitimation. Women's sexual desire would be regarded as a natural, acceptable urge, just as it was in the ancient matriarchal societies described by Bachofen and praised by both Bebel and Engels.[38] Sexuality as described in Bebel's text, however, was not to be completely freewheeling: "An excess of sexual pleasure is much more harmful than a deficit....*Moderation in sexual relations is just as necessary as in eating and drinking.*"[39] If moderation in quotidian life, as Michel Foucault describes it, signifies self-mastery and therewith an avenue to power, then excess reveals a lack of control that undermines power.[40] The excess and deviance of the bourgeoisie described in *Women and Socialism* serve as reason enough for it to be overthrown by the more respectable, healthy, and robust proletariat. Yet the text leaves readers wondering what life would really be like for women in the new socialist society. Would they follow the model of the intellectual, sexual libertines represented by George Sand, or would their sexuality be domesticated and channeled, whenever possible, into their "natural purpose" (*Naturzweck*)—motherhood?[41] Highlighting the tension between Bebel's call for women's emancipation and his domestic agenda, Mosse writes: "Socialism, while championing the rights of women, would strengthen and not weaken a happy family life."[42] Would this emphasis on healthy domesticity ultimately yoke women with the double burden of work and family as many women were—and often still are—in bourgeois capitalist society and in "real existing" socialism?

And what of the "losers" in the battle between the bourgeoisie and the proletariat? If prostitution were to vanish with revolution, as Bebel predicts, how would former prostitutes be integrated into the new socialist order? As markers of past bourgeois moral corruption, might they not still be treated as pariahs, as they often

---

38. See Bebel, *Die Frau und der Sozialismus,* 9, 11–23; and Engels, *The Origin of the Family,* 75–78, 113. For Bebel's vision of the future under socialism, particularly the aspects I have described, see *Die Frau und der Sozialismus,* 330–42.

39. I have slightly modified the translation; the German original reads: "Ein Übermaß geschlechtlicher Genüsse wirkt noch schädlicher, als ein Zuwenig....*Maßhalten* im Geschlechtsverkehr ist ebenso nötig wie im Essen und Trinken." Bebel, *Die Frau und der Sozialismus,* 158, emphasis in original; *Women in the Past, Present, and Future,* 104.

40. Michel Foucault, *The Use of Pleasure,* vol. 2 of *The History of Sexuality* (New York: Vintage, 1990), 80; Foucault, *The Care of the Self,* vol. 3 of *The History of Sexuality,* trans. Robert Hurley (New York: Vintage, 1988), 124–44.

41. On George Sand, see Bebel, *Die Frau und der Sozialismus,* 338–40; and for his repeated use of the term *Naturzweck* in relation to motherhood, see 80, 82, 117, 129.

42. Mosse, *Nationalism and Sexuality,* 185.

were in some working-class neighborhoods during Bebel's time?[43] These questions are left open by Bebel's text and by much of the socialist rhetoric on prostitution, which gives prostitutes sympathy as victims of the bourgeois capitalist order yet denies them potential identities as workers and fails to address pragmatic questions about social attitudes toward women's sexuality and domesticity. Sexism was not an alien concept to the working-class world, nor can it be claimed that proletarian men had no use or desire for prostitution. Although Bebel was right to point out the significant rise in middle-class patronage of prostitutes in the nineteenth century, this cannot cloud the fact that men of all classes purchased sex from prostitutes, just at different prices.[44] Examining the French socialist rhetoric on prostitution and the influence that Bebel's text had on it, Alain Corbin argues: "The socialists...did not explain in detail how the disappearance of any prostitutional demand in a socialist society would occur in practice. Here the discourse on prostitution turns into a utopia whose optimism resulted in a lack of interest in the struggle then being waged by those who were working toward an immediate improvement of the prostitute's lot."[45] As hopeful as Bebel's predictions for women's sexual and economic equality may have been, they constituted a social utopia that was not realized in his lifetime and that, despite the dramatic increase in women's autonomy, has yet to come to pass. Whereas Bebel's text offers few practical considerations for the current or future treatment of prostitutes, Georg Simmel's early essay on prostitution advocates an improvement in their social and moral status within bourgeois society, and his monumental work *The Philosophy of Money* presents prostitutes as quintessentially modern figures central to the understanding of life within what he called the "mature money economy."

Free Love or Freedom *from* Love? Georg Simmel on Money, Gender, and Desire

Georg Simmel was a keen observer of bourgeois life in Wilhelmine Berlin. A prolific scholar and public intellectual, he published numerous articles and essays, both in Europe and abroad, that spanned multiple fields of inquiry, including sociology, aesthetics, gender relations, and philosophy. Many of his contemporaries contended, and recent scholars do as well, that Simmel's work "could only [have been]

---

43. Lynn Abrams's historical analysis of the poor treatment of prostitutes by many working-class citizens certainly casts doubt on prostitutes' smooth social integration. See Abrams, "Prostitutes in Imperial Germany," 198–99. Richard Evans, on the other hand, argues that working-class attitudes toward prostitutes improved in the decades following the publication of Bebel's book, and that working-class men began to sympathize with prostitutes as fellow "victims of 'class justice.'" Evans, *Proletarians and Politics: Socialism, Protest, and the Working Class in Germany before the First World War* (New York: St. Martin's Press, 1990), 166.

44. On working-class men's patronage of prostitutes, see Abrams, "Prostitutes in Imperial Germany," 198; and Evans, *Tales from the German Underworld,* 5–6.

45. Corbin, *Women for Hire,* 238.

written in these times and in Berlin."[46] Like August Bebel, Simmel did not shy away from criticizing "'proper' society" for its moral hypocrisy and its gendered division of labor.[47] Like Bebel, he compared bourgeois wives with household possessions and the financially arranged marriage (*Geldheirat*) with prostitution.[48] Yet unlike Bebel, Simmel made only vague predictions for the future, and those he made did not include proletarian revolution. Although his early essays on prostitution and gender relations reveal his awareness of class struggle and his criticism of bourgeois men's exploitation of working-class prostitutes, he plainly states that such a radical overhaul of society via revolution was about as likely as "a sudden miracle from heaven." Societal change would come only through gradual reform.[49] An acknowledgment of social realities and problems was, for Simmel, the essential prerequisite for reform, and he therefore devoted much of his work to examining the intricacies of social life within urban capitalist modernity. Put plainly, his writings are more descriptive than they are prescriptive, more adept at "capturing the nuances of bourgeois culture" than undermining it.[50] One of his central objects of analysis, through which he studied modern social relations, was money.

By the time Simmel published *The Philosophy of Money* in 1900, money had become both the means (*Mittel*) and the end (*Zweck*) of modern existence. In other words, it was more than a means to acquire possessions; it had become a possession and a sign of wealth and status in its own right. With the growing prevalence of money, Simmel's study argues, quantitative value replaces qualitative

---

46. David Frisby, *Georg Simmel* (London: Tavistock, 1984), 34. Georg Simmel (1858–1918) grew up in the center of Berlin and became one of the most popular academics at the University of Berlin, where he worked from 1885 to 1900 as a Privatdozent and then as Ausserordentlicher Professor (an honorary and hence unpaid position) until the beginning of the First World War. His late promotion to the rank of professor was due to the insidious anti-Semitism of the German university system. With high enrollments in all of his lectures, he was also one of the first professors at the university to permit women to attend lectures. Simmel and his wife ran a literary salon that attracted such writers as Stefan George, Lou Andreas-Salomé, and Rainer Maria Rilke. In 1914 he took a Chair (*Ordinarius*) of Philosophy at the University of Strasbourg, which he held until his death in 1918. Biographical information comes from Frisby, *Georg Simmel;* Gianfranco Poggi, *Money and the Modern Mind: Georg Simmel's "Philosophy of Money"* (Berkeley: University of California Press, 1993), 38–52; Heinz-Jürgen Dahme and Klaus Christian Köhnke, introduction to *Schriften zur Philosophie und Soziologie der Geschlechter,* 10–12.

47. Simmel, "Einiges über die Prostitution," 60.

48. Simmel refers to the financially motivated marriage as "a means of permanently prostituting oneself" (*eine chronische Prostituierung*), implying that women are bought and used for repeated sexual encounters. Once she enters into such a marriage, the wife becomes an object, a body expected to fulfill her husband's sexual needs and reproductive demands in exchange for financial support and security. See Simmel, *Philosophie des Geldes* (1900, 1907; repr., Frankfurt am Main: Suhrkamp, 1989), 522, translated by Tom Bottomore and David Frisby as *The Philosophy of Money* (London: Routledge & Kegan Paul, 1978), 381.

49. Georg Simmel, "Der Frauenkongreß und die Sozialdemokratie," *Die Zukunft,* October 10, 1896, 80–84; reprinted in Dahme and Köhnke, *Schriften zur Philosophie und Soziologie der Geschlechter,* 134.

50. David Frisby, *Fragments of Modernity: Theories of Modernity in the Work of Simmel, Kracauer, and Benjamin* (Cambridge, MA: MIT Press, 1986), 39. For other works on Simmel that emphasize his bourgeois perspective, see Poggi, *Money and the Modern Mind,* 181, 185; and Suzanne Vromen, "Georg Simmel and the Cultural Dilemma of Women," *History of European Ideas* 8, no. 4/5 (1987): 563–79.

value, resulting in a devaluation of the individual person (*Persönlichkeit*) as well as an emphasis on rational over emotional life.[51] Money's function as a leveling mechanism—as something used to equate things with things, people with people, and even people with things simply by articulating a price—exists in an ineradicable tension with the opposing tendency that Simmel observed in modern culture: the supposedly high value placed on the individual. This tension is present in both the public and the intimate spheres, and it also illuminates a gender divide. Bourgeois society's proclaimed emphasis on individual fulfillment and achievement compels its members to search for the perfect companion, the "completely sympathetic complement to themselves," yet the difficulty or even futility of such a search often leads people (presumably men) to simply "buy" themselves a mate. The marriage of convenience allows for a choice of companion based on more tangible, material (quantitative) rather than elusive, personal (qualitative) criteria. Yet, when marriage becomes just another financial exchange, Simmel argues, human relations become increasingly alienated, and the effects on women are particularly detrimental.[52]

Why is it the case, however, that men are less adversely affected by the act of marrying for money? The answer lies in Simmel's analysis of Wilhelmine gender relations, in which men—as those who work, accumulate wealth, and are allowed access to a variety of activities and social circles—are more capable of "differentiation." They are able to fragment their selves into various parts, dedicating certain sides or parts of their personality to work and other sides to recreation and private life. As full participants in "objective culture," which can be defined as the external world of things and ideas, men have the power to attribute value to individuals and objects.[53] Women, whom Simmel describes as oppressed beings confined to the private sphere, have remained more unified, organic beings who cannot divide themselves into multiple subjectivities. The "undivided unity of her nature" allows therefore for the purchase of a woman's whole being in the marriage of convenience and also implies that when a woman gives herself sexually to a man, she gives herself completely.[54] By equating women's personalities with their physical bodies, Simmel's text anticipates what the young Berlin doctor and writer Alfred Döblin went on to argue in 1912—that dominant male culture equates women with their sex organs, whether they are used, in the case of the prostitute, for intercourse, or, in the case of the wife and mother, for reproduction.[55]

51. Simmel, *The Philosophy of Money*, 228–57.
52. Simmel, *The Philosophy of Money*, 381–82.
53. Simmel makes this argument most clearly in his 1902 essay, "Weibliche Kultur"; reprinted in Dahme and Köhnke, *Schriften zur Philosophie und Soziologie der Geschlechter*, 160–61; translated by Guy Oakes as "Female Culture," in *Georg Simmel: On Women, Sexuality, and Love*, ed. Oakes (New Haven, CT: Yale University Press, 1984), 65–101. See also Simmel, *The Philosophy of Money*, 382.
54. Simmel, "Female Culture," 71; Simmel, *The Philosophy of Money*, 377–78.
55. Alfred Döblin, "Über Jungfräulichkeit" and "Jungfräulichkeit und Prostitution," in *Kleine Schriften*, ed. Anthony W. Riley (Freiburg im Breisgau: Walter, 1985), 1:117–28.

It seems that Simmel offered women little hope for a way out of this oppressive, essentialist economy. But upon closer examination, his *Philosophy of Money* and his essays on gender do posit the possibility of women's differentiation between body and personality and identify narrow spaces in modern society for nonalienated, loving relationships. Curiously, it is not in his discussion of "free love" but in that concerning prostitution that such possibilities can be found. Although Simmel briefly explores the concept of free love in his 1892 essay on prostitution, he does not deem it a feasible option within a society that continues to idealize monogamous marriage. He simply cannot fathom a world in which women engage in premarital sex without hampering their own psychological and physical development.[56] Later he implies that the modern sense of freedom automatically makes the terms "free" and "love" incompatible, for the definition of freedom as the very absence of emotional or communal ties is incongruous with the bond of love. Indeed this negative definition of freedom is one of the central concepts of *The Philosophy of Money:* "Freedom seems to possess a merely negative character. It only has meaning in contrast to the concept of bondage; it is always freedom from something and corresponds to the concept by expressing the absence of obstacles."[57] In a society based on money, individuals purchase their freedom from various bonds by paying taxes in order to free themselves from the responsibility of political engagement, for example, or by paying a prostitute in order to enjoy a "completely fleeting inconsequential relationship" (in the German original, Simmel calls prostitution a "Beziehung, die keine Spuren hinterläßt"). In fact, Simmel describes prostitution and money as analogous, for both are characterized by an inherent "lack of attachment" (*Treulosigkeit*), by their "objectivity" (*Sachlichkeit*), and by a sheer indifference to the personal qualities of the individuals involved in the exchange. It is the indifferent nature of prostitution and the ease of the financial transaction that cause both the client and the prostitute to view each other as means to different ends—sexual gratification for the man and financial gain for the prostitute. Prostitution is a money-based relationship taken to its extreme: absolute indifference...and absolute freedom. "The relationship is more completely dissolved and more radically terminated by payment of money."[58] If money is a means to freedom, and prostitution is equated with money, then prostitution is also a way to freedom. In its tracelessness, prostitution becomes the only viable form of "free love" (albeit not "free" as in *gratis*) found in Simmel's *Philosophy of Money.*

But if prostitution is the only form of free love found in Simmel's text, does the prostitute achieve the same degree of freedom as her male client? Proper society, as the book describes it, associates the prostitute completely with the sexual act,

---

56. Simmel, "Einiges über die Prostitution," 67.
57. Simmel, *The Philosophy of Money,* 400; for similar passages on the negative concept of freedom, see also pp. 342–43.
58. Simmel, *Philosophie des Geldes,* 513–14; *The Philosophy of Money,* 376–77.

perceiving her to sell "her most intimate and most personal quality," and thereby "irredeemably renders [her] déclassé."[59] In Simmel's own analysis, however, people not only pay for freedom; they can also be paid for it. One of the examples he gives in the text is that of the peasant who allows his land to be purchased by the state in order to be freed from both labor and property and to acquire new buying power. "Certainly it is possible to experience the transformation of a tangible possession into money as liberation," Simmel writes. "With money in our pocket we are free."[60] If the peasant farmer can use money to separate himself from his work and his land, then perhaps the prostitute can do something similar with her body. If she gives her body just for the money, she attains a certain freedom from it, or at least she achieves a sense of distance between body and personality. It could even be argued that the ability of the prostitute to consciously fragment herself into subject and object allows her to bridge the gender gap between differentiated men and undifferentiated women. Fritz Breithaupt draws a conclusion similar to this when he argues that, within the modern money economy described by Simmel, freedom is found in self-objectification: "Objectification offers everyone a possibility of liberation; even the prostitute is emancipated if she succeeds in viewing the act of prostitution as an objective function, which means distancing herself from her body."[61] The image of prostitution in *The Philosophy of Money* differs in subtle yet important ways from the one offered by Simmel in his 1892 essay, which lends prostitutes a great deal of sympathy but little or no agency in its repeated reference to them as victims.[62] The essay admonishes those who morally condemn prostitutes and fail to concede the crucial role prostitution plays in protecting the sanctity of bourgeois marriage. It places the onus on bourgeois society to remove the moral stigma from prostitution and to raise prostitutes' social status.[63] In Simmel's later work, the prostitute is no longer a helpless victim or mere object. If she can successfully separate herself from her body by viewing sex as a physical function that she performs, then she becomes a self-conscious commodity, a subject and object at the same time, an agent who recognizes and capitalizes on the value of her body as an object of male desire. This act of fragmentation—this alienation of the body from the self, and the recognition of that alienation—is what makes the prostitute one of Simmel's most quintessentially modern figures. She is "the female figure...at the centre of the mature money economy," because she serves as the key to understanding how monetary exchange creates both social distance between people and frag-

59. Simmel, *The Philosophy of Money,* 377, 378.
60. Simmel, *The Philosophy of Money,* 399.
61. Fritz Breithaupt, *Der Ich-Effekt des Geldes: Zur Geschichte einer Legitimationsfigur* (Frankfurt am Main: Fischer, 2008), 194.
62. He describes prostitutes as "victims of [male] desire" (*Opfer der Triebe*), "victims of [bourgeois] sin" (*Opfer ihrer Sünde*), and "objects of social guilt" (*Objekte sozialer Schuld*). Simmel, "Einiges über die Prostitution," 64, 68, 69.
63. Simmel, "Einiges über die Prostitution," 68–69.

mentation within the individual.[64] In contrast to Marx, Simmel does not negatively judge this process of alienation, and he certainly does not define it as a symptom of class oppression; rather, he presents it objectively as a reality of modern social life.[65]

If, as David Frisby argues, "reconciliation with the objectified world takes place within the context of our creation of distance from it," does Simmel leave his readers with any hope for intimacy?[66] Does the prostitute, as an outlet for male desires, have an outlet for her own desires? Even though he presents romantic love as a virtual impossibility in the mature money economy, Simmel discovers a potential emotional and physical refuge for prostitutes in the lesbian relationship. He explains "the frequently reported cases of lesbianism among prostitutes" thus: "Because the prostitute has to endure a terrible void and lack of satisfaction in her relations with men, she searches for a substitute relationship in which at least some other qualities of the partner are involved."[67] As a relationship that lies outside the heterosexual economy—outside the division of labor within heterosexual marriage and the transaction between male client and prostitute—lesbianism offers the prostitute the possibility of fulfillment (Simmel uses the word *Ergänzung*) through a complementary partner who balances out her empty, objectified relations with men. Prostitutes, then, seem to be the only figures that can occupy two different worlds: the world of alienated, traceless sexual relations with men for money and that of intimate, nonalienated (or at least less alienated) relationships with other women. This rare example of a nonalienated coupling in a book that focuses on the alienating effects of money allows the reader a brief glimpse of a loving relationship that seems accessible only to women. But it also leaves the reader wondering if, in Simmel's work, heterosexual love is always alienated in some way and if women's desire is always absent from it.

There is, however, a space for heterosexual desire that resides somewhere between the lifelong bond of marriage and the fleeting, mechanical transaction of prostitution; it is the space for playful interaction between men and women that Simmel describes in his 1909 essay on flirtation (*Koketterie*).[68] Unlike marriage, flirtation requires no commitment, and unlike prostitution (and marriage), it

---

64. David Frisby, *Cityscapes of Modernity: Critical Explorations* (Cambridge: Polity, 2001), 149. Prostitutes today often identify this type of distancing as a common occupational strategy, as a way for them to separate their professional use of their bodies for commodified sex from their private, personal relationships with their friends, lovers, or husbands. Hydra's Stephanie Klee describes it matter-of-factly: "Ich gefalle einem Mann, fein, dann gebe ich ihm meinen Körper, bitte, und dafür gibt er mir Geld, also ein Stück Freiheit." (If a man likes me, great, then I give him my body, here you go, and for that he gives me money, a piece of freedom.) Quoted in Hoppe, "Die bürgerlichen Huren," 90. See also Bernstein, *Temporarily Yours*, 48–50.

65. For a more in-depth analysis of the differences between Marx's and Simmel's concepts of alienation, see Poggi, *Money and the Modern Mind*, 185–212; Frisby, *Fragments of Modernity*, 69, 89, 91, 104, 107–8; Frisby, introduction to *The Philosophy of Money*, by Georg Simmel, 11, 22–29, 36.

66. Frisby, *Fragments of Modernity*, 105.

67. Simmel, *The Philosophy of Money*, 379.

68. Simmel, "Psychologie der Koketterie," *Der Tag*, May 11–12, 1909; reprinted in Dahme and Köhnke, *Schriften zur Philosophie und Soziologie der Geschlechter*, 187–99; translated by Guy Oakes as "Flirtation," in Oakes, *Georg Simmel*, 133–52. All subsequent quotes come from Oakes's translation.

requires no money. It requires instead a subtle form of play that simultaneously promises and withholds sexual fulfillment; "it represents a mysterious interpenetration of consent and refusal, of giving and rejecting."[69] A game that renders gendered power structures unstable, flirtation often gives women the power to choose their objects of desire and to determine, yet not divulge, the outcome of the game. Flirtation "debases neither its subject nor its object," and indeed Simmel deliberately confuses the reader's sense of subject and object in this essay, making it all the more clear that both parties involved in flirtation assume both roles. They project desire, but they also want and need to be desired in return.[70] The essay argues that those relations that are still saturated with desire carry the greatest erotic value. The pleasure of flirtation is to be found in uncertainty, in the *possibility* of fulfillment rather than in fulfillment itself. This is perhaps the reason that Simmel refrains from an outright discussion of sex, for the magic of the game disappears as soon as erotic desire is fulfilled. Pleasure resides in the constant tension between having and not-having:

> There is a sense in which flirtation lends a positive concreteness to not-having, making it tangible for the first time by means of the playful, suggestive illusion of having, just as, conversely, flirtation intensifies the attraction of having to the most extreme degree by means of the threatening illusion of not-having. And if this fundamental relationship shows that in definitive having, there is still a sense in which we do not have, flirtation ensures that in definitive not-having, there is still a sense in which we can have.[71]

Just as flirtation allows for—albeit fleeting—moments of closeness between men and women, it also retains an element of distance. It still relies on differentiation, on the ability of the individuals involved to engage only partially in the relationship. And yet there is something about the fleeting pleasure of flirtation that Simmel regards as fundamental to "the relationship between the sexes," for flirtation is "the relationship that conceals within itself perhaps the most mysterious and tragic relation of life in its ultimate ecstasy and most glittering attraction."[72] By focusing on the transitory, uncertain, yet thrilling nature of flirtation, Simmel entices his readers into an intellectual game that ponders the very ambivalence of sexual desire and gender relations, "but to an end it cannot fathom."[73] The future of gender relations remains, in both Simmel's early and later works, unclear—always "mysterious," possibly "tragic," but not without a glimmer of hope, an element of play, and a tinge of desire.

---

69. Simmel, "Flirtation," 148.
70. Simmel, "Flirtation," 149; see also 145 for the desire to be desired.
71. Simmel, "Flirtation," 150.
72. Simmel, "Flirtation," 152.
73. Guy Oakes, "The Problem of Women in Georg Simmel's Theory of Culture," in Oakes, *Georg Simmel*, 6.

What's Love Got to Do with It? Prostitutes, Lovers, and Wives in Otto Erich Hartleben's Satirical Dramas

Arriving in Berlin just as the antisocialist legislation lapsed in 1890, Otto Erich Hartleben waxed enthusiastic about leftist politics in his diary, thrice proclaiming: "Long live international Social Democracy!" By 1896, however, his unbridled enthusiasm had waned significantly. He wrote: "I believed for a while that I had to be a Social Democrat"; but he came to prefer Nietzschean individualism over socialism in the end.[74] Between the years in which these two diary entries were written, Hartleben wrote several satirical dramas that reflect the influence of social democratic thought on his work, as well as his skepticism toward and eventual rejection of socialism. His 1893 play *Die Erziehung zur Ehe* (Education for Marriage) reveals Bebel's influence in its comparison of bourgeois marriage and prostitution, its critique of bourgeois marriage as loveless and bourgeois morality as hypocritical, and its representation of free love as a chosen relationship that falls outside the bounds of social legitimacy. Written one year earlier and immediately banned by the Prussian theater censor, Hartleben's drama *Hanna Jagert* also grapples with the issue of free love, yet it provides a stinging critique not of bourgeois society but of socialist male chauvinism. Both plays examine free love as an alternative to marriage or prostitution by featuring a financially independent and sexually liberated female protagonist, and yet neither play allows free love to flourish in the end. Marriage and forms of commodified sexuality—embodied by the prostitute, the kept woman, and the mistress—are the only relations that survive, and, as in Bebel's and Simmel's respective texts, prostitution is depicted as a more favorable option than marriage. Hartleben ventures a step further than the other two authors by presenting his audience with women who consciously choose prostitution over other work. In so doing, he challenges the audience to contemplate the limited options available to women who strive for both economic and sexual autonomy. Portraying his female characters—especially the prostitutes—as modern and rational, Hartleben also destabilizes the gender stereotypes of his time and sketches a personality profile that anticipates what would become known in the 1920s as "Neue Sachlichkeit," a cool objectivity that was deemed the most fitting attitude for modern urban life.[75]

Despite the fact that he was a best-selling author who was, during his lifetime, well known in literary and intellectual circles in both Berlin and Munich, little has

---

74. Otto Erich Hartleben, *Tagebuch: Fragment eines Lebens* (Munich: Albert Langen, 1906), 145, 228–29.

75. Simmel, too, offers readers one of the best-known descriptions of the blasé attitude of the cool, rational urbanite, in "Die Großstädte und das Geistesleben" (1903; repr., Frankfurt am Main: Suhrkamp, 2006); translated as "The Metropolis and Mental Life," in *Georg Simmel: On Individuality and Social Forms*, ed. Donald N. Levine (Chicago: University of Chicago Press, 1971), 324–39. On "New Objectivity," see Sabina Becker, *Neue Sachlichkeit* (Cologne: Böhlau, 2000).

been written about Otto Erich Hartleben and his works.[76] Likened to the medieval trickster Til Eulenspiegel and to the French chanson writer François Villon by his contemporaries, Hartleben was born in 1864 in Clausthal near Hannover and died in 1905 in Salò, Italy. Orphaned at a young age, he was supported for most of his life by his wealthy grandfather. After completing a law degree, Hartleben worked briefly at the court in Magdeburg, where he developed a greater liking for his defendants than for his bourgeois colleagues. In 1890, he gave up his law career and moved to Berlin to become a full-time writer. He lived the life of a bohemian in the capital city, circulating between various cafés and bars and writing satirical pieces for Berlin newspapers and for such journals as *Die Jugend* and the *Freie Bühne,* which later became the *Neue Rundschau.* His circle of friends, which included the publisher Samuel Fischer, the cabaret artist and composer Otto Julius Bierbaum, and the naturalist playwright Gerhart Hauptmann, appreciated his "brilliant sarcasm," his cynicism, and his disdain for philistinism, bourgeois or otherwise.[77]

While Hartleben's early plays drew the attention of the theater censor and hence ensured him a degree of notoriety within Berlin, his theatrical breakthrough and subsequent national success came with the premiere of his tragedy *Rosenmontag* in 1900. It was through the success of *Rosenmontag* that a wider German public discovered Hartleben's earlier plays; until then, they had been performed almost exclusively on Berlin stages.[78] This is not surprising, considering that both *Education for Marriage* and *Hanna Jagert* are clearly set in the German capital and make frequent reference to its streets and districts, and their risqué content likely kept them off the repertoire of more provincial theaters. Even in Berlin, playwrights such as Hartleben resorted to creative tactics in order to have their plays performed.

---

76. The only recent work that analyzes Hartleben's plays is Karl Leydecker's article "Prostitution, Free Love, and Marriage in German Drama in the 1890s," in Schönfeld, *Commodities of Desire,* 31–45. Otherwise, Hartleben receives passing mention in Repp, *Reformers, Critics,* 74, and Matthew Jeffries, *Imperial Culture in Germany, 1871–1918* (Basingstoke, UK: Palgrave, 2003), 149. Because Hartleben is not nearly as well known as Bebel and Simmel, I have chosen to place a brief biographical sketch in the body of the text. I will do the same in subsequent chapters, particularly for lesser-known writers and artists. Biographical information on most writers, thinkers, and artists appears in the notes.

77. Alfred von Klement, *Die Bücher von Otto Erich Hartleben: Eine Bibliographie* (Salò: Halkyonische Akademie für unangewandte Wissenschaften, 1951), 9. Von Klement's bibliography begins with an autobiographical segment written by Hartleben and includes quotes by contemporaries written at the time of Hartleben's death. The quote cited is attributed to Carl Hauptmann, Gerhart's brother. While the publisher of von Klement's book may sound like a hoax, it is actually the name of a group formed by Hartleben at his "Villa Halkyon" in Salò. Other biographical sources include Hartleben's *Tagebuch,* his *Briefe an seine Frau: 1887–1905* (Berlin: Fischer, 1908), and Julius Bab's description of Hartleben as an exemplary bohemian in *Berliner Bohême* (Berlin: Seeman, 1905), 41.

78. Hartleben's first play, *Angele,* premiered in November 1890 at the Residenz-Theater in Berlin, a stage run by the Freie Bühne cooperative, and its first performance outside of Berlin took place in 1904 in Vienna. After a lengthy censorship trial, *Hanna Jagert* opened in April 1893 at Berlin's Lessing Theater and was performed only in the large cities of Leipzig and Munich before the close of the century. *Die Erziehung zur Ehe* was first performed in September 1893 at the Neue Freie Volksbühne in Berlin and then again at the Lessing Theater in 1899. Subsequent performances, held in Bremen, Nuremberg, Wiesbaden, and Hannover, took place only after the success of *Rosenmontag.*

The Freie Bühne (Free Stage), for example, was a privately run theater founded in 1889 by a group of young journalists, actors, and intellectuals and spearheaded by the theater critic Otto Brahm as a way of evading the Prussian theater censor. It was one of the first theaters to stage plays that not only criticized bourgeois mores but also thematized the proletarian plight. The founders' decision to stage Gerhart Hauptmann's controversial plays, beginning with *Vor Sonnenaufgang* (Before Sunrise) in the fall of 1889, scandalized some of their own financial backers and audience members, many of whom were bourgeois citizens. In an attempt to expose the broader public to such plays, Bruno Wille founded the Freie Volksbühne (Free People's Stage) in 1890. This theater for the working class was also independent of the censor, allowing its founders to choose a repertoire that would provide its audience with an aesthetic education and foster within them a sense of community. Because of political tensions with the theater's board members, who championed a more radically Social Democratic repertoire, Wille split from the Freie Volksbühne in 1892 to form the Neue Freie Volksbühne (New Free People's Stage). It is fitting that Hartleben's *Education for Marriage* premiered at the Neue Freie Volksbühne, a stage less concerned with reflecting partisan interests in its program.[79]

What makes Hartleben's plays so important for this study is their portraits of women, which include a tyrannical bourgeois matriarch, a sassy maid, a level-headed accountant, a savvy businesswoman, a frail wife-to-be, and a seamstress who prostitutes herself on the side. Instead of proselytizing against prostitution by depicting prostitutes as social victims or as monstrous femmes fatales, Hartleben creates prostitutes who are street-smart, cool, and matter-of-fact, who are comic or "sachlich" rather than tragic figures. And yet for all his criticism of bourgeois mores, he has difficulty keeping his female characters from collapsing into the more traditional models of wife, mother, and whore created by respectable society. Still, even if such models remain intact, Hartleben's juxtaposition of prostitutes with other women struggling to maintain sexual and financial autonomy allows his readers to contemplate alternatives to prostitution and marriage, even if fleetingly.

Education for Marriage

Hartleben satirized the institution of bourgeois marriage and experimented with the concept of a free-love relationship in his 1893 tragicomedy *Education for Marriage*. The play's plot centers on the love affair between Meta Hübcke, an accounting clerk, and Hermann Günther, a young law student still living at home and dependent on his deceased father's money. In Meta, Hartleben offers his audience a character who is, at first glance, both financially stable and sexually liberated.

---

79. For information on the various "Free Stage" movements, see Jelavich, *Berlin Cabaret,* 62–63; and Julius Bab, *Das Theater der Gegenwart: Geschichte der dramatischen Bühne seit 1870* (Leipzig: Weber, 1928), 53–59.

Although the text hints at Meta's lower-class background by noting that she lives in Wedding, a distinctively working-class neighborhood in Berlin, her white-collar job seems to give her a level of autonomy that makes her relationship with Hermann more about mutual respect and affection than money. Their love affair comes to an abrupt end, however, when Hermann's staunchly bourgeois mother, Frau Günther, intervenes. Having already arranged for her son to marry the shallow and waifish Bella König, daughter of a wealthy textile factory owner, Frau Günther commands her son to end his dalliance with Meta immediately, and he obeys. She then calls on her brother-in-law, Onkel Otto, to come to Berlin and educate Hermann on the "virtues" of marriage. In a bewildered tone, she expresses her distress and confusion concerning Meta and Hermann's affair, telling Onkel Otto: "It really appears as if she [Meta]...bound herself to him not simply out of calculation, but rather, how shall I say this—out of love?"[80] The question mark that follows the word "love" shows that Frau Günther can barely grasp the concept. Expecting Meta to be a gold digger bargaining for her share of Hermann's monthly allowance, Frau Günther's incredulity intensifies when she finds out that Meta is a "solid" and "respectable" young woman who has never accepted money from Hermann. Frau Günther's solution to the problem is to raise her son's monthly allowance. This, she explains, will keep his relations with women "on the right level," for "had he had more money, she would undoubtedly have quickly become dependent on him." Instead, Meta's lack of dependence on Hermann allows a "kind of camaraderie" to develop between them, a bond that Frau Günther perceives as a sincere threat to the business deal she is hoping to seal, namely Hermann's marriage to Bella.[81] Although she thoroughly expects her son to engage in premarital sexual relations, she expects them to be purely physical and financial, not emotional, entanglements. In Frau Günther's view, money creates the desired asymmetry of power needed to keep bourgeois gender relations intact. The "comradely" relationship between Meta and Hermann involves no such imbalance of power; they have chosen each other freely and have formed a romantic bond that, because of Meta's financial independence, lies outside the bourgeois marital economy. Free love and the working woman, therefore, threaten to undermine the marriage of convenience and hence to destabilize traditional gender relations as Frau Günther understands them. Through the character of Frau Günther, a female enforcer of patriarchal capitalism, the play conveys what Simmel would claim nearly a decade later—that the moment money becomes the basis for a relationship, love is out of the question.

Lest the reader begin to pity Hermann, as the play unfolds, his actions reveal him to be anything but a victim of his mother's machinations. A playboy to the core, he makes regular passes at the family maid, Jenny, before he breaks off his

---

80. Otto Erich Hartleben, *Die Erziehung zur Ehe*, in *Ausgewählte Werke*, vol. 3, *Dramen* (Berlin: Fischer, 1913), 165.
81. Hartleben, *Die Erziehung zur Ehe*, 167.

love affair with Meta. When Frau Günther discovers this, she immediately fires Jenny in order to keep her household "pure" of sexual mischief. Hermann, pockets bulging with his increased allowance, arranges a rendezvous with Jenny on Potsdamer Platz—the location of one of Berlin's best-known prostitution markets—an arrangement that marks Jenny's new employment as Hermann's mistress and her likely entry into prostitution. Despite her firing, Jenny is not a tragic figure. Indeed, when Frau Günther offers to write Jenny an excellent letter of reference so that she may continue to work in domestic service, Jenny flatly refuses. Portrayed by Hartleben's text as sassy and street-smart, Jenny chooses commodified sexual relations over domestic service, claiming that she would rather "live like a baron" (*baronisieren*) than work as a maid.[82] The text leaves little doubt as to how Jenny will earn her money, for the use of the verb *baronisieren* insinuates that she hopes to become the mistress of a wealthy baron. Before she finds him, however, she will make do as the mistress of the bourgeois law student Hermann. In the scene in which Jenny agrees to become his mistress, Hermann rips her maid's apron from around her waist and waves it triumphantly over his head, proclaiming: "It belongs to me now!…The symbol of servitude has been taken from you—see: you are de-aproned!" (Hartleben uses the equally awkward term *entschürzt*.)[83] Here the apron is both a sign of Jenny's domestic servitude and a sexual fetish object that is, to quote Krafft-Ebing, "reminiscent of a female undergarment."[84] Hermann's gesture of holding up the garment and claiming his ownership of it clearly presents him as a *Schürzenjäger* (skirt chaser), which translates literally from the German to "apron hunter." The removal of Jenny's apron, however, also shows that she has been "freed" in more ways than one: she has been literally stripped of her profession as a maid by Hermann's antics, and at the same time she has been set free from the moral constraints of Frau Günther's bourgeois household. And yet Hermann's possession of the apron also underscores his new role as Jenny's employer or patron, a role that Onkel Otto applauds at the end of the play as part of Hermann's appropriate "education for marriage."

In the final scene, just after Hermann and Onkel Otto leave Frau Günther's house to join Jenny for a night on the town, it is Bella, the bourgeois wife-to-be, who enters the stage and sits alone, waiting for Hermann and waiting for marriage. In her 1893 review of the play, Lou Andreas-Salomé, a respected member of Berlin's intellectual circles who also contemplated the issue of free love in her writings, remarks that Bella's solemn, wordless, and solitary presence closes the play with a scene in which the "specter of marriage" looms largest.[85] With Meta's forced

82. Hartleben, *Die Erziehung zur Ehe*, 170.

83. Hartleben, *Die Erziehung zur Ehe*, 172.

84. Krafft-Ebing, *Psychopathia sexualis*, 223. See also Corbin, *Women for Hire*, 207, for a discussion of the French maid as fetish figure.

85. Lou Andreas-Salomé, "Hartlebens 'Erziehung zur Ehe,'" *Die Neue Rundschau* 4 (1893): 1165.

exit from Hermann's life, Hartleben's play leaves its readers with two images of dependent women: Jenny the mistress and Bella the wife. In so doing, it criticizes the bourgeois economy of the day, implying, just as Bebel's work argues, that it fosters loveless relationships based on sex and money. In its depiction of Jenny's choice to earn her living on the Potsdamer Platz rather than to serve the bourgeois household, it also bolsters Bebel's contention that prostitutes enjoy greater freedom than bourgeois wives. Jenny chooses both her new way of life and her first client, while Bella gloomily waits for her arranged marriage to commence. Hermann, a man who is free to take a lover (Meta) or mistress (Jenny) while his future wife must wait until marriage, clearly personifies the double standard. The free-love relationship that seems to be a viable option at the beginning of the play is quickly extinguished. Just as Bebel and Simmel argue, in Hartleben's play love has no place in the bourgeois order.

After her love affair with Hermann ends, even the venerable Meta chooses a loveless yet financially advantageous relationship with the charming aristocrat Herr von Bohling. Although Karl Leydecker claims in his reading of Hartleben's play that Meta "opts for the security of a *marriage* to a man whom she does not love," the text itself implies that she agrees to become Bohling's mistress or kept woman, a much more likely scenario considering the class difference between Meta and Bohling.[86] Meta's disillusionment with love and her struggle to remain economically independent lead her to accept Bohling's advances. She reveals her turn toward pragmatism by refusing to talk with her new suitor about love; she wants to discuss "facts...just facts." When Bohling mentions that although he is more than willing to offer her money, he had been told that money was of no consequence to her, Meta retorts: "Who told you that?—It all depends!—And one eventually learns....One evolves."[87] How is the audience supposed to read Meta's "evolution?" Andreas-Salomé's review expresses frustration regarding Meta's pragmatic turn and reads Meta as a tragic figure who does not develop but rather relinquishes both her freedom and her romantic fantasies. Although Meta's failed attempt at love does lend her elements of a tragic figure, the interpretation offered by the theater program at the Neue Freie Volksbühne offers greater agency and rational choice to Meta by reading her evolution as a freely chosen turn away from the "moral stuffiness" of bourgeois culture.[88] The play itself leaves little doubt that its main purpose is to offer the audience a biting "satire of *Spießbürgertum*," as Hartleben himself put it, and Meta demonstrates this in her statement that bourgeois society "judges life, people, everything...completely wrong. Much too—morally."[89] And yet Meta's

---

86. Leydecker, "Prostitution, Free Love, and Marriage," 35, emphasis added.
87. Hartleben, *Die Erziehung zur Ehe,* 155–56.
88. Both interpretations appear in Andreas-Salomé, "Hartlebens 'Erziehung zur Ehe,'" 1167.
89. The term *Spießbürgertum* defies any simple and direct translation, but it refers to a segment of the self-identified bourgeoisie that clings desperately to what it perceives to be bourgeois morals. It usually connotes a certain moral stuffiness, rigidity, and a judgmental nature. This quote appears in a letter

sense of resignation is palpable as she deliberates whether or not to take Bohling up on his offer. What Andreas-Salomé fails to mention in her review, however, is the socioeconomic critique contained within Meta's deliberation: "Hard, monotonous work . . . Even harder, more monotonous poverty.—And nothing more?—Nothing more? . . . No! I won't do it anymore! What for? Whatever for? . . . Now let's just try this."[90] With these words, she strikes a provocative and flirtatious pose, stretching out her arms and placing her hands on the back of her head, enticing and alluring Bohling. There are no words exchanged between Meta and Bohling about marriage, but it is clear from the quote above that, even as a woman employed in a white-collar job, Meta struggles with boredom and low wages and can barely maintain financial autonomy. Realizing that, for a woman, economic freedom is hard to come by, and sexual freedom has barred her entrance to respectable society, Meta exits the bourgeois economy for good, with the aristocratic Bohling enabling her exit. Trading in the fantasy of free love for a profitable business arrangement with a man who stands outside the bourgeois economy, Meta takes on the role of the kept woman, a form of commodified sexuality that seems to be the only—or, as the characterization of Jenny implies, the better—role available to single, economically vulnerable, and sexually active young women in Wilhelmine society.

Hanna Jagert

Hartleben's preoccupation with questions of free love and of women's financial independence is evident in his other major play from the early 1890s, *Hanna Jagert*. Although the play was scheduled to premiere at the Lessing Theater in Berlin in the spring of 1892, the Prussian theater censor banned it in March of that year. The Lessing Theater's director, Dr. Oskar Blumenthal, and Hartleben filed a joint lawsuit to have the ban lifted, and after a hard-fought battle that lasted into December 1892, the play opened on Easter Sunday 1893. The censor viewed the protagonist Hanna Jagert's tendency to follow her "carnal desires" from one man to the next as both morally reprehensible and politically dangerous, for free love was, in the eyes of Prussian state officials, a scandalous product of the socialist movement that threatened "the moral laws that form the basis of our state- and social order."[91] The play itself, however, advocates neither socialism nor free love unequivocally. Through the figure of Hanna, who has abandoned the socialist movement by the

---

written by Hartleben to his wife, on August 18, 1893; *Briefe an seine Frau: 1887–1905*, 178. For Meta's statement, see Hartleben, *Die Erziehung zur Ehe*, 148.

90. Hartleben, *Die Erziehung zur Ehe*, 159.

91. The court proceedings and the correspondence exchanged between the state authorities and Hartleben's lawyers, Richard and Ernst Grelling, are documented in Richard Grelling, "Censur-Prozeß betreffend 'Hanna Jagert' von Otto Erich Hartleben," in *Streifzüge: Gesammelte Aufsätze* (Berlin: Verlag des Bibliographischen Bureaus, 1894), 227–52, here 229. The primary documents pertaining to this case are also available at the Landesarchiv Berlin (LAB), A. Pr. Br. Rep. 030–05, Tit. 74, Th 666.

first act of the play, Hartleben's text delivers a strong critique of the persistent male chauvinism within that movement. In contrast to Meta, the struggling clerk in *Education for Marriage*, Hanna runs her own coat-making business and achieves a comfortable level of financial security that makes a man's support unnecessary. However, considering that Hanna's ascent from a working-class seamstress to an entrepreneur is made possible only through her affair with Alexander Könitz, a bourgeois factory owner, this play, too, grapples with the complexities of erotic and financial entanglements. By the end of *Hanna Jagert,* the "specter of marriage" conquers free love and turns Hanna from a successful businesswoman into a wife and mother, causing the reader to wonder if women's economic independence is irreconcilable with marriage and motherhood.

Set in Berlin between the years 1888 and 1891, *Hanna Jagert* captures much of the political turmoil and gender trouble stirring in the capital at the time. The protagonist Hanna is based on the historical figure Johanna Jagert, a young coat seamstress from a working-class family who was active in both the women's and the socialist movements in the 1880s but withdrew from the latter before leaving Germany for London in 1889.[92] Like her historical antecedent, Hanna abandons her working-class lover for a bourgeois one. In the first act of the play, Hanna is engaged to the hotheaded socialist Konrad Thieme, who has been imprisoned for political agitation. Konrad is released early and returns home only to find to his great chagrin that Hanna no longer belongs to the socialist movement and, even worse, is romantically involved with Alexander Könitz. Once Hanna admits to her affair with the bourgeois Könitz, both Konrad and Hanna's parents barrage her with insults and throw her out of the house. Blinded by jealousy, Konrad shoots and injures Alexander, who remains with Hanna and loans her the money to set up her own coat-making business. Once she has earned enough money to repay her debt to him, however, she ends their relationship. Over the course of three acts, Hanna climbs the social ladder as she goes from one lover to the next: from her "comrade" Konrad to the bourgeois Alexander to the aristocrat Bernhard von Vernier. Although Hanna is financially autonomous by the end of the second act and repeatedly voices her objections to marriage, her unplanned pregnancy leads her to accept Vernier's proposal of marriage in the end.[93]

Three aspects of *Hanna Jagert* merit close investigation. The first is the prostitute figure, Hanna's cousin Lieschen Bode. Perhaps a prototype for Jenny in *Education for Marriage,* Lieschen is blond and sexy as well as frank and street-smart. Full of pluck and speaking in Berlin dialect, she is clearly meant to represent the so-called *Dirnenmilieu.* The censor indeed described her as "a common prostitute," especially when compared to her "serious, austere, competent,

92. Grelling, "Censur-Prozeß," 235–36.
93. Hartleben, *Hanna Jagert,* in *Ausgewählte Werke,* 3:39–116.

industrious" cousin Hanna.[94] Yet the censor's description constitutes an oversim-
plification of the character, for Lieschen actually works as a seamstress as well,
but her wages keep getting cut, causing her to supplement her income by working as an occasional prostitute. Although Lieschen feigns offense when Hanna's
mother calls her a "Flittjen" (Berlin argot for *Flittchen,* meaning "floozy") in the
play's first act, in the third act she unapologetically admits that her fashionable
wardrobe is paid for by her various lovers and that she views her lifestyle as
"modern."[95] Her matter-of-fact attitude toward selling herself for clothes and
money anticipates Simmel's description of the prostitute as one who consciously
distances herself from her body to gain freedom from the oppressive bonds of
modern heterosexual and class relations, while also calling attention to the restrictive nature of women's work at the turn of the century. Lieschen also serves
as a figure of comparison for Hanna, and a closer reading of Hartleben's play
reveals that these two women have more in common than meets the eye. Having recently spotted Hanna riding in a private carriage with Alexander on the
central Berlin promenade Unter den Linden, Lieschen hints that Hanna has
sold herself to her bourgeois lover, a contention that Hanna does not refute.
In fact, she even admits in the presence of her family that she is "just like her"
(*ihresgleichen*).[96] Because she is dependent on Alexander for financial support
until the end of the second act, Hanna does see her position as akin to that of Lieschen, who works hard and yet must ultimately rely on her male lovers' money
to make ends meet. This is perhaps the reason that Hanna does not protest when
Konrad blatantly accuses her of selling herself to Alexander. At the beginning of
the third act, however, once she has paid her debts to Alexander and is truly autonomous, she becomes noticeably irritated when Lieschen asks her how much
her new aristocratic lover, Bernhard, pays her. Shooing Lieschen out of her
apartment, Hanna closes the door on her, drawing a visible line between herself
and her prostitute cousin.[97] This juxtaposition, followed by a clear distinction
between the two women, was intentional. As Hartleben's lawyer explained to
the authorities, "There is a difference between the prostitute's indiscriminate
surrender in exchange for money and the free choice of a lover based on affection
and made by a woman who demonstrates character and independence in both
her thoughts and her economic existence."[98] The initial blurring of lines between
Hanna and Lieschen encourages readers to recognize the difficulties that both
characters face as single, working women—difficulties that are nearly impossible to overcome without engaging in a form of prostitution. Hanna's later act of

94. Grelling, "Censur-Prozeß," 250.
95. Hartleben, *Hanna Jagert,* 48, 95.
96. Hartleben, *Hanna Jagert,* 49.
97. Hartleben, *Hanna Jagert,* 96.
98. Grelling, "Censur-Prozeß," 237.

slamming the door in Lieschen's face, however, slams the door to her own past as a dependent woman and underscores her role as an independent businesswoman involved in a free-love relationship.

Hanna's break with Lieschen constitutes just one of the family ties she severs during the course of the play; the other break is with her father. The socialist Eduard Jagert represents those working-class men who see emancipated women as a threat. He claims that women's work drives down wages and therefore has detrimental effects for male workers, a common argument made by working-class men at the time.[99] Konrad, Hanna's former fiancé, supposedly embraces the egalitarian principles of socialism. He initially praises Hanna's independence and accuses Eduard of being a tyrannical patriarch and a *Spießbürger* who clings desperately to respectability. Once he hears of Hanna's affair, however, Konrad is overcome by possessive rage and joins Eduard in cursing Hanna as a "slut" or "hussy" (*Luder*).[100] This clear depiction of socialist chauvinism is the second aspect of Hartleben's play that deserves critical attention. After enduring her father's and Konrad's verbal assaults and learning of Konrad's physical attack on Alexander, Hanna expresses her disenchantment with socialism in the starkest terms. She criticizes the movement's surreptitious domination of women and its potential for violence by portraying her own experiences in the party as a form of "rape" (*Vergewaltigung*) and concluding: "I saw how they functioned—these people who laid claim to a better future. The belief that one could save the world one day by replacing an established power...with this fledgling form—that was a belief I surely lost."[101] Hanna thus raises the possibility that women's emancipation might be found neither in the bourgeois nor in the socialist order. Her explicit reference to violence—including the sexual violence of rape—classifies both systems as forms of male tyranny, and her description of socialism as a "fledgling form" of power (or violence, as her use of the term *Gewalt* can also convey) implies that there is much work to be done within the movement before a promising future for both genders is possible. Hanna's criticism of the treatment of all women within socialist circles has certain parallels to Simmel's claim concerning prostitution's place in a hypothetical postrevolution socialist order: "Prostitution's status depends on the social feelings that it evokes, and we cannot know if or how such feelings will actually shift as a result of the eradication of capitalism and its consequences."[102] Would political and economic revolution truly change social attitudes toward prostitution, female sexuality, and women's rights or not? This is one of the critical questions raised by Hartleben's play.

---

99. Hartleben, *Hanna Jagert,* 58. On socialist male chauvinism, see Canning, *Languages of Labor and Gender,* 70–81; and Evans, *Proletarians and Politics,* 163.

100. Hartleben, *Hanna Jagert,* 60, 65.

101. Hartleben, *Hanna Jagert,* 111–12.

102. Simmel, "Einiges über die Prostitution," 69.

Although male chauvinism, both bourgeois and socialist, is clearly condemned in the play, this does not mean that Hanna's sexual and financial autonomy is unconditionally celebrated. In contrast to Meta in *Education for Marriage,* who makes the transition from romantic to realist, Hanna is portrayed until the very end of the play as objective, cool, and pragmatic. For instance, when Hanna explains how she came to take Konrad as her fiancé, she describes her feelings toward him not as love, but as admiration and comradeship. Konrad, on the other hand, is a fiery romantic who claims that he fell deeply in love with Hanna.[103] In fact, all of the men in the play are markedly more emotional than Hanna, and while Hanna is shown both at work and at home, the men are relevant only in terms of their private relations with Hanna. This textual gesture could be read to subvert gender stereotypes of the day, which associated the "masculine" with the public realm, with rationality and objectivity, and the "feminine" with the private sphere and emotional subjectivity. This subversion could also be read, in anticipation of Simmel's works, as a portrait of Hanna as the ultimate capitalist urbanite. Living the fast-paced life of a business owner, Hanna embodies the rational, objective attitude (*Sachlichkeit*) that holds dominion over feelings, a personality type attributed most often to the modern masculine subject in Simmel's writings.[104] Hanna's "cool persona," however, is not always portrayed in the most positive light. As a self-employed woman who categorically rejects marriage, Hanna is described as "unnatural" by both Alexander and Bernhard. The aristocratic Bernhard, who lives comfortably off his inheritance, fails to understand Hanna's desire to work and is uncomfortable in his relationship with her. As he tells Alexander, it's "really not the appropriate relationship between man and woman," and he elaborates by saying that he feels that their gender roles are reversed, causing him to feel that he belongs to Hanna, rather than that she belongs to him. Alexander, in turn, criticizes Hanna's aversion to marriage, saying that it "goes against nature."[105] Bernhard agrees with Alexander's sentiment and resolves that the only way to ensure "normal" gender relations between him and Hanna is to propose marriage. He does so impulsively, imploring Hanna to be his wife and telling her to show him that she loves him, "warmly and naturally, like we mortals should."[106] Bernhard's use of the word *Weib*—instead of *Frau*—for "wife" in his proposal marks his desire to transform Hanna into a more traditionally "feminine" woman, for as modernist literary scholars note, the term *Weib* signifies a femininity that is more closely tied to the body.[107] Indeed his proposal goes beyond a request

103. Hartleben, *Hanna Jagert,* 63.

104. See Simmel, *The Philosophy of Money,* 256–57, 474–79; and Simmel, "The Metropolis and Mental Life," 326–30.

105. Hartleben, *Hanna Jagert,* 102, 105. My use of the phrase "cool persona" refers to Helmut Lethen's study *Cool Conduct: The Culture of Distance in Weimar Germany,* trans. Don Reneau (Berkeley: University of California Press, 2002), which I discuss in greater depth in chapter 3.

106. Hartleben, *Hanna Jagert,* 114.

107. See, for example, Laurie Teal, "The Hollow Woman: Modernism, the Prostitute, and Commodity Aesthetics," *Differences* 7, no. 3 (1995): 82–83.

for marital commitment; in addition he asks Hanna to give up her business, her apartment in Berlin, and what he calls her "terrible independence" in order to become his wife. Hanna, who only moments earlier in the same scene had dismissed any talk of marriage and insisted that she would never consider abandoning her work, suddenly gives in and, to the reader's surprise, accepts Bernhard's proposal with all its stipulations. Laying her head on Bernhard's chest and thereby striking a more traditionally feminine pose of subjugation, she whispers that she would never have come to such a decision on her own, inferring that it is the best decision for their unborn child. When he realizes that Hanna is pregnant, Bernhard gleefully exclaims: "Now you're *really* my wife/woman!" (Jetzt bist du *erst* mein Weib!). He thus insinuates that motherhood has the power to transform Hanna into the more natural, corporeal woman he desires and can finally claim as his possession.[108] Hartleben's lawyer Richard Grelling cites this very scene in his defense of the play to the imperial authorities and claims that Hanna's ability to overcome her reservations about marriage and accept Bernhard's proposal gives credibility to the institution of marriage and restores the "social order." Hanna's acquiescence to marriage was in fact one of the primary factors that led the censors to lift their ban on the play, because it signified, in their eyes, the defeat of free love.[109]

Is free love truly defeated at the end of the play, or does Hartleben's work leave space for the audience to view both free love and marriage as legitimate options? Grelling carefully argues the latter in his final plea to the censor when he writes that those who attend the play might leave the theater with the impression that "a free union of hearts could, under certain circumstances, also be morally acceptable."[110] If free love is an intimate union between two financially self-sufficient persons, a union that balances out both sexual and economic power, then it exists in the play only briefly—in Hanna's premarital relationship with Bernhard. Hanna's decision to give up her job, marry, and become a mother seems to reinforce and privilege the bourgeois marital economy of independent man/dependent woman. This is complicated by the fact that, as an aristocrat, Bernhard stands outside the bourgeois order, at least economically. At first blush Hanna's marriage to Bernhard seems akin to Meta's liaison with Bohling at the end of *Education for Marriage*, for both relationships allow the female protagonists to exit the bourgeois economy for good. And yet Bernhard's essentialist rhetoric concerning what is natural or unnatural in the realm of gender makes him sound much more bourgeois than Bohling, who proudly refers to himself as "sinful" and actually seems to respect Meta's independence.[111] Hanna's pregnancy adds yet another dimension to the analysis of gen-

---

108. Hartleben, *Hanna Jagert*, 115–16, emphasis added.
109. Grelling, "Censur-Prozeß," 232, 250.
110. Richard Grelling to Königliches Oberverwaltungsgericht, September 19, 1892, LAB, A. Pr. Br. Rep. 030–05, Tit. 74, Th 666, p. 28.
111. Hartleben, *Die Erziehung zur Ehe*, 154–55.

der and sexuality in Hartleben's text, for her pregnancy binds her more closely to her physical body, and as the impetus for her decision to marry Bernhard, it causes the reader to wonder if motherhood is the ultimate barrier to women's autonomy. It is certainly used as a device to remove Hanna from the world of work and place her in the domestic sphere, to warm up what is portrayed throughout the play as her masculine "coldness," and hence to restore traditional gender relations. Hanna is no longer free; she is bound to Bernhard, his money, and their child. The only form of "free love" that remains intact at the end of *Hanna Jagert* is the kind that Simmel would outline in *Philosophy of Money*—the traceless sexual relationships of the occasional prostitute Lieschen.

Elusive Possibilities

Of the three influential writers discussed in this chapter, not one is truly able to imagine a world in which women can be both sexually and economically auton- omous. Still, to varying degrees, all three of them criticize the bourgeois patriar- chal order and its gendered division of labor within marriage, show sympathy for the social factors that lead some women to enter into prostitution, and support the presence of women in public life through increased educational and occupational opportunity.[112] With his vision of socialist revolution, August Bebel comes clos- est to championing women's absolute equality, and yet his emphasis on respecta- bility and moderation within postrevolution society casts doubt on his openness regarding sexuality. Would a complete overhaul of the bourgeois order be possi- ble, even after a revolution? Respectability's continued reign—even placed in the hands of socialists—leaves uncertain the fates of prostitutes, homosexuals, and all those who, in Bebel's words, engaged in the "unnatural satisfaction of sexual de- sire." Otto Erich Hartleben's plays expose the moral hypocrisy found in both the existing bourgeois order and the burgeoning socialist movement, but they pose only tentative alternatives to both. While they entertain the possibility of an indepen- dent, sexually active, working woman, his works do not allow his female protago- nists to remain completely autonomous, but rather transition them into marriage, motherhood, or forms of prostitution. It is certainly possible that Hartleben was merely appealing to the Prussian theater censor, and/or that his plays spoke to a prevailing "ambivalent attitude towards free love and the independent woman"

---

112. For example, for the tension between Simmel's analysis of gender roles as socially deter- mined—which has been praised as modern by both current and early twentieth-century scholars—and the limits to his vision of women's rights, see Lewis A. Coser, "Georg Simmels vernachlässigter Beitrag zur Soziologie der Frau," in *Georg Simmel und die Moderne: Neue Interpretationen und Materialien,* ed. Heinz-Jürgen Dahme and Otthein Rammstedt (Frankfurt am Main: Suhrkamp, 1984), 80–90. For an early twentieth-century reaction to Simmel's writings on gender, see Karen Horney, "The Flight from Womanhood: The Masculinity Complex in Women, as Viewed by Men and Women," *International Journal of Psychoanalysis* 7 (1926): 324–39.

held by the Wilhelmine audience, even in Berlin.[113] His most emancipated protagonist, Hanna Jagert, is portrayed as cold, pragmatic, and "unnatural"—read: too masculine—by the men around her. While Hanna's coldness could be interpreted as the rational, blasé attitude deemed necessary for survival in the modern metropolis and hence a foreshadowing of Simmel's work on the urban personality, it is important to note that "coldness" and "indifference" are also key attributes used by Lombroso and Ferrero in their description of the "morally insane" woman and the "born prostitute."[114] This problematic merger of critical social discourses with those on a pathological form of coldness or on forms of so-called sexual deviance is something that all of the works analyzed in this chapter have in common.

The supposed "coldness" of the prostitute seems, however, to have its advantages in the works of Simmel, for it allows her to achieve a separation or temporary alienation from her sexual transactions with men and to lend her more emotional and physical freedom than the bourgeois wife. While Bebel, too, uses prostitution as an instrument of conjugal critique by granting the prostitute more agency than the wife, Hartleben builds on Bebel's strategy and uses prostitution as a means to criticize the limitations placed on women's work. Instead of focusing on industrial laborers as Bebel does, Hartleben depicts women who choose a form of prostitution—that of the kept woman—over two of the other forms of women's labor prevalent at the time—domestic service (Jenny) and white-collar work (Meta). Indeed Hartleben's explorations of gray zones between prostitution and marriage, such as the figure of the mistress or kept woman, signify an attempt to offer his audience a "third type of woman, who is unmarried, engaged in sexual relations and yet is still respectable."[115] Both Meta and Hanna temporarily embody such a "third type," yet Meta intentionally exits "respectable" society when she accepts Bohling's money and his life of aristocratic decadence, and Hanna relinquishes her status as a single, working woman to take on the domestic roles of wife and mother.

Although all of the texts examined here use prostitution to criticize the institution of marriage, only Bebel's text offers—rather utopian—suggestions for marriage reform, and a firm belief in free love. Aside from revolution, however, it seems that no viable alternative is posed to marriage and prostitution, and certainly no solutions are given that could extricate the wife from the patriarchal family and the bourgeois division of labor. What is perhaps most striking is that these three writers leave very little room in their works for the consideration of women's sexual desire. In Simmel's *Philosophy of Money*, the prostitute is able to break out of the heterosexual economy and find intimacy in a lesbian relationship, a possibility neither Hartleben nor Bebel explores. Of the three, Simmel is the only one who

113. Leydecker, "Prostitution, Free Love, and Marriage," 41.

114. Lombroso and Ferrero, *The Female Offender*, 310–11. See also Dietmar Schmidt, ed., *Gebuchte Lust: Texte zur Prostitution* (Leipzig: Reclam, 1996), 58–59.

115. Leydecker, "Prostitution, Free Love, and Marriage," 32.

writes of the erotic pleasure of flirtation between men and women and its playful disruption of gendered power relations, but he is also the only one who openly admits how difficult it is to imagine gender equality. At the end of his 1892 essay on prostitution, Simmel himself flirts with the idea of women's increased intellectual, social, and financial autonomy and its possible effects on sexuality, yet he admits that the future of gender relations confounds him:

> If the pressure is taken off of women, if they are encouraged to test their own strength, to exercise their manifold talents, this difference from men might fade away as well, and women would then face a similar choice between either asceticism or premarital physical satisfaction. The consequences of such equality of conditions for both sexes are impossible to envision without getting lost in fantastic speculations; too limited is our grasp of all the changes in society that would have to occur simultaneously in order to affect the shape of gender relations.[116]

As unfathomable as women's equality and its accompanying sexual liberation may seem to Simmel, he does not deny their possibility. Within the first years of the twentieth century, Simmel was able to witness how some of the more radical members of the German women's movement dared to call for the abolition of state-regulated prostitution and to challenge the sexual double standard and the gendered division of labor. While some of them shied away from freeing women's sexual desire and favored premarital asceticism, others such as Helene Stöcker envisioned a "New Morality" that would create a space for women's sexual activity outside the conjugal model. Feminist writing on prostitution, although it did not necessarily favor prostitutes themselves, became a springboard for moral, marital, and sexual reform.

---

116. Simmel, "Einiges über die Prostitution," 70.

2

RIGHTEOUS WOMEN AND LOST GIRLS: RADICAL BOURGEOIS FEMINISTS AND THE FIGHT FOR MORAL REFORM

In 1907, the Berlin feminist Anna Pappritz published a collection of prostitutes' biographies entitled *Die Welt, von der man nicht spricht!* (The World of Which One Dares Not Speak!). A tireless critic of regulated prostitution, Pappritz directed the Berlin chapter of the International Abolitionist Federation (IAF), an organization that fought to end state regulation, its policing of prostitutes, and its implicit protection of men's sexual misbehavior. The brief case studies that appear in Pappritz's book, which she claims to have compiled from the papers of a policewoman, depict the vice squad in a particularly unflattering light. The story of the prostitute "W." is an excellent case in point, for the vice squad thwarts the young woman in her earnest attempts to leave prostitution. After W. has secured a job as the maidservant of a pious, charitable woman, the police show up and reveal her past, causing her to be fired from her job and leaving her with no option but to return to prostitution. The wardens of regulated prostitution are shown to be a punishing force that has no interest in the rehabilitation or reeducation of prostitutes. The so-called morals police serve the interests not of the women they monitor but of the "gentlemen" who make use of the services they provide, men whom Pappritz describes as shameless philanderers.[1]

---

1. Anna Pappritz, *Die Welt, von der man nicht spricht! (Aus den Papieren einer Polizei-Beamtin)* (Leipzig: Felix Dietrich, 1907), 18–19, 32. The title page claims that Pappritz is the organizer and editor

The melodramatic title of Pappritz's exposé is meant to decry the shroud of silence that enveloped the topic of prostitution within bourgeois circles, especially when it came to the patronage of prostitutes by bourgeois "gentlemen." Although the 1891 murder trial of Hermann and Anna Heinze, a pimp and his prostitute wife, garnered widespread attention in the urban and national press and drew spectators from well-to-do social circles, bourgeois observers could take comfort in the fact that the Heinzes came from a distinctively working-class milieu in Berlin-North and thus were not part of bourgeois society. Pappritz's book, however, seeks to disabuse her readers of the assumption that the so-called underworld and respectable society can be so clearly separated from one another. Eschewing hierarchical distinctions, Pappritz uncovers a world that "exists neither outside nor beneath 'our world,' but rather is tightly intertwined with it."[2] Just as the book reveals the central role that men play within the institution of prostitution, it shows that even young women like W., who grew up in affluent households, were well educated, and were employed in white-collar positions, could become prostitutes. But Pappritz's title, and with it her claims of novelty, are overstated, for her text was neither the first to present readers with biographies of prostitutes nor the first to point an accusatory finger at bourgeois men. As evidenced in chapter 1, August Bebel's *Women and Socialism*, which was widely read by late nineteenth-century feminists and would surely have been familiar to Pappritz, had exposed the connections between bourgeois society and prostitution long before the publication of Pappritz's collection. Bebel, too, had highlighted bourgeois men's culpability in the spread of venereal disease and the decline of the family.[3] Indeed by the time Pappritz's book came out in 1907, case studies of prostitutes had already proven to have popular appeal.

Filtering the life stories of prostitutes through the analytical lens of a medical professional, for example, the venereal disease expert Dr. Wilhelm Hammer published *Zehn Lebensläufe Berliner Kontrollmädchen* (Ten Biographies of Berlin's Registered Prostitutes) in 1905. Based on excerpts from prostitutes' diaries and from interviews that Hammer conducted with registered women, many of whom he treated for venereal infection, the biographies and Hammer's extensive commentary on them appeared in Hans Ostwald's multivolume series on metropolitan life, the *Großstadt*

---

of the materials provided to her by a policewoman, and yet the fact that portions of the text constitute excerpts from Pappritz's own polemics on prostitution is evidence of her (co)authorship. Although female police officials who worked with prostitutes or women at risk of entering prostitution were more prevalent during the Weimar years, they did exist in small numbers in imperial Germany, usually as ambassadors of social welfare organizations. See Ursula Nienhaus, "Einsatz für die 'Sittlichkeit': Die Anfänge der weiblichen Polizei im Wilhelminischen Kaiserreich und in der Weimarer Republik," in *"Sicherheit" und "Wohlfahrt": Polizei, Gesellschaft und Herrschaft im 19. und 20. Jahrhundert*, ed. Alf Lüdtke (Frankfurt am Main: Suhrkamp, 1992), 243–66.

2. Pappritz, *Die Welt, von der man nicht spricht!*, 6. The Heinze trial is described in greater detail in chapter 1 in this book.

3. On Bebel's widespread influence beyond Social Democratic circles, particularly on leading bourgeois feminists, see Repp, *Reformers, Critics*, 118–19; see also Canning, *Languages of Labor and Gender*, 104–5.

Dokumente (Documents of the Big City).[4] Although Pappritz explicitly sets the case studies in *The World of Which One Dares Not Speak* apart from Hammer's work in a footnote, the two texts have several key commonalities: both claim to debunk the Lombrosian theory of the "born prostitute" by showing the various ways that women can "fall" into prostitution, both are highly critical of state regulation, and both critique the double standard that morally condemns prostitutes yet exonerates their male clients. In a clear denouncement of the double standard, Hammer writes: "If men engage in intercourse with prostitutes without being deemed immoral, then the prostitutes cannot possibly be judged as immoral for offering themselves to men for intercourse." Hammer's and Pappritz's works differ, however, in two important ways. The first difference has to do with their perspectives on extramarital sex. In his attempt to protect prostitutes from moral stigmatization, Hammer asserts that if men are allowed to engage in sexual intercourse outside the boundaries of conjugality, then there need to be "morally acceptable extramarital forms of intercourse" available to all women as well.[5] Pappritz, in contrast, holds fast to marriage as the privileged site for heterosexual intercourse. Although she does not condemn women who, like W., engage in premarital sex and become pregnant, she presents most of them as victims—as women who are seduced, impregnated, and then abandoned by their boyfriends or lovers. This is, of course, a subtle difference between the two texts, but it is a crucial one. Hammer advocates an opening up of sexual possibilities for both men and women, while Pappritz strives to rein in male sexuality.

The divergence between Pappritz's and Hammer's texts in regard to gender parity and nonmarital sex is indicative of their second, larger difference. Unlike Bebel and Hammer, who identify class difference and poverty as the primary causes of prostitution, Pappritz is concerned, first and foremost, with gendered power dynamics. This difference is evident in the biographies themselves, for while Hammer's "control girls" (the literal term for registered prostitutes) hail from working-class or petit-bourgeois backgrounds, Pappritz offers a significant number of examples of women from the middle classes, some of whom held white-collar jobs before turning to prostitution. Whereas Hammer, like Bebel, points to socioeconomic factors that lead women to prostitute themselves, Pappritz focuses on moral stigmatization. She shows how respectable women, like the former accountant W., are judged harshly for their sexual transgressions, cast out of bourgeois society by their own families, and forced to fend for themselves and their illegitimate children.

---

4. Wilhelm Hammer, *Zehn Lebensläufe Berliner Kontrollmädchen (und zehn Beiträge zur Behandlung der Geschlechtskrankheiten)*, vol. 23 of *Großstadt-Dokumente*, ed. Hans Ostwald (Berlin: Seeman, 1905). For an in-depth analysis of Hammer's work and its connection to both the scientific and the cultural discourses of its time, see Dietmar Jazbinsek, "Lebensgeschichte und Eigensinn: Über die Biographie und die Biographieforschung des Dirnenarztes Wilhelm Hammer," *Mitteilungen der Magnus-Hirschfeld-Gesellschaft* 37/38 (June 2007): 32–61.

5. Hammer, *Zehn Lebensläufe*, 49; both quotes cited can be found on this page. The footnote in Pappritz's text assures readers that the life stories of prostitutes given in her text "are not identical to those presented" in Hammer's work. See Pappritz, *Die Welt, von der man nicht spricht!*, 14.

Pappritz's book, therefore, connects the life stories of prostitutes and an exposé on the perils of state regulation to a broader narrative that decries gender oppression and the moral condemnation of single mothers—topics that, this chapter will show, became rallying points for bourgeois feminists in turn-of-the-century Berlin.

While Pappritz explicitly mentions Hammer's text in her exposé, it seems a curious oversight that she fails to acknowledge the best-selling novel that brought the life story of a prostitute to a wide bourgeois readership in the same year that Hammer's case studies appeared, a novel that Pappritz herself had read and reviewed positively upon its release: Margarete Böhme's *Tagebuch einer Verlorenen* (Diary of a Lost Girl, 1905). The novel, which was presented to readers as the authentic diary of the bourgeois-daughter-turned-prostitute Thymian Gotteball, with Böhme acting as editor rather than author, enjoyed immense popularity, selling 90,000 copies in its first year and nearly two million copies by 1933. It was not only widely read; it also elicited a multitude of sympathy letters from concerned readers who, believing the novel to be a real diary, wished to pay their respects at Thymian's grave in Berlin-Schöneberg, and it inspired numerous imitations and spoofs, including the bogus autobiography of the prostitute "Hedwig Hard," written by none other than Hans Ostwald.[6] Böhme's influential book resonated within feminist and sex reform circles, garnering praise from Pappritz for "casting a glaring light on the 'double standard'" and for revealing the dangers of male sexuality run rampant. A rival of Pappritz's, the prominent feminist radical Helene Stöcker, reviewed Böhme's novel in one of the first issues of *Mutterschutz* (1905), the official journal of Stöcker's newly founded organization, the Bund für Mutterschutz (League for the Protection of Mothers; BfM). Citing Böhme's book as a laudable example of "new morality in artistic form," Stöcker argues in her review that Böhme's text admonishes conventional bourgeois morality for scorning the seduced and pregnant Thymian and facilitating her entrance into prostitution. In contrast to Pappritz's review, Stöcker contends that the novel's less judgmental stance on women's sexual behavior offers hope for the possibility of a new morality that would allow greater sexual freedom to all individuals, regardless of gender.[7] For the purposes of my own analysis, Böhme's novel and Pappritz's and Stöcker's positive— yet strikingly different—reviews of it demonstrate the cross-fertilization between the cultural and social discourses on prostitution in imperial Berlin. Although the title of Pappritz's 1907 collection, *The World of Which One Dares Not Speak!*, suggests the requisite propriety that mutes discussion of prostitution, the text itself, along with those

---

6. Böhme's *Tagebuch einer Verlorenen* sold more copies than Thomas Mann's novel *Der Zauberberg* (*The Magic Mountain*). Publication statistics are taken from Günther, *Weiblichkeitsentwürfe*, 245; and Donald Ray Richards, *The German Bestseller in the Twentieth Century: A Complete Bibliography and Analysis* (Bern: Herbert Lang, 1968), 55. For readers' reactions to the book, see Anna Richards, "Sense and Sentimentality? Margarete Böhme's *Tagebuch einer Verlorenen* in Context," in Schönfeld, *Commodities of Desire*, 98–109, here 98. On the various copycat texts, including Ostwald's, that appeared in the wake of Böhme's novel, see Jazbinsek, "Lebensgeschichte und Eigensinn," 41–43.

7. Pappritz, "Die Sittlichkeitsfrage in der 'schönen' Literatur," *Der Abolitionist* 4, no. 9 (1905): 99–101, here 101; Helene Stöcker, "Neue Ethik in der Kunst," *Mutterschutz* 1, no. 8 (1905): 301–6.

by Böhme and Stöcker, stands as evidence that women, both authors of fiction and feminist activists, did dare to speak openly about the world of prostitutes and its inextricable connection to bourgeois mores.

Pappritz's critique of the double standard and Stöcker's quest for an alternative morality critically inform my close reading of Böhme's *Diary of a Lost Girl*, but my reading also shows how the fictional biography of a bourgeois prostitute reveals the limits of turn-of-the-century radical feminism. While Margaret McCarthy's interpretation of the novel questions its ability to function effectively as a social critique, analyses by Richard J. Evans and Stephanie Günther find Böhme's novel to be critical of bourgeois moral codes and of the bourgeois feminists who upheld those codes.[8] Surprisingly, none of these readings analyzes the novel in light of the concurrent rise of feminist campaigns for the rights of unwed mothers, despite the fact that both Pappritz and Stöcker praised Böhme's book precisely for its potential impact on attitudes toward illegitimate pregnancy. By reading the novel in this context, I show that it does deliver a strong critique of traditional bourgeois norms, even if the critique was still packaged in a way that made the book palatable enough to become a commercial success among bourgeois readers. Much like Stöcker's essays on love and sexuality, Böhme's novel creates a privileged space for a form of emancipated, educated motherhood, from which the prostitute Thymian ultimately remains isolated. However, the book's immense popularity generated widespread public sympathy for the prostitute in a way that the turn-of-the-century feminist movement could not.

Daring to Speak about Prostitution

Up until the final decade of the nineteenth century, the term "prostitution" was widely used within the women's movement as an accusation denoting questionable morals or, at the very least, a questionable stance on sexual morality. Turn-of-the-century feminist rhetoric sometimes used the word "prostitution" as a polemical device to discredit rival feminists, and the issue of prostitution clearly highlighted the divisions between moderate and radical feminists within the women's movement. Gertrud Guillaume-Schack, a devoted follower of August Bebel, was the first activist to speak openly about prostitution. As early as 1880, she spoke out against the state regulation of prostitution to an audience at Berlin's city hall, and in an 1882 public lecture in Darmstadt that was cut short by the police, she urged feminists to act as "guardians of the moral order."[9] Women like Guillaume-Schack, who

---

8. Margaret McCarthy, "The Representation of Prostitutes in Literature and Film: Margarete Böhme and G. W. Pabst," in Schönfeld, *Commodities of Desire,* 77–97; Evans, *Tales from the German Underworld,* 166–212; Günther, *Weiblichkeitsentwürfe,* 310–18.

9. Gertrud Guillaume-Schack, "Über unsere sittlichen Verhältnisse und die Bestrebungen und Arbeiten des Britisch-Continentalen und Allgemeinen Bundes," in Marie-Louise Janssen-Jurreit, *Frauen und Sexualmoral* (Frankfurt am Main: Fischer, 1986), 61. Guillaume-Schack's ideas found few listeners

dared to mention the subject of prostitution in public—even critically—were initially treated as pariahs. Respectable bourgeois ladies did not speak of such things. Prostitution became a more acceptable topic among feminists only once England's Josephine Butler and her crusade to abolish the state regulation of prostitution began to gain momentum on the European continent, inspiring the creation of a German branch of the Abolitionist Federation founded by Anna Pappritz and Katharina Scheven in 1899.

By the start of the twentieth century, sexual morality and the various topics it encompassed—prostitution, love, and marriage; motherhood and child rearing; sexual desire—had become central issues in the German bourgeois feminist movement, particularly in its radical wings. While the activists and authors discussed in chapter 1, August Bebel, Georg Simmel, and Otto Erich Hartleben, certainly wrote critically about the restrictiveness of bourgeois marriage, its inherent gendered division of labor, and the moral condemnation of those women who stood outside of this institution, only Bebel pointed out the potential danger and destructiveness of male desire, and when he did so, he couched his critique in socioeconomic terms. He made a particular class, the bourgeoisie, responsible for the social ills of prostitution and venereal disease. Outspoken activists within the women's movement, in contrast, argued that it was not a particular class but the male-dominated state that had allowed men's sexuality to run rampant and had thereby jeopardized both public health and private bliss. The abolitionists vociferously opposed the state's forced registration and medical examination of prostitutes, a system that exonerated male clients from sexual and moral responsibility. With their fires fueled by rising rates of venereal disease in the capital city and throughout the country, which they saw as a direct effect of the state's regulation of prostitution, feminists placed themselves in the position of higher moral authority and admonished men for consorting with prostitutes and spreading disease into the domain of the family. In their moral vigilance, many feminists fought against the double standard by promoting a single standard of premarital abstinence for both men and women and spousal fidelity within marriage, and by demanding that men be held legally accountable for their transgressions.[10] Such demands served to erode

---

within the bourgeois feminist movement of the 1880s; indeed many women actually plugged their ears at the mere mention of prostitution. Some women were also deterred by the Prussian Law of Association, which placed restrictions on women's rights to meet in public and discuss political and social issues. The law remained in effect until 1908. Guillaume-Schack went into exile in London in 1886, where she continued to fight for women's and workers' rights until her death in 1903. Janssen-Jurreit describes the negative reactions among feminists to the topic of prostitution and sexuality in *Frauen und Sexualmoral,* 70, 154. On Guillaume-Schack's work with Bebel, see also Lopes and Roth, *Men's Feminism,* 166–76.

10. On the feminists' critique of male sexuality and the emergence of sexual morality as a central issue within the women's movement, see Ann Taylor Allen, "Feminism, Venereal Diseases, and the State in Germany, 1890–1918," *Journal of the History of Sexuality* 4 (1993): 27–50; Richard J. Evans, *The Feminist Movement in Germany, 1894–1933* (London: Sage, 1976), 2, 10; Barbara Greven-Aschoff, *Die bürgerliche Frauenbewegung in Deutschland 1894–1933* (Göttingen: Vandenhoeck & Ruprecht, 1981), 17, 43, 70, 79–82, 104–5; see also Frevert, *Women in German History,* 126–27, 131–37; Mosse, *Nationalism*

the boundaries between the public and private, disrupting what Isabel Hull calls the "bestowal of silence on men and moral judgment on women in matters sexual" that had played such a formative role in the nineteenth-century sexual system.[11] The increasingly public focus on the private realm of sexual behavior was meant to produce tangible results, not the least of which would be the elimination of prostitution.

Prostitution was an issue that divided women and men, but also women and other women. Abolitionism's growing popularity within the bourgeois feminist movement initially alarmed the more moderate members of its central organization, the Bund deutscher Frauenvereine (Federation of German Women's Organizations; BDF), who wanted to maintain their focus on social welfare and the expansion of professional and educational opportunities for women. The idea of offering social aid to prostitutes or of engaging in open discussions of sexual morality remained abhorrent to many women, and this led to a split within the movement.[12] In 1899, a faction of radical feminists including Anita Augspurg, Lida Gustava Heymann, Minna Cauer, and Maria Stritt broke away from the BDF to form a group called the Verband fortschrittlicher Frauenvereine (League of Progressive Women's Organizations; VfF). Many members of this new organization had already been active in the Verein Frauenwohl (Women's Welfare Association), founded by Cauer in 1888, which took on such controversial issues as pornography, venereal disease, and prostitution and was also the first group to endorse woman suffrage, an issue that found little resonance within the larger women's movement in Germany.[13]

Contemporary historians of the German feminist movement such as Ann Taylor Allen and Barbara Greven-Aschoff have argued that it was the feminists' relatively weak stance on suffrage, even among the radicals, that allowed campaigns for moral reform to take such a prominent place within the movement. By focusing their energies on marriage, the family, and sexual behavior rather than on the more blatantly

---

and Sexuality, 109–13; Repp, *Reformers, Critics,* 121; Roos, *Weimar through the Lens of Gender,* 98, 101; Schmidt, *Geschlecht unter Kontrolle,* 346.

11. Hull, *Sexuality, State, and Civil Society,* 406.

12. The BDF, formed in 1894, served as the umbrella organization for various middle-class women's associations and clubs. By the advent of the First World War, it represented nearly 500,000 women. See Ann Taylor Allen, *Feminism and Motherhood in Germany, 1800–1914* (New Brunswick, NJ: Rutgers University Press, 1991), 136; Frevert, *Women in German History,* 113; Greven-Aschoff, *Die bürgerliche Frauenbewegung,* 54, 88. Repp clearly states that it was the taboo topic of prostitution that "led to the crystallization of the left wing" of the feminist movement (*Reformers, Critics,* 120). See also Evans, *Feminist Movement,* 42; and Greven-Aschoff, 105.

13. Despite their formation of a new organization, many members of the VfF remained active within the BDF, particularly on its legal committee. On both the Verein Frauenwohl and the VfF, see Allen, *Feminism and Motherhood,* 136; Frevert, *Women in German History,* 129; Greven-Aschoff, *Die bürgerliche Frauenbewegung,* 91. For the classification of "moderates" and "radicals" within the bourgeois feminists movement, see Evans, *Feminist Movement,* 38–47; Heide Schlüpmann, "Radikalisierung der Philosophie: Die Nietzsche-Rezeption und die sexualpolitische Publizistik Helene Stöckers," *Feministische Studien* 3 (1984): 10–34, here 21; and Christl Wickert, *Helene Stöcker 1869–1943: Frauenrechtlerin, Sexualreformerin und Pazifistin* (Berlin: Dietz, 1996), 49–50. On the movement for woman suffrage as relatively weak in comparison to the push for moral reform, see Allen, *Feminism and Motherhood,* 148; Greven-Aschoff, *Die bürgerliche Frauenbewegung,* 91–92, 125–47.

public arena of political enfranchisement, feminists sought to carve out a particularly "feminine" sphere of influence within German society, a more motherly or nurturing approach to social reform that underscored rather than undermined gender difference. This "maternal feminism" has prompted some historians to present the German women's movement as particularly weak or even reactionary, but scholars like Allen argue that maternal feminism or "social motherhood" was a complex strategy employed by women to "create alternative views of the world by exposing the contradictions and exploiting the unexplored possibilities of dominant discourse."[14] Quite cannily, feminists used the assumed public/private split to their advantage, claiming expertise in the ostensibly private domestic realm rather than clamoring for the public rights of citizenship. But while feminists' family- and marriage-oriented rhetoric seemed to reinforce the traditional public/private divide, their public criticism of male sexuality undermined that very divide. By debating such hot-button issues as prostitution, venereal infection, and sex education, issues that were once deemed to be private but were discussed in a variety of public forums at the turn of the century, women were able to occupy prominent positions not only within the feminist movement, but also in influential public health organizations such as the Berlin-based Deutsche Gesellschaft zur Bekämpfung der Geschlechtskrankheiten (German Society for Combating Venereal Diseases; DGBG). Within these organizations and forums, prostitution formed the nexus for intersecting discourses on sexual morality, public health, and marriage reform. As Julia Roos has shown in her analysis of the bourgeois feminists' push for prostitution reform during the Weimar Republic, feminist discourse on prostitution exposed both the viability and the limitations of maternalism as a strategy for improving women's status, for it "combined genuinely emancipatory goals with more problematic efforts to control 'illicit' female sexuality."[15] However, as this chapter will show, such tensions between the emancipatory and oppressive elements of maternal feminism were already evident at the turn of the century, when key perspectives on prostitution were formulated.

Three bitter rivals, Hanna Bieber-Böhm, Anna Pappritz, and Helene Stöcker, exemplify the diverse aspects of radical feminist rhetoric on prostitution in turn-of-the-century Berlin. Despite their differences, their writings converge in important ways. All three women agreed that prostitution was the main cause of venereal disease and thereby constituted a major public health risk that somehow needed to be controlled or eradicated. All three spoke out against state-regulated prostitution and noted the system's failure to fight venereal disease effectively, but each outlined

---

14. Allen, *Feminism and Motherhood*, 11. Evans's book *The Feminist Movement in Germany, 1894–1933* serves as the most obvious example of the view of German feminism as weak and reactionary. For the argument that reads nineteenth-century maternal feminism as a precursor to the coercive familial and reproductive policies of the Nazi era, see Claudia Koonz, *Mothers in the Fatherland: Women, the Family, and Nazi Politics* (New York: St. Martin's Press, 1987), xx—an argument that Allen fiercely contests. Roos offers a cogent summary of this debate in *Weimar through the Lens of Gender*, 99–101.

15. Roos, *Weimar through the Lens of Gender*, 107.

different alternatives to it. Bieber-Böhm criticized the regulatory system as too lax in its failure to punish male clients for their moral transgressions, and she petitioned the state to extend its regulatory and punitive powers to the men who frequented prostitutes. Both Pappritz and Stöcker admonished the system for its surveillance and harsh control of women's public behavior, yet they diverged on the question of how the regulatory system could actually be abolished and what would be put in its place. Pappritz prescribed the moral education of the German youth of both genders, who would be instructed on the values of premarital abstinence and mutual respect within marriage. Stöcker, on the other hand, cited conventional bourgeois morality and philistinism—which she called "the old morality"—as the principal causes of prostitution. She pushed for marital reform and promoted a "new morality" that would create a space for women's sexual fulfillment and intimate relationships outside the boundaries of marriage. From Stöcker's perspective, only the broad acceptance of women's sexual autonomy could bring an end to prostitution. Perhaps the clearest point of convergence in these women's writings, however, is the effort they put into drawing a clear line between themselves and their "fallen sisters," the prostitutes.[16]

Feminist claims of solidarity or sisterhood with prostitutes were fraught with ambivalence, for as much as they claimed to speak *for* the prostitutes, they spoke twofold *against* them. Even in their attempt to speak *for* prostitutes, they did so on the assumption that prostitutes were unable to articulate their own interests and motivations, that they were, to use a German word that appears repeatedly in feminist texts of the time, *unmündig*—lacking in maturity, and hence incapable of making rational, moral decisions. Portraying prostitutes as childish or immature allowed feminists to occupy a position of power over them, making their relationship to prostitutes "hierarchical, controlling, and punitive."[17] In other words, feminists allowed themselves to speak *for* prostitutes by denying the prostitutes a voice and by refusing to consider prostitutes' decisions as valid choices. In speaking *against* prostitutes, they criticized both the social causes of prostitution and the women who engaged in it, portraying them not only as helpless victims but also as inherently lazy, and even physically and mentally ill. Indeed all three feminists whose works are examined in this chapter employ, to varying degrees, a language of pathology when discussing prostitutes.[18] In so doing, feminists bolstered their own desired role to act as moral authorities in the social control of sexuality. The price they paid for

---

16. Janssen-Jurreit, *Frauen und Sexualmoral,* 63–65; and Petra Schmackpfeffer, *Frauenbewegung und Prostitution* (Oldenburg: Bibliotheks- und Informationssystem der Universität Oldenburg, 1989), 142.

17. Judith Walkowitz, *Prostitution and Victorian Society: Women, Class, and the State* (Cambridge: Cambridge University Press, 1980), 131. Corbin also documents the charge of immaturity as a common description of French prostitutes in *Women for Hire,* 7.

18. Dietmar Schmidt aptly states that, in their attempts to explain prostitution's existence, most feminists vacillated "between the poles of social and constitutional (hereditary or pathological) causes of prostitution" (*Geschlecht unter Kontrolle,* 39). See also Roos, *Weimar through the Lens of Gender,* 148–51.

this authority was the isolation and condemnation of an entire group of women—prostitutes—and, with the exception of Stöcker, the continued denial of women's sexual desire. That said, it would be unjust to oversimplify these feminists' ideas, for although they were clearly condescending and dismissive toward prostitutes, their discourse surrounding prostitution represents a serious and complex discussion of its myriad causes, and their texts empowered women to speak out against male oppression and to take a public stand on issues of sexuality and public health.

Locking up Sex: Hanna Bieber-Böhm's Program of Punishment

Gertrud Guillaume-Schack, who because of her outspoken views on sexual morality and prostitution and her socialist sympathies, was barred from entering her native Silesia and from speaking in various cities throughout Germany, left for England in the late 1880s. After her departure, the next woman who dared to raise the subject of prostitution in the public arena was Hanna Bieber-Böhm. A painter from Berlin, she founded the Verein Jugendschutz (Youth Protection Association) in 1889 in order to educate young Germans on the virtues of chastity and temperance and to steer them away from what she deemed an immoral path leading to sexual promiscuity, alcoholism, and visits to seedy entertainment locales.[19] Bieber-Böhm's crusade against both prostitution and alcohol exemplifies the widespread influence of the temperance movement throughout western Europe and the United States in the latter half of the nineteenth century. For many a social crusader, "the excesses of drink and of the brothel became joined" and therefore had to be fought simultaneously.[20] Although Bieber-Böhm was initially ostracized by the mainstream women's movement for her willingness to speak so openly about prostitution, the moral outrage sparked by the 1891 Heinze trial may have inspired the women of the BDF to lend Bieber-Böhm their ears. The moral panic surrounding the trial was just what Bieber-Böhm needed to rally feminist support for her petition to the German parliament entitled *Vorschläge zur Bekämpfung der Prostitution* (Suggestions for the Fight

---

19. For secondary sources and further biographical information on Bieber-Böhm (1851–1910), see Evans, *Feminist Movement*, 41–47; Evans, *Tales from the German Underworld*, 202–3; Ute Gerhard, *Unerhört: Die Geschichte der deutschen Frauenbewegung* (Reinbek bei Hamburg: Rowohlt, 1992), 235, 245; Greven-Aschoff, *Die bürgerliche Frauenbewegung*, 80–81, 86; Lees, *Cities, Sin, and Social Reform*, 109; Repp, *Reformers, Critics*, 120–21; Schmackpfeffer, *Frauenbewegung und Prostitution*, 32–37.

20. David J. Pivar, *Purity Crusade: Sexual Morality and Social Control, 1868–1900* (Westport, CT: Greenwood, 1973), 23. Pivar's study focuses on the moral crusades in the United States. On the link between feminist abolitionism and temperance in Great Britain, see Walkowitz, *Prostitution and Victorian Society*, 123; and in Germany, see Allen, *Feminism and Motherhood*, 224; and Repp, *Reformers, Critics*, 268.

against Prostitution). Written in 1895, her petition portrayed prostitution as the gravest moral and physical threat to the German populace.[21]

Like the women of the abolitionist movement who would take her place at the podium by the century's close, Bieber-Böhm chastised the state regulatory system, claiming that it did nothing to hinder the spread of venereal disease and that it officially sanctioned prostitution by presenting registered prostitutes with "working papers" (*Gewerbescheine*). Still, she was not in favor of decriminalizing prostitution. Quite the contrary, she proposed a broadening and tightening of state controls, characterized by a shift in power that would allow for the surveillance of prostitutes and for their punishment and moral rehabilitation to be placed in the hands of "older, honorable, educated women."[22] The idea of appointing respectable women to positions of power over morally corrupt ones constitutes an essential dichotomy between women that Bieber-Böhm sets up at the very beginning of her petition— between the "thinking women" (*denkende Frauen*) of the bourgeois feminist movement and the "frivolous girls" (*leichtsinnige Mädchen*) who fall into prostitution.[23]

Prostitutes were not the only ones to be subject to this new system of control. Since the system run by men had obviously failed to protect society from disease and moral corruption, Bieber-Böhm argued, "the punishment of the moral transgressions of both genders" was in order. Punishment would no longer be a brief arrest for the prostitute and a mere slap on the wrist (if that) for the male client; under Bieber-Böhm's proposed doctrine, both the prostitute and her client would be imprisoned for one to two years, during which time they would undergo a moral reeducation led by none other than "educated women." Respectable, educated women were also to take over positions as guards (*Polizeimatronen*), as doctors who would conduct gynecological exams on prostitutes and run special clinics for those infected with venereal disease, and even as cultural censors who would advise the state on how to prevent the spread of vice in German society, including the closure of bars and entertainment venues.[24]

Balancing punishment with prevention, Bieber-Böhm claimed that doctor-patient privacy should no longer apply in cases of venereal infection. Doctors should be obligated to divulge their patients' health status in order to prevent the spread of venereal disease. She also recommended preemptive moral education for those whom she defined as "morally vulnerable adults" and "endangered children of immoral parents."[25] But what, in Bieber-Böhm's mind, constituted moral danger or vulnerability? Both her petition and the lectures she delivered in the mid-1890s reveal a clear class bias in her description of those who live a healthy, clean life and those who have

---

21. Hanna Bieber-Böhm, *Vorschläge zur Bekämpfung der Prostitution: Petition des Bundes deutscher Frauenvereine an den Reichstag betreffend Aufhebung der gewerblichen Prostitution* (Berlin: Osterheld, 1895).

22. Bieber-Böhm, *Vorschläge*, 12.

23. Bieber-Böhm, *Vorschläge*, ii.

24. Bieber-Böhm, *Vorschläge*, ii, 6–9.

25. Bieber-Böhm, *Vorschläge*, 8.

taken the wrong path. Clean living is attributed to the bourgeoisie, while the upper classes lead lives of indulgence and excess, and the poor are described as badly educated, malnourished, and plagued by alcoholism. Bieber-Böhm writes in a tone of indignation about working-class men and women, whom she refers to as "the ignorant and those burdened by illness," and she condemns their engagement in premarital intercourse as a form of prostitution.[26] Her equation of unsanitary living with moral deficiency places her work within the discourse of "social hygiene," a movement designed to "spread hygienic values among individuals and their offspring" that gathered momentum in the first years of the twentieth century with the establishment of the German Society for Combating Venereal Diseases (DGBG).[27] At the DGBG's first conference in 1903, members discussed the cramped, dirty living conditions of the urban proletariat, which speakers such as the leftist publicist from Berlin Paul Kampffmeyer associated directly with such sexual transgressions as incest, prostitution, and the spread of venereal disease.[28] Several years before the DGBG presented its case for "clean living," Bieber-Böhm proposed appointing bourgeois women as guardians not only of prostitutes, but also of any nonbourgeois men, women, and children who needed moral guidance and a social hygienic education. Simply put, she wanted to give bourgeois women carte blanche on policing social morals.

Preaching strict premarital abstinence and conjugal fidelity, Bieber-Böhm's petition articulated the bourgeois feminists' consensus on sexuality at the close of the nineteenth century: it was to remain within the parameters of monogamous marriage, and, outside of marriage, chastity was the key to moral and physical health. In addition, the petition supported the view that the bourgeois order was the cleanest, most moral order, particularly when placed up against the decadence of the upper classes and the moral chaos and poverty of the proletariat. Perhaps most important, it contained concrete plans for creating employment for older, morally sound, educated women—an apt description of the BDF membership—as doctors, educators, guards, and even ersatz mothers, whose task it would be to teach the central principle of moral reform: self-control (*Selbstbeherrschung*).[29] And yet the closing lines of Bieber-Böhm's petition made it clear that the ultimate power for reform would remain within the hands of the paternalistic state. Women would act as "helpers and

---

26. Bieber-Böhm, *Vorschläge*, 10–11; and Bieber-Böhm, *Die Sittlichkeitsfrage, eine Gesundheitsfrage, 2 Referate, gehalten beim Internationalen Frauen-Congress in Berlin, 1896* (Berlin: Reinke, 1896), 4, 9; the quote cited appears on p. 4.

27. Paul Weindling, *Health, Race, and German Politics between National Unification and Nazism, 1870–1945* (Cambridge: Cambridge University Press, 1989), 221. See also Repp, *Reformers, Critics,* 299–304.

28. For an in-depth reading of Kampffmeyer's speech, see Schmidt, *Geschlecht unter Kontrolle,* 335–37.

29. Bieber-Böhm, *Vorschläge,* 10, and *Die Sittlichkeitsfrage,* 4–5. On the principle of self-control as the central idea of feminist moral reform, see Greven-Aschoff, *Die bürgerliche Frauenbewegung,* 104–5.

advisers" within an expanded penal system run by men.[30] In its proposed tightening of controls over sexual behavior and its implicit portrayal of prostitutes as immoral, fallen women, Bieber-Böhm's document was ideologically akin to the goals of the conservative male morality associations of the day, such as those led by the infamous anti-Semite Adolf Stöcker.[31] Bieber-Böhm's punitive approach to vice was, however, not in line with the more nurturing approach propagated by maternal feminism, which sought to morally educate socially disadvantaged women rather than punish them. Therefore, by the advent of the new century, the new left wing of the BDF had discovered and embraced abolitionism.

Of Abolition and Abstinence: Anna Pappritz's *Frauenmoral*

The abolitionist movement in Europe was formed to protest the state registration and regulation of prostitution. The system of state-regulated prostitution had been the brainchild of Napoleon Bonaparte, who insisted that prostitutes be registered with the state and subjected to routine medical examinations in order to protect French soldiers from the debilitating effects of venereal disease. The soldiers themselves were never tested for infection. After Napoleon, it was the British who enforced regulatory measures in their country under the Contagious Diseases Acts in the 1860s, which met with staunch opposition from both the working class and feminist activists, the most famous of whom was Josephine Butler. Butler's efforts as the leader of the Ladies' National Association in England were essential to the ultimate repeal of the Contagious Diseases Acts in the 1870s and 1880s. It was Butler who chose the term "abolitionism" for the movement to free prostitutes from forced registration and venereal-disease testing—a term that had originally referred to the nineteenth-century struggle in the United States to free black slaves. Considering this choice of terms, it is not surprising that Butler also led the international battle against the highly sensationalized phenomenon of "white slavery," the sex trafficking of European women to North and South America.[32]

---

30. Bieber-Böhm, *Vorschläge*, 13.

31. Despite sharing the same last name, Adolf and Helene Stöcker were not related. On the men's moral purity movement, see John C. Fout, "Sexual Politics in Wilhelmine Germany: The Male Gender Crisis, Moral Purity, and Homophobia," in *Forbidden History: The State, Society, and the Regulation of Sexuality in Modern Europe,* ed. John C. Fout (Chicago: University of Chicago Press, 1992), 259–92. For a comparison of feminists' and male moral crusaders' discourse on prostitution in the British context and further evidence that "sexual politics makes strange bedfellows," see Judith R. Walkowitz, "Male Vice and Female Virtue: Feminism and the Politics of Prostitution in Nineteenth-Century Britain," in Snitow, Stansell, and Thompson, *Powers of Desire,* 419–38.

32. On Butler's choice of the term "abolitionism," see Walkowitz, *Prostitution and Victorian Society,* 123–24; and Wickert, *Helene Stöcker,* 50. Walkowitz's study is also an excellent source on the Contagious Diseases Acts and Butler's abolitionist campaign. For further information and critical perspectives on the turn-of-the-century debates on "white slavery," see Donna J. Guy, *Sex and Danger in Buenos Aires: Prostitution, Family, and Nation in Argentina* (Lincoln: University of Nebraska Press, 1991), which

In 1875, Butler extended her cause to continental Europe, seeking to open chapters of an International Abolitionist Federation in various western European countries, an initiative that Guillaume-Schack praised in her speeches of the 1880s. It was not until the 1890s, however, that Butler's ideas began to take hold in Germany, after members of the BDF's left wing such as Augspurg and Cauer had heard her deliver public lectures in Paris and Zurich. Bringing Butler's influence into the BDF, these women succeeded in isolating the punitive Bieber-Böhm and gaining a stronghold for abolitionism within the German women's movement. In 1898 and 1899, the first German branches of the IAF were formed in Hamburg by Lida Gustava Heymann and in Berlin by Anna Pappritz. Despite the fact that the IAF membership numbers barely exceeded one thousand, in the decades that followed, Pappritz became one of the most influential figures in the German feminist movement. She worked alongside Katharina Scheven as the editor of the IAF's periodical, *Der Abolitionist*, from 1902 to 1914; she served on the BDF's executive board for many years; and from 1902 on she was a member of the board of directors for the DGBG. Despite recurring health problems, she remained the leader of Berlin's chapter of the IAF, which in later years called itself the Bund für Frauen- und Jugendschutz (League for Protection of Women and Youth) until it disbanded in 1933. During the Weimar Republic, Pappritz remained a key figure in the movement for prostitution reform, which resulted in the abolition of state regulation under the 1927 Law to Combat Venereal Diseases.[33] Even before this important victory for the abolitionists, they succeeded in convincing the BDF to articulate a clear abolitionist stance on prostitution in its 1919 platform. The fact that the 1907 platform of the BDF includes a prominently placed paragraph on moral reform and prostitution can no doubt be credited to the tireless work of Pappritz and the abolitionists.[34]

While the alternatives the abolitionists posed to the regulation of prostitution were far less punitive in nature than Bieber-Böhm's, their reasons for opposing the system were the same. Regulation reinforced the double standard by putting only

discusses the trafficking of European women—particularly Eastern European Jewish women—to Argentina; and Melissa Ditmore, "Trafficking in Lives: How Ideology Shapes Policy," in *Trafficking and Prostitution Reconsidered*, ed. Kamala Kempadoo (Boulder, CO: Paradigm, 2005), 107–26.

33. Biographical information on Pappritz (1861–1939) comes primarily from her papers (Nachlaß Anna Pappritz), including all of her published writings, protocol books from IAF meetings, her correspondence with other leaders within the women's movement, her diary, and her memoirs. LAB, Helene-Lange-Archiv (HLA), B. Rep. 235–13. See also Allen, "Feminism, Venereal Disease, and the State," 28–29; Evans, *Feminist Movement*, 49; Greven-Aschoff, *Die bürgerliche Frauenbewegung*, 81, 105–6; Janssen-Jurreit, *Frauen und Sexualmoral*, 93–94; Lees, *Cities, Sin, and Social Reform*, 110–11; Repp, *Reformers, Critics*, 120–21; Schmackpfeffer, *Frauenbewegung und Prostitution*, 45. For Pappritz's activism during World War I and the Weimar Republic, see Laurie Marhoefer, "Degeneration, Sexual Freedom and the Politics of the Weimar Republic, 1918–1933," *German Studies Review* 34, no. 3 (2011): 533, 536–37; and Roos, *Weimar through the Lens of Gender*, 97–98, 101–4, 107–14, 136.

34. In her 1902 report on the BDF's fifth annual conference, Pappritz praised the harmonious atmosphere and the open discussion of sexual issues, stating that such discussions seemed unfathomable just several years before. LAB, HLA, B. Rep. 235–13, Nr. 3434. The BDF's platforms from 1907, 1919, and 1920 are reprinted in Greven-Aschoff, *Die bürgerliche Frauenbewegung*, 287–90, 294–98.

prostitutes under police surveillance while male clients were free to satisfy their sexual urges with impunity. In its forced medical examination of only prostitutes, the state's policy ignored male clients who were just as likely to be infected with venereal disease and who could then spread the disease to their unknowing wives and children, as well as to other prostitutes. Plainly stated, regulation failed to foster a sense of moral and physical responsibility among German men. The state's implicit support of unrestrained male sexuality and its apparent disregard for the health and well-being of German women and children was what Pappritz called *Herrenmoral*, a term that cleverly combines the "master's morals" with "men's morals." As in Bieber-Böhm's work, abstinence was the moral heart of the abolitionist platform. At the 1903 conference of the DGBG, Pappritz went to great lengths to cite medical experts who claimed that sexual abstinence posed no physical or psychological danger to those who abstained. Never questioning the institution of bourgeois marriage as the authors discussed in chapter 1 did, the abolitionists held fast to the notion that monogamous marriage was the cornerstone of a moral society and the privileged realm of "normal sexual intercourse."[35] Unlike Bieber-Böhm, however, the abolitionists insisted on loosening rather than tightening controls on prostitution. Their ultimate goal was the decriminalization of prostitution through the erasure of Clause 361/6 from the legal code, and their alternatives to the system focused on the principles of "care, rescue, and education." They proposed the creation of nurturing educational structures such as sex education—preaching abstinence, of course—for German youth of both genders and the founding of special homes or guardianship programs that would offer vulnerable young women a moral education as well as training for jobs in domestic service, the textile industry, and clerical positions. Being careful not to argue for the disbanding of the vice squad, they suggested that its work be redirected toward monitoring and censoring any public venues—theaters, low-brow cabarets, window displays—involved in the visual showcasing of sex.[36] This emphasis on "care, rescue, and education" highlights the most important difference between the abolitionists and Bieber-Böhm, for it entails a shift in the view of prostitutes, whom the abolitionists saw primarily as victims of both poverty and uncontrolled male desire rather than as inherently corrupt beings deserving of punishment. In their attempt to express "deep female anger at male sexual license" and hence to rally feminist support for their cause, Judith Walkowitz argues, abolitionists "found it politically expedient to depict 'fallen women' as pas-

---

35. Pappritz, "Herrenmoral" (1903), in Janssen-Jurreit, *Frauen und Sexualmoral*, 83–94. For Pappritz's reprint of her own remarks at the 1903 conference of the DGBG, see her *Einführung in das Studium der Prostitutionsfrage* (Leipzig: Ambrosius Barth, 1919), 230; and Schmackpfeffer, *Frauenbewegung und Prostitution*, 47.

36. Anna Pappritz and Katharina Scheven, "Die positiven Aufgaben und strafrechtlichen Forderungen der Föderation," *Abolitionistische Flugschriften* 5 (1913): 12; see also Pappritz, "Frauenarbeit und Volkssittlichkeit: Volksgesundung durch Erziehung," *Monatshefte für Lebenserziehung im Haus, Gesellschaft, Staat, Schule und Kirche* 7 (1911): 1–28.

sive victims of evil machinations."[37] It is in this very strategy that the link between the American and European abolitionist movements becomes apparent. Transferring the mark of enslavement from African American laborers to European prostitutes, the women abolitionists portrayed themselves as liberators, and prostitutes as victims in need of rescue.

Pappritz's bitterly satirical essay of 1903, "Herrenmoral," is a prime example of a turn-of-the-century text that expresses the deep-seated anger toward men's sexual misbehavior. Pushed to its logical extreme, the essay argues, men's/the master's morals would see all women working in a mass brothel or whores' town (*Bordellstadt*) located just outside the city limits of Berlin. Some of the women would work as prostitutes, sexually servicing men from the city, while the others would run the post offices, bakeries, drug stores, and hospitals of the town. Women doctors would give the prostitutes regular physical checkups, and midwives, wet nurses, and nannies would help to deliver and care for any resulting babies. The paternity of these babies would never be investigated, and men could come and go as they pleased. The clear message of Pappritz's parody of the brothel town is that women in turn-of-the-century German society existed only to serve the needs of an audacious, freewheeling male sexuality.[38] Its mention of illegitimate children and the lack of interest in paternity also points to the contentious debates, particularly within the women's movement, surrounding the German Civil Code (Bürgerliches Gesetzbuch) and its lack of proper legal and financial support for unwed mothers. The Civil Code, which was passed in 1896 to the great chagrin of many feminists, contained a key contradiction that absolved the fathers of illegitimate children of any social or financial responsibility. While it dictated on the one hand that fathers should pay financial support at a level commensurate with the mother's standard of living, it stated on the other hand that fathers and their illegitimate children were "not considered to be related," a loophole that allowed fathers to shirk financial support rather easily.[39]

Beyond its thinly veiled reference to the Civil Code, Pappritz's text, in its depiction of *all* women as isolated from city life and placed at the service of male desire, serves primarily as a critique of regulated prostitution and its broader repercussions for mobile or public women. As Evans notes in his description of the vice squad's sanctioned capriciousness, "the police gave themselves the power to intervene arbitrarily in the lives of Germany's female citizens when they thought any of them was overstepping the invisible lines laid down by social and sexual convention.... Thus regulation facilitated in the most direct possible way the intimidatory exercise of the male claim to monopolize this public sphere."[40] The

---

37. Walkowitz, *Prostitution and Victorian Society*, 146, 110.
38. Pappritz, "Herrenmoral," 86–88.
39. Allen, *Feminism and Motherhood*, 142–43.
40. Evans, *Tales from the German Underworld*, 204–5.

serious concern that emerges from behind the satirical facade of Pappritz's text is that in a state with regulatory laws that gave police license to arrest any woman off the street suspected of prostitution, *any* woman—even a respectable one like herself or one of her activist sisters—could be labeled as and treated like a prostitute.[41] This concern is most apparent when she departs from the language of parody and adopts a polemical tone, asking: "Do men really have no idea that merely being suspected of 'prostitution' causes a woman to feel horrible shame?" She sharpens this sense of shame by imagining what it must be like for a respectable woman (*eine anständige Frau*) to undergo a forced medical examination, to bare her body for the inspecting eyes of a doctor, even if that doctor is a woman, in order to prove her moral integrity or honor, which reads clearly as sexual purity. What Pappritz depicts in her text is not the victimization of the prostitute but rather the potential victimization of the respectable woman, whose arrest would strip her—both literally and figuratively—of her honor. Through her repeated use of the first-person plural pronoun *wir,* she shows her solidarity with the honorable, yet vulnerable, women. What she creates in this polemic is a distinct separation between those who feel shame—the upstanding women—and those who are shameless—the licentious men who frequent the brothel town and, implicitly, the prostitutes who allow them to indulge their desires.[42]

Embedded in Pappritz's narrative and its evocation of the concepts of shame and honor, then, is a desire to create a clear separation—a separation between those who have their own internal controls and those who need to be controlled. There is a compulsion to prove that there are women who are sexually modest and morally proud and that those women deserve to walk the streets unmolested. In their crusade to abolish regulation, respectable feminists such as Pappritz herself offer themselves as models of self-control, as agents out to reform *Herrenmoral* into *Frauenmoral* (women's morals). By scrutinizing male sexuality and distinguishing themselves from sexually active prostitutes through their promotion of abstinence, abolitionist feminists refuted sensationalist and essentialist turn-of-the-century representations of female sexuality as uncontrolled and dangerous, the most notorious of which was Otto Weininger's contention that *all* women were prostitutes with an insatiable desire for coitus.[43] If anything, it was male desire that was out of control. This turning

41. These fears were realized in 1902, just one year before Pappritz wrote "Herrenmoral," when the leading feminist activist Anita Augspurg was falsely arrested in Weimar on charges of prostitution. See Schmackpfeffer, *Frauenbewegung und Prostitution,* 50; and Schmidt, *Geschlecht unter Kontrolle,* 34.

42. Pappritz, "Herrenmoral," 90. I have translated Pappritz's use of the phrase "gewerbsmäßige Unzucht" simply as "prostitution," rather than more literally as "commercial immorality" or "commercial fornication." Pappritz herself puts the phrase in quotation marks to show that this is the official term for registered prostitution used in Clause 361/6.

43. Weininger, *Geschlecht und Charakter,* 337, 341–45. On Weininger's use of the prostitute to demonize female sexuality, see Chandak Sengoopta, *Otto Weininger: Sex, Science, and Self in Imperial Vienna* (Chicago: University of Chicago Press, 2000), 118–20.

of the tables challenged the gendered mind/body split that associated women with corporeality and men with rationality and intellect, and cleared room for "educated women" to dictate societal morals.

Pappritz's effort to establish clear boundaries between respectable women and prostitutes is also an implicit acknowledgment that state regulation caused confusion that ran in both directions. For if respectable, mobile, working women could be mistaken for prostitutes, then prostitutes, as women provided with valid working papers by the state, could also be mistaken for respectable women. By issuing work permits to registered prostitutes with clean bills of health and by designating spaces in which the exchange between prostitute and client could and should take place, the regulatory system created a class of professionalized prostitutes. In its depiction of a fictional brothel town in which all forms of women's work exist for the sole purpose of keeping the mass brothel running, Pappritz's text raises the concern that if the only work available to women is that which services male desires, prostitution might become the most valued form of work within a society ruled by *Herrenmoral*. Such concerns come more explicitly to light in an essay that Pappritz wrote shortly after "Herrenmoral" in the DGBG's main periodical, *Zeitschrift für Bekämpfung der Geschlechtskrankheiten*.[44] Although the primary aim of this particular essay is to debunk the theory that state-regulated brothels or zones of prostitution—that is, particular streets or districts that house registered prostitutes—protect the broader population from venereal disease and moral corruption, Pappritz dedicates a considerable portion of her text to examining the daily lives and attitudes of the regulated prostitutes who inhabit such spaces. In this text, which predates her collection of prostitutes' biographies (*The World of Which One Dares Not Speak!*) by several years, she incorporates statements by the prostitutes themselves, and yet she does not let their perspectives stand without editorial comment. She admits, at several points in the text, that the prostitutes' actions, opinions, and attitudes leave her feeling "agitated" or "stirred up" (she uses the term *frappieren*). Her agitation is most evident when she describes prostitutes who bear outward signs of respectability: they are kind to children, they show generosity by sharing their earnings with less fortunate relatives and friends, they display Christian religious values by hanging crucifixes and passages from scripture above their beds, and they even express moral disdain for their male clients. It is the prostitutes' expressed judgment of their male clients, combined with their refusal to play the socially dictated role of "repentant sinners," that so irritates Pappritz. Yet nothing provokes a stronger negative reaction from her than the registered prostitutes' definition of themselves as workers, as state employees entitled to the requisite benefits of such a position:

---

44. Pappritz, "Welchen Schutz können Bordellstraßen gewähren?," *Zeitschrift für Bekämpfung der Geschlechtskrankheiten* 3, no. 11 (1904/5): 417–24.

The fact that she [the prostitute] considers her activity to be "a legitimate profession" is the consequence of a state-sanctioned regulation and bordello system. Given the enormous legitimizing authority we attribute to the state, especially here in Germany, it is perfectly natural that individuals working within any government institution consider themselves to be civil servants, and such is the case with the girls from the brothels: I have often found that they deem themselves "entitled to a pension" and complain bitterly that these well-deserved funds were withheld from them. It is thus self-evident that attempts to save them (with a few rare exceptions) will be pointless given such views, the fact notwithstanding that the afflicted persons have been so softened and physically degraded by their ways of life that they are unable to do any systematic, vigorous work.[45]

While Pappritz's article, which appeared before Hammer's case studies of registered prostitution were published, is certainly unique for its time in its attempt to give prostitutes a voice and in its mere mention of the concept of prostitution as work, its outright rejection of a professional identity for prostitutes exemplifies the condescending tone adopted by turn-of-the-century abolitionists toward prostitutes. Pappritz's language of rescue and her use of the passive voice to describe the detrimental effects of prostitution on the women in the brothels are clearly meant to classify prostitutes as victims, a much more acceptable role from the abolitionists' point of view, but also one that was, to use Walkowitz's words, "a restrictive and moralistic image, one that inhibited a more searching inquiry into the motives and self-perception of the women themselves."[46] What Walkowitz's analysis of abolitionist discourse in England reveals is the implicit moral judgment contained within the label of victim, especially in the case of prostitutes, for it implies that they are incapable of recognizing and choosing the "right" moral path. As much as Pappritz claimed to stand in opposition to Lombroso's idea of the "born prostitute," her writing often lapses into pathological descriptions of prostitutes that are reminiscent of misogynist rhetoric.[47] There are hints of this in the above passage, but her later writings—particularly those written in the midst of the First World War—are rife with such degrading language. More heavily entrenched than ever in the fight against venereal disease, she authored a pamphlet entitled *Prostitution and Abolitionism*, in which she describes prostitution as "an antisocial phenomenon" that presents "a real danger to the people's health." Like her rival Bieber-Böhm, Pappritz portrayed prostitutes as mentally impaired (*schwachsinnig*).[48] In a document

---

45. Pappritz, "Welchen Schutz," 420–421; all of the quotations cited from the text thus far are from these pages.

46. Walkowitz, *Prostitution and Victorian Society*, 146–47.

47. For Pappritz's direct reference to and rejection of Lombroso's concept of the "born prostitute," see Pappritz, *Die Welt, von der man nicht spricht!*, 33.

48. Pappritz, *Prostitution und Abolitionismus*, Flugschriften der Deutschen Gesellschaft zur Bekämpfung der Geschlechtskrankheiten, vol. 21 (Leipzig: Barth, n.d. [1917?]), 4, 8.

from 1919, Pappritz referred to prostitutes as "crippled souls" and insisted that it was the state's duty to watch over them and prevent them from causing harm to themselves and the German public.[49]

This sudden turn to the state for increased control over prostitutes seems, at first blush, particularly odd coming from a woman who usually spoke so vehemently against the state regulation of prostitution. And yet, as scholars of German feminism such as Ann Taylor Allen, Atina Grossmann, and Julia Roos all note, both criticism of the state and calls for its intervention were quite common, especially as the Wilhelmine era drew to a close and World War I heightened nationalist sentiments among feminists.[50] In the wake of Germany's defeat and massive loss of life in the First World War, the organizations to which Pappritz devoted most of her energies, the BDF, IAF, and DGBG, all contributed to what the historian Annette Timm has identified as "a massive increase in rhetorical allusions to *Bevölkerungspolitik* [population politics] as justification for new health and welfare policies," initiatives that emphasized increased "VD control" and encouraged the production of healthy offspring.[51] Having observed the debilitating effects of the First World War on the German population, Pappritz dedicated herself and her fellow abolitionists to the rehabilitation of the body politic by combating any perceived dangers to that body. She emphatically argued: "It is time to fill in the horrible holes that this war has ripped in the ranks of our people; we can do so only by means of intelligent population politics. Therefore we must fight with all of our energy against the antisocial tendencies that threaten the health of our people."[52] If it is the abolitionists' job to rid German society of its "antisocial tendencies," and if prostitution is, as Pappritz states earlier in the same text, "an antisocial phenomenon," then prostitutes are no longer victims of the state, but enemies. As a destructive force rather than a reproductive one, prostitutes in Pappritz's World War I texts become women whose moral and physical "illness" prevents them from contributing to the population; they become antimothers.

In the first two decades of the twentieth century, the increasing centrality of sexuality, eugenics, and sexual hygiene to discourses of nationhood and public health offered feminists like Anna Pappritz a modicum of social power, for as women they could claim privileged knowledge of female sexuality and reproduction. Although Pappritz remained active within the women's movement, the DGBG, and the IAF until the end of the Weimar Republic, she looked back wistfully at the late imperial period as the pinnacle of women's activism. In a letter to the federal representative Marianne Weber dated December 1919, Pappritz expressed her disappointment that women's

49. Pappritz, *Einführung*, 243.
50. Allen, "Feminism, Venereal Diseases, and the State," 37, 41–42; Atina Grossmann, *Reforming Sex: The German Movement for Birth Control and Abortion Reform, 1920–1950* (New York: Oxford University Press, 1995), 37; Roos, *Weimar through the Lens of Gender*, 105–8. See also Marhoefer, "Degeneration, Sexual Freedom," 530, 532.
51. Timm, *The Politics of Fertility*, 35, 37.
52. Pappritz, *Prostitution und Abolitionismus*, 24.

newly gained citizenship rights did little to increase women's active participation in the formulation of public health policy. Despite having been invited to attend a meeting with the minister of the interior to discuss venereal disease prevention, Pappritz's views were silenced, and the meeting was prematurely cut off. Recounting this experience for Weber, Pappritz contends that the political representation of women in the Reichstag had, "in a very cowardly and dishonest way," circumvented the power of the grassroots women's movement. In Wilhelmine Germany, she writes, "one could fight and protest more forcefully, whereas now our hands are tied, just because we are proclaimed to be equals on paper."[53] The social power gained by the abolitionist feminists in the decades preceding the First World War, however, came at the expense of female sexuality, which under abolitionism remained confined within nineteenth-century values of chastity and marriage. The activist force of feminism that Pappritz lauds in her letter came at the expense of a certain group of women—prostitutes, who, as erotic women standing outside the bounds of chastity and marriage, were isolated and silenced by the very women who claimed to be their liberators.

Sex and the Single Mother: Helene Stöcker's New Morality

Despite the general radicalization of the bourgeois women's movement at the turn of the century, one thing that did not accompany this shift to the left was the feminists' willingness to openly acknowledge and discuss women's sexual desire. Reflecting on the self-proclaimed progressive feminist Minna Cauer in her autobiographical sketches, Helene Stöcker wrote that Cauer "repressed everything that had to do with erotic life and did not wish to be reminded of it."[54] At the outset of the twentieth century, Stöcker's writings were already getting her into trouble with the women of the BDF for her frank discussion of sexual desire and rejection of chastity as women's most natural and moral state. Her claims that married women were entitled to both professional careers and a family, her penchant for Nietzschean philosophy, and especially her promotion of sexual fulfillment for both men and women alienated her from the majority of feminists, who accused her of promoting sexual permissiveness and "prostitutes' morals" (*Dirnenmoral*).[55] In 1905, joined by Ruth Bré, Lily Braun, Maria Lischnewska, and Hedwig Dohm, Stöcker broke away from the mainstream feminist movement to form the League

---

53. Pappritz to Marianne Weber, December 22, 1919, LAB, HLA, B. Rep 235–13, MF 3462.

54. Helene Stöcker, "Lebensabriss," unpublished typescript, Box 1, Helene Stöcker Papers, Swarthmore College Peace Collection (SCPC), 5. The English translation is quoted in Allen, *Feminism and Motherhood*, 174.

55. On the labeling of Stöcker's ideas as *Dirnenmoral*, see Evans, *Feminist Movement*, 138; Janssen-Jurreit, *Frauen und Sexualmoral*, 37; Schmackpfeffer, *Frauenbewegung und Prostitution*, 55. On Stöcker's isolation from the mainstream feminist movement, see Amy Hackett, "Helene Stöcker: Left-Wing Intellectual and Sex Reformer," in *When Biology Became Destiny: Women in Weimar and Nazi Germany*, ed. Renate Bridenthal, Atina Grossmann, and Marion Kaplan (New York: Monthly Review Press, 1984), 112–15; and Repp, *Reformers, Critics*, 123–25.

for the Protection of Mothers (BfM) in Berlin. By 1908, the BfM had 3,800 registered members, making it nearly four times the size of Pappritz and Scheven's Abolitionist Federation.[56]

Central to the BfM's platform was Stöcker's "new morality," which promoted
not only women's educational and occupational self-fulfillment but the satisfaction
of their physical desires as well. What set Stöcker apart from abolitionists like Pappritz was her outspoken opposition to abstinence and the clear focus of the BfM
on single mothers, some of whom had been forced into prostitution by the moral
condemnation of society. Seeking to remove the social stigma from women who
bore children outside of wedlock, Stöcker's movement challenged the idea that
women who engaged in extramarital intercourse were automatically to be branded
as "whores." It was precisely such challenges to traditional morality that drew attention to Stöcker's movement, and although much of that attention was negative,
it still served to make the new morality one of the most discussed topics within the
women's movement in the period 1905–10.[57]

In their divergence from the program of the bourgeois women's movement,
Stöcker's ideas more closely resembled those articulated by Bebel, Hartleben, and
Simmel. Like Hartleben and Bebel, Stöcker criticized bourgeois philistinism for its
damning portrayal of "the sexual urge as evil incarnate" and cited it as the cause of
loveless and "unnatural" relationships such as prostitution and arranged marriage.[58]
Challenging the notion of marriage as a "moral" institution, she argued that the
very same people who championed traditional marriage and condemned intimate
relationships that were formed outside of it as immoral often allowed prostitution
to thrive as a "necessary evil."[59] Reminiscent of Bebel's political treatise, Stöcker's
writings depict marriage and prostitution as institutions based on money, and they
attempt to find a space for relationships that lie outside those institutional boundaries. It is not the case that Stöcker rejected marriage completely; rather, she sought

---

56. Information on Stöcker (1869–1943) and the BfM comes from her papers at the SCPC and from
Allen, *Feminism and Motherhood*, 149–87; Evans, *Feminist Movement*, 115–38; Frevert, *Women in German History*, 130–31; Greven-Aschoff, *Die bürgerliche Frauenbewegung*, 66–67, 95; Hackett, "Helene
Stöcker," 109–21; Schlüpmann, "Radikalisierung der Philosophie," 10–34; Schmackpfeffer, *Frauenbewegung und Prostitution*, 55–63; Wickert, *Helene Stöcker*.

57. Allen emphasizes the BfM's broad influence on the women's movement and beyond, despite its relatively small size. See Allen, *Feminism and Motherhood*, 175; also Evans, *Feminist Movement*, 138; Greven-Aschoff, *Die bürgerliche Frauenbewegung*, 67; Schmackpfeffer, *Frauenbewegung und
Prostitution*, 55.

58. Stöcker, "Zur Reform der sexuellen Ethik," *Mutterschutz* 1, no. 1 (1905): 4, 6–7.

59. Stöcker, *Die Liebe und die Frauen* (Minden: J. C. C. Brun, 1906), 97. Stöcker was not the only
radical feminist to celebrate human desire, to bemoan the current state of marriage, and to criticize the
"old morality" as a principal cause of prostitution. The aristocratic socialist feminist Lily Braun articulated arguments similar to Stöcker's in her essay "Die Entthronung der Liebe," *Die Neue Gesellschaft* 1,
no. 22 (1905), translated by Alfred G. Meyer as "The Dethroning of Love," in *Selected Writings on Feminism and Socialism*, ed. Alfred G. Meyer (Bloomington: Indiana University Press, 1987), 117–23. For
more on Braun's perspective on prostitution, see Meyer's introduction to *Selected Writings*, xiv, xvi; and
Roos, *Weimar through the Lens of Gender*, 141–44, 163.

to reform married life and foster acceptance of relationships that departed from the conventional model. In two separate essays written in 1911, for example, she explored two alternatives to monogamous marriage: heterosexual companionship and the lesbian relationship. Just like Simmel, Stöcker shied away from using the term "free love," for she, too, defined love as a bond between two individuals that did not fit with the modern sense of freedom as freedom *from* commitment or attachment. Where she differed from Simmel was in her explicit mention of sexual desire as a key component of such a love bond, stating that a union between two individuals must be both physical and emotional.[60] In defining love, she wrote in nongendered terms, using the German word *Mensch* (person, human being) rather than *Mann* and *Frau*. Although she clearly privileged heterosexuality in many of her works, she admitted that heterosexual relations were strained by the unequal division of labor in both public and intimate life, and, again like Simmel, she expressed sympathy for women who sought intimacy in lesbian relationships or "tender friendship with women."[61] As critical as she was of marriage in its current state, however, she still held the opinion that a loving conjugal relationship between two equals should be the ultimate goal.[62]

Reforming marriage therefore meant taking a close look at the economic power dynamics between husband and wife, and so Stöcker spoke out against the gendered division of labor and the hindrances to women's financial autonomy. Although she was greatly influenced by socialism and by Bebel's ideas in particular, Stöcker was not willing to wait for political revolution to resolve women's plight.[63] Emphasizing the urgency of women's rights, she explored ways to alleviate their domestic burdens, including seeing motherhood as a woman's decision rather than her duty and pressing for the acknowledgment of domestic labor as work. Stöcker's intention was to raise women's value in society by both promoting economic independence for those who wanted to work outside the home and defining the role of the housewife and mother as an important "economic and social contribution." It would be up to each individual woman to decide which path to take.

Stöcker's focus on the individual woman is symptomatic of her enthusiasm for Nietzschean individualism, an aspect of her work that is yet another point of convergence with writers like Hartleben. Not only did Nietzschean philosophy inform her critique of bourgeois philistinism, but it also shaped her own development as a feminist. In her autobiographical writings, Stöcker recalls how, as a young scholar,

---

60. Stöcker, "Das Werden der sexuellen Reform seit hundert Jahren," in *Ehe? Zur Reform der sexuellen Moral,* ed. Hedwig Dohm (Berlin: Internationale Verlagsanstalt, 1911), 56.

61. Stöcker, "Die beabsichtigte Ausdehnung des §175 auf die Frau," 1911, in Janssen-Jurreit, *Frauen und Sexualmoral,* 191–201, here 194. Allen, *Feminism and Motherhood,* 170–71, highlights the tensions between Stöcker's pro-lesbian activism—her organization of public protests against the possible criminalization of lesbianism—and her "privileging of heterosexuality over other sexual and social choices."

62. Stöcker, "Zur Reform der sexuellen Ethik," 10.

63. Stöcker, *Die Liebe und die Frauen,* 36.

she was captivated by Nietzsche's affirmation of life (*Lebensbejahung*) and his call to individual perfection. Admitting that she disagreed with Nietzsche's "definition of the 'master and slave dynamic,' his lack of understanding for poverty, his particular glorification of hardness and violence," she still chose to interpret his philosophy as championing gender-blind individual self-fulfillment.[64] This interpretation led Stöcker to articulate a more personalized concept of morality. To be moral was to reach one's full potential as a human being. In the very first issue of the BfM's journal, *Mutterschutz,* she wrote: "According to the laws of the *true* morality there is only one sin: to betray one's own highest ideals."[65] Each individual man and woman was to seek fulfillment by harmonizing physical urges with intellectual development, and those who chose to "separate the intellect from emotional life or desire" were, according to Stöcker, "low, contemptible, immoral."[66] The balance between body and mind that Stöcker advocated would be thrown off by the denial of desire, and the clearest form of such denial was abstinence.

After attending a conference of the DGBG in Berlin in 1904, Stöcker gave one of her strongest indictments of sexual asceticism in an essay entitled "Prostitution und Enthaltsamkeit" (Prostitution and Abstinence). In it she laments the gendered split among the presenters, with men representing what she calls "sex egoism" and the immediate satisfaction of physical urges and women representing sexual repression by means of "abstract asceticism." In other words, men support prostitution, while women support abstinence. According to Stöcker, such a dichotomized debate is absurd, and both sides offer false, and in her opinion, unhealthy solutions. She expresses her incredulity at their failure to propose alternatives, writing: "It seemed that they no longer perceived that both [prostitution and abstinence] are abnormal deviations from that which is healthy and life-sustaining. And even though abstinence may be a lesser evil than prostitution, it remains an evil just the same."[67] By referring to both prostitution and abstinence as "abnormal deviations," Stöcker deliberately employs the very language of pathology that was often used by pro-abstinence feminists to defame all forms of sex outside of marriage. In Stöcker's mind, debating the problem of venereal disease via the question of regulated prostitution versus abstinence only deepened the rift between the genders, strengthened the double standard, and fostered neither sexual responsibility among men nor an open discussion of women's desire. A respectful, loving, sensual relationship forged

---

64. Stöcker, "Lebensabriss," 2. Steven E. Aschheim describes Stöcker as "the most prominent and effective Nietzschean feminist in Germany" and argues that the philosopher's "devastating indictment of the bourgeoisie" for its rigid definition of good and evil resonated with Stöcker. Aschheim, *The Nietzsche Legacy in Germany, 1890–1990* (Berkeley: University of California Press, 1992), 89, 166. On Stöcker's interpretation of Nietzsche's ideas, see Evans, *Feminist Movement,* 28; and Schlüpmann, "Radikalisierung der Philosophie."

65. Stöcker, "Zur Reform der sexuellen Ethik," 11, emphasis in original.

66. Stöcker, *Die Liebe und die Frauen,* 16.

67. The essay appears in Stöcker, *Die Liebe und die Frauen,* 122–26, here 122.

by two individuals—married or not—may not have been on the docket at the DGBG's conference, but it was an essential component of the new morality espoused by Stöcker and the BfM.

Closely tied to the BfM's acknowledgment and even celebration of relationships that fell outside of the traditional conjugal model was its support for single mothers. As the leader of the BfM, Stöcker promoted the image of the independent, educated woman, who, married or not, pursued her "deepest natural desire" to become a mother.[68] Seeking to make single motherhood a viable and socially legitimate option, the league petitioned the state for improved legal rights for illegitimate children and founded homes for single mothers, the first of which was in Berlin. The goal of such efforts was to change the societal perception of single mothers as "fallen women," a perception that often barred them from "respectable society" and hence from employment opportunities, social networks, and welfare services. Altering moral attitudes toward single mothers would protect one of the groups of women most vulnerable to prostitution, for prostitution was one of the few ways for women who had been marked as fallen to make a living and support their children. By stating in 1908 that the formulation of the new morality was inextricably linked to the "fight against prostitution," Stöcker added a deeper dimension to the name of her organization. The BfM provided protection *of* mothers (*Mutterschutz*) by giving them shelter and rallying for their increased legal rights, but it also protected mothers *from* the unwanted and unwarranted stigma of prostitution.[69]

The BfM may have portrayed motherhood as an honor and a privilege, but it also claimed that there were certain women who should be prevented from reproducing altogether. Prostitutes made up one such group. The BfM advocated eugenics programs that not only encouraged healthy reproduction but also discouraged reproduction among those deemed "unhealthy" or "degenerate." While articulating the goals of the fledgling BfM in 1905, Stöcker stated without a hint of subtlety that "one will have to find ways to prevent degenerates from reproducing."[70] Although Stöcker generally delivered an institutional critique of prostitution and only rarely mentioned the women working within that institution, her classification of prostitutes as "degenerates" occasionally surfaces. In a pamphlet written during the First World War, Stöcker relates the tale of a "lazy and unruly child" who, when warned by her teacher that she will never amount to much if she fails to learn the meaning of work, merely shrugs off the warning and replies: "I'll become

---

68. Stöcker, *Die Liebe und die Frauen,* 85.

69. Stöcker, "Die Neue Ethik und ihre Gegner," manuscript for the BfM's journal *Die Neue Generation,* Box 6, Helene Stöcker Papers, SCPC, 11. On the BfM's efforts to remove the stigma of the "fallen woman" from single mothers, see Allen, *Feminism and Motherhood,* 180; and Evans, *Tales from the German Underworld,* 180.

70. Stöcker, "Zur Reform der sexuellen Ethik," 116.

a prostitute; then I won't have to work."[71] This brief anecdote illustrates Stöcker's affinities with Pappritz and Bieber-Böhm in her tendency to describe prostitutes in pathological terms (lazy, childish) and in her refusal to define prostitution as work.

The strongest indictment of prostitutes in Stöcker's work, however, came when the BfM became the Bund für Mutterschutz und Sexualreform (League for Protection of Mothers and Sex Reform; BfMS) in 1911. Joined in the BfMS by such prominent feminists as Hedwig Dohm and Maria Stritt, the Berlin artist Käthe Kollwitz, as well as male scientists, sexologists, and writers, Stöcker stressed the increased importance of eugenics for the organization, creating an expanded sex reform agenda that helped to revitalize it in the wake of the BDF's conservative backlash in 1908 and the BfM's internal scandals of 1909–10.[72] The intensified focus on sex reform and eugenics was not exclusive to Stöcker's organization; rather, it was symptomatic of the influence that social Darwinism, hereditarianism, and campaigns for the betterment of public health had within the feminist movement and scientific organizations during the first decades of the twentieth century.[73] In its first mission statement, written by Stöcker, the BfMS cites the "preservation of the health of the race" as one of its primary goals and pinpoints prostitution as one of the greatest dangers to a healthy society: "We see contemporary sex life…dominated by open and clandestine *prostitution,* the indiscriminate sexual surrender for the sake of material gain. We see it infested with *venereal diseases* that tear at the core of the people and, in countless marriages, prevent the fulfillment of their highest *purpose* in the service of the species."[74] The rhetorical vehemence of this statement presents prostitution not as a social problem but as a ruling enemy as well as a deadly infection. The first two italicized terms—*prostitution* and *venereal disease*—give the reader a sense that there is a causal relationship between them and hence depicts prostitution as the primary source of venereal infection. The third italicized word represents the dire consequences of such diseases—the inability for married

---

71. Stöcker, *Sexualpädagogik, Krieg und Mutterschutz,* pamphlet, Box 10, Helene Stöcker Papers, SCPC, 3.

72. Among the male members of the BfMS were the sexologists Iwan Bloch, Havelock Ellis, August Forel, and Magnus Hirschfeld, the psychoanalyst Sigmund Freud, and the writer Frank Wedekind. For a complete list of the founding members of the BfMS, see Stöcker, "Aufruf der Internationalen Vereinigung für Mutterschutz und Sexualreform," in Janssen-Jurreit, *Frauen und Sexualmoral,* 202–6. There seems to be some confusion among historians about when the BfMS was actually founded, for some cite the year of the BfM's founding (1905). I have based my chronology on Helene Stöcker's own papers, SCPC, and Allen's meticulous research in *Feminism and Motherhood.* The "internal scandals of 1909–1910" to which I refer involved the public airing of Stöcker's longtime affair with Dr. Bruno Springer, one of the BfM's major financial contributors. This led to a rift between Stöcker and one of the organization's most visible and active members, Adele Schreiber. See Evans, *Feminist Movement,* 137; and Schmackpfeffer, *Frauenbewegung und Prostitution,* 60.

73. Timm, *The Politics of Fertility,* 5–8. On the prevalence of hereditarianism in the Wilhelmine women's movement and the broader "reform milieu," see also Allen, *Feminism and Motherhood,* 156, 172; Evans, *Feminist Movement,* 163, 167–69; Repp, *Reformers, Critics,* 128, 130.

74. Stöcker, "Aufruf der Internationalen Vereinigung für Mutterschutz und Sexualreform," 202, emphasis in original.

couples to fulfill their "highest purpose," which is understood to be procreation. Because prostitution was seen as a destructive power, its eradication became a goal of sex reform programs, and prostitutes became potential targets for sterilization. If prostitution and its consequent spread of disease hindered motherhood, prostitutes were to be kept from mothering.

When one reads Stöcker's texts today, it is, without a doubt, shocking to find words such as "degeneration" or "sterilization" with the knowledge of how, in the 1930s and 1940s, the National Socialists twisted sex reform programs such as those promoted by the BfMS into policies of forced sterilization and euthanasia. In order to counter notions of continuity between the early twentieth-century sex reform movement and Nazism, some recent studies highlight the subtle yet clear differences between the types of eugenics espoused by reformers like Stöcker and Nazi racial ideology. When Stöcker uses the word *Rasse* or *Gattung*, Kevin Repp argues, she refers not to a master race but to the entire human race. Amy Hackett notes that eugenics was by no means a uniquely German phenomenon but one that originated in Great Britain in the writings of Francis Galton and Havelock Ellis, and was also embraced by scientists and lawmakers in the United States.[75] In her monograph *The Politics of Fertility in Twentieth-Century Berlin*, however, Annette Timm argues that, when discussing figures like Helene Stöcker, dichotomized paradigms of historical continuity versus break or progressive versus reactionary thought simply do not apply. She writes: "Negative eugenic thought and progressive ideas about sexuality coexisted in this era, often in the same individual.... The ideological and practical boundaries between these two spheres were permeable, and it is impossible to support an argument that takes 'eugenics' to be an antonym for 'progressive.'" What sets the sex reform movement of the Wilhelmine and Weimar eras apart from the years of National Socialist rule, Timm contends, is that "harsher...eugenic policies" like sterilization failed to gain political traction.[76] Ideas that were at the center of heated debates before 1933 became practice under the Nazis. Stöcker's rhetoric on prostitution and sterilization "divided women into the responsible worthy and the 'asocial,'" and the rhetoric of asociality was later put into action by the National Socialists to "select" prostitutes for forced sterilization and even death.[77]

---

75. Kevin Repp, "'Sexualkrise und Rasse': Feminist Eugenics at the Fin de Siècle," in Marchand and Lindenfeld, *Germany at the Fin de Siècle,* 120; Hackett, "Helene Stöcker," 118.

76. Timm, *The Politics of Fertility,* 87–88. For a similar argument, see also Grossmann, *Reforming Sex,* 136.

77. Grossmann, *Reforming Sex,* 70. Bieber-Böhm and Pappritz also referred to prostitutes as "degenerates"; see Bieber-Böhm, *Vorschläge,* 10; and Pappritz, *Einführung,* 282–83. On Nazi policies toward prostitutes, including forced sterilization, see Gisela Bock, "'Keine Arbeitskräfte in diesem Sinne': Prostituierte im Nazi-Staat," in Biermann, *"Wir sind Frauen wie andere auch!": Prostituierte und ihre Kämpfe* (Reinbek bei Hamburg: Rowohlt, 1980), 70–106; Christa Paul, *Zwangsprostitution: Staatlich errichtete Bordelle im Nationalsozialismus* (Berlin: Hentrich, 1994); and Julia Roos, "Backlash against Prostitutes' Rights: Origins and Dynamics of Nazi Prostitution Policies," *Journal of the History of Sexuality* 11 (January/April 2002): 67–94.

Although Helene Stöcker's writings clearly revile prostitution and with it prostitutes themselves, in their search for prostitution's causes and its eradication, her texts open up a critical discursive space between the poles of prostitution and marriage for the exploration of women's sexuality. It is a space that allows for criticism of feminists who cling to repressive bourgeois values such as chastity; it challenges the "old morality" and even names it as a cause of prostitution; and it suggests possible alternatives to traditional monogamous marriage. What makes Stöcker's texts progressive are the variety of possibilities they open up for women, presenting their readers with new models of individual women—the single mother, the lesbian, the intellectual, the career woman—models that transcend the traditional dichotomy of wife/mother and prostitute.

Sympathy for the Prostitute: Margarete Böhme's Best Seller, *Diary of a Lost Girl*

Perhaps the nicest words that Helene Stöcker ever wrote about a prostitute were about a fictional one. In her 1905 review of Margarete Böhme's newly published *Diary of a Lost Girl,* Stöcker described the novel's protagonist, Thymian Gotteball, thus: "Here we see inside the soul of one whose warmth and genuineness of emotion and whose sense of respectability is a thousand times greater than that of many average human beings, but who is still not able to lift herself out of the unfortunate profession of the prostitute."[78] By making the prostitute Thymian respectable, Böhme's novel inspired readers to think more critically about what does and does not constitute correct or "moral" comportment. In so doing, Stöcker argues, the novel departs from traditional definitions of respectability and makes the articulation of a new morality possible. Despite Stöcker's conclusion that Böhme's work constitutes a clear departure from bourgeois norms, scholars today continue to grapple with the question of whether the book undermines or reinforces turn-of-the-century bourgeois norms, whether it criticizes or panders to bourgeois society.[79] That the novel provoked a significant response from its readership is indisputable; Böhme received numerous letters from concerned bourgeois readers who expressed their dismay over her protagonist's fate and prodded the self-proclaimed "editor" Böhme for additional information about Thymian's life and Böhme's own role in it.[80]

---

78. Stöcker, "Neue Ethik in der Kunst," 306.

79. For secondary literature on *Tagebuch einer Verlorenen,* some of which also focuses on G. W. Pabst's 1929 film version of the book, see Borst, *Über jede Scham erhaben,* 115–42; Evans, *Tales from the German Underworld,* 166–212; Günther, *Weiblichkeitsentwürfe,* 310–18; McCarthy, "The Representation of Prostitutes," 77–97; Heide Schlüpmann, "The Brothel as Arcadian Space? *Diary of the Lost Girl,*" in *The Films of G. W. Pabst: An Extraterritorial Cinema,* ed. Eric Rentschler (New Brunswick, NJ: Rutgers University Press, 1990), 80–90; Schmidt, *Geschlecht unter Kontrolle,* 196–209.

80. Examples of the readers' letters are reprinted in Arno Bammé, ed., *Margarete Böhme: Die Erfolgsschriftstellerin aus Husum* (Munich: Profil, 1994), 203–4. See also Günther, *Weiblichkeitsentwürfe,*

The readers' concern most likely stemmed from the fact that Thymian, an upstanding bourgeois daughter, came from their milieu and yet suffered a fate considered most unrespectable. In the book, Thymian loses her mother to illness at a young age and is raised by her father, an apothecary who, after his wife's death, does his share of philandering with the family housekeepers. At the age of sixteen, Thymian is seduced and impregnated by her father's assistant, Meinert. Cast out of the house by her own family, forced to give up her child for adoption, sent to a reform school, and ostracized by polite society, Thymian eventually turns to a life of prostitution. Although she achieves financial success as a prostitute with bourgeois and aristocratic clients, her life is cut short by tuberculosis. She is able to tell her story only by passing her diary on to her friend Grete. Böhme's literary double, it is Grete who becomes, upon Thymian's death, the true heroine of the novel.[81]

Thymian's death and Böhme's hidden authorship are the linchpins of most scholarly analyses of *Diary of a Lost Girl*, which raise the following important questions: Does Thymian's death serve as an admonishment of the respectable society that turned its back on her, as Richard J. Evans argues, or is the protagonist's untimely demise, as Margaret McCarthy reads it, a distancing gesture, chosen to appease readers who likely believed that the only good prostitute was a dead one? Would there have been such an outpouring of sympathy for Thymian had she remained alive? Furthermore, would there have been such a show of concern for the plight of a dead prostitute had Böhme revealed her own authorship and thereby Thymian's fictional status? While McCarthy interprets Böhme's denial of authorship as a business tactic that uses the claim of authenticity to entice readers, and argues that the book's best-seller status undermined its critical potential, Evans sees Böhme's claim of the diary's authenticity as a clever strategy that protected both the integrity of the novel's social criticism and Böhme's own reputation. After all, he argues, had Böhme revealed herself as the true author of the novel/diary, she might have exposed herself to accusations of moral corruption or *Dirnenmoral* such as those slung at Helene Stöcker.[82]

Despite the critical attention it has received in the past two decades, Böhme's *Diary of a Lost Girl* has yet to be closely analyzed in light of Stöcker's new morality and her campaign for the support of single mothers, and Stöcker's own explicit praise of the novel has never been mentioned.[83] Böhme's text offers more insightful

306–9; and Jazbinsek, "Lebensgeschichte und Eigensinn," 42–43.

81. Margarete Böhme, *Tagebuch einer Verlorenen: Von einer Toten* (1905; repr., Witzwort: Kronacher, 1988). There is no available English translation of the novel.

82. Evans, *Tales from the German Underworld,* 168, 211; McCarthy, "The Representation of Prostitutes," 81–83. Eva Borst makes arguments similar to Evans's; see her *Über jede Scham erhaben,* 117.

83. This is not to say that scholars have not mentioned this context in relation to Böhme's novel. Heide Schlüpmann, for example, praises Böhme for her "keen awareness of social environment" and her "markedly emancipatory sexual politics. She defends the rights and dignity of unwed mothers, as well as the 'morality' of prostitutes, against the dominant bigotry, including the hypocrisy of middle-class charity groups run by women" ("The Brothel as Arcadian Space," 80). The reference to Stöcker's

criticism of the social climate of its time than contemporary scholars give it credit for; it chastises bourgeois society for its double standard, its moral hypocrisy, and its stigmatization of unwed mothers. By presenting its readers with a protagonist who is educated, charitable, and who is not afraid to express sexual desire, it seems to support greater sexual autonomy for women. And yet Böhme does seem to pander to a bourgeois readership in two seemingly contradictory ways: by giving her prostitute protagonist an air of respectability, on the one hand, and by keeping her at a safe distance from the privileged maternal figure of the novel, the writer Grete, on the other. By twice denying Thymian the chance to be a mother, by relegating her to the grave at the end of the text, and allowing Grete to censor the diary, Böhme ultimately denies Thymian both productive and reproductive power. Garnering sympathy for Thymian without making her into a role model, the novel capitalizes on the deceased Thymian's status as a victim of both an outdated morality and a fatal disease. Omitting the pages in which Thymian begins working as a prostitute allows the "editor" Böhme to avoid a crucial turning point and hence to portray prostitution as a fate imposed on the protagonist rather than a choice she makes.[84] In the end, the character who is granted the most agency is Grete, who, as a divorced working mother represents a new, more palatable model of autonomous womanhood for the book's bourgeois readers.

It could certainly be argued that Margarete Böhme had a personal stake in advocating the rights of single mothers. At the time she was writing the *Diary of a Lost Girl,* she was living in Berlin as a divorced single mother and supporting herself and her daughter with her writing. Born Margarete Fedderson in 1867 in the northern coastal town of Husum, Böhme started writing fiction at the age of seventeen under the pseudonym Ormanós Sandor, and she published her work in various northern German and Austrian newspapers. In 1894 she married the newspaper publisher Friedrich Theodor Böhme, with whom she had a daughter, Katharina. The marriage ended in divorce six years later, and in 1902 Böhme moved with her daughter to Berlin-Friedenau. The *Diary of a Lost Girl* was her literary breakthrough, and it secured her financial autonomy. Böhme remarried in 1911, this time to the Berlin bread manufacturer Theodor Schlüter. Moving from Berlin to Hamburg during the final years of the Weimar Republic in order to be closer to her daughter, she died in 1939.[85]

---

movement, however, remains implicit in Schlüpmann's piece, whereas it is explicitly yet fleetingly mentioned in Borst, *Über jede Scham erhaben,* 120, 141; and Evans, *Tales from the German Underworld,* 207.

84. The editor's voice in the novel claims, with more than a hint of melodrama, that the pages of the diary were removed by Thymian herself, and explains her alleged actions as a means of forgetting the point at which "she crossed, with quivering feet, the last, shaky bridge between two worlds." Böhme, *Tagebuch,* 118.

85. Biographical information on Böhme comes from Bammé, *Margarete Böhme;* Borst, *Über jede Scham erhaben,* 121; Jürgen Dietrich's foreword to the 1988 reprint of *Tagebuch einer Verlorenen;* and Günther, *Weiblichkeitsentwürfe,* 214–17.

Much like Helene Stöcker's activist texts, Böhme's novel conveys the message that bourgeois morality is damaging to women and deserves to be questioned and reformed. The dynamics in Thymian's household after her mother's death exemplify the double standard and its dire consequences for women. Thymian is expected to remain chaste until marriage and is therefore kept in the dark about sexual matters, while her father and Meinert actively pursue women sexually without any regard for the consequences. Male desire is allowed to surface and remain visible, and it is consistently represented in the novel by the trope of the "glimmering eyes" (*flimmernde Augen*), a motif used to signal scenes of seduction in the first third of the text, most notably when Thymian's father, Herr Gotteball, gazes at the young and attractive maid Elizabeth and when Meinert seduces Thymian. While Eva Borst reads the men's glimmering eyes as an "omen of sexual violence" and describes Thymian's seduction by Meinert—with late twentieth-century sensibilities—as a rape, there is no clear evidence in the text that this was Böhme's intention. Indeed there are two instances in which the trope of the glimmering eyes is used without a hint of violence or coercion: when Thymian and her childhood friend Count Osdorff first become lovers, and when she spends a platonic yet desire-laden night in the company of a gentleman in Hamburg.[86] Through the genre of the diary and Thymian's first-person narrative, the reader observes how the protagonist gradually learns to decipher the meaning of the glimmering eyes and thereby to read male desire. This slow process begins as the most ominous sides of that desire are revealed, first through Herr Gotteball's impregnation of Elizabeth, who drowns herself in despair when he refuses to marry her, and then in the pivotal seduction scene of Thymian by Meinert. It is indeed only once Elizabeth is dead and Meinert has deflowered Thymian that the protagonist understands the sexual dynamics at work in her own home and in bourgeois society. Her own eyes are opened, and she plainly states: "Now I see with both eyes what is happening around me."[87] She suddenly comprehends the double standard that forced Elizabeth to drown herself in shame while her own father continues with his dalliances, and she also knows that when men like Osdorff or the man in Hamburg stroke her cheek and look at her with a twinkle in their eyes, they desire her. Thymian's gradual enlightenment reveals Böhme's cleverness in choosing the diary as her genre for a novel on prostitution, for by giving a voice to the innocent, preseduction Thymian, the book dispels the myth of the "born prostitute" as naturally morally corrupt. By tracking her growing knowledge of desire and moral dynamics, the novel serves first and foremost as a critique of bourgeois society's tendency to withhold information about sexuality from its young women and the resulting unpleasant initiation to sexual life experienced by those women. Perhaps, in showing how Thymian's eyes are opened by her experiences, the book served to educate its—possibly

---

86. The "glimmering eyes" appear in Böhme, *Tagebuch,* 40, 56, 59, and 100, in the scenes described. For Borst's reading of the "glimmering eyes," see *Über jede Scham erhaben,* 130.

87. Böhme, *Tagebuch,* 58.

naive—turn-of-the-century bourgeois women readers. Perhaps Thymian's seduction was theirs as well.

After her seduction by Meinert, Thymian begins to feel her own sexual desire awakening, and she becomes more brazen in her interactions with the fumbling Osdorff. Strangely fascinated by his black leather boots and soft hands, she admits she feels "a strong urge to let [herself] be hit by those beautiful, smooth, white hands." When she actually verbalizes her masochistic desire to Osdorff, he is stunned and refuses to fulfill her wishes, yet he still chooses to read those wishes as an invitation to sex. Once they become lovers, Thymian never again expresses her wish to be beaten, yet she reiterates her desire for Osdorff, saying: "those hands, those hands—they really make me crazy."[88] Although Thymian's expression of masochistic desire appears to follow Krafft-Ebing's theory that masochism is simply a more extreme form of women's natural inclination toward sexual passivity, Böhme's book presents Thymian's relations with Osdorff with greater complexity—as a phase of sexual experimentation that falls between Thymian's seduction by Meinert and her turn to prostitution, during which she displays both sexual agency and passivity. In contrast to the sexual aggressor Meinert, the obviously "feminized" Osdorff gives Thymian the chance to occupy the subject position and allows her to love him "like an object,...like a thing."[89] McCarthy, too, reads Osdorff both in Böhme's novel and in G. W. Pabst's 1929 film version of the text as a figure that "enables Thymian to occupy both feminine and masculine positions and thus both sides of the sado-masochistic divide."[90]

Thymian's ability to see herself as both subject and object, and to vacillate between sexual agency and passivity, becomes even more evident once she is an experienced prostitute and professional mistress. On the one hand, she is represented as a desiring subject who acts on her own physical urges. On a trip to Vienna

---

88. Böhme, *Tagebuch,* 59. Osdorff's boots and gloves, which serve to protect his soft hands, mark him as an aristocratic dandy, and it is notable that black boots and white gloves such as his were also essential accessories for turn-of-the-century pimps, a role that Osdorff takes on later in the novel. See Evans, *Tales from the German Underworld,* 187. The expression of masochistic desire, particularly by bourgeois girls, seemed to be in vogue in turn-of-the-century German literature, most likely influenced by the popularity of Krafft-Ebing's *Psychopathia sexualis* and the writings of Leopold von Sacher-Masoch. The best-known literary example of masochism expressed by a bourgeois adolescent girl is Frank Wedekind's play *Frühlings Erwachen* (Spring Awakening), in which the female protagonist Wendla insists that one of the boys, Melchior, repeatedly strike her on the thighs. Although it was completed in 1891, Wedekind's play first premiered in Berlin in 1906; Max Reinhardt directed. See Frank Wedekind, *Frühlings Erwachen* (repr., Stuttgart: Reclam, 1995), 22, 93. As Barbara Mennel reminds her readers, masochism is not to be read simply as subversive, but it does encourage the contemplation of power dynamics: "Masochistic aesthetics stages power, begging the question whether this inverted and exaggerated staging of power relations reproduces existing power differentials or whether it offers ways to work through power differentials and resignify symbols of power." Barbara Mennel, *The Representation of Masochism and Queer Desire in Film and Literature* (New York: Palgrave Macmillan, 2007), 9.

89. Böhme, *Tagebuch,* 59–60.

90. McCarthy, "The Representation of Prostitutes," 97.

financed by her wealthy patron Count Y, she yearns for a casual sexual encounter, "to engage in a small intermezzo" as a form of erotic "refreshment," and she also pines for the doctor Julius, the only man in the diary for whom she expresses both love and desire.[91] Thymian furthermore recognizes her physical body as a desired commodity, and in one key scene she displays her entrepreneurial talents by charging men a fee to touch her luxurious dark hair: "All the other girls were jealous, and that pleased me, and that evening I let my hair hang wild, and every man who came near me wanted to touch and tousle my hair, but I wouldn't stand for that and made everyone who wanted to do so pay five marks first, and soon I had gathered about sixty marks altogether, so I bought myself a Parisian hat with yellow feathers the very next day."[92] This is one of the rare moments in the text when Böhme represents Thymian as a self-conscious commodity, a woman who consciously reaps financial benefits from her body. She captures attention, and she takes pride and pleasure in that attention. The fact that the scene is set in a Berlin *Nachtcafé*, a combination of café and bar generally frequented by a mixed-class clientele and a locale for clandestine prostitution, points to the confluence of urban leisure and commercial sex for which the capital city was already becoming known at the turn of the century. Thymian's mention of the "other girls" and their jealousy serves to set her apart from common prostitutes; indeed she remarks at several points in the text that her respectable appearance allows her to continue to pass as an upstanding lady. She even boasts that when she is out strolling the city streets, she is "never jostled in a lascivious manner," unlike her "colleagues," who "wear the stamp of their profession on their faces."[93] Not only does Thymian look respectable, she is also well mannered, articulate, and well educated; she speaks several languages and reads scientific, philosophical, and literary works. As an educated bourgeois woman, she attracts an upper- and middle-class—and mostly married—clientele. Her purchase of the "Parisian hat with yellow feathers" with the money she receives in the café underscores her status as a specific type of prostitute, a fashionable Parisian import of sorts who capitalizes precisely on her ability to appear respectable: a cocotte.[94]

By offering its readers the tale of a bourgeois daughter turned cocotte that takes place in a predominantly middle-class milieu, Böhme's "Kokottentagebuch" (diary of a cocotte), as it was dubbed by one turn-of-the-century critic, ignores socioeconomic realities such as limited employment opportunities, poor working conditions, and low wages as factors that often caused petit-bourgeois and working-class

---

91. Böhme, *Tagebuch*, 208.
92. Böhme, *Tagebuch*, 153.
93. Böhme, *Tagebuch*, 163.
94. The motif of the cocotte surfaces even before Thymian becomes one herself. It refers to her great-grandmother, a mobile and independent woman who hailed from the streets of Paris and left her husband (Thymian's great-grandfather) to run off with a rich Indian merchant. Thymian's Aunt Frieda claims that the great-grandmother infused the family with "the blood of a cocotte" (*Kokottenblut*). Böhme, *Tagebuch*, 71.

women to enter into prostitution. As Evans observes, "The working class is nowhere to be seen."[95] The novel's choice of a bourgeois protagonist, however, fits its aim of raising the awareness of its middle-class readership regarding the contradictions and restrictions inherent in their own rigid code of morality. Like feminists such as Anna Pappritz and Helene Stöcker, Böhme portrays the primary cause of prostitution as moral rather than economic. Branded as "fallen women" or "lost girls" by respectable society, young women such as Thymian were left with prostitution as their only chance for survival, as Thymian laments the double standard: "A man never runs into a dead-end street like we women; everywhere a door remains open for him; his existence is not destroyed by a misstep as is ours."[96] Exposing the moral hypocrisy of bourgeois society is *the* central critical point of the novel. Such hypocrisy is exemplified first by Thymian's own family, then by the brutal pastor and his wife who run the reform school to which Thymian is sent, and finally by a group of feminist charity workers who ostracize her when they discover the truth about her past. After watching the pastor cheat on his wife and his wife verbally and physically abuse the household servants, Thymian turns a deaf ear to their pious words. Questioning the very concept of moral reform as it is carried out at the school, she writes of the pastor and his wife in her diary: "They are desperately trying to better me, but whether or not they actually 'make me better' is another question. To me it seems like the opposite, as if the atmosphere of God fearing, moral strictness, and chastity in the pastor's home were teeming with the bacteria of malice, hypocrisy, greed, cruelty, and deceitfulness that one breathes in and absorbs against one's will."[97] Reversing the discourse of feminists and social hygienists who described immoral sexual behavior as an epidemic, Böhme employs the terminology of illness and infection to describe moral rigidity and expose its falseness and destructiveness. Thymian suffers the brunt of the abuse in the pastor's house because of her illegitimate pregnancy, and the fact that she runs straight from the reform school to her future madam causes the reader to ponder whether or not Thymian would even have become a prostitute had she not been subjected to the pastor's scorn. In a statement that could just have easily appeared in one of the BfM's pamphlets or journals, just before her flight from the reform school Thymian airs her dismay over the ostracization of single mothers, saying: "If people were really serious about their religion, they would not curse and deride the unwed mother and make it impossible for her to freely and openly acknowledge her child."[98] This plea for the

---

95. Evans, *Tales from the German Underworld,* 169. It was the literary critic Franz Diederich who called Böhme's novel a "cocotte's diary," in his review "Aus den tiefen des Lebens," *Das literarische Echo* 8 (1905): 177–81, here 179, quoted in Jazbinsek, "Lebensgeschichte und Eigensinn," 42.

96. Böhme, *Tagebuch,* 228.

97. Böhme, *Tagebuch,* 82.

98. Böhme, *Tagebuch,* 94.

fair treatment of unwed mothers marks one of Thymian's first efforts to define an alternative morality, a new morality that shifts its focus away from sexual behavior and recognizes, quite simply, human goodness.[99]

In the book's articulation of a new morality, traditional structures central to bourgeois culture melt away, the most important of which is marriage. Indeed, if marriage exists in the text at all, it is presented as a failed enterprise. When her family tries to force her to marry Meinert once her pregnancy is revealed, Thymian states that she would "rather be dead" than be his wife and hence his property.[100] Böhme's book continues to depict marriage as a business transaction through Thymian's eventual sham marriage to Osdorff, which she enters into for the sole reason of taking on the title Countess. The title, however, is not enough to lift her out of prostitution, since Count Osdorff has squandered the family fortune and has himself found a home in the so-called sexual underworld of Berlin. Interestingly, the only people in the diary who show genuine compassion and goodness are those from that very underworld who come to Thymian and Osdorff's aid once Osdorff falls ill. Sitting at his bedside for hours and offering gifts of food and flowers, their tough-talking friends from Friedrichstrasse prove themselves to be caring and loyal, causing Thymian to ask rhetorically whether "this amount of devotion and self-sacrifice by friends and colleagues can also be found in bourgeois circles."[101] Having already shown such "bourgeois circles" as the family and the reform school to be virtually devoid of kindness and understanding, the book shifts its critical gaze to a circle that, at the time that Böhme was writing Thymian's story, had proclaimed its moral authority—the bourgeois feminist movement.

Following Osdorff's death, Thymian secures her financial standing as Count Y's mistress and joins a bourgeois women's charity organization. At first Thymian fits in well with the educated and polite feminist charity workers, but she is soon angered by their harsh moral judgment of prostitutes and what they call the "demimonde" (*Halbwelt*). The feminists may present themselves as charitable, yet they place themselves on a moral pedestal and speak of less fortunate women with disdain, showing little actual compassion. Thymian experiences their misanthropic side firsthand when a former suitor recognizes her at one of the ladies' fund-raising events. Once her past is revealed, Thymian is expelled from the organization. Months later, she runs into the women during an outing at the Berlin zoo, where they meet her gaze with scornful sneers. Their expression of moral disdain confirms the doubts that Thymian had about the women's capacity for goodness even before they cast her out, doubts that cause her to wonder "whether or not these fine, upstanding ladies morally tower above the other world that they so disdainfully call the demimonde." Pondering such a question leads her to the clearest articulation of

---

99. The concept of goodness (*Güte*) comes up multiple times in Thymian's narrative. See Böhme, *Tagebuch*, 97, 129, 273.

100. Böhme, *Tagebuch*, 64–65.

101. Böhme, *Tagebuch*, 192.

new morality found in the diary; she writes: "From my perspective the word 'morality' is a universal term for all beautiful human qualities and not just for the narrow scrutiny of each person's sex life." In their exclusive focus on sexual morality, the feminists in the novel, much like most of the feminists of Böhme's time, wind up discriminating against the very women they claim to want to help.[102]

Despite their astute readings of Böhme's novel, neither Evans nor McCarthy mentions the obvious criticism of feminist charity workers in *Diary of a Lost Girl.* Böhme herself made few direct statements concerning her own views about feminism, but in a brief article written for the popular periodical *Die Welt am Montag* several months after the publication of her book, the author took issue with Anita Augspurg's review of the diary and distanced herself and her text from the work of bourgeois abolitionist feminists.[103] Beyond that, Böhme said little about her own stance on the women's activism of her time. Still, *Diary of a Lost Girl*'s critique of turn-of-the-century feminism must have made quite an impression on the filmmaker G. W. Pabst, who directed the 1929 cinematic interpretation of the novel.[104] Pabst devoted the final scene of his film to a confrontation between Thymian and a group of bourgeois feminists, set in the same strict reform house Thymian flees in the middle of the narrative. Although the scene begins with Thymian posing as the venerable count's niece in order to appear respectable in the eyes of the feminists, she eventually reveals herself in order to protest the reformatory master's treatment of her friend, the prostitute Erika, a character who does not exist in Böhme's novel.[105] Glaring at the women who give their financial support and moral approval to the reformatory's punishment of "lost girls" such as Erika, Thymian openly admits to her own past as a prostitute. As the women stare at Thymian in stunned silence, the count rushes to her side and delivers the final line of the film: "With a little more

---

102. Böhme, *Tagebuch*, 273; for the entire episode with the bourgeois feminists, see pp. 271–291.

103. Böhme, "Tagebuch einer Verlorenen: Eine Entgegnung," *Die Welt am Montag* (Beilage) 11, no. 36 (1905): n.p. Borst and Schlüpmann are the only two scholars who call attention to Böhme's negative portrait of the feminist movement of her day, and to my knowledge, no scholar has ever analyzed the particular passages from the novel cited above. Böhme maintained her critical stance toward bourgeois feminism in the novel that followed *Diary of a Lost Girl,* called *Dida Ibsens Geschichte,* lamenting once again the deliberate distance feminists placed between themselves and prostitutes. Borst, *Über jede Scham erhaben,* 163–64, mentions this particular passage and, in an editorial comment, describes Böhme's lack of solidarity with the feminists as "annoying" (*irritierend*).

104. Pabst's film celebrated its German premiere on October 15, 1929, in Berlin and received mixed but generally favorable reviews in the press. After playing in German cinemas for nearly two months, however, the film was pulled from theaters by the censor and subjected to extensive cuts, including the final scene. On the film's complex censorship history and eventual reconstruction, see Matthias Knop, "G. W. Pabsts *Tagebuch einer Verlorenen:* Zensur und Rekonstruktion," unpublished essay, BArch-Film Sg. 1_16488. Pabst's film is the only surviving version and the best-known of three cinematic renditions of Böhme's novel; the first was made in 1912 and directed by Fritz Bernhardt, and the second was made in 1918 by Richard Oswald, whose social hygiene films will be discussed at length in chapter 3.

105. It is possible that Pabst took the name Erika from the book, for that is the name of Thymian's daughter who is put up for adoption and perishes at a young age. The rebellious and sexually audacious prostitute Erika who appears in Pabst's film, however, constitutes a particular "Weimar twist" to the film's rendition of Böhme's novel. See the final pages of this chapter, below.

love, no one on this earth would ever be lost." The events unfold less dramatically in the novel, and yet the critical message is the same. Despite feminists' claims of solidarity, there was no sisterhood between feminists and prostitutes. The hope for a new morality, however, is also found in the count's plea for "a little more love," a broader, more accepting form of morality similar to the novel's focus on "goodness."

While Pabst's film ends with Thymian standing defiantly side by side with Erika, only one woman is left standing at the end of Böhme's novel, and that is Grete. Grete is quite obviously Böhme's literary double—a divorced fiction writer who lives in Berlin-Friedenau with her daughter Käte—and her introduction to the narrative offers readers a new image of the financially autonomous woman. She is many things that Thymian is—educated, attractive, creative, and savvy, and yet she is also what Thymian cannot be: a mother. As much as Thymian dreams of motherhood as a young woman, she is twice prevented from fulfilling that dream. First, her own daughter is put up for adoption and then dies at a young age, and then later in the text she is struck by a carriage and is subsequently informed that the blow caused a miscarriage. Her reaction to the loss of her first child is utter despair, but her reaction to the miscarriage of her second child is cool, rational, and resigned: "It didn't terribly upset me; I think it's for the best; what was I supposed to do with a child?"[106] The episode involving the miscarriage seems at first to be superfluous, but when read in the context of Grete's imminent appearance it can be interpreted as a distancing gesture between the two women.

As Dietmar Schmidt has pointed out, Grete and Thymian are contrasting figures: Grete is a successful mother, and Thymian loses both of her children; Grete is divorced and lives alone with her daughter, while Thymian shares her bed with multiple men; Grete produces novels and articles for the popular bourgeois women's journal *Die Gartenlaube*, and Thymian consumes great quantities of money on jewelry and clothing; Grete is financially independent, while Thymian depends on her wealthy male patrons for income.[107] But while Schmidt sees Grete as fitting easily into the bourgeois milieu of her sleepy Berlin suburb, the book suggests otherwise. Grete enters the scene immediately after Thymian encounters the disdainful feminists at the zoo. Disillusioned by the behavior of the charity workers, Thymian plans to close herself off to contact with women until she meets Grete, who seems to fall somewhere in between the morally rigid bourgeois feminists and the world of prostitution. Indeed Grete's background remains vague, and the fact that she is revealed to be an old acquaintance of Thymian's from Hamburg—where Thymian first started working as a prostitute—is briefly mentioned but never discussed in depth.

---

106. Böhme, *Tagebuch*, 246.

107. See Schmidt, *Geschlecht unter Kontrolle*, 201–4, for a similar analysis of the figures of Thymian and Grete. Schmidt, however, approaches the text psychoanalytically and reads the two women as representing the author Margarete Böhme's two sides: one sexually liberated (Thymian) and the other sexually repressed (Grete). See also McCarthy, "The Representation of Prostitutes," 82–83.

When Thymian suggests that she and Grete meet up, Grete responds in a way that both seals the two women's relationship with one another and, at the same time, ensures that there will be distance between them. She begins by saying that she lives a rather "withdrawn" life, set apart from her own bourgeois milieu and from the urban underworld that she knows to be Thymian's. The separation between Grete and Thymian's milieu is made clear by Grete's request that the two women meet only alone, a request that betrays her discomfort with the idea of running into any of Thymian's associates. She also plainly states her most important priorities, saying: "I have my work and my child, and both fill up my life."[108] It is lines such as these that remind the reader of what makes Grete different from the protagonist. In Grete's presence, the reader is reminded of Thymian's lost children and also of entries in the diary that express the emptiness of Thymian's existence, entries that express her listlessness and her longing for "activity" and "honest work."[109] Such passages insinuate that prostitution is not work, and at the very least it is not honest work, and they betray Thymian's own feeling that she is not a productive member of society. She is unable to produce healthy children like Grete's rosy-cheeked Käte, and she relinquishes her one product, her diary, to Grete by the end of the novel.

The start of Thymian and Grete's friendship marks the beginning of Thymian's rapid physical decline and the end of her creative productivity. Having promised her diary to Grete, who admits she will have to dilute and sweeten its contents "with water and patchouli" in order to make it more marketable to the "readers of a family publication," Thymian allows her own production to trickle out, leaving only her illness to quite literally consume her.[110] Like so many fictional prostitutes, among them Émile Zola's Nana and Alexandre Dumas's Violette, she dies of tuberculosis. It is Grete who is left to edit the diary, to insert her own commentary, to censor any parts "that are absolutely unfit for publication," and to ensure that it will not be placed in the ranks of "titillating literature."[111] Pieced together by Grete, the diary is made fit for consumption by a respectable reading public. Grete's own privileged status in the novel serves to present readers with a new model of motherhood that could exist outside the confines of marriage; like Helene Stöcker's BfM, Böhme's book added to a turn-of-the-century discourse that allowed the single mother to emerge "as a new icon celebrating the triumph of life-giving nature."[112] Taking great pains to keep this new mother figure separate from the prostitute in their works, however, both Stöcker and Böhme ultimately deny prostitutes productive and reproductive rights. Sympathy for the prostitute had its limits.

---

108. Böhme, *Tagebuch*, 298.
109. Böhme, *Tagebuch*, 141.
110. Böhme, *Tagebuch*, 296.
111. Böhme, *Tagebuch*, 3.
112. Allen, *Feminism and Motherhood*, 182.

Although the progressivism of Stöcker's activist texts and Böhme's novel, particularly their critiques of hypocritical bourgeois morality, should not be understated, neither can their lingering prejudice against prostitutes be ignored. They distinguished themselves from both the mainstream feminist movement and the abolitionists by advocating greater sexual freedom for women and by fighting to erase the stigma of unwed motherhood; yet Böhme and Stöcker still maintained that the way of the prostitute was a sure way to the grave. The final words of Böhme's novel, spoken by Grete after Thymian's funeral, are "God protect our children."[113] Both children and mothers are to be protected from Thymian's fate, the fate of a prostitute. Even though it is written by an author who was critical of the turn-of-the-century women's movement, this plea aptly reflects the tenuous relationship between bourgeois feminists—from Bieber-Böhm to the women of the BfM—and prostitutes. Feminists and prostitutes were not sisters. At best, feminists saw themselves as mothers and guardians, and at worst, as wardens keeping the lost girls under control.

From Wilhelmine to Weimar Berlin

The predominant images of prostitutes as social victims and public health threats found in turn-of-the-century feminist discourse did not vanish with time, but new, more complex images did develop. The vague contours of such images were already visible within certain Wilhelmine texts and artifacts: the artist Heinrich Zille's plucky and robust prostitutes from Berlin's working class resisted the definition of prostitutes as victims and instead served to popularize their urban *Milljöh*. At the same time, writers such as Otto Erich Hartleben and Margarete Böhme confronted their readers with images of respectable women—bourgeois and petit bourgeois—who quite consciously engaged in various forms of commodified sexuality that catered primarily to a bourgeois clientele, cocottes who blurred the lines between "upstanding" and "fallen" women that feminists fought so hard to define. The Weimar Republic, I argue in the following chapters, blurred these lines even more, producing multiple discourses on prostitution and new womanhood, influenced by such phenomena as economic instability, the increased public presence of women in the workplace and in places of leisure, and the rise of popular entertainment and consumer culture. In particular, with the proliferation of visual media in the 1920s, discourses on prostitution underwent a significant shift from print to visual culture, as prostitutes were portrayed in paintings, drawings, photographs, films, and on the stages of Weimar Berlin. Print culture itself became more visual in nature with the rise of illustrated magazines, mixed-media travel guides and "moral histories" (*Sittengeschichten*), and novels that incorporated the visual

---

113. Böhme, *Tagebuch,* 308.

language of film. This shift into the visual realm, and the myriad possibilities for spectatorial interpretation it provided, opened up an even greater space for images of prostitutes that defied those of victim or monstrous, disease-spreading whore.

G. W. Pabst's film *Diary of a Lost Girl* (1929) exemplifies this shift from print to visual media and its concomitant complex depiction of prostitutes. Although Böhme's story of the fallen bourgeois daughter remains, the visual representation of the prostitutes in the film is quintessential to the 1920s. Played by the American actress Louise Brooks, Thymian no longer boasts the cascading tresses given to her by Böhme; instead she sports the signature haircut of the 1920s emancipated woman—the bob. Recent scholarship on the film questions how Thymian's story may have resonated with audiences of Weimar women. Heide Schlüpmann, who focuses on the protagonist Thymian as a victim and as an object of a sadistic, patriarchal gaze—even if that gaze is, at certain points in the film, embodied by women—argues that viewer identification with Thymian can be read only as "naïve" and "masochistic." McCarthy, on the other hand, points to ways in which the film "exceed[s] female masochistic pleasure." She does so by reading the two seduction scenes, in which Thymian swoons, as ones that combine "masochistic pleasure with the pleasures of transformation, refiguring a presumed loss of self as a recreation of self."[114] McCarthy's reading of the seduction scenes as offering Thymian even the slightest hint of agency seems untenable—after all, she falls into a state of *Ohnmacht,* which translates literally as "without power," a state that clearly depicts her sexuality as passive. That said, McCarthy's efforts to locate "multiple and often conflicting points of identification" within Pabst's film are well worth further investigation.[115]

Even more so than in Böhme's novel, in the film Thymian appears as both victim and agent, object and subject. She transforms from a seduced, fallen bourgeois daughter to a prostitute who orchestrates her own fate and consciously embraces her commodity status. For example, after Thymian becomes acclimated to life in the brothel, she is shown in a dance hall, surrounded by adoring patrons. The film's dance-hall scene is an updated version of the novel's scene in the *Nachtcafé,* in which Thymian charges men to touch her hair. In Pabst's version, Thymian organizes a lottery to raise money for a friend and offers herself as the prize (fig. 6). By writing her name on the winning ticket, she displays her awareness of her status as desirable commodity, and her deliberate use of that status for financial gain. Before Thymian's father and his new wife arrive in the dance hall and subject her to their disapproving looks, she is shown as blissful and carefree, and the lottery tickets

---

114. Schlüpmann asserts that the "male gaze" in the film is channeled through such a character as the sadistic reformatory matron played by an androgynous Valeska Gert and even through the kindly brothel madam (Emmy Wyda), arguing that these women merely serve as vessels for the male-controlled camera and cinematic apparatus. See Schlüpmann, "The Brothel as Arcadian Space?," 86, 89. For McCarthy's arguments, see "The Representation of Prostitutes," 89.

115. McCarthy, "The Representation of Prostitutes," 86.

Figure 6. Louise Brooks as Thymian in G. W. Pabst's *Das Tagebuch einer Verlorenen* (Diary of a Lost Girl), 1929. Courtesy of Deutsche Kinemathek—Museum für Film und Fernsehen.

sell quickly, causing the viewer to ponder Richard W. McCormick's question as to whether or not there is "more agency to this supposed commodity status than critics have assumed," a question I discuss in the following chapters as I continue to explore and define the concept of the self-conscious commodity.[116]

The following chapters also continue to analyze how prostitution is used by some artists and authors to interrogate bourgeois structures, even while it is seen by others to be even more entrenched in those structures. Like Böhme's novel, Pabst's film exposes bourgeois hypocrisy and presents the brothel prostitutes as an alternative community for the shunned Thymian (fig. 7). The film, however, also captures the sexual audacity of the era in which it was filmed. Unlike the novel, which offers its readers a new model of respectable single motherhood through the figure of Grete, the film gives its viewers Erika, the reformatory inmate who introduces Thymian to the brothel as a place of refuge. The irrepressible Erika is unapologetic about her life as a prostitute, and perhaps even more than Thymian, she can be

---

116. Richard W. McCormick, *Gender and Sexuality in Weimar Modernity: Film, Literature, and "New Objectivity"* (New York: Palgrave, 2001), 35.

Figure 7. Emmy Wyda, Edith Meinhard (as Erika), Louise Brooks, and Speedy Schlichter in G. W. Pabst's *Das Tagebuch einer Verlorenen* (Diary of a Lost Girl), 1929. Courtesy of Deutsche Kinemathek— Museum für Film und Fernsehen.

read as a figure that offers both men and women viewers a variety of possibilities for pleasurable spectatorship. In the Weimar film press, the actress Edith Meinhard was praised for her portrayal of Erika, just as Pabst's favorable depiction of the brothel was reviewed positively. Critic Ernst Blass wrote in the *Berliner Tageblatt:* "Finally! The bordello with the good-natured and jovial madame...and the obviously talented Edith Meinhard's cheerful and charming cocotte creates a gentle, soft, seductive effect....It was extraordinarily good to present things like this for a change: the world of the demimonde as a possible remedy to the cruelty and the lovelessness of what came before it. That is good and courageous."[117] Erika is a defiant figure who challenges the rules of the girls' reformatory by wearing makeup. Violating the home's strict code of appearance, with its simple and shapeless frocks and its prohibition of makeup designed to desexualize the girls' bodies, in one of the scenes in the reformatory Erika is shown gazing into a compact mirror and applying forbidden lipstick. Taken with the seductiveness of her own image, she

---

117. Ernst Blass, "Tagebuch einer Verlorenen," *Berliner Tageblatt,* October 20, 1929, n.p. Neither Schlüpmann nor McCarthy discusses the character of Erika in her interpretation of the film.

winks flirtatiously at herself, failing to notice the thuggish reformatory warden lurking behind her. In this scene Erika is both the object of the warden's punitive—yet also lascivious—gaze and the somewhat narcissistic subject, keenly aware of her own attractiveness. Despite the warden's plan to "punish Erika," a sentence he writes into his calendar with the confiscated lipstick, Erika escapes the fate that would serve to place her alongside numerous fictional erotic women punished for their misdeeds. In fact, Erika escapes this fate at two key points in the film. First, in a delicious reversal of fortune, it is Erika who instigates the just punishment of the sadistic reformatory matron and warden doled out collectively by the "lost girls," which enables her and Thymian to escape to the brothel. At the end of the film, just when Erika's punishment and humiliation at the hands of the feminists seems inevitable, her alliance with Thymian saves her from the feminists' retribution. In the end, it is not prostitution from which Erika is saved, but rather the very system that claims to want to save her.

The figure of Erika contains many of the salient issues addressed in the coming chapters. Her active display of desire and pleasure marks the Weimar era as one of sexual experimentation and of a broader acceptance of active female sexuality. The scene in which she applies lipstick emphasizes the important function of makeup as a tool for women's self-fashioning, and it displays women's increased eroticization and commodification within the consumer culture of the Weimar era, a process that blurred lines between prostitutes and other public women. Erika's allure, her ability to appeal to her male clients, to the warden, and to Thymian as well, reveals the prostitute as a figure that captured attention and captivated 1920s audiences across gender lines. Finally, Erika's alliance with Thymian and the count at the end of the film raises the possibility of alternative configurations to the traditional bourgeois family. The former-bourgeois-daughter-turned-prostitute Thymian enters into a financially advantageous yet tender companionship with the kindly, aging count, and they welcome into their fold the prostitute Erika. This ending, which in contrast to the novel leaves Thymian very much alive and Erika unpunished, demonstrates that in Weimar culture power relations were less clearly defined by respectability, and that bourgeois values—already under scrutiny at the turn of the century and weakened further by war and economic uncertainty—were crumbling.

3

Naughty Berlin? New Women, New Spaces, and Erotic Confusion

If traditional bourgeois morality and social structures came under fire in Wilhelmine Berlin, then the First World War, the political revolution of 1918 and 1919, and the inflation years that followed "destroyed conventional notions of respectability and faith in authority."[1] Turn-of-the-century activism on the part of social reformers and progressive feminists certainly laid the groundwork for change, making modest inroads toward marital reform and calling bourgeois moral conventions into question. In Berlin, many of the key participants in the debates on prostitution and sexual mores—August Bebel, Anna Pappritz, Helene Stöcker, and Magnus Hirschfeld, just to name a few—remained the same before and after the war. But as Hirschfeld openly admitted, the war acted as a catalyst, speeding up the changes that had slowly begun to take place during the Wilhelmine era. Two million German men lost their lives to the violence of modern warfare, nearly one-third of whom were married. The war, with its unprecedented casualties and its immense social upheaval, dealt a devastating blow to the bourgeois family, its gendered division of labor, and its restrictive sexual standards. In so doing, the First World War created, in Hirschfeld's words, "a moral vacuum where experiments

---

1. Eric D. Weitz, *Weimar Germany: Promise and Tragedy* (Princeton, NJ: Princeton University Press, 2007), 11.

could be carried out."[2] The grandest sociopolitical experiment of all was Germany's first democracy, the Weimar Republic, which was founded in the wake of wartime devastation.

The war caused a proliferation in public roles for women, particularly in urban industrial centers like Berlin. With millions of German men between the ages of seventeen and forty-five enlisted in the armed services, women were propelled out of the realm of the family and into jobs in offices and factories that had previously been filled by men.[3] As Belinda Davis has shown, women in the capital city organized demonstrations and strikes in order to protest food shortages and the state's inability to provide for its citizens on the home front, actions that caused "a broad population of Germans" to see women "as the 'protagonists' in the social and political conflict that marked the era."[4] Looking back at the war and the advent of the Weimar Republic from the perspective of the republic's final years, the social commentator and cultural critic Curt Moreck described the drastic changes in gender roles caused by the First World War: "With father and son torn from the family by the call to arms, mother and daughter were compelled to work with their hands. Through the urgent call to labor, through the fight for their daily bread, mother and daughter joined the ranks of working men."[5] The changes wrought by women becoming more active and visible in the workplace, however, were

---

2. Magnus Hirschfeld, *Sittengeschichte der Nachkriegszeit* (Leipzig: Verlag für Sexualwissenschaft Schneider & Co., 1931), 1:4. For contemporary scholarship that highlights the continuities between the late Wilhelmine era and the Weimar Republic, specifically in regard to sex reform and the more open discussion of sexuality, see Dagmar Herzog, *Sex after Fascism: Memory and Morality in Twentieth-Century Germany* (Princeton, NJ: Princeton University Press, 2005), 259; Marchand and Lindenfeld, introduction to *Germany at the Fin-de-Siècle*, 3–4, 6; Weitz, *Weimar Germany*, 329. On German war casualties, see Richard Bessel, *Germany after the First World War* (Oxford: Clarendon Press, 1993), 10, 225. See also Elisabeth Domansky, "Militarization and Reproduction in World War I Germany," in Eley, *Society, Culture, and the State in Germany*, 442. Domansky cites a higher number of deaths among married men, claiming that they constituted 50 percent of the casualties, but most historians of World War I corroborate Bessel's statistics.

3. As Ute Frevert notes, the impact of the war on women's employment is often exaggerated, for numbers were already rising steadily around the turn of the century. By compelling women to take jobs in sectors previously dominated by men (i.e., commerce and industry), however, "the war caused the female labour force not to grow more rapidly than it would normally have done, but to relocate." Frevert, *Women in German History*, 157.

4. Belinda Davis, "Homefront: Food, Politics, and Women's Everyday Life during the First World War," in *Home/Front: The Military, War, and Gender in Twentieth-Century Germany,* ed. Karen Hagemann and Stefanie Schüler-Springorum (Oxford: Berg, 2002), 115. See also Davis's book-length study, *Home Fires Burning: Food, Politics, and Everyday Life in World War I Berlin* (Chapel Hill: University of North Carolina Press, 2000).

5. Curt Moreck, "Frauenideale der Nachkriegszeit," in Hirschfeld, *Sittengeschichte der Nachkriegszeit,* 1:403. Curt Moreck was born Konrad Haemmerling in Cologne in 1888. During the 1918 German revolution he was active in several radical artists' groups. A popular figure in Weimar Berlin's intellectual circles, he worked as a writer, editor, translator, and cultural critic. Because of their focus on the erotic side of city life and mass culture, and their celebration of women's emancipation and sexual experimentation, Moreck's books were burned by the National Socialists in 1933. He remained in Germany during the "Third Reich" but was forbidden to write. He died in 1957. For biographical information on Moreck, see Rudy Koshar, *German Travel Cultures* (Oxford: Berg, 2000), 83–84.

not limited to shifts in women's social roles. Such transformations also resulted in reconfigurations of social space.

In Moreck's view, the increased contact between men and women in spaces devoted to work and play heightened the sense of collegiality and camaraderie between them and signified a clear departure from the gendered division of labor and leisure of the Wilhelmine era. As he portrayed the situation, women had earned their right to take advantage of metropolitan nightlife: "They stood side by side with the man in the factories, in the offices, and at the machines; and through him they became acquainted with various places of pleasure...and in his company they spent their hours of leisure, in need of distraction: in the cafés, pubs, liquor lounges, and bars." Untainted by any sense of threat or resentment toward their new colleagues, the "working men" in Moreck's synopsis played a significant role in introducing women to spaces that were previously closed off to them, particularly urban entertainment venues. It was "through" the man and "in his company" that a Weimar woman gained legitimate access to cafés and taverns, spaces that in the pre-Weimar era had been generally considered to be sites of sexual solicitation for prostitutes. Exploring the interdependence of spatial proximity and the democratization of gender, Moreck goes on to describe women as both "masculinized" and "eroticized" by their experience of public life, and he defines the "feminization" of men in post–World War I Germany as a necessary step toward the social and sexual "emancipation" of both men and women.[6] Here, emancipation implies not just the transgression of traditional gender roles but also experimentation with sexual intimacy that transcended the institutions of marriage and prostitution. As both Atina Grossmann and Annette Timm document in their work on sex reform, the majority of young Weimar Berliners who visited "eugenic counseling centers" in the capital city did so more for free birth control and sex advice than for eugenic screening or health certificates, and many doctors who worked at the centers "promoted a particular vision of responsible companionate heterosexuality."[7]

As a result of the more freewheeling female sexuality of the Weimar Republic and the growing social acceptance of companionate relationships, Moreck suggests that "prostitution traditionally defined—as the old form of trading 'love' for cash on the more or less public markets—lost significance."[8] But what exactly does Moreck mean by this? Does prostitution become obsolete once female sexuality is less restricted by bourgeois morality, or does it merely lose its ability to mark

---

6. Moreck, "Frauenideale der Nachkriegszeit," 403. In the same essay, Moreck uses the terms *Vermännlichung* and *Erotisierung* in reference to Weimar women, and he claims that men's "Einbuße an physischer Männlichkeit" in the wake of the war was a crucial part of "der fortgeschrittenen Emanzipation"; see pp. 392, 394, 395.

7. Grossmann, *Reforming Sex*, 10, 69. Timm notes that 66.7 percent of young women who visited the counseling centers did so for access to birth control (*The Politics of Fertility*, 111). See also Weitz, *Weimar Germany*, 305.

8. Moreck, "Frauenideale der Nachkriegszeit," 408.

illicit sexuality? It could certainly be argued that prostitution had already taken on myriad meanings during the Wilhelmine era, when social reform discourses used prostitution as a site for critical discussions of female sexuality, agency, marriage, and respectability. What seems to concern Moreck is the increase in public forms of erotic intimacy or "love trades" in Weimar society that makes it nearly impossible to distinguish between professional prostitutes and other sexually active women. As Daphne Spain postulates in her book *Gendered Spaces*, the "spatial integration" of men and women constitutes "a route to higher status of women," but how is women's status affected by the act of occupying spaces that are historically associated with commodified female sexuality?[9] Instead of *prostitution* losing significance, the meanings attributed to *prostitutes* and sites of prostitution multiply and become increasingly complex in the cultural discourses of the Weimar Republic. Moreck's own work provides an example of this. In his essays in Magnus Hirschfeld's multi-volume moral histories of the First World War and the interwar period, in his own moral histories of film and Weimar society, and in his 1931 *Führer durch das "laster-hafte" Berlin* (Guide to "Naughty" Berlin), Moreck offered readers a broad range of images of prostitutes and emancipated women, and he often deliberately conflated the two.[10] As Moreck's texts and the diverse cultural phenomena examined in this chapter demonstrate, the obvious public presence of women in Weimar Berlin met with a variety of responses, many of which intertwined cultural discourses of sexually and financially emancipated womanhood with those about prostitutes, thereby creating "the elision of the woman *on* the street with the woman *of* the street."[11]

Indeed the proliferation of public roles for women was concurrent with a proliferation of discourses on prostitutes. With class divisions and gender roles destabilized by the war and ensuing inflation, Weimar Berlin replaced Paris as the

---

9. Daphne Spain, *Gendered Spaces* (Chapel Hill: University of North Carolina Press, 1992), xv. In her study, Spain reveals how the spatial organization of men and women contributes to "gender stratification," a social hierarchy in which men are granted unrestricted access to public life, while women's access is restricted.

10. Moreck contributed to all four volumes of Hirschfeld's moral histories: *Sittengeschichte des Weltkrieges,* 2 vols. (1930), and *Sittengeschichte der Nachkriegszeit,* 2 vols. (1931). One of the difficulties in citing these works is the fact that these volumes were produced as a collaborative project, with Hirschfeld acting as the executive editor. It is therefore not always clear who has authored the various chapters; Moreck's essays are directly attributed to him in only two cases. For more on the other contributors to Hirschfeld's project and the organization and impact of the project itself, see Richard Kühl, "'Aber in unserem Buch, Herr Sanitätsrat': Fragen an Magnus Hirschfelds Publikationspraxis 1929/30," *Mitteilungen der Magnus-Hirschfeld-Gesellschaft* 41/42 (2009): 32–42; and Kühl, "Zur Wirkung und Wahrnehmung von Magnus Hirschfelds *Sittengeschichte des Weltkrieges,*" *Mitteilungen der Magnus-Hirschfeld-Gesellschaft* 39/40 (2008): 23–35. Moreck also wrote *Sittengeschichte des Kinos* (Dresden: Paul Aretz Verlag, 1926), *Kultur- und Sittengeschichte der Neuesten Zeit: Geschlechtsleben und Erotik in der Gesellschaft der Gegenwart* (Dresden: Paul Aretz Verlag, 1928), and *Führer durch das "lasterhafte" Berlin* (Leipzig: Verlag moderner Stadtführer, 1931). Although I recognize that the word *Sitte* refers to social habits and customs as much as it does to moral conventions, both Hirschfeld's and Moreck's deliberate focus on sexual behavior and the shifts in the moral climate caused me to choose "moral history" as the most fitting translation for the term *Sittengeschichte.*

11. Meskimmon, *We Weren't Modern Enough,* 38.

European capital of sexual experimentation and display, and prostitutes—both real and imagined—were central figures in the metropolis's bawdy entertainment culture. Images of prostitutes pervaded visual and popular culture in Berlin; they could be seen on stage at the city's numerous cabarets, revues, and theaters and on movie screens, posters, and postcards. During the revolution, as public officials and health-care professionals debated the future of regulated prostitution, Berlin's prostitutes organized to form support organizations like the Hilfsbund der Berliner Prostituierten (Auxiliary Club of Berlin Prostitutes), where they discussed "issues such as prices, competition, the conduct of the police and physicians, and effective protections against professional hazards."[12] Along with the increased cultural currency and social activism of prostitutes came the eroticization of the younger generation of bourgeois and petit-bourgeois women. Some of these women had grown up during the war with a father at the front and a mother who worked in the war industry or stood in line for hours waiting for food rations, while others had entered the workforce prematurely to help support their families. Some saw their family's financial security evaporate during the years of inflation and hyper-inflation, when reversals of fortune became the order of the day. Many experienced their bodies differently, feeling the pangs of hunger and the effects of malnutrition for the first time, but they also learned to see their bodies as sources of labor and perhaps even as desirable commodities that could help them survive the years of upheaval. With bourgeois respectability compromised, fascination with the so-called sexual underworld grew as middle-class patrons and the nouveaux riches went "slumming" in Berlin's many dive bars and *Tingeltangels*.[13] The city streets that Walter Benjamin describes as clearly marked by the "sign of prostitution" during his childhood in Wilhelmine Berlin were also traversed, during the Weimar era, by other women on their way to work or to urban entertainment venues such as the café or cinema.[14] In other words, just as prostitutes seemed to inhabit more public spaces than ever before, working women from bourgeois backgrounds were increasingly occupying spaces that before the war were considered to be the exclusive domain of the prostitute.

---

12. Roos, *Weimar through the Lens of Gender*, 78.

13. On the lack of parental surveillance of the German youth during the war, see Bessel, *Germany after the First World War*, 23, 25, 225; and Roger Chickering, *Imperial Germany and the Great War, 1914–1918* (Cambridge: Cambridge University Press, 1998), 122–25. On the years of inflation, the impoverishment of the German middle classes, and the social effects on women, see Bernd Widdig, *Culture and Inflation in Weimar Germany* (Berkeley: University of California Press, 2001), 22, 169–220; and Weitz, *Weimar Germany*, 131–45. A *Tingeltangel* was, to quote Alan Lareau, "a low-class music hall" or "any disreputable barroom entertainment," in which the performers were often prostitutes "noted for the vulgarity of their repertoires." Alan Lareau, *The Wild Stage: Literary Cabarets of the Weimar Republic* (Columbia, SC: Camden House, 1995), 4. See also Jelavich, *Berlin Cabaret*, 1, 21.

14. Walter Benjamin, "Berliner Chronik," in *Gesammelte Schriften*, ed. Rolf Tiedemann and Hermann Schweppenhäuser (Frankfurt am Main: Suhrkamp, 1985), 6:472.

In contrast to Moreck's depiction of men who invited and welcomed women into the public sphere, some other male observers saw the increased public presence of women in Weimar Berlin as an alarming trend, and the image of the prostitute was evoked as a way of criticizing this change. When they encountered financially and sexually independent women in spaces traditionally associated with sexual exchange, these men failed to see women as "an increasingly autonomous and observing presence."[15] Instead they simply saw whores. Journalist Thomas Wehrling's 1920 article "Berlin Is Becoming a Whore," for example, creates an image of Berlin's public spaces as "overrun" by corrupt, permissive women who once hailed from respectable bourgeois households. Wehrling calls for "strong, sustaining men" to bring these women back to their senses and back into the private space of the home—a call that clearly reflects a discourse of postwar anxiety concerning female sexual autonomy and male weakness.[16] Readers familiar with Maria Tatar's study *Lustmord: Sexual Murder in Weimar Germany* could easily interpret Wehrling's vicious verbal assault on the women of Berlin as a "strategy for managing certain kinds of sexual, social, and political anxieties."[17] Tatar argues that this strategy was used by Weimar men who perceived themselves to be victims—of war, disease, the whims of the economy—to retaliate against their imagined enemies: women. Only the destruction of the erotic woman would allow the male subject to reassert himself. With brushstrokes performing slashes of the knife, the artists George Grosz and Otto Dix enacted aesthetic revenge on erotic women in their *Lustmord* paintings of the early 1920s, and this revenge was read as justifiable murder. According to Tatar, if "the victims are prostitutes—women marked with the signs of corrupt and corrupting sexuality—the killer is not infrequently judged to be a normal person provoked to an act of violence or his victims are seen as complicitous in their murders."[18] In this analysis, the two most common depictions of prostitutes, that of the threatening femme fatale and that of the victim, are collapsed. The former provokes male violence while the latter falls prey to it.

It is not the aim of this chapter to simply add to Tatar's discourse on the prostitute and emancipated women as objects of male fear and anxiety, although it is certainly worth noting that she often conflates the two without critical consideration. I examine instead the complexities of this conflation of prostitute and "New Woman" and pose the following questions: Did the sexually freewheeling atmosphere of Weimar Berlin actually make the overt expression of female desire and

---

15. Deborah L. Parsons, *Streetwalking the Metropolis: Women, the City, and Modernity* (Oxford: Oxford University Press, 2000), 43.

16. Thomas Wehrling, "Berlin Is Becoming a Whore," translated and reprinted in *The Weimar Republic Sourcebook*, ed. Anton Kaes, Martin Jay, and Edward Dimendberg (Berkeley: University of California Press, 1994), 721–23.

17. Tatar, *Lustmord*, 6.

18. Tatar, *Lustmord*, 54. For similar readings of Dix's and Grosz's *Lustmord* paintings, see Irwin Lewis, "*Lustmord*"; and Täuber, *Der häßliche Eros*, 113–33. Täuber places greater emphasis on the aesthetic agendas of Dix and Grosz in her analysis and offers more nuanced interpretations of their works.

financial independence more socially acceptable? Or did the lack of a social code for distinguishing sexually aggressive working women from paid prostitutes cause *all* publicly visible women simply to be marked as prostitutes? The latter is clearly the case in Wehrling's indictment of Berlin's "whores." By invoking the image of the prostitute as a method of insult, however, Wehrling's text demonstrates the prostitute's potential power to act as a social irritant and indicator of change. Offering an alternative to Tatar's morbid conclusions in her research on prostitution in the Weimar Republic, Julia Roos asserts: "To view Weimar's economic and political crises *solely* from the vantage point of their negative impacts on women's emancipation is problematic. Such an analytical perspective risks obscuring consequential shifts in conventional power relationships between the sexes during the Weimar period."[19] The concepts of crisis and male anxiety so prominent in studies of gender and sexuality in the Weimar era have recently been reexamined and evaluated more positively by scholars such as Roos, Kathleen Canning, and Richard W. McCormick, who claims that "what ought to be celebrated includes precisely that which has been derided as decadence and 'effeminate weakness' by many writers." By thematizing male crisis, McCormick argues, many Weimar artists and writers openly acknowledged "the blurring of traditionally gendered roles and behavior."[20] Prostitutes were also central figures in the debates surrounding such palpable changes in gender roles, and this chapter therefore maps a range of cultural discourses on prostitutes and emancipated womanhood that link the two in more complex ways, some of which present obstacles to women's autonomy and some of which move beyond misogynistic representations of public women and beyond images of prostitutes as mere "fantastic ciphers of debauchery."[21] Such blending and blurring of prostitutes and New Women connect the popular image of the cocotte, a prostitute who looks and acts like a respectable woman, with a new kind of coquette, a seemingly respectable woman who looks and acts like a prostitute, both of whom occupied public spaces in Weimar Berlin.

Close analysis of Weimar-era texts that explore spaces of public contact between male cultural critics and young working women reveals what Spain describes as "the reciprocity between the social construction of space and the spatial construction of social relations."[22] While Spain's discussion of the "spatial construction of

19. Roos, *Weimar through the Lens of Gender,* 8.

20. McCormick, *Gender and Sexuality,* 4–5. There is a growing body of Weimar scholarship that reads "crisis" as a complex term, often to connote "opportunity" or an opening up of possibilities. See Canning, *Gender History in Practice;* 48, 61; Moritz Föllmer and Rüdiger Graf, eds., *Die "Krise" der Weimarer Republik: Zur Kritik eines Deutungsmusters* (Frankfurt am Main: Campus, 2005); Birthe Kundrus, "Gender Wars: The First World War and the Construction of Gender Relations in the Weimar Republic," in Hagemann and Schüler-Springorum, *Home/Front,* 160; Patrice Petro, *Joyless Streets: Women and Melodramatic Representation in Weimar Germany* (Princeton, NJ: Princeton University Press, 1989), xix.

21. Meskimmon, *We Weren't Modern Enough,* 30.

22. Spain, *Gendered Spaces,* 29. Of course Spain's work takes Edward W. Soja's work on the "sociospatial dialectic" as one of its central theoretical paradigms; see Soja's book, *The Political Organization of*

social relations" is primarily concerned with the actual building practices that serve to either prevent or enable gender integration, my argument focuses on how the imagined meaning of particular urban spaces gets grafted on those who occupy such spaces, particularly when those occupants are women. This is most striking in the case of the cinema, one of the spaces most highly theorized in cultural criticism by Weimar intellectuals such as Siegfried Kracauer and in current scholarship on the Weimar Republic.[23] Critics' skepticism toward the new mass medium of film reveals itself most clearly in their disparagement of filmgoers themselves, who, more often than not, were imagined to be women. The controversy surrounding the popular hygiene films (*Aufklärungsfilme*) at the advent of the republic exemplifies how political debates concerning the reinstatement of artistic censorship, aesthetic discussions of the competing media of film and theater, and social discourses on prostitution and female sexuality became intertwined. After engaging with gendered representations of cinematic space, I turn to the more ambiguous and less often theorized spaces of the street, cabaret, club, and café, spaces that seem to offer greater possibilities for the construction of female agency and emancipated sexual relations, opportunities for the "social construction of space."

Although, with the notable exception of visual artworks by Jeanne Mammen, most of the works I use to access these spaces are produced by men, my approach to these texts recognizes subtle gradations and what Susan S. Friedman calls the "presence of hybridity" within seemingly hegemonic discourses. Friedman encourages critical readings that question to what degree the author's own gender identification may or may not influence how gender and sexuality are represented in his or her texts.[24] Thus, in what follows, texts by modern male writers and leftist intellectuals such as Bertolt Brecht, Magnus Hirschfeld, Siegfried Kracauer, Kurt Tucholsky, and Curt Moreck that represent urban spaces and the women who inhabit them can be read to express *both* men's anxiety in regard to women's emancipation *and* their acknowledgment or even celebration of it.

Space of Anxious Encounter: The Cinema

Even before the First World War and the Weimar Republic, modernist author Alfred Döblin marked the cinema as a feminized and eroticized space. In his essay

---

Space (Washington, DC: Association of American Geographers, 1971) and his essay "The Socio-Spatial Dialectic," *Annals of the Association of American Geographers* 70 (1980): 207–25.

23. For a compilation of texts that express a broad range of reactions to the new cinematic medium in Wilhelmine and Weimar Germany, see Anton Kaes, ed., *Kino-Debatte: Texte zum Verhältnis von Literatur und Film, 1909–1929* (Tübingen: Niemeyer, 1978).

24. Susan S. Friedman, *Mappings: Feminism and the Geographies of Encounter* (Princeton, NJ: Princeton University Press, 1998), 26–27. Friedman argues that the "new geography of identity insists that we think about…writers in relation to a fluid matrix instead of a fixed binary of male/female or masculine/feminine…. The interactional, relational, and situational constituents of identity for both male and female writers should be read together."

"Das Theater der kleinen Leute" (The Theater of the Little People, 1909), Döblin remarks on the predominantly working-class audience, the "couples making out in the background," the "children wheezing with consumption," and the "heavily made-up prostitutes leaning forward, forgetting to adjust their scarves."[25] The prostitutes are depicted as completely absorbed viewers, so absorbed in the filmic spectacle that their slipping scarves expose their cleavage to the audience members around them, reminding observers such as Döblin of their sexualized bodies. Their unveiled eroticism combined with their implicitly uncritical viewing of the filmic narrative make them, in Döblin's analysis, one with both the medium of film and the space of the cinema. Miriam Hansen convincingly reads Döblin's use of the image of the prostitute as "an epithet for the cinema as a whole." In his essay, she argues, prostitutes represent both the mass audience and the mass medium of film, "an openly commercial ('venal') art."[26] The permissive atmosphere of the cinema was underscored by its darkness; hence the disappearance of the physical space of the viewing room opened up a spatial imaginary, in which authors such as Döblin could connect the medium with whom he imagined to be its viewers. In fact, although Döblin portrays the prewar audience as proletarian, research into the social composition of Wilhelmine film audiences shows that they were made up of "women of diverse backgrounds, the 'little people,' the workers, and salaried employees."[27] Such findings show that even before the lavish film palaces of the 1920s were built to accommodate mass audiences, there was a significant degree of social mixing that occurred in the cinematic space. Hence, despite its temporal context, Döblin's critical notes on cinema can be read on a continuum with Weimar-era essays by Bertolt Brecht and Siegfried Kracauer, in which discourses on the cinema, sexuality, and women—be they prostitutes or salaried employees—converge.

With the lifting of film censorship in November 1918, prostitutes became a pervasive cultural presence on the movie screens of Weimar Berlin and throughout Germany.[28] The entertainment industry capitalized on the visual appeal of the prostitute, and this appeal concerned male cultural critics as they sat in the cinema and speculated about the effects that the popular social hygiene film (*Aufklärungsfilm*)

---

25. Alfred Döblin, "Das Theater der kleinen Leute," *Das Theater* 1 (1909): 191–92; translation quoted in Miriam Hansen, "Early Silent Cinema: Whose Public Sphere?," *New German Critique* 29 (1983): 174.

26. Hansen, "Early Silent Cinema," 174.

27. Heide Schlüpmann, *Unheimlichkeit des Blicks: Das Drama des frühen deutschen Kinos* (Basel: Stroemfeld / Roter Stern, 1990), 13; translation quoted in Peter Jelavich, "'Am I Allowed to Amuse Myself Here?' The German Bourgeoisie Confronts Early Film," in Marchand and Lindenfeld, *Germany at the Fin de Siècle*, 229.

28. Even after the much-scorned popularity of the social hygiene films that I will discuss in this chapter, prostitutes continued to grace the silver screen in films like *Die Straße* (The Street, 1923), *Die freudlose Gasse* (The Joyless Street, 1925), *Dirnentragödie* (Tragedy of a Prostitute, 1927), *Die Büchse der Pandora* (Pandora's Box, 1928/9), *Das Tagebuch einer Verlorenen* (Diary of a Lost Girl, 1929), and *Mutter Krausens Fahrt ins Glück* (Mother Krause's Journey into Happiness, 1929). For my reading of G. W. Pabst's *Diary of a Lost Girl*, see chapter 2.

might have on its female viewers. *Aufklärungsfilme* were sex education films that emerged amid the chaos of the First World War and employed a unique blend of titillation and education to warn the German populace of the dangers of venereal diseases, alcoholism, and prostitution. The use of film to educate the masses signaled a media shift within the public health, or social hygiene, movement, which before the war had limited itself to lectures and pamphlets. During the war, organizations such as the DGBG and institutions such as Karl Lingner's German Hygiene Museum in Dresden sought to harness the power of the visual image by organizing traveling hygiene exhibits, staging theatrical productions, and making short documentary films (*Lehrfilme*) that were usually shown to target audiences such as enlisted soldiers. As the rate of venereal disease spiked toward the end of the war, the *Lehrfilme* were shown to a broader audience, serving as public service documentaries that immediately preceded feature films. While the public was initially both fascinated and repulsed by the images of diseased bodies presented in such works, they were quickly bored by the dry, factual, scientific tone of the *Lehrfilme.*[29] It was the filmmaker Richard Oswald who realized that hygiene films first had to appeal to the viewing public before they could educate them, and in 1917 he teamed up with the DGBG's Alfred Blaschko to make the first feature-length social melodrama on venereal disease, *Es werde Licht!* (Let There Be Light!). The film's title, with its blatant call for illumination, directly linked Oswald's project with the enlightenment, or *Aufklärung,* of its audience. Its critical and popular success served to associate Oswald himself with the *Aufklärungsfilm,* for better or worse, for the rest of his career.[30]

---

29. For the shift to visual media within the social hygiene movement, see Ulf Schmidt, "'Der Blick auf den Körper': Sozialhygienische Filme, Sexualaufklärung und Propaganda in der Weimarer Republik," in *Geschlecht in Fesseln: Sexualität zwischen Aufklärung und Ausbeutung im Weimarer Kino, 1918–1933,* ed. Malte Hagener (Munich: Text + Kritik, 2000), 23–46. See also the work of the medical doctor Waldemar Schweisheimer, *Die Bedeutung des Films für soziale Hygiene und Medizin* (Munich: Georg Müller, 1920), 8.

30. Born Richard W. Ornstein to a middle-class Viennese Jewish family in 1880, Oswald initially embarked on a career in the theater. After fourteen years of acting, writing, and directing for the stage in Vienna, southern Germany, and Düsseldorf, he took up residence in Berlin in 1913 and began working as a director and screenwriter for Jules Greenbaum's film production company, Vitascope. Oswald spent the next twenty years of his life in Berlin and became one of the most popular and prolific filmmakers of his time. Between the years 1918 and 1933, he directed seventy feature films, most of which he also produced and wrote or cowrote. He founded his own film production company, Richard Oswald GmbH (Ltd.) in 1916. The breadth of Oswald's body of cinematic work is staggering, including detective films, social melodramas, adaptations of crime, fantasy, and romance literature, epic historical dramas, and, after the transition to sound film, musical comedies and operettas. Despite the sheer number of films and range of genres attributed to Oswald, he is best remembered for his *Aufklärungsfilme.* Incidentally, Oswald never used the term *Aufklärungsfilm;* he preferred to describe such works instead as "social hygiene films" (*sozialhygienische Filmwerke*). Biographical information on Oswald was compiled from a variety of sources, including Michael Berger, "Richard Oswald: Kitschkönig und Volksaufklärer," in *Pioniere in Celluloid: Juden in der frühen Filmwelt,* ed. Irene Stratenwerth and Hermann Simon (Berlin: Henschel, 2004), 201–5; Hans-Michael Bock, "Biographie," in *Richard Oswald: Regisseur und Produzent,* ed. Helga Belach and Wolfgang Jacobsen (Munich: Text + Kritik, 1990), 119–32; Jürgen Kasten and Armin Loacker, eds., *Richard Oswald: Kino zwischen Spektakel, Aufklärung und Unterhaltung*

During the final months of the war and within six months of the lifting of censorship, Oswald and the Berlin sexologist Magnus Hirschfeld raised eyebrows and tempers by collaborating on three controversial hygiene films, *Sündige Mütter (Strafgesetz, §218)* (Sinful Mothers [Penal Code §218]), *Die Prostitution* (Prostitution), and *Anders als die Andern* (Different from the Others).[31] With illegal abortion, prostitution, and homosexuality as their respective topics, these films challenged the German state's right to legislate sexual behavior. The topics of the three film projects undertaken by Oswald and Hirschfeld in 1918 and 1919 were clearly aligned with the goals of the sex reform movement, goals that had already been articulated in the Wilhelmine era. *Sinful Mothers* criticized antiabortion law by implying that it drives women to have back-alley abortions with fatal results. *Different from the Others* boldly called for the removal of laws penalizing homosexuals by concluding with a scene in which Hirschfeld's hand crosses §175 out of the law book for the new republic.[32] *Prostitution* is a film whose story depicts the downfall of a woman who has chosen prostitution, but the film's plot is introduced by and concludes with a fictional trial of prostitution itself. The defendant, an erotic woman with long, tousled hair, personifies the institution of prostitution. At the end of the trial, she sinks to her knees in relief, and the final words of the film read: "Prostitution is acquitted. We want to help to relieve need, to create humane laws, for we have no right to judge."[33]

(Vienna: Verlag Filmarchiv Austria, 2005), 9, 12, 547–59. For more information on *Es werde Licht!*, which premiered in Berlin on March 2, 1917, was produced and directed by Oswald and was based on a screenplay by Oswald and Lupu Pick, see Bock, "Filmographie," in Belach and Jacobsen, *Richard Oswald*, 144; and Kasten and Loacker, *Richard Oswald*, 86, 546.

31. *Sündige Mütter*, advertised as the fourth sequel to *Es werde Licht!*, premiered in October 1918 in Halle and was cowritten by Oswald and Ewald André Dupont, who went on to have an illustrious directing career during the Weimar Republic. Hirschfeld served as a consultant. For an analysis of this film and its abortion politics, see Ursula von Keitz, *Der Schatten des Gesetzes: Schwangerschaftskonflikt und Reproduktion im deutschsprachigen Film 1918–1933* (Marburg: Schüren, 2005), 81–84, 120–32. *Die Prostitution*, later renamed *Das gelbe Haus* (The Yellow House) and then *Im Sumpfe der Großstadt* (In the Mire of the Metropolis) to appease the censor, premiered on May 1, 1919, in Berlin. Richard Oswald wrote, directed, and produced the film in consultation with Magnus Hirschfeld. Anita Berber, Gussy Holl, Conrad Veidt, and Reinhold Schünzel starred in the film, which was banned in Bavaria soon after its release and was destroyed in 1922. Like many of Oswald's films that were lost or destroyed, *Die Prostitution* can be reconstructed only through a careful analysis of promotional materials, reviews in the press, notes from censorship proceedings, and written reactions by contemporary critics. For a case study of this film, see Jill Suzanne Smith, "Richard Oswald and the Social Hygiene Film: Promoting Public Health or Promiscuity?," in *The Many Faces of Weimar Cinema*, ed. Christian Rogowski (Rochester, NY: Camden House, 2010), 13–30. *Anders als die Andern* premiered to the general public on May 30, 1919, at the Prinzess-Theater in Berlin, nearly one month after *Die Prostitution*. The press screening on May 24, 1919, at the Apollo Theater in Berlin included introductory remarks by Hirschfeld. Oswald produced and directed, and he and Hirschfeld cowrote the screenplay. For an excellent discussion of this film as well as its censorship history and reception both in Germany and by gay audiences in the United States, see James D. Steakley, "Cinema and Censorship in the Weimar Republic: The Case of *Anders als die Andern*," *Film History* 11 (1999): 181–203. On all three films, see also Kasten and Loacker, *Richard Oswald*, 94–97, 101–12, 124–131, 274–87, 548–49.

32. Kasten and Loacker, *Richard Oswald*, 109; Steakley, "Cinema and Censorship," 187.

33. Instead of casting Anita Berber, who played the role of the prostitute in the film's main narrative, Oswald shrewdly chose the more innocent-looking Kissa von Sievers for the role of "Prostitution."

The freeing of prostitution from the realm of the court in *Prostitution* can be interpreted as a plea against the system of state regulation, a system already under serious attack since the turn of the century. In the wake of the First World War, the protests of abolitionists intensified, and their base of support grew. Oswald and Hirschfeld's film on prostitution signifies an important moment in this antiregulation discourse, for its release coincided with a number of public debates on the issue of prostitutes' rights and the abolition of state regulation. In the spring of 1919, liberal politicians in Berlin petitioned the city government to take away the punitive powers of the vice squad and place prostitutes under the protection of a Municipal Welfare and Rescue Center, an idea that was subsequently championed by the Berlin magistrate in a letter to the Prussian State Assembly.[34] Sex reformers and left-liberal politicians alike envisioned an alternative to legal regulation that would decriminalize prostitution and allow prostitutes access to private health care, provisions that were later included in the Law to Combat Venereal Diseases, passed in 1927. The most marked contributors to this discussion, however, were prostitutes themselves, who organized several mass meetings of prostitutes, pimps, and interested citizens in Berlin to rally for basic rights to privacy and unhindered mobility and to form the Auxiliary Club of Berlin Prostitutes, complete with membership cards and fees (fig. 8). Among the supporters whom the prostitutes elected to the executive council of this new organization was none other than Hirschfeld himself.[35]

While it is certainly fitting to view Oswald and Hirschfeld's film in the broader context of human rights activism and sex reform in the nascent democratic culture of the Weimar Republic, it is impossible to ignore the fact that there were medical

---

See the film program in the Schriftgutarchiv, Stiftung Deutscher Kinemathek (SDK). The description of the trial and the closing line of the film can be found in Kasten and Loacker, *Richard Oswald*, 128; and in Lothar Fischer, *Tanz zwischen Rausch und Tod: Anita Berber 1918–1929 in Berlin* (Berlin: Haude & Spener, 1996), 35. See also the censorship decisions documented in Herbert Birett, ed., *Verzeichnis in Deutschland gelaufener Filme: Entscheidungen der Filmzensur 1911–1920; Berlin, Hamburg, München, Stuttgart* (Munich: K. G. Saur, 1980). It comes as no surprise to learn that the trial scene was one of the first to be removed by local censors in Munich in 1919, where the repeal of national censorship laws seemed to be of little consequence (Birett, 561).

34. An advertisement for the film that appeared several months before its premiere shows that its critique of regulated prostitution is intentional, for it mentions the dangers of "garrisoned prostitution" (*kasernierte Prostitution*), a method of regulation that isolated prostitutes to certain streets or districts. The term *kaserniert*, however, also has particular resonance in light of the German military's use of the brothel system during the war as a way of maintaining soldiers' morale and keeping them ready for battle, a practice that was partially responsible for the wartime rise in venereal diseases. For the ad, see "Das soziale Filmwerk *Die Prostitution,*" *Der Film* 50 (1919). For the heated debates over the establishment of the Municipal Welfare and Rescue Center and the future role of the vice squad in Berlin, see Roos, *Weimar through the Lens of Gender*, 118–20. The letter from the Berlin magistrate to the Prussian State Assembly, dated July 8, 1919, can be accessed at the Geheimes Staatsarchiv Preussischer Kulturbesitz Berlin (GStA-PK) I, HA Rep. 77, Ministry of the Interior, Tit. 435, Nr. 1, Bd. 1, pp. 188–89.

35. Hirschfeld reports on the prostitutes' meetings he attended and on his membership in the Hilfsbund in *Sittengeschichte der Nachkriegszeit,* 2:96–98 and in *Geschlechtskunde* (Stuttgart: Julius Püttmann, 1930), 3:358. The organization's existence was short-lived. On Hirschfeld's view of the Hilfsbund, see Roos, *Weimar through the Lens of Gender*, 77–78, 94.

Figure 8. Membership Card, Hilfsbund der Berliner Prostituierten, ca. 1919. Courtesy of Magnus-Hirschfeld-Gesellschaft.

professionals, intellectuals, and politicians spanning the range of the political spectrum who accused Oswald and Hirschfeld of commercializing sexuality for the prurient masses. The popularity of the Oswald/Hirschfeld films, particularly with urban audiences, spawned an entire crop of films by lesser-known directors with titles meant to both allure and horrify: *Das Gift im Weibe* (The Poison in Woman, 1919), *Hyänen der Lust* (Hyenas of Lust, 1919), and *Im Rausche der Sinne* (Intoxicated with Sensuality, 1920), to name just a few. Although most film critics of the day raved about Oswald's film *Prostitution,* public officials excoriated it as the prototype for the multitude of sex-themed films that followed its release, works that members of the leftist Independent Social Democratic Party (USPD) simply labeled as exploitative "prostitution films" and defined as a "cultural disgrace of the highest order." In the German parliamentary debates on film censorship, the liberal representative of the German Democratic Party (DDP), Paul Ende, cited an anonymous literary critic who compared the permissive atmosphere of German cinemas with brothels.[36] This conflation of cinema and brothel, of film and prostitution, so reminiscent of Döblin's essay, is symptomatic of how criticism of specific films such as Oswald's *Prostitution* became unhinged from the individual works themselves to form a larger discourse, in which representatives from the political, scientific, and cultural fields vied for control over both the body politic and the new cinematic medium.

One of the most common criticisms leveled against *Prostitution* at the time of its release was that it presented prostitution not as dangerous and demeaning but as glamorous and inviting. In his 1920 study offering guidelines for the proper use of film in the social hygienic education of the masses, the medical doctor Waldemar Schweisheimer expressed his incredulity about the fact that Oswald's film made

---

36. Eva Sturm, "Von der Zensurfreiheit zum Zensurgesetz: Das erste deutsche Lichtspielgesetz (1920)," in Hagener, *Geschlecht in Fesseln,* 64, 72.

Figure 9. Film poster by Josef Fenneker for Richard Oswald's *Die Prostitution*, 1919. Courtesy of Deutsche Kinemathek—Museum für Film und Fernsehen. Copyright 2012 Stadt Bocholt / Stadtmuseum Bocholt.

no mention of the connection between prostitution and venereal diseases.[37] Before Schweisheimer's study even appeared, however, cultural critics including the young playwright Bertolt Brecht and the satirist Kurt Tucholsky had already voiced their concerns about the film, claiming that the scenes set in the brothel "do not deter, but rather, at the very least, excite."[38] The glamorized image of the prostitute was indeed used to promote social hygiene films such as Oswald and Hirschfeld's production, as one can see from the film poster for *Prostitution* (fig. 9). The poster shows a slim, attractive woman in a low-cut, yet tasteful gown placed in front of throngs of admiring gentlemen. Her heavy makeup and sunken eyes are the only physical markers that betray her profession and imply her possible sickness. The only other clue to her potential deadliness is the skeleton-like face in the lower far right corner of the poster, yet this is nearly hidden in the crowd of adoring men's faces. The prostitute herself looks not at her admirers, but at the poster's viewer, beckoning with a seductive look. Viewing this poster, one could see why Brecht and Tucholsky accuse the film of promoting prostitution. However, today's scholars of the *Aufklärungsfilme* remind us that while the films' sensationalistic advertising materials (titles, posters) may fit the popular appeal of sex in the early Weimar Republic, they rarely have much to do with the actual plot of the films they represent.[39] Indeed a brief review of *Prostitution* in one of Berlin's daily newspapers praises the film, its director, and its actors for treating this potentially sensational topic with "tact and taste."[40] The narrative constructed by Oswald seems to do little to entice its viewers into prostitution, especially when one considers the fates of the main female protagonists.

The film tells the tale of two sisters who live with their good-for-nothing father in a working-class neighborhood in Berlin. Oswald depicts the sisters as clear opposites in both appearance and character; Hedwig (Gussy Holl) is the good sister—a sweet, demure, and hardworking secretary—while Lona (Anita Berber) is the bad sister who seduces her sister's boss, Alfred Werner (Conrad Veidt), and then leaves him for a career as a prostitute in a luxury brothel. When Alfred goes to the brothel to retrieve Lona, he finds Hedwig there instead, who was, through the complicity of her own father, drugged, abducted, and brought to the brothel against her will. Struggling against the advances of her first potential

37. Schweisheimer, *Die Bedeutung des Films,* 71.

38. Kurt Tucholsky, "Die Prostitution mit der Maske," in *Gesammelte Werke,* ed. Mary Gerold-Tucholsky and Fritz J. Raddatz (Reinbek bei Hamburg: Rowohlt, 1960), 1:404. Brecht, too, wrote a scathing critique of the social hygiene films that, like Tucholsky's essay, makes specific mention of Oswald's film. See Bertolt Brecht, "Aus dem Theaterleben," in *Werke: Große, kommentierte Berliner und Frankfurter Ausgabe* (Berlin and Frankfurt am Main: Aufbau & Suhrkamp, 1989–97), 21:40–42.

39. Malte Hagener and Jan Hans, "Von Wilhelm zu Weimar: Der Aufklärungs- und Sittenfilm zwischen Zensur und Markt," in Hagener, *Geschlecht in Fesseln,* 17–19.

40. "Die Films der Woche," *Berliner Tageblatt,* May 4, 1919. Other rave reviews in the popular Weimar press include "Ein neuer deutscher Auslandsfilm," *BZ am Mittag,* April 29, 1919; and "Aus der Tiefe der Weltstadt," *Bühne und Film* 3 (1919).

Figure 10. Promotional postcard, Anita Berber and Werner Krauß in Richard Oswald's *Die Prostitution*, 1919. Courtesy of Bundesarchiv-Filmarchiv.

"John," Hedwig is aided by Alfred, who fights off the man and rescues her. Hedwig and Alfred find happiness together and get married, while Lona slides further into ruin. She works in the brothel until the madam casts her out, and once she is back on the street, she turns to another former lover Karl Döring (Reinhold Schünzel), who promptly becomes her pimp. Lona prostitutes herself willingly for Döring until she meets her grim end at the hands of a *Lustmörder* (sexual murderer) played by Werner Krauß (fig. 10). By organizing the plot around the fates of an opposing pair of sisters, one of whom finds marital bliss and one of whom is murdered, Oswald relies on a tried-and-true narrative formula: in the end, good is rewarded, and evil is punished. The familiar paradigm of good versus evil, Oswald himself argued, was crucial to educating the general public, which would be more apt to follow the path of the good character and read the punishment of the evil character as a clear warning against similar behavior. He wrote specifically about how filmmakers should portray prostitutes in such a way that would strike fear in the hearts of female viewers and actively deter them from following the same path.[41]

The figure of the *Lustmörder* is instrumental to Oswald's goal of deterrence. With a nod to his own beginnings in the theater, Oswald finishes off the prostitute

---

41. Richard Oswald, "Der Film als Kulturfaktor," in *Das Kulturfilmbuch*, ed. Edgar Beyfuss and I. Kossowsky (Berlin: Cryselius & Schulz, 1924), 104.

Lona in the same way that Frank Wedekind offs the notorious social-climbing whore Lulu in his 1892 play *Die Büchse der Pandora* (Pandora's Box): with the knife of a Jack-the-Ripper character. The *Lustmörder,* who, incidentally, always goes free, can be read as Tatar would interpret him—as the ultimate vigilante who enacts justice by removing the dangerous erotic woman from society. However, Oswald's film—much like Hirschfeld's writings on the topic, which, in some cases, validated Lombroso's theory of the "born prostitute" and yet, in others, acknowledged the importance of socioeconomic factors in women's entrance into prostitution— remains ambivalent regarding the question of the causes of prostitution.[42] Is Lona, like Lulu, driven by an innately corrupt sexuality, or is she a victim of the social ills of prostitution (i.e., poverty and an alcoholic father)? Is *she* the dangerous woman, or does the danger lie in the institution of prostitution itself? The arrest of Karl Döring, Lona's lover and pimp, at the end of the main narrative suggests that gender and economic relations are somehow culpable, yet the film leaves these questions unanswered. Still, its ominous message rings clear: prostitution is an ill-fated enterprise. In contrast to the trial scene and its acquittal of prostitution, the film's main narrative delivers a wholesale condemnation of prostitution, and with it, of the prostitute herself. By placing the good sister in a happy marriage and the incorrigible prostitute in the grave, the message of the film is ultimately a conservative one and supports Malte Hagener's and Jan Hans's description of the social hygiene film as "an unprocessed relic from the Wilhelmine era," in which "alternative lifestyles... are punished and shown to be deviant."[43]

Despite *Prostitution*'s grim ending, however, critics of the film such as Schweisheimer claimed that even Lona's brutal death did not trump the film's glamorous (he uses the word *glänzend*) depiction of her life in the brothel.[44] Conflating the "shimmering nightclubs" depicted in the film with the bourgeois film palaces of the Weimar Republic, Bertolt Brecht also imagined how the on-screen action would translate into the real-life seduction of the women in the audience. Paying no attention to the on-screen secretary Hedwig, who successfully resists the sexual advances of the men in the brothel, Brecht was more concerned with the secretaries in the audience: "The young girls sitting in the cinema, most often next to the young man who bought their ticket, are enlightened to the fact that refusal... is pointless.... All the bosses are infused with male desire and pour their secretaries wine; there are *no* objections allowed."[45] In Brecht's view, the message conveyed to women by the *Aufklärungsfilm* is one of nonresistance; it is best to accept the

---

42. In his multivolume work, *Geschlechtskunde,* published as the culmination of his sexological research, Hirschfeld writes: "Prostitutes themselves are lamentable creatures, *no matter whether they become so due to external or internal reasons.*... But they also present a constant danger to others" (3:295, emphasis added).

43. Hagener and Hans, "Von Wilhelm zu Weimar," 8–9.

44. Schweisheimer, *Die Bedeutung des Films,* 72.

45. Brecht, "Aus dem Theaterleben," 41, emphasis in original.

movie ticket from one's boyfriend or the glass of wine from one's boss and give him what he expects in return. In other words, Brecht's essay blurs the line between the fictional prostitute in the film and those women the author imagines as her viewers, for both allow themselves not simply to be seduced but to be *bought*. Brecht's "concern" for the young women's personal welfare was echoed in more tempered terms by Tucholsky, who suggested that if sex education were truly the goal, then the most appropriate vehicle would be a scientific lecture, delivered separately to same-sex audiences. But it was Schweisheimer who argued the point in the starkest terms: *Aufklärungsfilme* had become "pornographic films" (*Animierfilme*) that encouraged premarital copulation and accelerated the spread of venereal disease.[46] In these texts by Schweisheimer, Brecht, and Tucholsky, the social space of the movie theater becomes a veritable den of iniquity that bears a striking resemblance to Döblin's vision of the prewar cinema.

Reading these men's arguments, it is clear that their critique of Oswald's film has less to do with the film itself and more to do with their views on its female spectators and with social anxiety regarding female sexuality. In fact, Schweisheimer's and Brecht's scant or inaccurate mention of *Prostitution*'s plot insinuates that they probably had not even seen the film but rather based their accounts of it on hearsay. Schweisheimer even has recourse to an urban legend published in *Die Weltbühne* about a man who boasted of how easily he seduced a sixteen-year-old girl in the cinema after he noticed that the *Aufklärungsfilm* had aroused her. The same anecdote also circulated on the floor of the German parliament during the debates on film censorship.[47] Oswald's particular film on prostitution functioned, then, as a springboard for a more general critique of an entire filmic genre, the *Aufklärungsfilm,* and its presumably negative social effects on women. The concern expressed by Brecht, Schweisheimer, and Weimar politicians alike for the well-being of young women only thinly veils their anxiety over an active form of female sexuality that falls outside of the social institutions of marriage and prostitution. Portraying female film viewers as dupes or even potential victims of wily seducers seems far more palatable to them than portraying the women in the audience as socially savvy—cognizant of their own desirability and the advantages that desirability might offer them.

The biting criticism of the social hygiene films anticipates the feuilleton writings of Siegfried Kracauer, who also sat in the darkness of the cinema with his eyes and mind on female audience members, and who wrote one of the defining essays on film spectatorship, "Die kleinen Ladenmädchen gehen ins Kino" (The Little Shopgirls Go to the Movies, 1927). In Kracauer's work the moviegoers are nearly identical to the "young girls" and "secretaries" in Brecht's text; their designation

46. Tucholsky, "Die Prostitution mit der Maske," 406; Schweisheimer, *Die Bedeutung des Films,* 74.

47. Schweisheimer, *Die Bedeutung des Films,* 76. On the anecdote's airing in parliament, see Sturm, "Von der Zensurfreiheit zum Zensurgesetz," 72, 78–79; and on its status as urban legend, see Moreck, *Sittengeschichte des Kinos,* 200–201.

as "little shopgirls" is meant to signify their limited education and gullibility. Kracauer portrays them as easily duped; they are naive girls who confuse film with reality, perceiving adventure films as true getaways or believing in fairy-tale endings filled with riches and romance.[48] The cinema offers them a temporary escape from the drudgery of their lives tending shop, an escape that allows them to dream or cry for a few hours without critical thought or reflection. Kracauer observes the shopgirls as they dab tears from their cheeks, and remarks: "Crying is sometimes easier than contemplation."[49] Their rapt attention betrays their inaction. Instead of inspiring social or political activity among the girls, the escape to the cinema simply perpetuates other forms of escape by encouraging the female audience members to visit dance halls and search for wealthy men. Kracauer remarks: "No film without a danceclub, no tuxedo without money. Otherwise women would not put on and take off their pants. The business is called eroticism, and the preoccupation with it is called life."[50] By holding out the hope of a financially advantageous relationship, the films keep the shopgirls content with their monotonous jobs and meager paychecks. Help, in the form of a rich cavalier, is on the way.

Anticipating Kracauer's explication of the shopgirls' passivity is pivotal to an understanding of how Brecht and Tucholsky depart from Schweisheimer in their critique of the *Aufklärungsfilme*. The real crux of Brecht's and Tucholsky's respective arguments is not that hygiene films should be indicting prostitution as a danger to public health, as Schweisheimer maintains. Their concerns are more of a cultural and political nature; put simply, they chastise both the film audience and the filmmakers for choosing sex and profits over political action. After all, the repeal of censorship laws in 1918 gave leftist intellectuals like Brecht and Tucholsky hope that the cinema would become a platform for diverse political voices. This hope was dashed by the immense popularity of the hygiene films and the financial success they brought to their creators. As Brecht ironically states in the final sentence of his essay, "Business is booming, *Prostitution* is extended by 'popular demand,' and freedom is the best of all circumstances." Tucholsky, too, laments that the people have been duped while "the false friends of the people make money."[51] In their respective essays, prostitution takes on a double meaning. It is both the title of Oswald's film and a cipher for the mass medium of film, whose existence is based on selling sex for money. Freedom, certainly not the kind that Brecht or Tucholsky envisioned, is defined not in political terms but rather in sexual and financial ones.

---

48. Siegfried Kracauer, "Die kleinen Ladenmädchen gehen ins Kino," in *Das Ornament der Masse: Essays* (Frankfurt am Main: Suhrkamp, 1977), 279–94; translated by Thomas Y. Levin as "The Little Shopgirls Go to the Movies," in *The Mass Ornament: Weimar Essays* (Cambridge, MA: Harvard University Press, 1995), 291–304.
49. Kracauer, "The Little Shopgirls," 302.
50. Kracauer, "The Little Shopgirls," 296.
51. Brecht, "Aus dem Theaterleben," 41; Tucholsky, "Die Prostitution mit der Maske," 406.

The essays discussed above can easily be read as precursors to a broader critical discourse on popular culture, exemplified by Theodor W. Adorno and Max Horkheimer's 1947 treatise "Culture Industry," which maligns the mass culture audience for its uncritical absorption of popular entertainment and its inability to recognize that modern mass culture does not come from the people but "is administered and imposed from above."[52] These essays could also be analyzed through a specifically gendered lens. As Andreas Huyssen has persuasively argued, mass culture was often feminized in modernist texts. Behind modernist critiques that portrayed popular culture as a threat to high culture, Huyssen contends, lay a fear of the working masses and also of women "knocking at the gate of a male-dominated culture."[53] With Huyssen's analysis in mind, it is perfectly plausible to read the essays by Döblin, Brecht, and Kracauer as responses to the perceived threat of both mass culture and masses of women. The presence of women in the movie audience, as depicted by these Weimar-era observers, indicated women's increased and unwanted presence in the public sphere—in the workplace and entertainment venues. The possible threat of the working woman is diffused by these authors in two strategic moves. The first move presents women as dim-witted dupes easily manipulated from above by their male bosses, lovers, or cultural institutions like film studios. These women are portrayed as having no agency; they place their bodies in service of industry, and they allow their minds to be shaped by the "culture industry." The second move is to depict these women in explicitly sexual terms—as passive sexual objects. All three authors use both the trope of prostitution and the darkened, eroticized space of the cinema to aid them in these moves.

A subtle shift occurs between Döblin's essay and Brecht and Kracauer's pieces, however. The shift that takes place is one from prostitute to white-collar worker, and yet this shift does not mean that the prostitute disappears from the scene. Whereas Döblin's prewar spectators are prostitutes with painted faces who represent the sexually permissive atmosphere of the cinema and its imagined working-class audience, the women in the essays by Brecht and Kracauer are white-collar workers who take social cues from on-screen prostitutes. Here prostitution takes on a variety of meanings. It can be read as the potential sexual objectification of white-collar women by the men who accompany them to the cinema, and it can also represent a rationalized eroticism that keeps women enslaved within an exploitative socioeconomic system. Certainly what all of these women have in common is that they do not possess a critical gaze; they are bad spectators. The authors, in contrast, are authoritative observers who have the power both to *see* the audience with a critical eye and *see through* the manipulative messages of the filmic

---

52. This particular quote comes from Huyssen, "Mass Culture as Woman," 48. The original essay by Theodor Adorno and Max Horkheimer is "The Culture Industry: Enlightenment as Mass Deception," in *Dialectic of Enlightenment,* trans. John Cumming (New York: Continuum, 1999), 120–67.

53. Huyssen, "Mass Culture as Woman," 47.

narratives. By foregrounding the deficiencies of the female spectators, these essays privilege male spectatorship, for they imply that the masculine subject can decipher the "truth" behind the image. As a darkened space that creates a clear delineation between on-screen actors and ostensibly passive spectators, Huyssen points out in a recent analysis of Kracauer's Weimar essays, the cinema is easily "transfigured" by modernist critics "into a spatial imaginary or even into a dream space" in which the thoughts and dreams of those who occupy the space are illuminated by the authors, for better or worse.[54] The cinema is thereby transformed from a space of anxious encounter between men and women into a pleasurable space, one in which men like Kracauer, Döblin, and Brecht could experience erotic pleasure by viewing women both in the audience and on the screen, and intellectual pleasure by analyzing "the secret mechanism" behind each film.[55]

This theoretical move by authors such as Kracauer to privilege male spectatorship at the expense of female spectatorship has been dismantled by feminist film scholarship, particularly by Patrice Petro, who implores readers to "challenge the assumption that cinematic vision is inherently masculine."[56] While Kracauer's text belittles the shopgirls' desire for pop cultural distraction, Petro reads Kracauer's own work against the grain, noting that it is *he* who is distracted and therefore may be misreading the girls' responses to the films. Attempting to read the girls' "state of concentration" as critical contemplation rather than naive absorption, Petro returns to the scene in which Kracauer admonishes the girls for crying, and argues: "While the emotional response of the little shop girls may reveal an acknowledgement of a loss of social mastery, their concentrated gaze involves a perceptual activity that is neither passive nor entirely distracted."[57] The same moment in Kracauer's text, however, leaves open the possibility for a different reading, one that still allows for the possibility of women as critical consumers of mass culture (fig. 11). Having just watched a tragic film in which the female protagonist commits suicide in order to save her lover's career, the shopgirls shed a few tears, but they "furtively… wipe their eyes and quickly powder their noses before the lights go up."[58] If one of Kracauer's main criticisms of the girls is that they do not recognize the disjuncture between filmic representation and their own drab lives, and therefore fail to take action toward social change, their act of powdering their faces could contradict his claim. Although Kracauer implies that their powdering constitutes an overidentification with the on-screen actress and their desire to participate in the film's plot, it is possible that their powdering is actually

54. Huyssen, "Modernist Miniatures: Literary Snapshots of Urban Spaces," *PMLA* 122, no.1 (2007): 33.

55. Kracauer, "The Little Shopgirls," 292. This discussion of the "male gaze" takes as its theoretical premise Laura Mulvey's work *Visual and Other Pleasures* (Bloomington: Indiana University Press, 1989).

56. Patrice Petro, "Perceptions of Difference: Woman as Spectator and Spectacle," in Ankum, *Women in the Metropolis,* 58.

57. Petro, "Perceptions of Difference," 57.

58. Kracauer, "The Little Shopgirls," 303.

Figure 11. Jeanne Mammen, *Im Aufklärungsfilm* (At the Hygiene Film), 1929. Courtesy of Jeanne-Mammen-Stiftung. Copyright 2012 Artists Rights Society (ARS), New York / VG Bild-Kunst, Bonn.

a moment of critical disjuncture. Drying their tears and dabbing their faces with powder *before* the cinematic space is illuminated, the shopgirls anticipate the transition from the darkened space of the theater to the space of the street and thereby display an awareness that they will be looked at. The city street, in contrast to the cinema, can be seen, Henri Lefebvre suggests, as "a form of spontaneous theater" that offers urban women and men opportunities to be "spectacle and spectator, and sometimes an actor."[59] Recognizing the difference between these spaces, with a dab of the powder puff, the supposedly passive "girls" move out onto the street and

59. Henri Lefebvre, *The Urban Revolution*, trans. Robert Bononno (Minneapolis: University of Minnesota Press, 2003), 18.

on to the next adventure. Perhaps, then, these shopgirls are not dupes but critical consumers, perfectly aware of the disjuncture between cinematic representations and reality and able to negotiate various urban spaces. Perhaps the cinema is not the site of their social and moral corruption but rather a place where they can exercise their buying power and satisfy their desire for entertainment at the end of a long workday. Perhaps they are *desiring subjects* as well as desired objects. And perhaps, before they exit the cinema, they pause to look in their compact mirrors for a second, casting quizzical glances at the intellectual in the back row and returning, even if just for a second, his studied gaze.

While this may seem like playful conjecture, these are all possibilities raised by writers and artists who encounter women in other urban spaces, ones that, unlike the darkened space of the cinema, require a more active negotiation of social and sexual relations. An examination of the widespread popularity of prostitutes' songs in Berlin's cabarets reveals discourses that do not attempt to render female sexuality or spectatorship passive, but rather acknowledge Weimar women's active search for entertainment and companionship, as well as their penchant for self-stylization and masquerade. Looking beyond the cinematic space allows us to see Weimar Berlin as a city filled with various performances of gender and sexuality, an urban environment in which sexual norms and essentialized definitions of gender are destabilized, all with the help of a powder puff.

Cabaret Coquette: Prostitutes Take Center Stage

In the final months of the First World War, the head of Berlin's theater censorship department, Kurt von Glasenapp, received a dismayed report from the police commissioner concerning both the repertoire and the audience of the capital city's many cabarets. Couched in a plea for stricter censorship of what the police report calls "beer-and-coffee cabarets" is a description of a new urban audience comprised mostly of women, and a repertoire consisting primarily of *Dirnenlieder,* or prostitutes' songs. Without censorship of these songs and their lewd lyrics, the police commissioner feared, audience members would gradually "get used to the idea that there is nothing extravagant or forbidden about such behavior." Much like Brecht and his concerns in his essay "From the Theater Scene," the police official was worried that, especially in a time of staggering food shortages and financial need, female audience members would take social cues from prostitutes. What sets this document apart from texts such as Brecht's, however, is its portrayal of the cabarets' women visitors. These were not the naive girls that Brecht and Kracauer would go on to depict. Quite the contrary, they were savvy Berliners and no strangers to "the follies of love" so common to "Berlin's metropolitan life." The report's author openly admitted that he had no problem with women expressing curiosity about sex, telling saucy jokes, or reading erotic novels as long as they did so among themselves and in private. As soon as they moved into the public realm and became part of a mixed audience, however, their behavior became a cause for concern. Unlike Brecht's imagined secretaries, who visited the cinema accompanied by men, the women who visited Berlin's cabarets made up nearly three-quarters of the audience, which means that they were either unaccompanied or going out in groups. The suspicion aired by the police report is not that these women would become the targets of unwanted attention, but rather that, like the prostitutes on stage, they might actively solicit too much attention.[60]

Four months after the above report was written, its plea for increased oversight of the cabarets was rendered moot by the official lifting of censorship, and new cabarets began opening up all over the city, most of them not much more than glorified strip clubs catering to the nouveaux riches. Even the literary cabarets such as Max Reinhardt's second incarnation of Schall und Rauch (Sound and Smoke), Rosa Valetti's Cabaret Größenwahn (Cabaret Megalomania), and Trude Hesterberg's Wilde Bühne (Wild Stage) catered primarily to a new bourgeois audience that preferred "spicy punchlines and champagne" to political satire.[61] Inspired by the Parisian cabarets that flourished in late nineteenth-century Montmartre and featured the talents of Aristide Bruant and Yvette Guilbert, the founders of Berlin's literary cabarets "longed to revolt but remain popular—and commercially successful." This proved to be a difficult balance to strike, and none of these cabarets lasted more than two seasons.[62] With the writing talents of Kurt Tucholsky, Friedrich Hollaender, Walter Mehring, and Klabund, and performers such as Paul Graetz, Kurt Gerron, Gussy Holl, and Valeska Gert, the literary cabarets owed much of their commercial success to their portrayals of colorful urban characters—cigarette vendors, thieves, vagabonds, pimps, and prostitutes. The underworld was chic. Women performers like Gert, Rosa Valetti, and Blandine Ebinger played prostitutes on stage, turning whores' songs—or, in the case of Gert, whores' dances—into what Alan Lareau calls "conventional fare."[63] And yet each of these performers had her own interpretation of the figure, and these interpretations were not necessarily conventional. Indeed they were quite different from most prostitutes' songs performed in turn-of-the-century cabarets in Berlin, which offered either overly

---

60. Police report sent to Oberregierungsrat Kurt von Glasenapp, dated July 9, 1918, LAB, A. Pr. Br. Rep. 030–05, Th 135, pp. 66–67. I am most grateful to Peter Jelavich for calling my attention to this document.

61. Lareau, *The Wild Stage*, 9. On literary cabaret in Weimar Berlin, see also Jelavich, *Berlin Cabaret*, 128–53; and Roger Stein, *Das deutsche Dirnenlied: Literarisches Kabarett von Bruant bis Brecht* (Cologne: Böhlau, 2006), 278–89.

62. The quote comes from Lareau, *The Wild Stage*, 188. Parisian influence on Berlin's cabaret scene was significant, as Jelavich and Stein both demonstrate. See Jelavich, *Berlin Cabaret*, 26–27, 85; and Stein, *Das deutsche Dirnenlied*, 107–21.

63. Lareau, *The Wild Stage*, 71–72. It is interesting to note that many of these women cabaret artists also appeared in feature films about prostitution during the Weimar Republic. Gussy Holl played Hedwig in Oswald's *Prostitution;* Gert appeared both as a procuress in *The Joyless Street* and as the sadistic matron of the home for lost girls in *Diary of a Lost Girl;* and Valetti played the aging cabaret artist Guste in Josef von Sternberg's hit talkie *The Blue Angel* (1930), starring Marlene Dietrich.

romanticized portraits of the underworld or dismal stories of the prostitute's grim fate. Weimar performers, particularly those in the literary cabarets, broke away from such clichéd representations. Before Sound and Smoke opened its doors in December 1919, its artists got together to write, play music, and test out possible performance pieces. In his memoirs, the lyricist and composer Friedrich Hollaender describes one of these improvisational sessions, where he met the woman who would become his first wife, Blandine Ebinger. It is without a tinge of fear, anxiety, or disgust, indeed it is with no small measure of fascination and respect, that he describes Blandine's off-the-cuff performance of a prostitute: "An almost-too-skinny girl with a face that's pale—paler—palest under the dark pageboy....Imitates a hooker in a bar. Sits down on a barstool that's not even there, crosses her legs, hikes her skirt up a bit, give me a glass of Cognac, and sings one straight from the soul, all about the business, what types of clients show up, does one have to, of course one has to, and it just pours out of her mouth, with such humor, with such keen powers of observation."[64] Ebinger's "bar hooker" is a plucky, yet slightly jaded, working-class prostitute. The line "does one have to, of course one has to" (hat man das nötig, klar hat man das nötig) plays with the German term *Not* (need) and is left ambiguous, referring simultaneously to the sexual needs of the clients and the financial need of the prostitute. Although Hollaender pokes fun at Ebinger's pale and masklike face peering out from under her bobbed hair, his memory of this event shows a clear appreciation for the sardonic wit of the performer and for her rendition of the subject.

Valeska Gert, an anarchic dancer and actress who also performed at Sound and Smoke in 1920 and became known throughout interwar Europe for her parodies of such popular dances as the Charleston, fox-trot, and tango, had a different take on the prostitute.[65] Portraying the prostitute as an unabashedly erotic figure, Gert "wanted to show [the prostitute] plying her trade." She stressed the novelty of her performance at the time, describing herself in her memoirs as "a sensitive whore, moving gently and sensually," exposing her thighs, gyrating her hips to the music, and making provocative gestures to the audience.[66] By giving her audience the most extreme version of what it surreptitiously wanted, Gert exposed to them their own sexual desires and made them squirm in their seats. As a contemporary critic noted of her performances, those who saw them as simply obscene were mistaken, for

---

64. Friedrich Hollaender, *Von Kopf bis Fuß: Revue meines Lebens* (Berlin: Aufbau, 2001), 80–81.

65. Jelavich, *Berlin Cabaret*, 184–85; and Lareau, *The Wild Stage*, 52. For more on Valeska Gert, see also Birgit Haustedt's popular history, *Die wilden Jahre in Berlin: Eine Klatsch- und Kulturgeschichte der Frauen* (Berlin: Edition Ebersbach, 2002), 15–49; and Ute Scheub, "Das Leben ist ein Kabarett: Die Kabarett-Gründerinnen Rosa Valetti, Trude Hesterberg, Dinah Nelken und Valeska Gert," in *Femme Flaneur: Erkundungen zwischen Boulevard und Sperrbezirk,* ed. Rita Täuber (Bonn: August Macke Haus, 2004), 85–91.

66. Valeska Gert, *Ich bin eine Hexe* (Reinbek bei Hamburg: Rowohlt, 1978), 39.

"Valeska Gert does not uncover herself, but rather the sexuality of dance."[67] By acting out the prostitute's sexuality, then, Valeska Gert did not mark that sexuality as deviant but as a type of sexuality that is often denied but secretly desired by bourgeois society. The prostitute's own desire, on the other hand, might be pure performance, just like Gert's dances.

Gert's blatant exposure of sexuality was a bit too much for Kurt Tucholsky, who described her dances as a mixture of "desire and agony."[68] In the songs he wrote for Sound and Smoke, Tucholsky took a subtler approach to eroticism and chose to stage a more refined type of prostitute—the youthful bourgeois cocotte from Berlin West. The cocotte was a figure that had fascinated Tucholsky since the final years of the Wilhelmine period when he observed the famed Berlin cabaret artist Fritzi Massary play a *grande cocotte*. Massary was no stranger to prostitutes' songs; she performed them regularly in popular revues at Berlin's Metropoltheater in the years leading up to the First World War, but it was her artful rendition of the *grande cocotte* that Tucholsky recounts in his 1913 essay "Massary."[69] In Tucholsky's opinion, Massary was the only performer who could walk the fine line between obscenity and respectability required by the figure of the cocotte, without ever stepping fully onto one side or the other. She coquettishly awaited each suitor, only to toy with his affections by inflaming his desire and then rejecting his "clumsy" advances. Admitting that he is embellishing a bit, Tucholsky describes Massary's staged rejection of her overeager suitor to his readers thus: "'O-ho! Dear Sir!' (The tone of her voice changes: for this moment, she has a wonderful, ethical bass at her disposal.) 'What do you take me for? I'm an upst...' And as soon as she says it, mocking laughter rings out."[70] The target of the audience's and Massary's mockery is not just the fumbling gentleman caller but the very concept of respectability (*Anständigkeit*), for the word *anständig* (upstanding) serves as the truncated punch line of the cocotte's joke. Massary's irreverent performance no doubt inspired

---

67. Anonymous review in *Kritiker,* November 1926, translated and quoted in Jelavich, *Berlin Cabaret,* 184.

68. Quoted in Frank-Manuel Peter, *Valeska Gert: Tänzerin, Schauspielerin, Kabarettistin* (Berlin: Frolich & Kaufmann, 1985), 45. Kurt Tucholsky (1890–1935) was one of the Weimar Republic's premier critics and satirists. He wrote song lyrics for Berlin's literary cabarets and penned political and cultural essays, short prose pieces, and verse for a variety of Weimar-era periodicals, including the *Berliner Tageblatt, Uhu,* and, most regularly, *Die Weltbühne.* He published under his given name and under four pseudonyms—Ignaz Wrobel, Kaspar Hauser, Peter Panter, and Theobald Tiger—each one befitting a different venue for or genre of his writing. Tucholsky left Germany for Paris in 1924 and moved to Sweden in 1929, where he committed suicide in 1935. For more on Tucholsky, see Jelavich, *Berlin Cabaret,* 131–41, 152–53.

69. Kurt Tucholsky, "Massary," in *Gesamtausgabe,* ed. Antje Bonitz, Dirk Grathoff, Michael Hepp, and Gerhard Kraiker, vol. 1, *Texte 1907–1913,* ed. Bärbel Boldt, Dirk Grathoff, and Michael Hepp (Reinbek bei Hamburg: Rowohlt, 1997), 347–51. The essay was originally published in the journal *Die Schaubühne* in November 1913. For more on Fritzi Massary's performances of *Dirnenlieder,* see Alan Lareau, "The Genesis of 'Jenny': Prostitute Songs, the Mythology of Pimps, and the *Threepenny Opera,*" in Schönfeld, *Commodities of Desire,* 167–90, here 168–69.

70. Tucholsky, "Massary," 349.

Tucholsky's own Weimar-era *Dirnenlieder,* in which the cocotte retains the upper hand over her bumbling, disarmed suitor, and in which male desire is portrayed as more of a laughable nuisance than a threat. The men described by Tucholsky's co-cottes are "bums" or buffoons rather than cunning seducers, a portrayal that likely appealed to the growing female cabaret audience.[71]

Although less overt in their eroticism than Gert's aggressive dances, Tucholsky's songs revealed to the audience its own demand for certain types of women and certain types of entertainment. His song "Zieh Dich aus, Petronella!" (Take It Off, Petronella!), written for Gussy Holl and set to music by Hollaender, mocked the postwar public's seemingly insatiable appetite for nude dance shows, exemplified in the early Weimar Republic by the popularity of performances by the notorious Anita Berber and by the Ballet Celly de Rheidt, and in the large-scale revues that had their heyday in the mid- and late 1920s. One version of the song ends with Petronella taking off her clothes in private for a wealthy patron and shows just how blurred the lines between erotic entertainment, private pleasure, and com-modified sex had become in Weimar Berlin.[72] It is exactly these erotic gray zones that Tucholsky's lyrics from the early Weimar years explore, and his female pro-tagonists are rarely working-class streetwalkers or seasoned bar hookers. They are less mature and intimidating than Massary's *grand cocotte,* but they are no less savvy about men's desires. Perhaps they are most aptly characterized as flirts, teases, or cocottes-in-training. The most striking example of an aspiring cocotte is Tucholsky's "Das Tauentzienmädel" (Girl from the Tauentzienstrasse, 1920), a fresh-mouthed fifteen year old who sneaks out to the cabaret when her well-to-do parents think she is taking French lessons instead. The prelude to the song is a flirtatious dialogue between the girl and the conférencier, loaded with double entendres concerning the girl's desire to learn French—"fränzösisch lernen" is a clear allusion to learning the art of fellatio—and her underage status. As the girl quips, although she may not yet have reached sixteen, the legal age of consent, the Weimar president might be able to issue an emergency decree if the conférencier is truly in need (again, the German term *Not* is used to signal male desire). By placing the girl in the audience during the prelude and having the conférencier invite her onto the stage to sing her song, Tucholsky denies his audience a clichéd

71. The female singer of Tucholsky's song "Die Dame mit 'n Avec" (The Lady with a Certain Something, 1920) starts the song by proclaiming brashly that the men in Berlin are "nothing but bums" (nischt wie Penner) and "can all kiss her ass" (Alle könn' sie mir). Literally translated, the joke of the title is "The Lady *with* the *Avec,*" which simply doubles the word "with" in both German and French and thereby pokes fun at the "lady" herself as well for putting on airs. See Tucholsky [Theobald Tiger], *Gesamtausgabe,* vol. 4, *Texte 1920,* ed. Bärbel Boldt, Gisela Enzmann-Kraiker, and Christian Jäger (Reinbek bei Hamburg: Rowohlt, 1996), 106–7; with commentary, 646.

72. Tucholsky [Theobald Tiger], "Zieh dich aus, Petronella!" (also listed as "An eine für viele"), in *Gesamtausgabe,* 4:10–11. The longer version of the song is reprinted in Stein, *Das deutsche Dirnen-lied,* 311–12, and is followed by Stein's analysis. On Anita Berber and Celly de Rheidt, see Haustedt, *Die wilden Jahre,* 15–35; and Large, *Berlin,* 179. On the Weimar revues and their commercialization of the female naked body, see Jelavich, *Berlin Cabaret,* 154–86.

portrait of the Berlin underworld and shines the spotlight on a figure from their own bourgeois milieu instead.[73]

Tucholsky's girl from the Tauentzienstrasse is just the type of female audience member about whom the police warned the censorship official Kurt von Glasenapp at the end of the war. A "cheeky chick" ("kesse Beere" in Berlin dialect), as the conférencier calls her, she deceives her parents and absconds to the cabaret, to dance balls, and to walk the "streets around the K.d.W." The K.d.W. is the Kaufhaus des Westens, one of Berlin's largest department stores, which still stands at the corner of Tauentzienstrasse and Wittenbergplatz in the heart of what was known in Weimar Berlin as the "new West."[74] While the reference to the K.d.W. evokes urban consumer culture, the reference to the streets that surround it evoke the brand of upscale, urbane (*mondän*) prostitution for which the area was known. Although Tucholsky's savvy girl repeatedly claims that she never goes beyond the "overture" in her relations with men, the song's multiple allusions to oral sex and the girl's admission that she likes to "try it out a little" make the audience wonder just how long and how expensive this "overture" might be. The "it" in "try *it* out a little" may be left open, but the lines that surround it are like the streets that surround the K.d.W.; they all point to prostitution.[75] The implicit references to prostitution, however, do not serve to undermine the girl's self-assurance and wherewithal. Instead, the song highlights both the erotic tension that lies in the girl's ability to vacillate between the roles of "innocent angel and cocotte" and the cool pragmatism with which she approaches sex:

I dance at every ball
with men over twenty—all.
Where children come from, God, do you think I'm dumb!
I really must protest!
After all, we have progressed,
I even already know how *not* to have 'em!

73. Tucholsky [Theobald Tiger], "Das Tauentzien-Girl" (prelude) and "Das Tauentzienmädel" (song), in *Gesamtausgabe*, 4:128–31; with critical commentary, 658–59. The song and prelude were performed by Ernestina Costa, with Hans von Wolzogen as the conférencier, in the April 1920 program of Sound and Smoke. References to "learning French" and to the emergency decree are on p. 129. The mention of an emergency decree refers to Article 48 of the Weimar Constitution, which gave the president the power to circumvent the parliament and rule by decree if necessary.

74. The city of Berlin expanded in 1920 to incorporate the districts of Charlottenburg, Köpenick, Lichtenberg, Neukölln, Pankow, Schöneberg, Spandau, and Wilmersdorf, causing the city's population to jump to nearly four million and thereby making it the third largest city in Europe. The streets of the "new West" were mostly in Charlottenburg. See Sabine Hake, *Topographies of Class: Modern Architecture and Mass Society in Weimar Berlin* (Ann Arbor: University of Michigan Press, 2008), 19, 36–37; and Large, *Berlin,* 171.

75. The song's full refrain, repeated three times, reads: "Und ich geh', und ich geh', und ich geh' / und probier es mal ein bißchen, / ein kleines bißchen; / kommt der Mann / aber dann näher ran, / wisch ich aus und rufe: 'Stopp! / Fauler Kopp! / Blonder Zopp! / Kühler Kopp!' / Was ich auch noch im Munde führe / ich bleib' stets bei der Ouvertüre! / Das macht, weil ich alles seh / in den Straßen rings um's K.d.W." Tucholsky, "Das Tauentzienmädel," 130–31.

Auf allen Bällen tanz ich
mit Herrn, die über zwanzig.
Wo Kinder herkomm'n, Gott, wer weiß das nicht!
Da muß ich schon sehr bitten!
Wir sind doch fortgeschritten,
ich weiß sogar schon, wie man keine kriegt.[76]

Sexual knowledge, including the art of flirtation and methods of birth control, is presented here as central to young Weimar women's emancipation. By consciously teasing the audience and the conférencier about her sexual availability, Tucholsky's Tauentzien-Girl embodies the game of flirtation as Simmel described it in 1909, for she "lends a positive concreteness to not-having, making it tangible for the first time by means of the playful, suggestive illusion of having" and at the same time "intensifies the attraction of having to the most extreme degree by means of the threatening illusion of not-having."[77] She may not quite be a cocotte, but she is certainly a Berlin coquette.

As a bourgeois girl who is "trying it out a little," Tucholsky's girl serves to further erode the boundaries between prostitutes and New Women, between polite society and the so-called underworld. But as small literary cabarets closed down in the early and mid-1920s, losing audience members to large-scale revues, prostitutes' songs performed by individual cabaret artists in an intimate setting gave way to elaborate tableaux vivants of naked or nearly naked women and to kicklines of girls who moved with mechanical precision. As Roger Stein documents, the *Dirnenlied* reached the pinnacle of its popularity in the early years of Weimar Berlin and had become a dying form by the mid-1920s.[78] It saw a brief revival, however, in one of the cultural works most often associated with Weimar Berlin: Bertolt Brecht and Kurt Weill's 1928 *Dreigroschenoper* (The Threepenny Opera). Although the primary textual source for *The Threepenny Opera* was the English playwright John Gay's *Beggar's Opera* (1728), Brecht also drew inspiration from the repertoires of Parisian and Berlin cabarets. Indeed Brecht took many of the song texts used to describe the underworld milieu of the opera's antihero, Macheath, and his former lover, the prostitute "Dive-Bar Jenny" (*Spelunken-Jenny*), most notably their duet called the "Ballad of the Pimp" ("Zuhälterballade"), directly from K. L. Ammer's German translation of the Parisian *chansonnier* François Villon's songs and ballads.[79] Because she is a prostitute and because she betrays Macheath for money, Dive-Bar Jenny has often been read as a critical figure personifying "the reduction

76. Tucholsky, "Das Tauentzienmädel," 131.
77. Simmel, "Flirtation," 150; this passage is quoted and discussed at greater length in chapter 1.
78. Stein, *Das deutsche Dirnenlied*, 476–77, 491–97.
79. Lareau, "The Genesis of 'Jenny,'" 177–82. On Villon's influence on German cabaret and on Brecht in particular, see also Stein, *Das deutsche Dirnenlied*, 110, 114–15, 450–51.

of human relations to financial transactions."[80] Lareau and Stein, however, argue that reading Jenny primarily as a critical, materialist figure neglects the prostitute's status as a popular figure of Weimar stage and screen. Jenny, after all, has three incarnations in Brecht's late Weimar operas: "Pirate-Jenny" (*die Seeräuber-Jenny*) and Dive-Bar Jenny in *The Threepenny Opera,* followed by the prostitute Jenny in *Aufstieg und Fall der Stadt Mahagonny* (Rise and Fall of the City of Mahagonny, 1929). In both works, some of the most memorable lines and songs are given to Jenny. Drawing attention to the popularity of Weill's music, Brecht's clever use of Villon's lyrics, and the play's focus on the urban milieu of beggars and prostitutes, Weimar cabaret scholars like Lareau and Stein claim that *The Threepenny Opera* is very much a period piece, intimately linked to the urban world of cabaret, music hall, and revue. It is a work that points to the ironic tension between Brecht's "appropriation of popular entertainment forms and his relentless satire of their illusory and manipulative nature." *The Threepenny Opera* enacts and thereby exposes the phenomenon of "underworld chic."[81] Just as it capitalizes on the popular appeal of underworld figures like the thief Macheath and the prostitute Jenny, it reveals those figures first as objects of bourgeois faddishness and then as completely bourgeois themselves. After all, the roguish Macheath wears spats, carries an ivory-tipped cane, and adorns the stable where he is about to consummate his marriage to Polly Peachum with stolen Chippendale furniture. Even his regular visits to the brothel, Isabelle Siemes points out, are simply "bourgeois rituals," habits that Macheath just cannot break.[82] The whorehouse is no less bourgeois than Mackie's lair; Brecht describes it in his stage directions as "a bourgeois idyll," where the prostitutes iron clothes, play cards, and bathe while Mackie's men sit quietly reading the newspaper.[83] If this conflation of the criminal underworld with the bourgeoisie is a form of ridicule, whom is Brecht's opera ridiculing and to what end? Is this a cultural critique, lamenting the ability of bourgeois culture to dictate theater repertoire and subsume all that lies outside of it? Does Brecht bemoan the mainstreaming of the margins, even as he attempts to appeal to a mainstream audience?[84] Does Brecht

---

80. Siemes, *Die Prostituierte in der literarischen Moderne,* 201; see also Jan Knopf, *Brecht Handbuch* (Stuttgart: Metzler, 1980), 1:58.

81. The given quotes come from Lareau, *The Wild Stage,* 7 and 72. Lareau's focused analysis of *Threepenny Opera,* however, appears in "The Genesis of 'Jenny.'" See also Stein, *Das deutsche Dirnenlied,* 446–53.

82. Siemes, *Die Prostituierte,* 201.

83. Brecht, *Die Dreigroschenoper,* in *Werke: Große, kommentierte Berliner und Frankfurter Ausgabe,* ed. Werner Hecht, Jan Knopf, Werner Mittenzwei, and Klaus-Detlef Müller (Berlin/Weimar and Frankfurt am Main: Aufbau and Suhrkamp, 1988), 2:269; translated by Ralph Manheim and John Willett as *The Threepenny Opera,* in *Brecht: Collected Plays,* vol. 2 (New York: Vintage, 1977), 186; all subsequent references are to this translated edition.

84. An apt theoretical frame for this discussion is Dick Hebdige's study *Subculture: The Meaning of Style* (London: Routledge, 1979). In it, Hebdige describes the process by which mainstream society interpolates the style (i.e., fashion, lingo, music) of groups one considered marginal or even deviant. Similar to the concept of "underworld chic" described by Lareau, Hebdige argues that if the group's style receives enough publicity, if it appears in "every…chain-store boutique," its prevalence diminishes the

succeed in his attempt to both provoke and entertain, revealing the hypocrisy of a
bourgeoisie that refuses to see the suffering of those whose stories they consume as
mere entertainment? Such questions, though much discussed, remain unanswered,
and it is this tension between social critique and popular appeal that allows *The
Threepenny Opera* to remain so appealing to twenty-first-century audiences.

These tensions are certainly evident in Polly Peachum's performance of "Pirate
Jenny." In *The Threepenny Opera* the roles of prostitute and bourgeois daughter,
while they seem to be reversed, are actually conflated. The prostitutes in the brothel
"perform" bourgeois domesticity, while the bourgeois Polly Peachum "performs"
lower-class prostitution. What is "Pirate Jenny" but a bourgeois daughter's performance of an underworld woman? As she stands up in front of her bridegroom
Macheath and his band of thieves, Polly announces: "I myself will sing a little song;
it's an imitation of a girl I saw once in some twopenny halfpenny dive in Soho."[85] It
is Polly's fascination with the low-class barmaid that leads her to stand up and sing
a song that became one of the show's greatest hits. It is also the song with the clearest revolutionary potential, for Pirate Jenny calls for the destruction of an entire
city and, with it, all those who have wronged her. As an avenger of both class and
gender oppression, Pirate Jenny evokes an ambivalent reaction from Macheath and
his men.[86] Whereas the thief Matthias describes Polly's performance as "pretty"
and even "cute," the newlywed Macheath is less amused and retorts: "What do you
mean pretty? It's not pretty, you idiot!" Although, in an ironic defense of culture,
Macheath defends Polly's song as "art" to his band of thieves, in a private aside to
his bride, he expresses his unease, saying: "I don't like you play-acting; let's not have
any more of it."[87] Women's agency—even its mere performance—is perceived by
Macheath as a threat. Brecht's *Threepenny Opera* reflects the paradox inherent in
the figure of the prostitute, a figure that can both affirm and subvert social structures. And yet compared to the more daring and complex portraits of prostitutes
performed by cabaret artists of the early years of the Weimar Republic, Brecht's
prostitutes seem, to use Stein's description, "more like inventory, backdrops to the
action"; they are on stage "just because they belong to the milieu."[88] This may be

---

group's perceived marginality. This creates a certain measure of distance between the group that originally defined the style and the style itself. "Stripped of its unwholesome connotations, the style becomes
fit for public consumption" (130).

85. Brecht, *The Threepenny Opera,* 164.

86. Anyone who has heard the African American jazz singer Nina Simone's 1964 version of "Pirate Jenny" knows that it can be used as an effective allegory for vengeance against racial oppression as well. Indeed the performance history of "Pirate Jenny" has become increasingly complex ever
since the song was sung by the prostitute Jenny (played by Lotte Lenya) in G. W. Pabst's film version of
The Threepenny Opera (1931), a decision that conflates the two Jenny characters and clearly underscores
the song's subtext of prostitution.

87. Brecht, *The Threepenny Opera,* 166.

88. Stein resists classifying the songs in *Threepenny Opera* as *Dirnenlieder,* for they do not fit in with
the self-assured, first-person narratives of unapologetic prostitutes that he tracks through the early years
of the Weimar Republic. "A *Dirnenlied* in its most specific terms cannot be found in *The Threepenny*

a slightly oversimplified reading of the original staging of *The Threepenny Opera*, but by the time Brecht staged the prostitute Jenny and the procuress Widow Begbick in *Mahagonny*, he had chosen to place "the milieu" of prostitution fully on the side of exploitative capitalism. This one-dimensional drawing of female characters as cold capitalists betrays a lack of critical interest in gender dynamics and thereby supports Christian Rogowski's diagnosis that "the world of Brecht's plays is a man's world."[89]

The world of early Weimar literary cabaret, however, was not exclusively a man's world. It relied just as much on the talents of women artists (Holl, Ebinger, Gert) and entrepreneurs (Hesterberg, Valetti) as it did on the writing talents of men like Tucholsky and Hollaender. These performers used the *Dirnenlied* both to entertain and to provoke their audience, and to explore the nuances of erotic femininity and commodified sexuality. The performance of a more audacious form of female sexuality, as Tucholsky's Tauentzien-Girl with her mention of the "streets around the K.d.W." implies, was not limited to the cabaret stage. It was happening on the streets and in the cafés and clubs of Weimar Berlin, as Curt Moreck shows in his *Guide to "Naughty" Berlin*. The guide takes its reader to the capital city's many entertainment venues and late-night haunts, paying special attention to the women who frequent these places. In its constant blending of prostitutes and New Women, as well as its repeated references to masks, mimicry, and makeup, Moreck's guide takes a more playful approach to gender and sexuality and calls on its readers to find out for themselves what might—or might not—be so naughty about Berlin.

New Men, New Women, and Masks: Curt Moreck's *Guide to "Naughty" Berlin*

Curt Moreck begins his *Guide to "Naughty" Berlin* with a familiar slogan: "A Visit to Berlin for Everyone!" (Jeder einmal in Berlin!).[90] This catchy phrase was the advertising slogan used by Berlin's municipal tourist agency in the 1920s to attract visitors to Germany's capital city. Ostensibly it worked. During the period of economic

---

Opera—for that, the prostitutes do too little to carry the plot; more appropriately, they are inventory, backdrops to the action" (Stein, *Das deutsche Dirnenlied*, 449).

89. Christian Rogowski, "Schattenboxen: Zum Warencharakter von Geschlecht und 'Rasse' in *Aufstieg und Fall der Stadt Mahagonny*," *The Brecht Yearbook* 29 (2004): 325. It is important to note that the success of Brecht's late Weimar productions can be attributed largely to the talents of the actresses whom he and Weill chose to play leading roles, such as Lotte Lenya and Carola Neher.

90. Moreck, *Führer durch das "lasterhafte" Berlin*, 6. Although Moreck's guide was recently rediscovered by German studies scholars, with a few notable exceptions it has received little more than cursory references in publications on gender and sexuality in the Weimar era. The most extensive reading to date is by Koshar, *German Travel Cultures*, 83–96, but even Koshar's convincing analysis does not look closely at how prostitution is represented in the text. For other brief readings of Moreck's guide, see also Deborah Smail, *White Collar Workers, Mass Culture, and "Neue Sachlichkeit" in Weimar Berlin* (Frankfurt am Main: Peter Lang, 1999), 147–86; and Roos, *Weimar through the Lens of Gender*, 67.

stabilization (1924–29), as many as two million tourists per year flocked to the city.[91] Many of those tourists were drawn to Berlin by more than the urge to stroll down Unter den Linden to see the Brandenburg Gate. Those visitors who were looking for sexual thrills that could not be found on a guided tour or in the bourgeois standard-bearer of travel guides, the Baedeker, those who wanted to explore the "confusing metropolis of pleasure," needed Moreck's guide.[92]

The guide is a mixed-media text that combines its alternative travel narrative with visual images. Moreck's witty style of big city reportage is accompanied by contemporary illustrations by Berlin artists such as Paul Kamm, Jeanne Mammen, George Grosz, Christian Schad, and Heinrich Zille. Moreck spends his first chapter, "We'll Show You Berlin," convincing the reader that the guide is, in many ways, indispensable to any traveler who wants to get beyond Berlin's "official side." Moreck claims to offer a way to experience rather than simply to see Berlin, a peek past the city's official mask:

> Every city has an official and an unofficial side, and it is superfluous to add that the latter is more interesting and more informative of the essence of a city. That which appears so clearly in the light of the arc lamps has a face more like a mask than a physiognomy. The smile it offers is more an appeal to the visitor's purse. It wears the makeup of the *coquette,* applied too thickly to permit the true features underneath to be recognized. Those who are looking for experiences, who long for adventure, who hope for sensations—they must go into the shadows.[93]

In this passage, Berlin's official tourist industry is likened to a painted "coquette," a particularly bold lady of the night who could just as easily be described as a "cocotte." Found under the "light of the arc lamp," the tourist industry/cocotte wears a smile only to entice the tourist to spend money. To use a contemporary phrase, she's a "tourist trap." Eager to please the eye, tourism cakes on its makeup, creating a mask that obscures the city's "essence." Interestingly, as much as Moreck promises to show his readers Berlin's "true features," most often he winds up showing them its many masks. Perhaps the masklike makeup—so garishly applied—is impossible to remove completely. One can only hope to examine its various layers. Moreck's use of prostitute imagery in his description of "official Berlin" can be read as further testament to the prostitute's mainstream status in Weimar Berlin, for in this passage the prostitute is associated with the moneymaking industries

---

91. Koshar, *German Travel Cultures,* 72.

92. Moreck, *Führer durch das "lasterhafte" Berlin,* 10.

93. Moreck, *Führer durch das "lasterhafte" Berlin,* 7, emphasis added. The translation of this particular passage is taken from Kaes et.al., *The Weimar Republic Sourcebook,* 564. The original German text uses neither the term *kokett* nor the word *Kokotte,* but the translators do capture the spirit of the passage by choosing the term "coquette." Still, the ambiguity is worth noting. All other translations of Moreck's text are mine.

of entertainment and tourism. Yet prostitutes in Moreck's guide also inhabit the "unofficial" world of shadows, embodying the "adventure" and "sensations" of sexual subcultures, as well as the "demimonde" in which they are virtually indistinguishable from the new generation of women who walk the streets of Berlin. The sheer variety and ambiguity of Moreck's representations of prostitutes place him in closer proximity to women artists of the Weimar period like Jeanne Mammen, whose works, the art historian Marsha Meskimmon argues, are effective in "dismantling...the marginality of sex workers as mere symbols of decadence, commodity capitalism, and the uncontrollable mass."[94] Indeed Moreck's guide repeatedly calls the very concept of social and spatial marginality into question by showing its readers a city with multiple centers of pleasure filled with a host of urban characters sporting playful masks.

Setting himself apart from Karl Baedeker's guidebook *Berlin and Its Environs,* which provides readers with recommendations for hotels and restaurants, detailed maps of the capital city's streets and transportation system, and helpful blueprints of churches, monuments, and museums, Moreck gives his readers neither maps nor diagrams. The visual elements of his guide are the artists' renditions of social spaces. Unlike traditional travel guides that feature state-sponsored cultural institutions and historic landmarks, Moreck steers his readers away from the more historic sections of the city, privileging spaces that more aptly reflect Berlin's youthful, erotic vibrancy. Instead of using streets as mere avenues to particular destinations or monumental sites, the streets themselves become destinations. In an essay written the same year as Moreck's guide, Kracauer himself identified the street as a space that can "escape the authority of urban planners and architects and reveal the heterogeneity that their designs deny."[95] However, as Moreck warns, some streets still cater to an older generation of tourists, naive "provincials" from "strict bourgeois" backgrounds still grounded in Wilhelmine morals.[96] The best case in point is his description of Friedrichstrasse, a popular destination for foreign and provincial visitors because of its geographical location close to one of Berlin's main train stations, and, incidentally, the only location for nightlife mentioned in Baedeker's

---

94. Meskimmon, *We Weren't Modern Enough,* 68. Mammen's work is only beginning to get the critical attention it deserves. For more complete information on Jeanne Mammen and her work, see the exhibition catalog *Jeanne Mammen 1890–1976: Gemälde, Aquarelle, Zeichnungen* (Cologne: Wienand, 1997); Annelie Lütgens, *"Nur ein paar Augen sein": Jeanne Mammen—Eine Künstlerin in ihrer Zeit* (Berlin: Erich Reimer, 1991); and Suzanne Nicole Royal, "Graphic Art in Weimar Berlin: The Case of Jeanne Mammen" (PhD diss., University of Southern California, 2007). On the representation of prostitutes in Mammen's work, see Täuber, *Der häßliche Eros,* 187–94; and Täuber, *Femme Flaneur,* 59–65.

95. Kracauer, *Berliner Landschaft,* translated and quoted in Courtney Federle, "Picture Postcard: Kracauer Writes from Berlin," in *Peripheral Visions: The Hidden Stages of Weimar Cinema,* ed. Kenneth S. Calhoon (Detroit: Wayne State University Press, 2001), 43. See also David Frisby, "Deciphering the Hieroglyphics of Weimar Berlin: Siegfried Kracauer," in Haxthausen and Suhr, *Berlin: Culture and Metropolis,* 152–65. Neither Federle nor Frisby engages the topic of gender in his analysis of Kracauer's writings on the street.

96. Moreck, *Führer durch das "lasterhafte" Berlin,* 14–15.

turn-of-the-century guide.[97] According to Moreck, "Were it not for the fact that the Friedrichstrasse is the most natural canal that takes in the stream of foreigners from the train station and directs it into the city…it would die out, for the democratic West, where the 'new men' live, is robbing it of its lifeblood."[98] It is in this passage that the author clearly makes the point that his is a new guide for a new generation of both men and women. For Weimar Berliners, Moreck claims, the Friedrichstrasse has become a "fossil," a vestige of the Wilhelmine era that once catered to the desires of bourgeois men but now caters only to unassuming tourists in search of what they believe to be "naughty" Berlin. The various entertainment venues scattered on or around Friedrichstrasse, with their many attractive women, help to maintain the image of Berlin as a city of sexual decadence, but this "comedy of 'Berlin, Babylon of Sin' is just a show put on for the traveling foreigners." Those who want to enter the "domain of the locals" and experience the streets that epitomize modern Berlin are directed to visit Berlin-West, where the shopping promenades of the Tauentzienstrasse and the Kurfürstendamm quiver with sexual energy and offer pleasures that are potentially more risqué.[99] Decked out in high boots of varying colors, prostitutes specializing in S & M aggressively proposition passersby. Admitting that these women may intimidate visitors to Berlin-West, Moreck engages in a project of demystification, telling his readers that these boot whores, once considered a kinky peculiarity, have become "fashionable items" appealing to a variety of customers (fig. 12). The same holds true for the city's many gay, lesbian, and transvestite clubs. Once seen as dens of iniquity, Moreck claims, some of these clubs now attract fashionable crowds interested in following a trend. Trendsetters looking for voyeuristic titillation find, however, that the clubs' atmospheres are actually quite bourgeois, just as those individuals who go searching Alexanderplatz for the danger of the Berlin underworld find themselves admonished by Moreck not to confuse exaggerated cinematic images of Berlin's criminal underbelly with reality. He instructs readers to be aware that, in many cases, the most dangerous criminals look the most benign, whereas those who truly look the part are mere mimics.[100] By simultaneously refuting and perpetuating the idea of "naughty" Berlin, Moreck's guide pokes fun at those who naively buy into the advertising slogans or the cinematic stereotypes of the metropolis as site of sexual decadence and danger. The very fact that the title of the guide places the word *naughty* in quotation marks underscores the tension between the reification of sexuality and danger and the demystification of the assumed link between sex and danger, a tension that Moreck's work fails to resolve. It does, however, depart from a common

---

97. Karl Baedeker, *Berlin und Umgebung: Handbuch für Reisende* (Leipzig: Verlag von Karl Baedeker, 1910), 48.

98. Moreck, *Führer durch das "lasterhafte" Berlin*, 12–14.

99. Moreck, *Führer durch das "lasterhafte" Berlin*, 18–19, 22.

100. Moreck, *Führer durch das "lasterhafte" Berlin*, 30, 32 (on the boot whores), 133 (on the gay and lesbian clubs), 212, 216 (on the so-called Berlin underworld). Moreck explicitly uses the term "mimicry" in his discussion of would-be criminals.

Figure 12. Jeanne Mammen, *In hohen Stiefeln* (In Tall Boots), 1930. Courtesy of Jeanne-Mammen-Stiftung. Copyright 2012 Artists Rights Society (ARS), New York / VG Bild-Kunst, Bonn.

understanding of sex tourism that presumes chauvinistic male agency and female passivity, for it resists mapping a clear path to the sexual satisfaction of male desire at the expense of female desire.

Who, then, is Moreck's intended reader? As previously mentioned, from the beginning Moreck makes it clear that the guide (the narrative "we") is addressing a new generation of reader similar to the "new men" of Berlin-West, a republican reader who is open to a more democratic view of gender and sexuality. Rudy

Koshar thoughtfully speculates on what this "new man" might look like, and he offers the following profile of Moreck's "imagined tourist":

> He was of course a male heterosexual who was drawn to the more salacious side of Berlin culture after World War I.... He was willing to concede the variety of sexual identities one encountered when traveling through a major city... where not only heterosexual women, but also male and female homosexuals operated as more than passive subjects, as more than objects of derision, or as more than players in eroticized *tableaux vivants*. In Moreck's Berlin, the Other looked back, and the possibilities of new representations and new sexual identities were contained in this returned gaze.[101]

Koshar convincingly argues that the guide caters primarily to a male heterosexual audience, yet the "male gaze" does not necessarily dominate the narrative, nor does it render the female gaze passive. If anything, in contrast to the texts on female spectatorship by Brecht and Kracauer, for instance, Moreck's text casts doubt on the authority given to men's cinematic vision by implying that the reader is prone to confuse film or sexual spectacle with reality. Additionally, by featuring spaces beyond the cinema—a space that is mentioned only fleetingly—the guide emphasizes the complex matrix of looks and gazes that exists in the city's clubs, streets, and cafés.[102] Such spaces are filled with women who are not just aware of being looked at but who *want* to be looked at and who look at others as well—sometimes at men, sometimes at other women. In the lesbian club and brothel Toppkeller, for example, only women can enter and choose a companion, after casting "scrutinizing looks" into the crowd of other women.[103] A male reader would have to come to terms with the fact that his own desire for sexual fulfillment may be thwarted or even subjugated by female desire. Plainly stated, this modern guide is pitched to a youthful, alternative reader.

The guide's generational focus, however, does not apply just to the "new man"; it also applies to the "New Woman" and a more open form of female sexuality. Young, single, sexually active women in the metropolis who adopt the open flirtatiousness and the once-distinctive style of the prostitute, particularly the prostitute's use of cosmetics and more revealing fashions, make such behavior and style into the new norm. Returning to the space of the street, consider Moreck's passage on the Tauentziengirls, fashionable prostitutes from Berlin-West, who before

---

101. Koshar, *German Travel Cultures,* 96.

102. Moreck, *Führer durch das "lasterhafte" Berlin,* 35, 76. Moreck mentions the cinema only in passing, identifying it as one of the many possible spaces in which Berliners might spend a few hours in the late afternoon or early evening.

103. Moreck, *Führer durch das "lasterhafte" Berlin,* 168. The Toppkeller actually housed multiple locales, including a cabaret stage. Moreck is most likely referring to the Damenklub Pyramide (Pyramid Women's Club), a well-known haunt of lesbians and women artists.

the First World War were notorious for their "refined femininity" and "demonically sparkling perversity" but are now virtually indistinguishable from their athletic and emancipated daughters:

> The Tauentziengirls of yesteryear have aged and now have daughters who, on the athletic fields, engage in a beautiful competition with their masculine peers. The Tauentziengirls of yesteryear have become mothers, even if, thanks to their bobbed haircuts and cosmetics, they look more like their daughters' older sisters. The Tauentziengirls of yesteryear now laugh over the fact that what one used to refer to as their vice and wickedness is considered perfectly natural today. Their extravagance of yesteryear is now taken for granted as the female youth's given right.[104]

Moreck's repetition of the phrase "the Tauentziengirls of yesteryear" constantly underscores the difference between the sexual mores of the turn of the century and those of Weimar Berlin. Assigning new meaning to the particular space of Tauentzienstrasse, a street once associated exclusively with *mondän* prostitution, this passage serves as an excellent example of how Moreck uses generational and spatial motifs to map out the domains of the New Woman. In this particular instance, prostitutes and New Women are—quite literally—related. This is quite a shift from Tucholsky's "Girl from the Tauentzienstrasse," who makes it clear that she knows more about sex than her prudish and well-to-do mother. Moreck's contention that the Tauentziengirls' matching makeup and hairstyles make them look more like sisters could be read in various ways: as "sisterhood," a form of solidarity between prostitutes and sexually emancipated women, or perhaps as a sign of their contemporaneous visibility in Berlin's social scene. But it is the motif of the mother that is most fitting to the tone of the travel guide, not only because prostitutes have traditionally been depicted, even in more progressive discourses, as antimothers, but even more because it implies that emancipated women are the figurative progeny of prostitutes. While the older generation of Tauentziengirls takes on the more traditionally "feminine" role of the mother and prostitute, the younger generation crosses gender boundaries, embodying both "masculine" brawn and athleticism and "feminine" extravagance. The prostitutes who caused a moral stir in Wilhelmine Berlin have given birth to a new generation of young women for whom sexual expression is a "natural right" and whose interaction with the men of their generation looks less like a threat and more like healthy competition and camaraderie.

The Weimar Republic brought with it what Moreck boldly labels "gender assimilation," in which women actively sought their own leisure activities and created a space for themselves on the athletic fields and the streets and in Berlin's

---

104. Moreck, *Führer durch das "lasterhafte" Berlin*, 24–25.

multitude of entertainment venues.[105] Proving themselves to be independent actors within spaces once—and perhaps still—dominated by men, these women could also be seen as potential readers of Moreck's guide. Descriptions of women's "desire to see and be seen" permeate the narrative, and the female gaze is visually represented by Jeanne Mammen's illustrations.[106] Mammen's fourteen contributions, second only to Paul Kamm's twenty, exemplify the presence of an active female gaze that makes Moreck's guide so unique. In many of Mammen's watercolors and drawings, women look at one another (as they do in her charcoal drawing of the boot whores in figure 12 above) or look confidently back at the viewer, and they do so with a gaze that is cool and casual, sometimes flirtatious and sometimes defiant. Take, for example, one of her illustrations commissioned for Moreck's guide, *Im Romanischen Café* (In the Romanische Café; fig. 13).[107] The artwork shows two elegantly dressed women on their way out of (or into) the café, a well-known haunt of bohemian culture and Berlin intellectuals, signified by the tight-lipped man in round spectacles reading the newspaper.[108] The women's red lipstick, scarves, bell-shaped hats, and clutch purses portray them as fashionable and possibly financially independent. Like the streets of Berlin-West, the urban café is portrayed by Moreck and Mammen as a space of welcome encounter between men and women, challenging its definition as a space frequented only by prostitutes or "lewd women." As current theorists of space point out, however, the café differs from the street in its simulation of a domestic environment and its role as the "poor man's sitting room." Michel de Certeau, for instance, writes of café interiors as clear examples of the "privatization of public space" that, by mimicking the look of familiar domestic spaces like kitchens or living rooms, invite guests to linger over newspapers and cups of coffee.[109] Even though the café can be read as a space where the public and private intersect and blend with one another, as a space where both intimate conversations and social experimentation can take place, in the cultural and literary discourse of the Weimar Republic, the Romanische Café is described as "first and foremost a democratic institution" where women from all walks of life, including writers such as Else Lasker-Schüler, found a home and experimented with

---

105. Moreck, *Führer durch das "lasterhafte" Berlin,* 42. The author uses the phrase *Assimilierung der Geschlechter,* but the translation of *Geschlechter* from German into English always poses a dilemma, considering that the German language makes no distinction between "sex" and "gender."

106. Moreck, *Führer durch das "lasterhafte" Berlin,* 50.

107. As was often the case with Mammen's works, the title was chosen by the publishers of the guide, not by Mammen herself. In the catalog of Mammen's work, authorized by the Jeanne-Mammen-Stiftung, it appears simply as *Berliner Café (Jeanne Mammen 1890–1976,* 150.)

108. This is most likely Mammen's portrait of the critic Max Hermann-Neisse, a regular fixture at the Romanische Café. He appears in the background of works by other Weimar artists as well; see Christian Schad's portrait of Sonja the secretary in the Romanische Café, in the exhibition catalog *Glitter and Doom: German Portraits from the 1920s,* ed. Sabine Rewald (New Haven, CT: Yale University Press, 2006), 146–47.

109. Michel de Certeau, Luce Giard, and Pierre Mayol, *The Practice of Everyday Life,* vol. 2, *Living and Cooking,* trans. Timothy J. Tomasik, revised and expanded ed. (Minneapolis: University of Minnesota Press, 1998), 24, 11.

Figure 13. Jeanne Mammen, *Berliner Café* or *Im Romanischen Café* (In the Romanische Café), ca. 1930. Courtesy of Jeanne-Mammen-Stiftung. Copyright 2012 Artists Rights Society (ARS), New York / VG Bild-Kunst, Bonn.

cross-gender identities.[110] As an "open, porous environment" that "offered women a more or less neutral space," the café lent itself well to the performance of different personas and to frank discussions of sexuality.[111] It was well known as a place where artists and intellectuals willingly subjected themselves to the gaze of others, regardless of gender. Elias Canetti reminisced: "The visits to the Romanisches Café...resulted from *a need to be seen* that nobody was immune to.... This applied to each rank and all stations of society."[112]

Mammen's artistic rendition of the café also draws the viewer's attention to the act of seeing and being seen. While the woman in profile takes a casual drag from her cigarette, the woman in the foreground pauses to look straight at the viewer. Her cool expression is softened only slightly by the coy shrug of her shoulder. The blank, narrow eyes—so typical of Mammen's style—coupled with pale cheeks and red lips give her face a masklike quality. The squinted eyes, made-up face, and coy pose could be read today through Helmut Lethen's explication of the "cool persona," the adoption of "strategic self-enactment" central to the age of New Objectivity. In the economically and politically unstable Weimar years, Lethen argues, many intellectuals and artists donned masks of impassivity or tested out various "codes of conduct" in order to protect their vulnerable inner "creature."[113] Because Lethen's study focuses almost exclusively on men, he fails to satisfactorily address the question of whether or not women can successfully try on the mask of the "cool persona." Mammen, however, draws her female subjects in masks that bear an uncanny resemblance to Lethen's description of the "cool gaze," a squinting of the eyes into narrow slits: "The impulse to squint is transmitted simultaneously to the muscles that lower the upper lids and raise the lower ones, and again to the muscles that open the eyes. A more or less narrow slit remains open, resulting in the familiar image of eyes peering between nearly closed lids."[114] Anyone familiar with Mammen's work will immediately acknowledge that the "image of eyes peering between nearly closed lids" is a trademark of her women's faces. If, as Lethen argues, "character" in the age of New Objectivity "is a matter of what mask is put on," then Mammen's images of women who exude "cool conduct" imply that they were just as adept at trying on masks as male intellectuals and artists were.[115]

---

110. Sigrid Bauschinger, "The Berlin Moderns: Else Lasker-Schüler and Café Culture," in *Berlin Metropolis: Jews and the New Culture, 1890–1918,* ed. Emily D. Bilski (Berkeley: University of California Press, 2000), 80, 82. On Lasker-Schüler's experimentation with gender, see Christanne Miller, *Cultures of Modernism: Marianne Moore, Mina Loy, and Else Lasker-Schüler* (Ann Arbor: University of Michigan Press, 2005), 80–89. See also Jürgen Schebera, *Damals im Romanischen Café: Künstler und ihre Lokale im Berlin der zwanziger Jahre* (Berlin: Das neue Berlin, 2005); and Haustedt, *Die wilden Jahre,* 51–79.

111. Miller, *Cultures of Modernism,* 33. For comments about how sexuality was one of the main topics of conversation at Weimar-era cafés, especially in Berlin, see Hirschfeld, *Sittengeschichte der Nachkriegszeit,* 1:236.

112. Quoted in Rewald, *Glitter and Doom,* 148, emphasis added.

113. Lethen, *Cool Conduct,* 17–18.

114. Lethen, *Cool Conduct,* 105–6.

115. Lethen, *Cool Conduct,* 12.

Both Mammen's artworks and Moreck's guide foreground the central role that makeup and masquerade played in Berlin street life and nightlife.[116] Makeup was the element of fashion that served most to eroticize and feminize 1920s women, and its widespread use did contribute to the blurring of lines between prostitutes and nonprostitutes. Sabine Hake notes: "Until the war, only prostitutes and demi-mondaines wore makeup during the day."[117] But in Weimar Berlin, New Women started wearing rouge and foundation to work and more dramatic makeup at night. The more widespread use of cosmetics robbed them of their power to mark illicit sexuality. Describing women on the streets of Berlin-West, Moreck raises this very point about makeup, remarking: "Makeup used to be a label, but today it has become part of the cosmetic uniform of the female sex."[118] A label is generally used on products to reveal to the consumer what is hidden inside, and although it does not have the strong negative connotations of a stigma, it nevertheless implies a kind of fixed categorization imposed from the outside. A uniform conjures, on the one hand, the women's uniformity of appearance, their possible indistinguish-ability. On the other hand, a uniform is also an article of clothing that one puts on and takes off. Therefore, Moreck's observation suggests that the widespread use of makeup, combined with the loosening of moral codes, made it virtually impos-sible to stigmatize women's promiscuity. Instead women could use makeup as a mask—as a medium through which to try out different looks and attitudes—to experiment with androgyny, to be hyperfeminine, to be flirtatious, or to appear cool and detached. As Hake notes, there were different cosmetic "uniforms" for different spaces: a more natural, professional look for the workplace and a more dramatic, masklike one for bars, dance halls, or nightclubs.[119] This concept of put-ting on a different face to suit each attitude, occasion, or space is one that dispels the myth of an ontological female "essence," for, as the feminist film theorist Mary Ann Doane argues, "to claim that femininity is a function of the mask is to dismantle the question of essentialism before it can be posed."[120] Following Doane's lead, Mark Wigley joins theories of space with those of gender and sexuality by drawing paral-lels between architectural theories on the decorative facades of buildings and the use of makeup and masquerade by women. He writes: "The mechanisms of the

---

116. The references to makeup and the mask in Moreck's guides are too numerous to cite in the main body of this text; see Moreck, *Führer durch das "lasterhafte" Berlin,* 25, 38, 42, 148, 190 for makeup; and pp. 186–87, 212, 227 for discussions of masquerade.

117. Sabine Hake, "In the Mirror of Fashion," in Ankum, *Women in the Metropolis,* 189.

118. Moreck, *Führer durch das "lasterhafte" Berlin,* 42. Once again, the inability to distinguish be-tween "sex" and "gender" complicates the translation of Moreck's phrase, particularly when one consid-ers that, as evidenced by Moreck's description of the transvestite haven "Eldorado," makeup in Weimar Berlin was used not only by women to create a playful mask of femininity (148).

119. Hake, "In the Mirror of Fashion," 189.

120. Mary Ann Doane, *Femmes Fatales: Feminism, Film Theory, Psychoanalysis* (New York: Rout-ledge, 1991), 37. Of course Doane draws inspiration from Joan Riviere's 1929 essay, "Womanliness as Masquerade," reprinted in *Formations of Fantasy,* ed. Victor Burgin, James Donald, and Cora Kaplan (London: Routledge, 1986), 35–44.

production of gender can be exposed as such in order to make a space for woman. The 'decorative layer'...can be manipulated to produce other spacialities, which is to say, other sexualities."[121] Moreck's guide and its accompanying illustrations show its readers a multitude of spaces in which notions of fixed gender and sexual identity no longer apply; instead the Berlin he portrays is one of layers, masks, and makeup applied by the New Women and new men who inhabit it.

In Moreck's guide, even if the masks and the makeup that comprise them have been adopted by new generations of women, the prostitutes remain some of the ultimate performers described in the text. The boot girls perform dominance, the Tauentziengirls perform youthful extravagance, and the prostitutes who duck into the lesbian bar Café Olala to have a quiet drink with their girlfriends between shifts perform heterosexual desire for their male clients.[122] The possibilities afforded by the mask are a large part of Weimar emancipation, and self-stylization is an act in which many a New Woman and new man is shown to take part. In Moreck's text, the state of confusion that results from not being able to discern the truth behind the mask, to tell prostitutes from nonprostitutes, heterosexuals from homosexuals, and sometimes even men from women, does not inspire fear but rather constitutes an erotic thrill. Just how naughty was Berlin, and where did this naughtiness reside if not in this sense of erotic confusion? By calling Berlin's naughtiness into question in his own title, Moreck's work satirizes what it defines as outdated moral codes, such as those represented in Thomas Wehrling's essay "Berlin Is Becoming a Whore" and texts that would define Berlin as the metropolis of vice and its public women as whores. By holding fast to rigid definitions of gender and sexuality or by theorizing gender in the darkened, enclosed space of the cinema, even writers such as Brecht and Kracauer were incapable of seeing the sexual pleasures enjoyed by New Women and new men, who confused and delighted each other by wearing playful masks on the streets and in the clubs, cabarets, and cafés of Weimar Berlin.

Mixing and Mingling in Berlin-West

On a crisp November evening in 1925, one of the preeminent film critics of the Weimar Republic, Willy Haas, found himself in the midst of a tumultuous street scene in front of a Berlin cinema. The occasion was the premiere of Richard Oswald's latest film, *Halbseide* (Half-Silk), and the reason for the hubbub was that the event had been oversold by one hundred tickets. Much more interesting than the film itself, claims Haas in his review, was the urban crowd wrangling to get into the premiere. Mingling with newspaper critics and businessmen were

---

121. Mark Wigley, "Untitled: The Housing of Gender," in *Sexuality and Space,* ed. Beatriz Colomina (Princeton, NJ: Princeton Architectural Press, 1992), 386.
122. Moreck, *Führer durch das "lasterhafte" Berlin,* 25, 30–32, 166.

"tuxedoed men with women in bright brocade coats" and "little hookers from the Kantstrasse—who [were] rightfully interested in a subject that [had] more to do with them than with anyone else."[123] The subject that Haas imagines being of such great concern to the prostitutes in the crowd is, at least in part, betrayed by the film's title, *Half-Silk*. It is about the creation of erotic confusion through the blurring of class boundaries and moral boundaries. The film's promotional brochure explains the concept of "half-silk" in greater detail by describing how the film begins with a game between two men, played out on the streets of Berlin: "The men amused themselves by checking out the passing women and guessing their value, which in this case meant their willingness. They classified the women as they would a commodity. Silk, that was a society lady, cotton was a little bourgeois girl, but half-silk had that certain thrilling something, of which one couldn't quite discern if [she] still belonged to society or just to so-called society, or [if she] vacillated between the two." One of the two men decides to follow "a blond, who was elegantly, not ostentatiously, but yet coquettishly dressed," and after a series of misunderstandings that make up the film's convoluted plot, the men's canny ability to classify women by their sexual availability, or "willingness" (*Willigkeit*), is exposed as a sham.[124]

Most film critics at the time agreed that Oswald's *Half-Silk* was a playful, harmless film and primarily a commercial enterprise, but they also agreed that there was something intangible about it that captured Weimar Berlin to a tee. One critic proclaimed: "Oswald, the Ur-Berliner from Vienna, has once again brought a slice of Berlin milieu to the screen." Film scholars who have recently rediscovered Oswald argue that his works offer unrivaled insight into popular Weimar films and the tastes and whims of that era's mainstream audience.[125] Certainly the film's sold-out premiere and the colorful crowd outside the cinema, as described by Willy Haas, speak to Oswald's ability to draw a large audience, just as Weimar-era reviews of the film tell us something about that audience's fascination with Berlin's urban milieu. But what made this film by Richard Oswald a "Berlin film?" It had something to do with the open acknowledgment of uncertainty, but it also raised the possibility that uncertainty, or confusion, could have a pleasurable side, making Berlin—as Moreck would call it—"the confusing metropolis of pleasure." Perhaps it was the murky legibility or even indecipherability of visual cues such as makeup and clothing that used to demarcate sexually available women from "respectable" ones, perhaps it was the openness of urban spaces that placed "little

123. Willy Haas, *"Halbseide," Film-Kurier,* November 27, 1925. Oswald's film has been lost; only promotional materials, reviews, and censorship cards remain.

124. Promotional brochure for *Halbseide* (Vienna: Kino-Reclame-Verlag Gustav Kübart, 1925), 1, courtesy of the Schriftgutarchiv, SDK.

125. The quote comes from an unsigned review of *Halbseide, Reichsfilmblatt,* November 1925, no. 48, p. 21. In his review of the film, the well-known Weimar critic Walter Kaul simply states: "Oswald is the man of the present." *Berliner Börsen-Courier,* November 29, 1925. For current studies that emphasize Oswald's importance as maker of popular Weimar films, see Kasten and Loacker, *Richard Oswald,* 12; and Jeanpaul Goergen, introductory essay on Richard Oswald, *Filmblatt* 12, no. 34 (Summer 2007): 3.

hookers" shoulder to shoulder with newspapermen and elegant ladies, and perhaps it was the knowledge—informed by the experience of war, political upheaval, and inflation—that the fates of any of these urban figures could change in an instant. As one contemporary observer reported, "Those were the years in which the ladies of the middle- and higher- social classes felt that the thing to do was to look like a cocotte," and he goes on to quip that this trend caused prostitutes to stop wearing makeup just to distinguish themselves from other women.[126] It is this playful approach to the conflation of prostitutes and New Women that is often missing from current scholarship on Weimar, which tends to read prostitution as a simple trope for gendered exploitation. By looking beyond the dominant scholarly narrative on the Weimar Republic and examining the correspondence, film reviews, popular artworks, cabaret songs, and social commentary written by those who experienced the era for themselves, we find a response to prostitution in Berlin that complicates and transcends the dichotomy of victim and whore and that portrays an urban population that embraced, rather than rejected, changes in gender roles and a more audacious expression of sexuality.

---

126. Bruno Vogel, "Geschichte der Prostitution seit dem Kriegsende," in Hirschfeld, *Sittenge-schichte der Nachkriegszeit,* 2:91.

4

Working Girls: White-Collar Workers and Prostitutes in Late Weimar Fiction

In the later years of the Weimar Republic, public officials grappled with the overt expression of female sexuality and struggled to redefine prostitution in light of new public health legislation. On October 1, 1927, the Law to Combat Venereal Diseases (Reichsgesetz zur Bekämpfung der Geschlechtskrankheiten; RGBG) went into effect, and with it, prostitution was officially decriminalized. Former "morals police" still patrolled Berlin's streets to maintain public order, but the monitoring of public health and any threats to it was handed over to the capital city's main health office (Hauptgesundheitsamt; HGA). Under Clause 4 of the RGBG, the medical authorities of the HGA had the power to place individuals who were suspected of carrying and potentially spreading venereal diseases under "hygienic supervision" and to require those individuals to obtain a health certificate (*Gesundheitszeugnis*) that documented the status of their infection and treatment.[1] In contrast to the policies that had accompanied the state regulation of prostitution, the RGBG did not force prostitutes to undergo humiliating pelvic exams in public facilities; instead, it allowed them to be examined by a private physician of their choice. Berlin was, in fact, one of the only cities in the Weimar Republic to pay for its citizens to have

---

1. Roos, *Weimar through the Lens of Gender,* 91. The following information on the RGBG comes from my own archival research; from Roos, 1–3, 10, 90–96, 113, 160–62; and Timm, *The Politics of Fertility,* 58–65.

access to private physicians, making it possible for prostitutes and individuals with lesser means to maintain a modicum of privacy.

As both Julia Roos and Annette Timm have shown in their historical analyses of the 1927 law, by removing the focus from prostitutes as the primary spreaders of disease, the RGBG "signified an important break with regulationism's blatant double standard."[2] By offering medical treatment and emphasizing the prevention of venereal disease over harsh penalties for those who spread infections like syphilis and gonorrhea, the law encouraged male and female citizens alike to volunteer for medical screening at one of the city's many VD clinics and to use prophylactics during sexual intercourse. In the months and years immediately following the RGBG's passage, improvements were made to the law that catered to the demands of Berliners, who were, according to Timm, "a demanding and opinionated clientele." Responding to public demand, Berlin officials offered increased access to health care and birth control by opening clinics and advice centers (*Beratungsstellen*) in the city's various districts and allowing condom dispensers to be installed in men's lavatories. At least in the German capital, the number of men who voluntarily visited clinics for VD testing or treatment reached nearly 20,000 within the first years after the passage of the RGBG, and medical officials noted marked improvement in venereal health.[3] The success of the new law in Berlin did not mean, however, that its implementation was smooth. Concerned citizens decried the rise in unabashed sexual solicitation on the streets of Weimar Berlin, despite claims by prominent health officials and the magistrate that "a noticeable deterioration of conditions in the street cannot be substantiated."[4] Confusion remained regarding the role of the police in the enforcement of the RGBG, and public officials of various stripes were acutely aware of how easily the "hygienic supervision" of the populace, particularly of prostitutes, could lapse back into regulation.[5] As the following case shows, the police themselves were confused about their role in the preservation of public order and what might constitute a disruption of that order, especially when it came to audacious displays of female sexuality.

---

2. Roos, *Weimar through the Lens of Gender,* 3. See also Timm, *The Politics of Fertility,* 61.

3. Timm, *The Politics of Fertility,* 109. On the number and distribution of clinics throughout the city, see Timm, 103–17; and on the sale of prophylactics, especially condoms, 71–77. Citing a report by the DGBG's secretary Georg Loewenstein, Timm writes: "Eschewing forceful tactics had encouraged 20,000 (mostly male) voluntary visits to Berlin clinics, whereas cities still relying on social control measures directed at prostitution had seen virtually no voluntary compliance" (*The Politics of Fertility,* 64).

4. Berlin magistrate's 1929 report to the minister of the interior, GStA-PK I, HA Rep. 76, VIII B, Nr. 3831, p. 68.

5. It is worth noting, however, that even while the regulation of prostitution was still in force in the early years of the republic, Berlin police were fairly careful to distinguish between professional prostitutes and sexually active women. When citizens filed complaints with the police, alleging that certain entertainment establishments were simply covers for prostitution or that individual women were working as prostitutes, the police conducted thorough investigations and often found the allegations to be false. For detailed reports on citizens' complaints, the police investigations, and their findings, see the documents from 1921–25 in GStA-PK I, HA Rep. 77, Title 435, Nr. 6, especially pp. 121–23, pp. 159–60, pp. 178–82.

Late in the evening of January 21, 1928, several policemen were walking the beat on the Kurfürstendamm when four young women caught their attention. The women were standing on the sidewalk, their backs to the shop windows, calling out and gesturing to men who passed by, and according to the report filed by Berlin's police commissioner to the minister of public welfare, the women's gestures and calls served a clear purpose: "to entice male passersby to engage in sexual intercourse" with them. The commissioner's use of the word *Unzucht* makes sexual intercourse sound like an offense and serves to chastise the four women for their blatant engagement in sexual solicitation. On the grounds that the women were disturbing the peace, and on the mere suspicion that they might pose a threat to public health, the police officers brought the women to the precinct for questioning and forwarded their names to the main health office. Several months later, after an investigation of the matter, representatives from the health office responded to the police, not to express their gratitude, but rather to issue a stern reprimand. Despite the fact that all four women openly admitted to the police that they made their living as prostitutes, this provided no proper basis for detaining them, as a result of the recent passage of the RGBG. In fact, even though one of the four women was indeed registered with the health office and undergoing treatment for venereal infection, there was no reason for the police to suspect that the women constituted a threat to public heath. As the health authorities argued in their reply to the police, "the mere fact that these persons engage in habitual promiscuity does not give us the right to demand a health certificate from them."[6] The terms used by the HGA in its response to the police reflect a concerted effort to enforce the RGBG on gender-neutral terms and without a bias against prostitutes, for the document refers to the women as "persons" (*Personen*) and to their acts as "habitual promiscuity" (*häufig wechselnder Geschlechtsverkehr;* hwG) instead of prostitution. In Weimar social reform circles, especially before the passage of the RGBG, the designation of "hwG" was given to women who were identified as being at risk of entering into prostitution and/or who were engaging in sexual intercourse with multiple partners, but not in exchange for money. As Timm rightly points out, "The category of hwG was always somewhat ambiguous in that it was sometimes synonymous with prostitution and sometimes not."[7] From its emergence in the social reform discourse of the Weimar Republic, the term "hwG" was used to navigate the extremely murky waters between prostitution and promiscuity, but the intent behind its creation was to ensure that there was a term that differentiated between women who frequently engaged in sexual intercourse and those who did so for money.

---

6. The arrest of the four women and the response of the health office is documented in a report from the police commissioner to the minister of public welfare, GStA-PK I, HA Rep. 76, VIII B, Nr. 3831, p. 41.

7. Timm, *The Politics of Fertility,* 171. I have adopted Timm's translation of "hwG" as "habitually promiscuous."

Rather ironically, with the end of regulated prostitution and the decriminalization of unregulated prostitution that were part and parcel of the RGBG, "hwG"
could be used, as we see in the HGA's report, as a blanket term for self-designated
prostitutes and promiscuous *persons* alike (read: not just women). At least in theory,
however, this broader designation of "hwG-Personen" was meant both to protect
prostitutes from stigmatization and to protect all sexually active women from gender discrimination.

The case of the four women arrested on the Kurfürstendamm did not end with
the HGA's written reprimand of the police. It was discussed at length by Berlin's
municipal government in June 1928, and the politicians' lively debate reveals how
the RGBG and its implementation raised key issues regarding gender equality, the
public display of sexual prowess, and the definition of prostitution. Leftist women
like the Communist Party representative Margarete Hoffmann-Gwinner and the
Social Democrat Käte Frankenthal did not hide their dismay over the police's actions, which they saw as an indication of blatant gender discrimination. Dr. Frankenthal reminded her fellow delegates that the RGBG and its provisions for public
health "refer to *persons*, not to women specifically." She then asked, rhetorically:
"Where would it lead us if the police rounded up and alerted the health authorities
of all persons who were observed while hitting on a person of the opposite sex?"[8]
She went on to answer her own question by implying that there would be very few
men left on the streets of Berlin if the police's actions, as they were carried out against
the four women in question, were truly applied to all. Hoffmann-Gwinner boldly
proclaimed that the RGBG rendered prostitution, as a term connoting criminal or
morally reprehensible activity, obsolete: "According to the law there are no more
prostitutes.... Ladies and gentlemen, there is no more prostitution according to the
law, and there are also no more witch hunts. Consequently, young women can stand
together on the street as much as they want."[9] In her opinion, it was the policemen
who were disturbing the peace and offending social mores by taking the women into
custody, for this was an example of the old regulatory system rearing its ugly head.
Hoffmann-Gwinner's and Frankenthal's impassioned pleas for women's autonomy
garnered applause from their colleagues in the Berlin senate. After a spirited discussion, the senate concluded "that it is inappropriate for the police to take action
against persons who engage in habitual promiscuity."[10] Like the response from the
HGA to the police commissioner, the senate's statement to the magistrate used the
concept of "hwG-Personen" to convey the fact that, under the new law, prostitutes

---

8. Official stenographic report of the meeting of the Berlin city government (Amtlicher stenogra-
phischer Bericht über die Sitzung der Berliner Stadtverordnetenversammlung), June 28, 1928. GStA-
PK I, HA Rep. 76, VIII B, Nr. 3831, p. 48, emphasis added.
9. Stenographic report, meeting of the Berlin city government, June 28, 1928, p. 46.
10. Stenographic report, meeting of the Berlin city government, June 28, 1928, p. 54.

had the same rights as all female citizens of the republic, and that the public expression of sexual desire—be it by a man or a woman—was not a crime.

Just as the RGBG inspired debate within social reform and political circles in Berlin, it also empowered prostitutes to exercise their rights as female citizens. Working prostitutes petitioned local and federal officials if they found that the police were overstepping their bounds and arresting women erroneously.[11] For example, in response to repeated raids on their lodgings, prostitutes from the working-class neighborhood surrounding Alexanderplatz wrote a letter of protest to the minister of the interior in 1930. Asserting the prostitutes' right to provide "the common man" with the "opportunity for sexual intercourse," the letter's author complained that the raids were motivated by class bias. After all, she argued, the "Dirnen" of Berlin-West conducted their business just as publicly, and yet they remained unmolested. In a clever employment of the discourse of respectability, the Alexanderplatz prostitutes claimed: "We conduct ourselves with discretion on the streets, while those in the better districts display brazen wantonness." The women of the Kurfürstendamm, whose arrest had caused such a stir in the Berlin senate just two years earlier, were now, according to the humbler prostitutes of Berlin-North, given free rein in the streets. Although there is no indication that the letter caused the raids to cease, the women of Alexanderplatz did receive a written apology from the minister.[12]

As these documents from the years immediately following the passage of the RGBG show, the discourse on prostitution was shaped by a variety of players, and complex negotiations regarding sexual behavior and its regulation took place between police, citizens, and politicians. Strikingly, both the prostitutes' petition and the Berlin senate's debate and decision demonstrate how the blurring of boundaries between working prostitutes and other publicly visible women could actually be used to defend women's rights rather than to curtail them. This chapter shows how a variety of social actors in late Weimar Berlin, most of whom were women, engaged in this type of strategic conflation of prostitutes with urban "working girls" in order to explore both the limits and the possibilities of female emancipation. Prostitutes asserted their rights to be treated like normal working women, while elected officials and authors of popular fiction fought to safeguard women's sexual freedom. Through open discussions and complex representations of "hwG" persons, politicians and writers revealed how prostitution, just like the law that decriminalized it, was intimately connected to issues of labor, public comportment, sexual choice, and gender parity.

11. The fact that the RGBG provided prostitutes with "new rights of legal redress" is one of the key arguments that Roos makes in *Weimar through the Lens of Gender,* especially pp. 10, 92.

12. Letter from the prostitutes of the District Alexanderplatz to the minister of the interior, April 1930, GStA-PK I, HA Rep. 77, Title 435, Nr. 6, pp. 239–40. In accordance with German privacy laws, I have withheld the name of the author. Roos cites this letter as well in *Weimar through the Lens of Gender,* 94, and I am indebted to her for directing me to this document.

Half-Silks and White-Collar Bohemians

If, with the passage of the RGBG, prostitutes were no longer legally different from habitually promiscuous women, then certainly the reverse was also true, making it even more difficult to distinguish between prostitutes and other sexually active women. It was against this social backdrop that authors, artists, and cultural critics in Weimar Berlin produced complex representations of prostitutes, working women, and desire. They did so by depicting women who are best described as "half-silks," to use the title of Richard Oswald's popular film: women whose appearance and sexual behavior made them difficult to categorize, both sexually and socioeconomically speaking.[13] "Half-silks," as the name implies, are women who can probably not afford to be draped in silk from head to toe, but they are fashionable, flirtatious, and visible figures within the urban landscape. Many of them are—as Siegfried Kracauer and Bertolt Brecht imagined the composition of the Weimar film audience—secretaries and shopgirls with dreams of big-city glitz and glamour who supplement their meager salaries by actively seeking generous suitors. By using their bodies as commodities, these "half-silks" are figures that exemplify just how blurred the lines between prostitutes and nonprostitutes had become during the Weimar era.

One prominent cultural critic who merged images of shopgirls and secretaries with those of prostitutes was Siegfried Kracauer. His groundbreaking study *Die Angestellten* (The White-Collar Workers, 1930) documents and analyzes the lives of white-collar workers both in- and outside the workplace, and many of his case studies focus on women.[14] The rationalization of the German workplace during the Weimar Republic caused a shift in the type of work open to women and placed them "at the forefront: in assembly-line factories; in mechanized offices with typewriters, filing cabinets, and switchboards; behind the sales counters of chain stores."[15] Young, single, and employed, by 1930 these women constituted one-third of the 3.5 million white-collar workers in Germany and almost half of Berlin's white-collar workforce. Images of the female white-collar worker were basically

---

13. See chapter 3 for a more extensive discussion of Oswald's *Half-Silk* (1925).

14. Siegfried Kracauer, *Die Angestellten: Aus dem neuesten Deutschland*, translated by Quintin Hoare as *The Salaried Masses: Duty and Distraction in Weimar Germany* (London: Verso, 1998). Kracauer's study was first published as a series of essays in the *Frankfurter Zeitung* in 1929 and 1930 and was subsequently published in book form. Although I have chosen to use Hoare's translation of the main text and will therefore cite its title in subsequent footnotes, I prefer Sabine Hake's translation of the work's title, *The White-Collar Workers,* and will refer to Kracauer's book as such in the body of my text. See Hake's discussion of *Die Angestellten* in *Topographies of Class,* 72–74.

15. Grossmann, *Reforming Sex,* 6. The aim of rationalization was to heighten productivity while lowering costs—efficiency made possible through increased mechanization (use of machine versus human labor). For more on the impact of American production processes on German business, see Mary Nolan, *Visions of Modernity: American Business and the Modernization of Germany* (New York: Oxford University Press, 1994). For further discussion of the shifts in women's work resulting in a marked increase in clerical workers, see Frevert, *Women in German History,* 177.

synonymous with those of the New Woman or Girl, and they dominated the visual and print culture of the mid- to late Weimar period, adorning the pages of illustrated magazines in colorful advertisements, and appearing as protagonists in popular novels and films.[16] Like the prostitute, the white-collar woman elicited a variety of competing responses from cultural critics and social activists. Her perceived lack of interest in getting married and starting a family, combined with her carefree penchant for urban nightlife, caused many to view her with skepticism, concern, and even alarm. As shown in chapter 3, the public visibility of these women extended beyond the shop or office; donning the latest fashions, sporting makeup and modern hairdos, they appeared both escorted and unescorted in cinemas, cafés, nightclubs, and crowded streets—spaces that had traditionally been associated with prostitution. In the minds of some Weimar-era observers, white-collar workers and prostitutes were not just physically proximate; they were one and the same. Such assumptions were, without a doubt, exaggerated and difficult to prove. However, as Roos's research shows, empirical data gathered in the mid-1920s does provide evidence that the job of "salesclerk" was the fourth most common occupational identity listed by prostitutes in Berlin, and physicians' interviews conducted with prostitutes in other large German cities such as Cologne revealed that poorly paid white-collar workers turned to prostitution for "economic incentives" and out of "the desire for a more independent and exciting life."[17] It is precisely this type of young woman—the woman in search of "a more independent and exciting life"— that Kracauer portrays in *The White-Collar Workers* as one of "a few choice specimens," as he characterizes her in the title of the chapter in which his description of a white-collar bohemian appears. By depicting himself as an explorer, botanist, and astronomer, Kracauer employs the language of natural science, thereby presenting white-collar workers as scientific specimens deserving closer inspection and giving

---

16. The statistics on white-collar workers in Germany and particularly in Berlin are taken from Kracauer, *The Salaried Masses*, 29; and Frevert, *Women in German History*, 177–79. My characterization of the female white-collar worker as New Woman or Girl is supported by various sources, most prominently by Grossmann, "The New Woman and the Rationalization of Sexuality"; and Grossmann, "*Girlkultur* or Thoroughly Rationalized Female: A New Woman in Weimar Germany?," in *Women in Culture and Politics: A Century of Change*, ed. Judith Friedlander, Blanche Wiesen Cook, Alice Kessler-Harris, and Carroll Smith-Rosenberg (Bloomington: Indiana University Press, 1986), 62–80. See also Elke Kupschinsky, "Die vernünftige Nephertete," in Boberg, Fichter, and Gillen, *Die Metropole*, 164–73; and Vibeke Rützou Petersen, *Women and Modernity in Weimar Germany: Reality and Representation in Popular Fiction* (New York: Berghahn, 2001), 51, 78. For analyses of white-collar women in print media, advertising, and popular literature, see Kerstin Barndt, *Sentiment und Sachlichkeit: Der Roman der Neuen Frau in der Weimarer Republik* (Cologne: Böhlau, 2003); Petro, *Joyless Streets*; and Janet Ward, *Weimar Surfaces: Urban Visual Culture in 1920s Germany* (Berkeley: University of California Press, 2001). The female secretary, particularly the private executive secretary, became a stock figure in the so-called *Angestelltenfilme* of the late Weimar Republic, including Richard Oswald's *Arm wie eine Kirchenmaus* (Poor as a Church Mouse, 1930) and Wilhelm Thiele's *Die Privatsekretärin* (The Private Secretary, 1931). On these films, see Angelika Führich, "Woman and Typewriter: Gender, Technology, and Work in Late Weimar Film," *Women in German Yearbook* 16 (2000): 151–66.

17. Roos, *Weimar through the Lens of Gender*, 74, 76.

his own narrative a veneer of objectivity. And yet some specimens seem to baffle or agitate the author/scientist so much that his appearance of objectivity is compromised and his ambivalence revealed. This ambivalence is particularly evident when he is confronted with women of the "salaried-bohemian" type, mobile adventurers who reject their bourgeois family backgrounds to come to Berlin and carouse with artists and students. Kracauer describes them as

> girls who come to the big city in search of adventure and roam like comets through the world of salaried employees. Their career is unpredictable and even the best astronomer cannot determine whether they will end up on the street or in the marriage bed. A perfect example of this genus is the nice manufacturer's daughter from western Germany who often resides in the Romanische Café. She likes it better there than with her family, from which she ran away one fine day.... Better too than in the big firm where she works at an adding machine for 150 Marks a month. What is one to do, if one wants to live, really live, and does not get the smallest allowance from home? To be sure, she wants to get herself a higher position and will do so; but office work for her is still always only the indispensable condition of the freedom she wants to enjoy. After closing time, at home in her furnished room, she first gulps down a strong coffee to freshen her up again, then it is off and away into the midst of life, to the students and artists with whom there is chatter and smoking and canoeing. More than that probably happens too. After a short while, she will disappear.[18]

Kracauer's comparison of the white-collar bohemian to a comet—an object that has inspired both fear and wonder in its observers for centuries—appropriately marks the tension that exists between the author's fascination with the woman's path (her orbit) and his rhetorical gestures to steer or determine that path. On the one hand, the passage seems to express sympathy for the woman's desire to escape a stifling bourgeois provincial lifestyle, to want something more than a meager monthly salary of 150 marks, and to strive for freedom and adventure in the metropolis. On the other, Kracauer begins the passage by speculating about the two possible ends to the woman's lightning-speed journey through the city: marriage or prostitution. Thereby, he winds up describing not an erratic orbit but a linear trajectory from bourgeois home to urban office job to café to either street or marriage bed. The young woman's flirtatious, permissive behavior in the café implies that she is more likely to end up "on the street." What seems to matter to the author is not these women's orbits—their experimental exploration of the urban universe—but rather their catastrophic crash.

This passage from Kracauer's *Angestellten* is paradigmatic in several ways. It is indicative of Kracauer's tendency to rhetorically deny white-collar workers—

---

18. Kracauer, *The Salaried Masses*, 73.

especially women—self-awareness and agency.[19] Like comets, their paths are often determined by external forces; they are easily swayed. The passage's emphasis on the erotic element of female office workers' lives is also typical for its time; particularly in its description of the young woman's flirtatious behavior with the "students and artists" in the café, it perpetuates the stereotype of the working girl as an object of male desire and hints that she might be a desiring subject as well. Finally, the passage from Kracauer's book reveals its ambivalence toward female sexuality by channeling it back toward the traditional dichotomy of bourgeois wife and whore. And yet, the author does not stage the white-collar bohemian's crash for his readers. The publicly visible, thrill-seeking, desiring woman simply vanishes from sight by the end of the passage, leaving it up to the reader to decide her probable fate.

It was not just male cultural critics like Kracauer who contemplated the blurred boundaries between prostitutes and New Women; women artists and writers did so as well. This chapter examines popular fictional texts by women authors that present readers with diverse forms of commodified sexuality, some of which can easily be classified as prostitution—the performance of sexual activities for money or material gain—and others that involve the conscious use of the female body or sexual allure to the same ends, such as posing naked or hustling men for free drinks and clothing. As Marsha Meskimmon demonstrates in her study of female visual artists in Weimar Germany, women artists tended to paint or draw prostitutes "as individualized and ordinary working women rather than as highly stylized images of decadence or seduction." This was not merely an attempt to apply some measure of dignity to the image of the prostitute; the prostitutes in these artworks "became the subject of a large-scale renegotiation of terms. Far from seeking to define a singular and homogenous symbol of woman through the representation of sex workers, women artists grappled with numerous issues raised by prostitution and commodified female sexuality in multiple contexts."[20] This very approach to prostitution is found in two of the most popular novels written by women in late Weimar Berlin: Vicki Baum's *Menschen im Hotel* (Grand Hotel, 1929) and Irmgard Keun's *Das kunstseidene Mädchen* (The Artificial Silk Girl, 1932). By examining the conflation of white-collar woman and prostitute in the figures of Flämmchen and Doris in Baum's and Keun's novels, respectively, my analysis shows that these figures offer both critical insights into white-collar employment *and* provocative depictions of "commodified sexuality in multiple contexts" that move beyond sexual deviance or social victimization. In their complex representation of commodified sexuality, Baum's and Keun's works simultaneously acknowledge the limits

---

19. Janet Ward, *Weimar Surfaces,* 34, describes Kracauer's writing as "ostensibly in league with, yet at times transparently condescending toward, the mass Other (particularly when that Other is gendered female)."

20. Meskimmon, *We Weren't Modern Enough,* 33, 29.

placed on women's emancipation and explore the possibilities for their financial and sexual autonomy. In both novels, prostitution is not a simple sign of the female protagonist's failure, as most current scholars have read it. Instead, it is portrayed by Baum as a more profitable option than white-collar work and a legitimate "way of getting on" in a modern urban society teetering on the brink of economic disaster.[21] In Keun's witty novel, Doris's resistance to being defined from the outside as a prostitute invites readers to examine more closely her numerous financial and sexual negotiations and to identify moments of autonomous female desire. Analyzing the blurred lines between prostitutes and New Women, then, provides a discursive space in which women artists and authors and the viewers or readers of their works can contemplate various experiences of urban life, economies of desire, and the opportunities and limitations of women's work.

Destinies beyond Typewriters: A Study of Flämmchen

Vicki Baum's novel *Menschen im Hotel,* serialized in the *Berliner Illustrierte Zeitung (BIZ)* and subsequently published by Ullstein Press in 1929, became "one of the most successful popular culture products ever created by a German-language writer."[22] Set in an opulent hotel in Berlin, the novel entangles the fates of a disparate group of strangers: the aging ballerina, Grusinskaya, and the charming, impoverished aristocrat-turned-thief, Baron von Gaigern, who fall in love on the very night that Gaigern plans to steal Grusinskaya's prized pearls; the maimed war veteran, Dr. Otternschlag, a lonely morphine addict who lives at the Grand Hotel; the

---

21. Corbin, *Women for Hire,* 364. I will engage with the works of specific scholars in my subsequent interpretation of each novel.

22. Lynda J. King, "*Menschen im Hotel/Grand Hotel:* Seventy Years of a Popular Culture Classic," *Journal of American and Comparative Cultures* 23, no. 2 (Summer 2000): 17. See also Sabina Becker, "Großstädtische Metamorphosen: Vicki Baums Roman *Menschen im Hotel,*" *Jahrbuch zur Literatur der Weimarer Republik: Frauen in der Literatur der Weimarer Republik,* ed. Sabina Becker (St. Ingbert: Röhrig, 2000), 167–69.

Hedwig (Vicki) Baum was born in 1888 to a middle-class Jewish family in Vienna. While studying harp at the Vienna Conservatory (1904–10), she began writing short stories, several of which she published in German magazines under the surname of her first husband, Max Prels. In 1912 she divorced Prels, left Vienna, and took a position in the Darmstadt city orchestra. She married the orchestra's conductor, Richard Lert, in 1916, bearing two sons during the First World War. The economic hardship of the war and postwar years convinced her to take up writing again, and she began publishing books with the Ullstein Press in 1920. In 1926 she moved to Berlin and signed an exclusive contract with Ullstein. From then on, she wrote short topical pieces for the publisher's illustrated newspapers and magazines (*Berliner Illustrirte Zeitung, Die Dame,* and *Uhu*) and wrote five serialized novels for the *BIZ* between 1926 and 1932. She also took regular boxing lessons from the Turkish trainer Sabri Mahir. The ominous political climate in Germany motivated Baum's emigration to the United States in 1932, which was expedited by her connections to the film industry. She continued to write magazine articles, novels for Doubleday press, and screenplays for various Hollywood studios until her death in Los Angeles in 1960, yet none of her works equaled the success of *Menschen im Hotel / Grand Hotel.* Biographical information on Vicki Baum comes from Baum's own memoir, *Es war alles ganz anders* (Berlin: Ullstein, 1962); and Nicole Nottelmann, *Die Karrieren der Vicki Baum: Eine Biographie* (Cologne: Kiepenheuer & Witsch, 2007).

provincial textile industrialist, Preysing, who purchases the secretarial services of Fräulein Flamm (a.k.a. "Flämmchen") for an important set of meetings at the hotel; and Otto Kringelein, an underpaid and fatally ill bookkeeper from Preysing's company, who has come to Berlin to live out his last days in luxury. It is a quintessential Berlin novel. It portrays the tempo of urban life through the nonstop comings and goings of people in the hotel lobby, the transitory relationships, and the swift reversals of fortune, all set to the din of ringing telephones and the sounds of a jazz band. The novel's success in Great Britain and the United States—it became an instant best seller after Doubleday published it under the title of *Grand Hotel* in 1931— made it ripe for a Hollywood script, and there can be no doubt that Baum's international success was sealed by MGM's 1932 Academy Award–winning film *Grand Hotel* starring Greta Garbo, John and Lionel Barrymore, and Joan Crawford.

Despite—or perhaps because of—its immense success, recent scholarship has given *Menschen im Hotel* little critical attention. Those secondary works that do analyze *Menschen im Hotel* focus primarily on defending the integrity of Baum's literary production.[23] Lynda J. King documents the novel's various incarnations, explaining their deviations from the original by examining the sexual politics of the time and place in which they were produced (i.e., the Weimar stage production, the 1930s Hollywood film, the 1950s German film, and the 1980s Broadway musical). It was the character of Flämmchen, who supplements her income as a temporary stenotypist with nude photo shoots and occasional prostitution, that was most often transformed—even censored—in the various adaptations of the novel. An unabashedly erotic figure, Flämmchen appeared naked on stage in the 1930 theatrical adaptation by Gustaf Gründgens at Berlin's Theater am Nollendorfplatz. Although the Berlin audience raised no objections to Flämmchen's peccadilloes, subsequent stage and screen adaptations for both American and German audiences eliminated her nudity and muted her sexual audacity.[24] But was it simply Flämmchen's naked body and sexual activity that needed to be hidden from audiences? What was it exactly that made Baum's depiction of Flämmchen so controversial?

---

23. King tries to depart from terms like *Trivialliteratur* and *Kitsch* by arguing that Baum's works occupy a literary space between "high" and "low" artistic production. See King's book-length study, *Best-Sellers by Design: Vicki Baum and the House of Ullstein* (Detroit: Wayne State University Press, 1988), 147. Kerstin Barndt documents how works by Baum were classified in their day, and thereby highlights the concept of the "gutgemacht[en] Mittleren" (well-made middle-brow literature) in *Sentiment und Sachlichkeit*, 22. Most scholarship on Vicki Baum concentrates on Ullstein's campaign to make her a best-selling author with a public profile as a New Woman, her life and work in U.S. exile, or her earlier novel, *stud. chem. Helene Willfüer*, giving short shrift to *Grand Hotel*. Even the newest scholarly works on *Grand Hotel* are devoted either to its aesthetic defense or to an analysis of its setting. See Becker, "Großstädtische Metamorphosen"; and Bettina Matthias, *The Hotel as Setting in Early 20th-Century German and Austrian Literature* (Rochester, NY: Camden House, 2006), 173–98, respectively. None of these works focuses exclusively on the character of Flämmchen, as my reading does.

24. Lynda J. King, "*Grand Hotel*: The Sexual Politics of a Popular Culture Classic," *Women in German Yearbook* 15 (2000): 187–89. See also Becker, "Großstädtische Metamorphosen," 178.

In the novel, Flämmchen first appears in the Grand Hotel as a personal typist hired by Preysing. She immediately fits both the physical image and the personality profile of the New Woman or Girl: Young and slim with an athletic figure, she wears makeup, perfume, and a stylish felt hat over her curly bobbed hair. Cool, rational, and unflappable, she prefers brief, casual relationships with men. As the narrator tells us, Flämmchen "picked up acquaintances the way you light a cigarette. You take a couple of drags, just the number that taste good, and then you extinguish it, treading out the last sparks."[25] Perhaps it is this cavalier attitude toward relationships and sex that causes King to characterize Flämmchen as "one of the many women in 1920s literature who on the surface represented emancipation, but actually were still portrayed as objects to be used by men or as ready willingly to submit to male domination in traditional relationships."[26] My reading of Flämmchen contradicts King's assessment by arguing that Flämmchen is a figure who resists male domination rather than "willingly submitting" to it. Indeed Flämmchen proves, in her interactions with Preysing, Gaigern, and Kringelein, to be the most modern character in the novel. With Preysing she is both a personal secretary and an escort who knows how to use her body for financial gain. When flirting and dancing the tango with Gaigern, she is a sexual agent unafraid to express her desires. But just as my reading runs counter to King's assertion of Flämmchen's submissiveness, it also challenges Vibeke Petersen's somewhat exaggerated analysis of Flämmchen as an "unfettered, free-floating libido" or "as the novel's metaphor for vice," for Baum's novel depicts her as pragmatic enough to know when and how to control her own desire.[27] Unsentimental as she may be, she shows compassion and sympathy for her fellow white-collar worker, Kringelein, who in the end becomes her companion. The novel's objective narrative tone resists passing moral judgment on Flämmchen, and it avoids making her a victim. Instead, it offers to its readers the possibility of a woman who can be many things—a desiring woman and a sympathetic companion, a typist, and a prostitute.

As one sees in Flämmchen's working relationship with Preysing, the bonds she forms are far from traditional. Although the power dynamics between boss and personal secretary are often perceived to be those of male domination and female exploitation, an assumption that categorically denies female agency, Flämmchen proves to be an astute businesswoman as she actively negotiates with Preysing for a more long-term and lucrative contract. Fully aware of her physical allure, she consciously portrays herself to Preysing as an erotic object while still maintaining

25. Vicki Baum, *Menschen im Hotel* (1929; repr., Cologne: Kiepenheuer & Witsch, 2002), 84; the physical description of Flämmchen appears on pp. 80–81. For my translations of Baum's texts, I consulted the 1931 English translation but made changes when necessary to best capture the tone of the German original. For the quoted passage, see Vicki Baum, *Grand Hotel*, trans. Basil Creighton (Garden City, NY: Doubleday, Doran & Company, 1931), 79.

26. King, *Best-Sellers by Design*, 193.

27. Petersen, *Women and Modernity*, 37, 63.

the upper hand in their negotiation. Typing a document for Preysing, she baits her hook, insinuating that she is perfectly willing to use her body as a commodity in exchange for money and adventure. She explains: "I'm often photographed for the newspapers and so on, for soap advertisements as well....I look very good in the nude, you know. But the pay is horrible. Ten marks a photo. Just imagine that. No, the best thing would be if someone would take me on a trip as his secretary this spring. Last year I was with a gentleman in Florence...Oh, well, something else will turn up this year too."[28] Flämmchen's strategy is clever. First she entices Preysing by encouraging him to imagine her naked body. Then she gains his sympathy by mentioning how little she is paid for posing nude. Having demonstrated her need for work, she presses on, expressing her wish to work as someone's personal secretary—preferably in an exotic location. Her last sentence—uttered in the future indicative rather than the wishful subjunctive or the passive—shows her determination to find work, and can even be read as a command: "Something else *will* turn up this year." By planting an erotic image of herself in Preysing's mind, she implies that she is willing to combine her secretarial services with sexual services.

Her plan works: Preysing becomes conscious of his desire for her. The day after their first meeting, he opens an illustrated magazine and discovers one of Flämmchen's nude photos. Mesmerized by the sight of her body, in his mind he begins to merge the images of secretary and sexual commodity: "Preysing kept hold of the magazine, lay back and closed his eyes. At first there was only red; then he saw Flämmchen. Not the clothed Flämmchen at the typewriter and not the unclothed Flämmchen in the black-and-white photograph, but *an incredibly exciting mixture of both*."[29] In this passage, the author Baum exposes the male fantasy of the eroticized woman office worker and the impulse to control and possess her as an object of sexual desire. The photograph, an effective advertisement, makes Preysing want to have what he sees. "He was done with looking. He wanted to grasp and feel."[30] But although Preysing immediately sets off to proposition Flämmchen, he finds her otherwise occupied, dancing an erotically charged tango with Baron von Gaigern, the man she actually desires.[31] When she and Preysing finally make a deal, it is Flämmchen who controls the arrangement: she names her price, and she makes it clear that sexual activity will happen only on her own terms. When Preysing tries to convince her to perform his fantasy of the half-clad office worker by requesting that she stand before him wearing only her stockings and heels, she refuses with a flat no. Flämmchen's behavior makes it clear that despite

28. Baum, *Grand Hotel*, 80–81; *Menschen im Hotel*, 85.
29. Baum, *Grand Hotel*, 209; *Menschen im Hotel*, 216–17, emphasis added.
30. Baum, *Grand Hotel*, 210; *Menschen im Hotel*, 217.
31. Baum, *Grand Hotel*, 214; *Menschen im Hotel*, 222. In this dance that oozes sensuality, the intimate contact between Gaigern and Flämmchen is emphasized by such words as *verschwistern* (used in reference to their thighs), which implies their mutual consent as well as their physical closeness, and *schmachten*, which underscores their intense desire.

Preysing's obvious desire for her, their relationship is a business arrangement; for her, sex with Preysing is part of her work. She has entered into the contract after "a clear and unsentimental survey of the chances the job offered her," weighing the suppression of her own desire for an "affair with the handsome Baron" against the material advantages of an arrangement with Preysing.[32] Pragmatically, she thinks to herself: "After all, a respectable person couldn't take a thousand marks and a journey to England and a new coatdress and various other perks and give nothing in return."[33] This sentence clearly reveals Flämmchen's view of her sexuality as an exchangeable commodity. But the most remarkable part of this passage is Baum's ironic, humorous use of the rhetoric of *respectability* in favor (rather than in judgment) of prostitution. The reference to Flämmchen as "a respectable person" (*ein anständiger Mensch*) consciously plays with the bourgeois concept of *Anständigkeit,* associating it with the act of making a fair trade. The fact that the fair trade in this context is actually a sex trade subverts traditional bourgeois notions of sexual morality—a value system that was shaken by late Wilhelmine reformers and cultural figures and was severely damaged by the First World War—and thereby dissociates respectability from normative sexual behavior.[34] As fair as her deal with the industrialist may seem, however, there is a bigger and more "respectable" deal in store for Flämmchen.

Unable to fulfill her contract with Preysing, who, in a complex and surprising turn of events, is arrested for Gaigern's murder, Flämmchen enters into a relationship with the accountant Kringelein that is both financially advantageous and comradely. The novel's pairing of the sexy, youthful Flämmchen with the feeble, ailing bookkeeper Kringelein certainly seems far-fetched. Yet Baum's strategy is actually quite cunning, for it is neither the gallant Baron von Gaigern nor the famous ballerina, Grusinskaya, who elicits the most sympathy from the novel's readers—it is the white-collar worker Kringelein.[35] He arrives at the hotel weakened by illness and carrying his pension money in a paper bag; he is the ultimate underdog. King attributes the book's tremendous success in part to the figure of Kringelein, whose "background and social class were chosen to make him especially relevant" to the (lower) middle-class, white-collar readership of the *BIZ.*[36] If Kringelein is the primary figure of reader identification, then his affection for Flämmchen gains the sympathy and understanding of the reader as well—sympathy for her social struggle and understanding for the choices she makes in order to remain relatively

---

32. Baum, *Grand Hotel,* 221–22; *Menschen im Hotel,* 229. The negotiations between Flämmchen and Preysing take place on pp. 228–31, 273–78 in the German original and pp. 220–23, 264–69 in the English translation.

33. Baum, *Grand Hotel,* 265; *Menschen im Hotel,* 274.

34. For a late Wilhelmine example of how cultural performers mocked the concept of *Anständigkeit,* see my reading of Kurt Tucholsky's 1913 essay "Massary" in chapter 3.

35. On Kringelein as the "unacknowledged protagonist of the novel," see Matthias, *The Hotel as Setting,* 188.

36. King, *Best-Sellers by Design,* 161.

autonomous. Upon closer examination, the pairing of Kringelein and Flämmchen makes perfect sense; after all, they are colleagues in the world of underpaid, insecure white-collar work.

Although most white-collar workers perceived themselves as middle class, their income—an average monthly salary of 120 marks for women and 150 marks for men—placed them in closer proximity to the working class, leaving them in a socioeconomic no-man's-land. Even before the world economic crisis hit in the autumn of 1929, the lack of job security permeated all levels of white-collar work in Germany, and rationalization was one of the main causes of this insecurity. Fordism, for example, broke down the production process into a series of functions or tasks, replacing skilled with unskilled labor. Kracauer underscored the lack of advanced training and skill required for white-collar work by arguing that it could not be defined as a "vocation" (*Beruf*) but rather as a series of "jobs" or "positions" (*Stellen*), like places on an assembly line that can be vacated and filled as needed.[37] The situation was precarious for both men and women, but it was especially so for aging male employees like Baum's fictional character Kringelein. As Kracauer's study shows, youth and beauty were prized over skill and intelligence and were therefore stipulations for finding and/or keeping a white-collar job. He describes the employees' desperate rush to the beauty salons and makeup counters in their efforts to look young at all costs. "For fear of being withdrawn from use as obsolete, ladies *and* gentlemen dye their hair, while forty-year-olds take up sports to keep slim."[38] Kracauer's emphasis on the "and" in "ladies *and* gentlemen" makes it clear that women are not the only ones being judged by their looks. Men, too, are subjected to the objectifying gazes of both their employers and their customers. Arguing that job security was drawn primarily along age rather than gender lines, Kracauer shows how white-collar work, with its emphasis on a youthful and attractive appearance, narrowed the gender gap between male and female employees. Both were potentially "feminized" by the discerning stares of their superiors and the stark realities of a volatile job market.[39]

In *Grand Hotel*, Baum reveals the empathy between her two white-collar characters through a conversation in which Kringelein asks Flämmchen why she became intimately involved with Preysing. In her matter-of-fact way, Flämmchen answers: "For money, of course." Kringelein does not question her further. He does not need to: "Kringelein understood at once. 'For money...' he replied, not as a

37. For a profile of white-collar workers' salaries, class identity, and the effects of rationalization on their sense of security, see Kracauer, *The Salaried Masses*, 29–31, 34–37. For the original German, see Kracauer, *Die Angestellten*, 11–13, 19–20. See also Hake, *Topographies of Class*, 69–70; and Weitz, *Weimar Germany*, 155–59. Weitz points out the downside of rationalization, showing that "while wages did rise between 1924 and 1929, so did unemployment" (152).

38. Kracauer, *The Salaried Masses*, 39, emphasis in original.

39. As McCormick, *Gender and Sexuality*, 85, claims, to be unwittingly "exposed to the gaze of others...is clearly to lose power (and thus to become 'feminized')."

question, but more like an answer. His life had been a struggle to make ends meet, so how could he fail to understand Flämmchen?"[40] This moment of understanding between Kringelein and Flämmchen dissolves any sense of moral reprehensibility that Kringelein may have projected on Flämmchen's relations with Preysing. His reaction to her answer portrays them as equals, partners in the "struggle to make ends meet," both determined to survive and even eke some pleasure out of life. It is this moment that seals their union, not a "traditional" union characterized by "male domination," but one based on mutual understanding and emotional security.[41] In keeping with the nontraditional definition of respectability proposed by the text, however, Flämmchen retains a certain degree of socioeconomic pragmatism in her bond to Kringelein. After all, she is set to reap the financial benefits of his recent gambling win—3,400 marks. The final pages of the novel may portray the little man Kringelein leaving the hotel "like a king," but it is Flämmchen who has made her best deal yet: a trip to England, new clothes, triple the amount of money offered her by Preysing, and an intimate companion.[42] Flämmchen's decision to leave the Grand Hotel on Kringelein's arm is not one based on sentiment or traditional values, but a rational choice to improve her fortune and take comfort in a relationship that is both emotionally *and* financially secure, no matter how long it may last.

In the character of Flämmchen, the novel creates—yet does not condemn—a woman who uses her body for profit, be it in nude photographs or as a female escort. Indeed *Grand Hotel* presents prostitution as a more lucrative alternative to white-collar work. As the following passage illustrates, Flämmchen recognizes that her body is worth far more than her office work: "She knew her price. Twenty marks for a nude photograph. A hundred and forty marks for a month's worth of office work. Fifteen cents per page of typing with carbon copy. A fur coat worth two hundred and forty marks for a week of physical surrender."[43] By comparing Flämmchen's earnings or "price" for each task, the passage reveals sex ("physical surrender," or *Hingabe*) to have the highest material value, allowing Flämmchen to earn more in one week than she would earn for a month of office work. In its comparison of white-collar jobs with prostitution, Baum's novel subtly documents and criticizes the meager pay, minimal benefits, and lack of security involved in white-collar work. The way Baum chooses to list these jobs—posing naked for advertisements (which some would consider pornography), office work, a page of dictation, sexual intercourse—presents them all as *work*. Most important, however, is the way Baum presents Flämmchen throughout the novel; she is neither victim nor whore

---

40. Baum, *Grand Hotel,* 283; *Menschen im Hotel,* 293.
41. If anything, Flämmchen is portrayed as the dominant figure in this pairing. Earlier in the novel, during their first meeting in the dance hall, it is Flämmchen who takes the lead when she dances with Kringelein. See Baum, *Grand Hotel,* 219; *Menschen im Hotel,* 227.
42. Baum, *Grand Hotel,* 288, 305; *Menschen im Hotel,* 298, 316.
43. Baum, *Grand Hotel,* 287; *Menschen im Hotel,* 297.

but a savvy, determined young woman who is very aware of the trade-offs involved in the work she takes. She is a self-conscious commodity, a figure who is fully aware of male desires to see her as an erotic object, and who consciously manipulates those desires to her own advantage, be it sexual, financial, or both. This is a complex and ambiguous position to occupy, for it involves the conscious adoption of the object position (or, at the very least, the *appearance* of occupying that position). More often than not, it also requires the suppression of physical desire; this is most evident when Flämmchen weighs the costs of giving up an affair with Gaigern—her own object of desire—in order to take Preysing's business deal.

Flämmchen's unsentimental view of sex as a means to financial autonomy anticipates the late twentieth-century image of the "call girl," a figure that recent writers on prostitution such as the former prostitute, activist, and Berlin-based author Pieke Biermann have proposed as a model for the "emancipated" sex worker. Alain Corbin describes the call girl as a woman of relatively high intelligence who selects her own clientele, works independently from a pimp or procurer, and "claims to be practicing a profession that gives her a certain independence, allows her to work when she feels like it, and, when the time comes, to change her way of life."[44] Baum's novel stands out as a work of popular fiction that explores the possibilities of autonomy *within* prostitution, possibilities that could offer a woman greater financial security than the factory, office, or shop. After all, at the end of the novel it is the secretarial work that Flämmchen abandons, not Kringelein and his new fortune. In the fleeting, flirtatious conversations between Flämmchen and Gaigern, the novel shows Flämmchen's ability to distinguish between the commodification of her body and her private desires. By pairing her with Kringelein in the end, however, Baum's book also offers the possibility that intimacy and pleasure could be found in the arms of the client, yet it leaves the fate of their relationship completely open, denying readers any sort of traditional "happy end." The novel's narrative voice rather drily warns readers not to expect a happy end, particularly one that would involve a traditional love story between Flämmchen and Kringelein: "It is not as if Flämmchen would fall in love with Kringelein. No, life is quite far from producing such sweet treats."[45] In her analysis of novels by Baum and

---

44. Corbin, *Women for Hire,* 358. King refers to Flämmchen as a "sometime call girl" in her most recent article ("Seventy Years," 17), but she does not elaborate on the meaning of the term. Matthias refers to her as an "escort" but claims, quite erroneously, that "she does not qualify as a call-girl or even as a prostitute" simply because "she does not count on making a living that way" (*The Hotel as Setting,* 190). Pieke Biermann, now an award-winning author of detective fiction who lives in Berlin, spearheaded the prostitutes' rights movement in Germany with the publication of her book *"Wir sind Frauen wie andere auch!"* in 1980. It was the first book on prostitutes' lives and struggles for civil rights to be written by a practitioner. For an astute analysis of Biermann's detective fiction and its crime-fighting network of Berlin-based prostitutes, see Katrin Sieg, "Postcolonial Berlin? Pieke Biermann's Crime Novels as Globalization Critique," "Writing and Reading Berlin," ed. Stephen Brockmann, special issue, *Studies in Twentieth- and Twenty-First-Century Literature* 28, no. 1 (Winter 2004): 152–82.

45. Baum, *Grand Hotel,* 286–87; *Menschen im Hotel,* 297.

Keun, Kerstin Barndt convincingly argues that the readership for Baum's novels was largely composed of white-collar working women capable of creating their own images of the "New Woman" in dialogue with writings by women authors. By denying her readers a happy end, Barndt asserts, Baum expressed an awareness of and sympathy for the "ongoing process of serial decision-making" faced by women like Flämmchen and the complex negotiations they undertake in their attempts to balance personal desires with social realities.[46]

Dynamics of Desire and Definitions of Work in *The Artificial Silk Girl*

The harsh social realities that confronted working women and men at the time of *Grand Hotel*'s publication in 1929 had become even more dire by the time Irmgard Keun's novel *Das kunstseidene Mädchen* (The Artificial Silk Girl) appeared in 1932. The German unemployment rate soared after the onset of the world economic crisis in the autumn of 1929, and by the end of 1932, five million Germans were out of work. The political arena became increasingly polarized, as voters turned to either the Communist Party or the reactionary Nazis in hopes of solving their woes. Street battles between Communists and Nazis became ever more common, especially in the working-class districts of the German capital. Even in the midst of socioeconomic and political turmoil—or perhaps especially then—glitzy advertisements for films, entertainment establishments, and consumer goods continued to adorn Berlin's landscape, and young men and women continued to dream of upward mobility.[47]

Keun's protagonist Doris is one such dreamer. One of the best-selling books of the early 1930s, *The Artificial Silk Girl* is the self-told story of Doris, an eighteen-year-old secretary who wants to see herself in pictures rather than take dictation from a pimply-faced lawyer.[48] Hoping to create a film-like life for herself, Doris

46. Barndt, *Sentiment und Sachlichkeit*, 26. *Grand Hotel* itself supports Barndt's reading in telling its readers that the fates of its characters "do not constitute entire human destinies complete and rounded off." See Baum, *Grand Hotel*, 299; *Menschen im Hotel*, 309.

47. For a cogent narrative on the German experience of the economic crisis, see Weitz, *Weimar Germany*, 161–68; for unemployment statistics, see Roos, *Weimar through the Lens of Gender*, 202–3.

48. Barndt documents that Keun's novel was the "summer book of the year" in 1932, selling 50,000 copies by the end of its first year (Sentiment und Sachlichkeit, 167).

Born in 1905 in Berlin-Charlottenburg, Irmgard Keun moved with her family to Cologne in 1913. She worked briefly as a stenographer and typist (1921–23) before going to drama school in Cologne (1925–27). After several years of formal study, she worked as an actress for three years, with engagements in Cologne, Hamburg (Thalia Theater), and Greifswald. In 1929 she began writing novels, publishing *Gilgi, eine von uns* in 1931 and *Das kunstseidene Mädchen* in 1932, both of which brought her popular and critical success. Blacklisted by the Nazis in 1933 for the overt sexual content of her work, she went into exile in 1936. Between 1936 and 1940, she led a vagabond's existence, living mostly in Belgium, but traveling to Switzerland, England, and even to North America. In 1940, an English newspaper erroneously announced Keun's suicide, and she returned to her parents' home in Cologne. Her postwar life was marked by financial hardship, alcohol abuse, and mental and physical breakdowns that

conducts various affairs with men in her hometown before being fired from her job for inviting, then refusing, her boss's sexual advances. After a brief stint acting in the local theater, she steals a fur coat from the theater's dressing room and, thinking herself a fugitive, flees to Berlin. A mobile, desiring woman like Flämmchen, Doris also uses sex to obtain new clothes and accessories, food and accommodations, from men in Berlin. Her sexual adventures bring her into contact with a broad spectrum of people, and she bounces between luxury and abject poverty, between a bohemian lifestyle and middle-class security. My reading of the novel begins by examining Doris's clear rejection of white-collar work and her subsequent quest for the elusive "Glanz" in Berlin. Locating a biting critique of white-collar work in the midst of the general social and economic chaos of Berlin in the early 1930s, *The Artificial Silk Girl* explores the employment alternatives open to women at that time and presents its readers with various forms of commodified sexuality, from Doris's hustling of men for food and gifts to the street prostitute Hulla's dismal existence. Like Baum, Keun conflates the figures of prostitute and white-collar worker in her novel's protagonist, Doris, yet she does so in a much more complex way. Like Flämmchen, Doris is a woman whose affairs with men vacillate between those based on her own desire and those based on material gain. Less pragmatic than Flämmchen, Doris refuses at several points in the text to suppress her desires in favor of financial security. More often than Baum, Keun allows her protagonist to exhibit and enjoy moments of desire that are free from financial deal-making and thereby challenge readers to recognize the difference between Doris's sexual agency and her objectification. Keun's novel encourages a differentiated reading of prostitution as something other than an ominous sign of Doris's impending doom or "failure" in Berlin, as scholars like Katharina von Ankum, Doris Rosenstein, and Vibeke Petersen have hitherto read it. Instead of interpreting the novel's depiction of prostitution as a feasible alternative to white-collar work, these scholars are quick to judge it as an automatic dead end.[49] Although this novel is very often judged by the perceived "success" or "failure" of its female protagonist, I argue that the work itself—through complex narrative strategies and its thematization of prostitution and other forms of commodified sexuality—questions the very validity of diametrically opposed concepts like success and failure in such a precarious time and place as early 1930s Berlin.

caused her to live most of her later years in various clinics in Bonn and Cologne. From 1977 to 1980, she and her works enjoyed a brief resurgence in popularity after the Claassen publishing house reissued her books. Known as both elusive and cantankerous, Keun died in 1982.

49. Katharina von Ankum, "Gendered Urban Spaces in Irmgard Keun's *Das kunstseidene Mädchen*," in Ankum, *Women in the Metropolis*, 180; and Ankum, "Material Girls: Consumer Culture and the 'New Woman' in Anita Loos' *Gentlemen Prefer Blondes* and Irmgard Keun's *Das kunstseidene Mädchen*," *Colloquia Germanica* 27, no. 2 (1994): 164. See also Petersen, *Women and Modernity*, 38; and Doris Rosenstein, "'Mit der Wirklichkeit auf du und du?' Zu Irmgard Keuns Romanen *Gilgi, eine von uns* und *Das kunstseidene Mädchen*," in *Neue Sachlichkeit im Roman: Neue Interpretationen zum Roman der Weimarer Republik*, ed. Sabina Becker and Christoph Weiß (Stuttgart: Metzler, 1995), 281.

Recent scholarship on *The Artificial Silk Girl* has centered on the following themes: the novel's depiction of cinema and consumer culture, the protagonist's limited intellect and how it affects her critical potential, and the question of whether Doris exemplifies women's autonomy or limitation within urban modernity. Numerous scholars have, with good reason, explored the filmic nature of Keun's narrative. Rejecting the archaic genre of the diary as a way to document her experiences, Doris prefers the modern medium of the film script.[50] Doris's insistence on making her life seem like a movie, however, also cautions readers to distrust her self-image. While both Anke Gleber and Monika Shafi read the novel as a "female 'Bildungsroman,'" in which Doris comes to recognize her cinematic ideals as mere illusions, other critics maintain that Doris's obviously limited viewpoint encourages readers to hold her ideals at a critical distance. A closer look at the novel's narrative techniques provides more evidence for the latter interpretation. The novel's open ending and its resistance to a linear trajectory make it difficult to classify as a bildungsroman. Keun's clever depiction of Doris's often exaggerated sense of self and limited education invites readers to actively scrutinize and even edit Doris's autobiographical screenplay. After all, how can readers trust a narrator who claims that she can dazzle Albert Einstein by telling him the chemical composition of water, or that her recitation of one line in a provincial play will put her well on her way to becoming a star?[51] The author's choice of the first-person narrative combined with the genre of the screenplay exemplifies what the feminist theater scholar Sue-Ellen Case calls "proximity effects." In contrast to Bertolt Brecht's materialist, empirical "alienation effects" (*Verfremdungseffekte*), Case defines proximity effects as devices used by early twentieth-century women authors and playwrights such as Marieluise Fleißer and Else Lasker-Schüler to confront and interrogate gender relations, sexuality, and structures of desire. The story of Doris, as it is told in Keun's

---

50. In an oft-cited passage, Doris claims: "And I think it will be a good thing if I write everything down, because I'm an unusual person. I don't mean a diary—that's ridiculous for a trendy girl like me. But I want to write like a movie, because my life is like that and it's going to become even more so." Keun, *Das kunstseidene Mädchen*, translated by Katharina von Ankum as *The Artificial Silk Girl* (New York: Other Press, 2002), 3. For analyses of Keun's filmic, or "visual," writing, see Anke Gleber, *The Art of Taking a Walk: Flanerie, Literature, and Film in Weimar Culture* (Princeton, NJ: Princeton University Press, 1999), 195–208; Leo Lensing, "Cinema, Society, and Literature in Irmgard Keun's *Das kunstseidene Mädchen*," *Germanic Review* 60 (1985): 129–34; Patrizia McBride, "Learning to See in Irmgard Keun's *Das kunstseidene Mädchen*," *German Quarterly* 84, no. 2 (Spring 2011): 220–38; McCormick, *Gender and Sexuality*, 130; Monika Shafi, "'Aber das ist es ja eben, ich habe ja keine Meinesgleichen': Identitätsprozeß und Zeitgeschichte in dem Roman *Das kunstseidene Mädchen* von Irmgard Keun," *Colloquia Germanica* 21, no. 4 (1988): 314–25.

51. On the classification of the novel as a "female 'Bildungsroman,'" see Gleber, *The Art of Taking a Walk*, 193; and Shafi, "Identitätsprozeß und Zeitgeschichte," 320. For readings that argue for a distrust of Doris's perspective, see Hiltrud Häntzschel, *Irmgard Keun* (Reinbeck bei Hamburg: Rowohlt, 2001), 39; McCormick, *Gender and Sexuality*, 134; and Rosenstein, "Mit der Wirklichkeit," 281. McBride's recent analysis balances and then transcends these two discussions, arguing that Keun's novel offers "parodic commentary on the genre of the *Bildungsroman*" ("Learning to See," 223). For the given examples of Doris's inflated view of herself, see Keun, *The Artificial Silk Girl*, 13, 44.

novel, offers readers "the close-up, the in-the-midst-of dramaturgy that is unstable in its referents and narrative and therefore well-suited to the *operations of desire and its oppression*."[52] It is through Doris's highly personal yet unreliable narrative that readers are given both a sense of the protagonist's struggles, limitations, and efforts to carve a space for her own desires, as well as the freedom to develop a separate perspective—independent from the protagonist's—regarding Doris's views on the social and sexual dynamics depicted in the novel.

As a recurring motif in the text, prostitution plays a key role in the novel's examination of what Case calls "operations of desire and its oppression," in several ways. Throwing various dynamics of work and desire into relief, prostitution acts on the one hand—as it does in Baum's novel—as an instrument of social critique of white-collar employment. Sensitive to the dangers inherent in this very critique, particularly in the portrayal of prostitution as *preferable* to white-collar work, Keun's novel reminds her readers through the depiction of the impoverished and battered prostitute Hulla of the potential for victimization that exists in what Richard McCormick identifies as "prostitution in its clearest and least attractive form." Finally, by locating less easily definable forms of prostitution in the text and drawing attention to the contrast between Doris's genuine expressions of sexual desire and her more calculated, emotionally detached use of her body for food, clothing, and shelter, Keun's text or "script" invites readers to define what is and is not prostitution and to acknowledge that such a distinction is hardly clear-cut. As McCormick argues, "The reader/viewer is confronted with the dilemma of determining whether |prostitution| actually occurs," yet even his nuanced reading of Keun's novel does not offer an in-depth analysis of the multiple ways in which its depiction of prostitution and prostitutes casts light on Doris's complex negotiations.[53]

As in *Grand Hotel*, when prostitution and white-collar work are compared with one another in *The Artificial Silk Girl*, it is prostitution that seems to offer a higher salary and a greater chance for autonomy and adventure. If given the choice of returning to an office job, being "kept" by a wealthy industrialist, or walking the streets, Doris claims toward the end of the novel that she might just as well become a "whore." In a literary nod to Kracauer's study of white-collar workers, she bemoans her own lack of education, the monotony of office work, its meager pay, and its rigid schedule:

> As if someone like me, who has no education and no foreign language skills except for olala and has no high school diploma and nothing could get anywhere through work. And no knowledge of foreign currencies and opera and all the rest of it. And no degrees. And no chance to get more than 120 in an honest way—and to always

52. Sue-Ellen Case, *The Divided Home/Land: Contemporary German Women's Plays* (Ann Arbor: University of Michigan Press, 1998), 3, 20–21, emphasis added.

53. McCormick, *Gender and Sexuality,* 132, 135.

be typing files and more files, so boring, without any motivation and no risk to win or lose. And just more of that nonsense with commas and foreign words and all that.... You have 120 marks with deductions to turn in at home or live on.... And you want a few nice clothes, because at least then you're no longer a complete nobody. And you also want a coffee once in a while with music and an elegant peach melba in very elegant goblets—and that's not at all something you can muster alone, again you need the big industrialists for that, and you might as well just start turning tricks. Without an eight-hour day.... A whore's life is more interesting. At least she's got her own business.[54]

At first glance, Doris could be read as a lower-class version of Kracauer's white-collar bohemian whose path seems to be propelling her toward life on the streets. Her desire for consumer goods and entertainment would no doubt have met with Kracauer's disdain. In one of the most critical moments in *The White-Collar Workers,* he describes the leisure-time pursuits of employees as empty and superficial, writing: "Nothing is more characteristic of this life, which only in a restricted sense can be called a life, than its view of higher things. Not as substance but as *glamour* (nicht Gehalt, sondern *Glanz*)."[55] For Kracauer, the term *Glanz* signifies various surface aspects of 1920s consumer culture: affordable new fashions, garish advertisements, and the blinking, glittering neon signs of the city's entertainment venues—diversions that made the *Angestellten* even more dependent on their humdrum jobs. Keun's novel, although it satirizes Doris's desire to become a *Glanz* (here a star or glamorous figure), lends its protagonist a more critical perspective on secretarial work than one finds in Kracauer's book.

Indeed Keun's text debunks one of the celluloid dreams that Kracauer deplores yet perpetuates in the opening pages of *The White-Collar Workers:* the secretary's fantasy of marrying the boss. In his writings on film, Kracauer bemoans the popularity of the Weimar *Angestelltenfilm,* which typically starts with a pretty, young woman from the provinces trying to make it in the big city and ends with an engagement to her boss.[56] Wilhelm Thiele's 1931 hit film *Die Privatsekretärin* (The Personal Secretary) relies on this exact formula: the film's protagonist, Vilma,

---

54. Keun, *The Artificial Silk Girl,* 158–60. I do, at times, take issue with Ankum's translation. For example, in this passage, she translates *inneres Wollen* as "motivation." While this does indeed fit in the context of this passage, the concept of "inneres Wollen," when viewed in the context of Keun's novel, can also be translated as "desire." For the original German, see Keun, *Das kunstseidene Mädchen* (1932; repr., Munich: List, 2000), 181–83.

55. Kracauer, *The Salaried Masses,* 88; *Die Angestellten,* 91, emphasis added. Friedrich A. Kittler claims that Keun was "obviously under the influence of Kracauer" when she wrote *The Artificial Silk Girl;* see Kittler, *Gramophone, Film, Typewriter,* trans. Geoffrey Winthrop-Young and Michael Wutz (Stanford, CA: Stanford University Press, 1999), 81.

56. Kracauer, *The Salaried Masses,* 28. On white-collar films and the fantasy of marrying the boss, see Kracauer, "The Little Shopgirls," 300; and Kracauer, *From Caligari to Hitler,* 213. For more references to the *Angestelltenfilme* and Keun's critique thereof, see Lensing, "Cinema, Society, and Literature," 130; and Rosenstein, "Mit der Wirklichkeit," 287.

comes to Berlin "first to find a job and with that...to find happiness." To use the words of the Weimar illustrated film press, Vilma's boss, the bank director Arvai, "recognizes in a flash...that Vilma is not the type of frivolous girl who can be had in exchange for flashy trinkets. Such a girl is well worth marrying."[57] In these films, the boss is portrayed as an object of romantic love (the potential husband) and/ or a clever, benevolent ruler. Countering Kracauer's portrait of the easily duped shopgirl who would gladly buy into the idea of romance between the desirable boss and the "girl worth marrying," Keun's Doris does not even fleetingly entertain the idea of marrying her pimply boss. Instead, she rewrites the script of the typical working-girl comedy when she gruffly rejects the boss's sexual advances and asks him: "Have you ever looked at yourself in the mirror? I'm asking you, what sex appeal could you possibly have?" Her incredulous boss fires her immediately. In this scenario the boss is neither an object of desire nor an employer with heart who deserves the loyalty of his workers. This scene clearly shows Doris's reluctance to suppress her own desires and give in to the boss's advances just to save her job. In her film neither marriage nor the white-collar job is the goal, but rather the controversy of getting fired, the excitement—the "sensational event"—of starting a new life, and the will to preserve her sexual autonomy.[58] Keun's novel presents the pursuit of *Glanz* as exactly that which lures Doris *away* from her desk job, quite contrary to Kracauer's definition of *Glanz* as the culture of distraction (cinema, nightclub) that keeps white-collar workers bound to their monotonous work. Doris's decision to steal the fur coat and live unregistered in Berlin forces her—or perhaps, more appropriately, allows her—to make a permanent break with the world of white-collar work.

Without a regular office job Doris visits cafés and bars throughout the city, hustling men for food, drinks, and fashionable clothing, sometimes sleeping with them and sometimes not. Like Baum's Flämmchen, Doris displays a range of motivations for sex, including desire, compassion, love, and financial need. As she herself states, "Men always think it's love or sensuality or both...but what they don't know is that there are a million reasons for a girl to sleep with a guy."[59] Doris's survival in Berlin is often based on her ability to use her body as a commodity in her relations with wealthy men such as the "Onyx" and Alexander (whom she calls "a jolly pink rubber ball"), both of whom offer to make her their mistress. But what makes Doris different from Flämmchen is that she is unwilling to suppress her sexual attraction for men like the Onyx's handsome friend, "the hunk," just to make a good business

57. Both of the above quotes come from the *Illustrierter Film-Kurier* 171 (1931), featuring *Die Privat-sekretärin,* Schriftgutarchiv, SDK. The film itself, which exists only in truncated form, can be viewed at the Bundesarchiv-Filmarchiv in Berlin. Wilhelm Thiele's work is just beginning to garner critical attention from contemporary scholars of Weimar film, but his films starring Lillian Harvey were some of the most beloved of the era. On Thiele, see Rogowski, *The Many Faces of Weimar Cinema,* 10, 239–42.

58. Keun, *The Artificial Silk Girl,* 18, 19.

59. Keun, *The Artificial Silk Girl,* 11.

deal. Likening her desire for "the hunk" to glittering diamonds, she gladly sleeps with him, only to be fired the next day by the Onyx, who calls her a "whore."[60] This episode simultaneously celebrates Doris's sexual fulfillment and exposes the hypocrisy of the Onyx and his wife, whose marriage of convenience implies that "socially sanctioned sex for money and without desire is...rewarded, while desired but unsanctioned sex meets with scorn."[61] The brilliance of Keun's text, however, lies in its examination not only of the difference between these two types of sex identified here by McCormick, but also of the many gray areas in between. For Doris, who must constantly decide between financial survival and sexual autonomy, being labeled a "whore" by a man who had previously offered her money for sex is an outrage. Her expression of rage toward such labels fits well with her repeated rejection of those men on the street who mistake her for a prostitute. Her resistance to this external designation signifies her continued efforts to define her sexual behavior and her survival tactics on her own terms.

The Artificial Silk Girl involves readers in this renegotiation of terms by providing numerous examples of commodified sexuality—some of which are consciously chosen and some of which are externally imposed, some that offer opportunities for increased financial autonomy and some that are clearly oppressive. These examples span the entire socioeconomic spectrum, from the luxurious—yet also boring—life of a kept woman that Doris leads with Alexander to the poverty and violence experienced by the street prostitute Hulla. Keun provocatively intertwines Hulla's story with Doris's narrative of temporary luxury and *Glanz* as Alexander's mistress, thereby inviting the reader's close scrutiny of both.[62] Beaten beyond recognition by her pimp, Hulla temporarily saves herself by turning him in to the police. She continues to work the streets, subjecting herself to taunts about her bandaged, deformed face and accepting a pittance—several marks—for her services. When her pimp is released from prison, she anticipates his wrath and commits suicide. After her death, Doris prays for her, saying: "And when there're no men who pay, there won't be any Hullas—no man is allowed to say anything bad about that Hulla. I really wish her a heaven that has use for the good in her eyes. And when she's become an angel, she should have wings without any bandaids on them."[63] In death, Hulla becomes, in Doris's eyes, an angel, or a "hooker with a heart of gold." In her attempt to proclaim Hulla's innocence, however, Doris falls back onto clichés, rationalizing Hulla's fate (and the existence of prostitution writ large) by blaming the

---

60. Keun, *The Artificial Silk Girl*, 74–75. It is in this aspect of my analysis of Keun's novel that I differ with McBride's assertion ("Learning to See," 224) that Doris "strenuously endeavors to restrain her sexual desire," or "has learned to delay gratification until after securing a material gain." The episode with the "hunk" suggests otherwise.

61. McCormick, *Gender and Sexuality*, 137.

62. Keun, *The Artificial Silk Girl*, 105–15. Doris's affair with Alexander begins on p. 106 and ends on p. 113, while Hulla is first mentioned on p. 105 and meets her tragic end on p. 115.

63. Keun, *The Artificial Silk Girl*, 119.

male demand for venal sex and men's willingness to pay for it.[64] By making Hulla into a martyr, Doris is able to keep the victimized prostitute at a safe distance (in the grave, in heaven) and ignore the fact that her own survival in Berlin depends on "men who pay." But there is even more at stake for Doris in this distancing gesture, for what Hulla's life and death represent is a complete loss of self—and with that, a complete relinquishment of desire. Observing the meandering gait of various prostitutes throughout the city, Doris claims that it is this gait that identifies them as prostitutes—"they walk in such a hesitant way...as if their heart had gone to sleep."[65] This description resonates with the previously cited passage on secretarial work as something Doris engaged in "without motivation," or, perhaps more aptly worded, "without desire" (*ohne inneres Wollen*). By resisting definition as a prostitute, Doris clings desperately to the idea that she can still play an active role in her own fate and that hope for intimacy is not lost.

"I want—I want—what do I want?" This is what Doris asks herself as she sits in the waiting room of Berlin's Zoo station and contemplates her next move. This turning point in the text leads Doris through a week of poverty and homelessness, through a decision to prostitute herself "just once, and never again," and into an unexpected comradely relationship with the middle-class modern man Ernst, Doris's most significant relationship in the novel.[66] It is an arrangement that allows Doris to find pleasure in domestic work—work she chooses to do—and intimacy in the company of a sensitive, educated man. Rarely given more than passing mention in secondary texts on Keun's novel, Ernst is a far cry from the nineteenth-century bourgeois husband who believes in the traditional gendered division of labor. The Bauhaus-inspired furniture adorning his apartment, his self-sufficiency, the literature he reads (poetry by Baudelaire, Van de Velde's *The Ideal Marriage*), the films he views (Leontine Sagan's *Girls in Uniform*), his genuine concern for Doris, and his enduring love for his unfaithful wife—all of these factors combine to depict him as Weimar's modern or "new" man: sensitive and caring, and also hardworking, rational, and intellectual.[67] Ernst does not fit the image of men that Doris has constructed in her script, for even though he approaches her on the street just as she decides to prostitute herself, he doesn't want sex. He simply wants a companion.

---

64. This was an argument that early twentieth-century social scientists like Abraham Flexner (*Prostitution in Europe*, 46, 69) found to be only partly true, but that continues to resurface in feminist debates on prostitution.

65. Keun, *The Artificial Silk Girl*, 125.

66. Keun, *The Artificial Silk Girl*, 123, 133.

67. See Keun, *The Artificial Silk Girl*, 133–82. No other character besides Doris commands as much space as Ernst, and yet he is the character who has received the least amount of attention in scholarship on the novel. McCormick (*Gender and Sexuality*, 138, 140), one of the only scholars to mention Ernst, credits him with "saving" Doris from prostitution but also criticizes him for making her into an "ersatz-housewife" in a relationship that simulates a passionless bourgeois marriage. Ankum ("Gendered Urban Spaces," 178), the same scholar who assumes that Doris decides to prostitute herself at the end of the novel and therefore "fails" in Berlin, also laments her "retreat into the limited experiential sphere of the housewife."

Doris can hardly fathom a relationship in which men give without expecting something in return, but Ernst gives her food, shelter, and money without laying claim to her body or demanding her labor. Only when she insists on giving something in exchange does he tell her that if she so chooses, she can tidy up the apartment while he is at work. It is Doris who gradually takes charge of the entire household by shopping, cooking, cleaning, and decorating the apartment. "I have a lot to do. I'm in charge of the entire household," she proudly proclaims. Unlike Ernst's estranged wife, Hanne, who fled the domestic sphere to pursue her dance career, Doris finds freedom and pleasure in her time with Ernst, calling it in retrospect "the most wonderful time of |her| life."[68] Her daily shopping trips allow her to remain mobile and in touch with urban street life, joking, chatting, and haggling with various vendors.

The sense of autonomy and happiness conveyed by Doris during this phase stands in contrast to some recent feminist scholarship, which negatively depicts the woman shopper by claiming that she "does not represent the new image of a self-determined female subject of the streets" because she is "mobilized by bourgeois consumption." Anke Gleber, for instance, lumps the woman shopper together with the prostitute and the bag lady, arguing that "these women form nothing if not the cynically distorted female images of consumption and flanerie in an age of capitalist and sexist exploitation," while Katharina von Ankum reads Keun's novel as one that "negates the possibility of female *flânerie.*"[69] Culture studies scholars like Meaghan Morris, however, who examine the spaces of shopping centers and the various forms of women's consumption in more nuanced ways, warn of the "danger of constructing exemplary allegorical figures" such as the "female flaneur" that Gleber and Ankum seek to define, against which all women are unfairly measured. Morris also cautions that some feminist scholarship could "become cruelly bound by repetition, confined by the reiteration of the terms we're contesting."[70] In her insistent use of the terms "capitalist and sexist exploitation," Gleber in turn continues to define and confine women within those terms, denying agency to prostitutes, women consumers, and female vagabonds. Although it is impossible to deny that capitalism and sexism place constraints on women, is it not more fruitful to examine what women do to gain relative autonomy within those boundaries, or how they continue to push or contest those boundaries? This is the type of critical reading that Keun's text invites, for it provokes readers to consider the emancipatory potential of roles that are often disregarded as traditional or exploitative, such as the roles of prostitute and homemaker.

It is through Doris's dialogue with Ernst that prostitution, housework, and office work are compared and contrasted, bringing forms of women's public and

---

68. Keun, *The Artificial Silk Girl,* 153, 184.

69. Gleber, *The Art of Taking a Walk,* 183–84; Ankum, "Gendered Urban Spaces," 163.

70. Meaghan Morris, "Things to Do with Shopping Centres," in *The Cultural Studies Reader,* ed. Simon During (London: Routledge, 1993), 397, 409.

private labor to light and inviting readers to contemplate the possibilities and limitations of each form. In a segment of their conversation that immediately follows Doris's statement that "a whore's life is more interesting. At least she's got her own business," Ernst challenges Doris's own definition of work. Despite her adamant refusal to find work, Ernst counters by arguing: "But Miss Doris, you're working for me too, when you cook for me and when you wash my curtains." She responds: "I'm working for you because I enjoy it, not because I'm afraid I won't be able to make a living. I'm not really working. I just do it like that."[71] For a woman with Doris's previous experiences and class background, it is understandable that she does not view work as something that people do for pleasure; it is what they do to survive. By challenging her views, Ernst may not change Doris's mind, but his point of view does serve to engage readers in their debate as well and encourages an expansion of their view of work to include domestic labor. The recognition of housework as work was something that feminists like Helene Stöcker had been advocating since the turn of the century, and it is also an issue that many contemporary prostitutes' rights activists deem to be clearly connected to prostitution and other underacknowledged, socially stigmatized, or underpaid forms of women's work.[72]

Ernst's perspective on work, enlightened as it may seem, is, as McCormick points out, surely skewed by his own "unacknowledged level of material comfort."[73] As much as she wants to stay with Ernst, Doris cannot ignore the differences in their class and educational backgrounds, nor can she replace Ernst's wife, Hanne, with whom he is still very much in love. Deciding to leave him in a selfless attempt to reunite him with his wife, at the end of the novel Doris stands alone in the waiting room of the train station. She weighs her options, deciding between a relationship with the proletarian Karl, who lives outside Berlin in a workers' garden colony, becoming a star, and/or choosing prostitution: "I want—want—I don't know—I want to be with Karl. I want to do everything with him. If he doesn't want to—I won't work, I'd rather go on the *Tauentzien* and become a star. But I could just as well turn into a Hulla—and if I became a star, I might actually be a worse person than a Hulla, who was good. Perhaps glamour isn't all that important after all."[74] This is the passage that Ankum uses as evidence of Doris's "failure in Berlin."[75] Yet such criticism misses the mark, for it neglects to consider the novel's skeptical stance toward the very notion of "success," as represented by the elusive concept of *Glanz*. It fails, as well, to acknowledge that just because Doris lists prostitution as one option, this does not mean that it is the option she will choose. Furthermore, Ankum's reading

---

71. Keun, *The Artificial Silk Girl,* 162; the entire conversation about work can be found on pp. 158–62.

72. See, for example, Biermann, "Wir sind Frauen," 12–21.

73. McCormick, *Gender and Sexuality,* 143.

74. Keun, *The Artificial Silk Girl,* 192.

75. Ankum, "Gendered Urban Spaces," 180. See also Rosenstein, "Mit der Wirklichkeit," 281; and Shafi, "Identitätsprozeß und Zeitgeschichte," 319.

assumes that if Doris does indeed choose prostitution, this would constitute the ultimate failure. Such an interpretation imposes the structure of a linear narrative on a novel that resists that very structure. The novel's open ending, and, to return to Case's theory of feminist dramaturgy, the denial of "aesthetic closure and sentimental release," force readers to interrogate the social and sexual dilemmas left unsolved by the text and to recognize "the continuing suffering of both women and men."[76] Reading Doris's final decision—a decision that the novel leaves completely open—as an example of women's resignation to patriarchal authority minimizes her struggle throughout the novel to maintain a certain degree of control over her own choices and to remain a desiring woman. It ignores the striking similarity between this passage and the one that begins the third chapter and that Doris also articulates in the train station's waiting room—"I want—I want—what do I want?" Her repetition of the phrase "I want" (*ich will*) offers readers a sense of hope rather than defeat for Doris. After all, her "inneres Wollen," the manifestation of her active desire and her determination to retain some measure of autonomy in her life, remains intact.

Readings that judge the novel's ending as a sign of Doris's "failure" also fail to acknowledge the general economic instability for both men *and* women that pervades the entire text. *The Artificial Silk Girl* is often erroneously read as a "women's novel" with Doris at the center, and yet it focuses not just on women but on gender, offering readers a broad spectrum of male characters who challenge more traditional definitions of masculinity, from the bourgeois "new man" Ernst to the plucky proletarian Karl to the blind war veteran Brenner. Doris's descriptions of streets in Berlin are replete with homeless, jobless men, from the gritty Münzstrasse near Alexanderplatz, where "there are unemployed people … who don't even own a shirt, and so many of them," to the more upscale Kurfürstendamm, where a man wears a sign around his neck that reads: "'I will accept any work' with 'any' underlined three times in red."[77] That it is a woman who gives this man money may seem a small detail, but it is one that addresses one of the central themes of the novel that has heretofore been overlooked by scholars. Shifting the focus away from Doris, whose self-image and definition of work are unreliable as they are, readers find a novel filled with working women. These women represent various forms of work open to women during the Weimar Republic: from office work (Doris's friend Therese) to service (Doris's mother works in the theater coatroom) to entertainment (Ernst's wife, the dancer Hanne). While Therese is single and self-sufficient,

76. Case, *The Divided Home/Land*, 27.

77. Keun, *The Artificial Silk Girl*, 56, 87. Kracauer also reports having sighted a jobless man on the Kurfürstendamm with a sign around his neck that reads as a desperate plea for work: "From the text written in bold characters passers-by could discover that the man was a 25-year-old unemployed salesman who was seeking work on the open market—no matter what kind" (*The Salaried Masses*, 53). Employed salesmen also walked the streets of Berlin as commodities, with signs draping their bodies, serving as moving advertisements for various products; see Ward, *Weimar Surfaces*, 93–94, 96.

Hanne struggles to make a living, telling Doris: "It's so tough out here."[78] Quite a few of the women support dependent men. Doris's mother supports her unemployed, alcoholic husband, and Doris's landlady in Berlin, Tilli, supports her husband, Albert, once he loses his job, in part by taking on Doris as a tenant. These are all examples of women who struggle to survive on their own, and help others to survive as well. They stand as evidence that "unemployment meant less work for men but more work for women, regardless of whether they were working for a wage."[79] By acknowledging women's efforts to keep their heads above water in a flood of unemployment, and by granting legitimacy to their choices, Keun's novel encourages readers to look beyond traditional forms of wage labor in the attempt to explore and define (and perhaps even redefine) women's work.

Sink or Swim

At first glance, Flämmchen and Doris bear a striking resemblance to other fictional white-collar protagonists of the late Weimar period, such as Vilma in Thiele's 1931 film *The Personal Secretary*. Flämmchen and Doris certainly fit the description that was given to Vilma in the Weimar film press as "one of the courageous, self-confident, energetic girls of our time, who does not hesitate to take on the struggle with life, a life that is anything but easy." Like Vilma, they are ambitious *Girls* who fight to survive in Berlin during a time of great hardship and misfortune. Yet unlike Vilma, Flämmchen and Doris are women "who can be had in exchange for shiny trinkets," and their stories do not end with a kiss and a marriage proposal from a debonair boss.[80] Indeed there is no simple, satisfying end to their stories at all. There is, however, much more room in Keun's and Baum's novels than there is in Thiele's hit film for the critical contemplation of the social and sexual struggles that white-collar working women confronted in the final years of the Weimar Republic. There is also a resistance on the part of the novels' authors, as there was in the sociopolitical discourse of the time on hwG persons and prostitutes, toward categorizing women like Flämmchen or Doris simply as prostitutes or whores, despite the fact that they are sexually active women who use their own bodies as marketable commodities. As Erhard Schütz argues in his analysis of Weimar-era white-collar novels and their heroines, "Female figures, as described by women, show that the literary stereotypes of men and women no longer apply. The traditional clichés of women, the familiar dichotomies of saint and whore, mother and lover, the cliché of the sexually aggressive, uncontrollable woman on the one hand,

78. Keun, *The Artificial Silk Girl*, 187.
79. Grossmann, *Reforming Sex*, 113. See also Weitz, *Weimar Germany*, 164–65.
80. *Illustrierter Film-Kurier* 171 (1931), featuring *Die Privatsekretärin*, Schriftgutarchiv, SDK.

the motherly nurturing…woman on the other, no longer fit these 'Girl'-stories."[81] Although Schütz focuses his interpretation on women, he acknowledges, albeit fleetingly, that in their production of new and less stereotypical images of men, *Angestelltenromane* thematized gender more broadly. In contrast to the rags-to-riches stories perpetuated by the illustrated press and popular films, late Weimar novels gave readers a more complex view of the possible trajectories that the lives of white-collar men and women could take.

In their exploration of complex gender dynamics and in the tension they create between the evocation of urban visual culture and its demystification, the novels by Baum and Keun could be read in tandem with another popular white-collar novel of the time, Erich Kästner's biting satire, *Fabian: Die Geschichte eines Moralisten* (Fabian: The Tale of a Moralist, 1931). Toward the end of Kästner's novel, his protagonist Jakob Fabian, an unemployed advertising copywriter with a doctorate in Germanistik, finds himself, much like Keun's Doris, in one of Berlin's main train stations. Leafing through the pages of an illustrated newspaper, he sees a photo of his former lover, Cornelia Battenberg, under the caption "Lady Lawyer Becomes Movie Star." What the photos of Cornelia in the boulevard press show are a successful young woman in a lightweight fur coat, sitting "behind the wheel" of a luxury car, but what Kästner's written narrative reveals is Cornelia's anguished decision to sleep with the film producer Makart in order to financially support both herself and the newly jobless Fabian.[82] Attempting to keep her financial autonomy and to maintain her companionate relationship with Fabian, Cornelia strikes a deal with Makart and becomes a kept woman. In a book filled with voracious, sexually aggressive women—the most striking example of whom is the "man-eater" Irene Moll, Cornelia stands out as a mild-mannered, educated woman who desires love and intimacy in her relationship with Fabian, but who, in her effort to provide an income for herself and Fabian, is also willing to deny her sexual impulses in exchange for financial security. As Fabian tells her, life in Berlin demands such an exchange: "People here have to make a trade. Those who want have to give whatever there is to give." What Cornelia winds up giving to Makart is her body, and what she sacrifices in the process is her sexual desire, a price that the men in the novel are never asked to pay. As she writes to Fabian, "I feel as though I have sold myself to the anatomy class."[83]

While I agree with McCormick's view that *Fabian* portrays "the autonomous expression of desire…by women" as a threat to male agency, I read Kästner's novel as an equal-opportunity satire, a satire that is directed not only at the loosened

81. Erhard Schütz, "Girls: Frauenfiguren in Angestelltenromanen," in *Romane der Weimarer Republik* (Munich: Fink, 1986), 170.

82. Erich Kästner, *Fabian: Die Geschichte eines Moralisten* (1931; repr., Munich: dtv, 2004), 211, 161–62.

83. Kästner, *Fabian,* 177, 162.

sexual mores and political polarization of late Weimar Berlin, but also at the novel's own protagonist, the cynical and hypocritical "moralist" Fabian.[84] As a character who admits that he is "watching and waiting...for the triumph of respectability (*Anständigkeit*)," a concept that was parodied by Kästner's peers Vicki Baum, Bertolt Brecht, and Kurt Tucholsky alike, Fabian stands as the novel's clearest example of what Kästner later called "the epidemic paralysis" of the republic's end.[85] This paralysis, Kästner wrote in his 1950 prologue to a new edition of *Fabian,* was one of the main targets of his satire. When Fabian does actually make a move, he moves backward by hopping a train out of Berlin and returning to his provincial childhood home. Far from offering the antidote to urban anomie, however, life in the provinces is maligned in the novel for its preservation of outdated gender roles: femininity appears only in the figures of doting mother and downtrodden brothel prostitute, and only sadistic, militaristic masculinity thrives. Although it is certainly true that Kästner's novel fails to offer any solutions to Fabian's paralysis, its message is not, as McCormick reads it, a "nostalgic one" that longs for a return to traditional gender roles.[86] In the end, Fabian jumps into the river in hopes of saving a young boy, and he does so without pausing to remember that he is unable to swim. As Fabian's absurd death by drowning shows, dynamic action without contemplation results in self-destruction. Despite the fact that Cornelia has, by this point in the novel, faded back into the pages of the illustrated press, readers of Kästner's novel can assume that she continues to contemplate her strategy for survival in Berlin. Fabian may sink, but Cornelia swims.

Much like Kästner's Cornelia, Flämmchen and Doris engage in various forms of commodified sex in order to stay afloat in late Weimar Berlin. And yet the novels by Baum and Keun explore self-conscious commodification in much more intricate ways than Kästner's text, and they provide a space in which prostitution can be defined as work. In so doing, their works pose alternative models of morality and examine possibilities for the expression of female desire. The forms of desire depicted in these Weimar *Zeitromane* may not always be completely autonomous, but as Isabel Hull reminds us, perhaps desire never is: "Desire is not a 'force' that must be constrained, but something that actually comes into being within a set of circumstances. It is an act of will, but it is never free. It is how a person walks through the landscape in which she finds herself."[87] By analyzing how Baum's and Keun's protagonists use their own acts of will (their *inneres Wollen*) to navigate the thorny landscape of late Weimar Berlin, eking out moments of pleasure and forming

---

84. McCormick, *Gender and Sexuality,* 108. McCormick (101) draws explicit comparisons between Kästner and Kracauer in his analysis of *Fabian.*

85. Kästner, *Fabian,* 100; Kästner, "Vorwort des Verfassers / Zur Neuauflage dieses Buches," (1950), in *Fabian,* 9–10, here 10.

86. McCormick, *Gender and Sexuality,* 109. For the depiction of Fabian's hometown (presumably Dresden), see Kästner, *Fabian,* 216–36.

87. Hull, *Sexuality, State, and Civil Society,* 47.

companionate relationships, no matter how fleeting, we get away from a scholarly narrative that insists on women's failed emancipation and their "willing return to traditional gender roles" in the twilight years of the republic.[88] In her thoughtful critique of this type of "historiographical boundary-drawing," Kathleen Canning argues that an insistence on women's oppression or willing submission threatens to make gender seem marginal rather than central to the study of Weimar. She writes: "A different interpretation is certainly thinkable, one that might probe the *fragility* rather than assert the completion of such projects of restoration [of gender roles]. Not only would this approach make it more difficult to marginalize gender but it would also help to excavate its place in the key chapters of Weimar history."[89] The close examination of cultural texts with a critical focus on prostitution, one that resists reading prostitution simply as an indicator of women's oppression, reveals the fragility of gender relations and new modes of sexual expression in the Weimar era without resorting to defeatist conclusions. Close cultural analysis and a more open approach to the various meanings that prostitution can take on shows that if we look carefully enough, we might just learn that when we want to know more about the lives of Weimar working girls (and boys), we really can "find all that in novels."[90]

88. Ankum, introduction to *Women in the Metropolis*, 6.

89. Canning, *Gender History in Practice*, 48, emphasis added. In the passage quoted, Canning is responding directly to Ankum's introduction to *Women in the Metropolis* as well.

90. Kracauer, *The Salaried Masses*, 28.

CONCLUSION: BERLIN COQUETTE

Without question, between the years 1890 and 1933, Berlin was known as a city of whores.[1] Berlin-based writers, artists, social reformers, journalists, municipal politicians, police officials, and prostitutes themselves acknowledged this, and many of them fed this image. Consider, for example, the voices that emanate from various documents of the Weimar era: "Sexual intercourse with prostitutes is unavoidable in a city like Berlin," wrote the working-class streetwalkers of Alexanderplatz in their 1930 letter to the minister of the interior, justifying the existence of their profession while appealing to the minister for fair treatment by the police.[2] At the height of hyperinflation in 1923, the mainstream newspaper *Berliner Tageblatt* reported that there were at least forty to fifty entrepreneurial madams at work in the German capital, catering to a worldly, upscale clientele. Taking advantage of the dire economic situation, the madams held a veritable army of "young girls at the ready," many of them still schoolgirls or students hailing from newly impoverished bourgeois families. "With a mere phone call" the madams sent their girls to one of

---

1. When I use the word *whores* here, I am deliberately conflating professional prostitutes with other sexually available women. Although I do not use the term in a derogatory manner, I am fully aware that it can be construed as such.

2. Prostitutes of the District Alexanderplatz to the minister of the interior, letter, April 1930, GStA-PK 1, HA Rep. 77, Tit. 435, Nr. 6, p. 239.

the city's many hotels and pensions that catered to wealthy foreign tourists.[3] In a report to the minister of welfare in 1925, Berlin's police commissioner admitted that myriad forms of prostitution thrived in both "the entertainment district for foreign visitors" and "the places where the locals like to stroll and browse." And yet, the commissioner contended, the city was not nearly as overrun with prostitutes as it was perceived to be; images of widespread destitution and debauchery were, he argued, most often the products of popular fiction and the *feuilleton*.[4]

Taken together, these snippets from the archives offer readers brief glimpses into the various forms that prostitution may have taken in the German metropolis during the Weimar years. The letter written by the streetwalkers of Alexanderplatz reveals a self-confident professional identity and stands as a clear example of how prostitutes articulated their rights as citizens of the republic. The boulevard press's report on upscale "call girls" is evidence both of the loosening of social mores during the inflation years and of the diversification of sex commerce within Berlin in order to cater to clients from across the socioeconomic spectrum. No matter what the reality on the streets might have been, the police commissioner's report claims that when it came to prostitution, Berliners were more likely to believe what they read in the newspapers and in the pages of imaginative texts. Images and representations mattered just as much, if not more, than hard statistics. The mere fact that a police official mentioned the power of cultural representations in his letter to the minister of welfare shows just how intricately intertwined the social and cultural spheres were in Wilhelmine and Weimar Berlin. However, contrary to the police commissioner's claim that cultural works on prostitution in Berlin were sensationalistic, aiming to shock and/or titillate urban readers, the works explored in this book invite readers to critically examine prostitution, its causes, and its broader social and sexual implications.

Much like the Weimar-era police commissioner, turn-of-the-century social reformers openly acknowledged the cultural sphere's potential to influence public views on prostitution, but unlike the commissioner, they viewed the role of culture more positively. For example, when Anna Pappritz reviewed Margarete Böhme's novel *Diary of a Lost Girl* shortly after its release in 1905, she admitted to the readers of her antiregulation periodical *Der Abolitionist* that social activism had its limits. Reformers who wanted to influence how people thought about prostitution, sexual morality, and issues of "illegitimate parenthood" needed to form alliances with those who had the greatest power to shape public opinion: writers and artists. According to Pappritz, "Every person who aims to convince the public of new ideas or to cause a change in perspective has to see true art as a most distinguished ally, for

---

3. "Toshiwara im Zentrum Berlins," *Berliner Tageblatt,* August 29, 1923.

4. Police commissioner to the Prussian minister of welfare, letter concerning "the Nature of Prostitution in Berlin," March 27, 1925, GStA-PK 1, HA Rep. 76 (Ministry of Culture), VIII B, Nr. 3812, pp. 2–4.

the sociopolitical activist [*Sozialpolitiker*], even with all of his know-how, cannot influence the judgment of the masses nearly as profoundly as the true writer."[5] True works of art (*die echte Kunst*), by Pappritz's definition, do not simply reflect the sociohistorical contexts in which they are created; they *reflect on* social issues and inspire visions for change within their readers. As a reader of Böhme's text herself, Pappritz cheered the novel's bold critique of "male vice" and expressed her hope that the book could be used to educate men on the virtues of "sexual purity" and to ease the harsh moral judgment of women who became pregnant out of wedlock.[6] For other turn-of-the-century readers like Helene Stöcker, Böhme's fictional biography of the prostitute Thymian transcended traditional bourgeois morality and its cult of purity to open up new sexual and moral possibilities.[7] By offering readers the image of a smart, elegant, and kind-hearted cocotte in the protagonist Thymian, as well as that of a single working mother in Grete, Böhme's novel challenged the accepted definition of respectability by seeking to remove sexual behavior from the equation. In its creation of a respectable prostitute and a financially independent, unmarried woman, Böhme's text is similar to Otto Erich Hartleben's late nineteenth-century plays, which offered their audience a range of women characters who defied the traditional roles of bourgeois wife and victimized prostitute. And yet, whereas Hartleben's independent women are ultimately forced to choose marriage and motherhood (Hanna Jagert) or a form of prostitution (Meta's choice to become a kept woman at the end of *Education for Marriage*), Böhme's novel leaves her readers with a model of single motherhood that is allowed to stand on its own. Although the prostitute characters in both Böhme's and Hartleben's works fade gradually from the scene, prostitution functions as a venue for criticizing existing moral and sexual systems and for posing alternatives to those systems.

Wilhelmine writers, cultural critics, and social reformers used prostitution as a site for productive discussions of female sexuality, marriage, respectability, and women's work. In so doing, their texts transformed marriage from an unshakable institution to one in need of reform, called greater attention to the conditions under which women work, and challenged polarized definitions of female sexuality as either destructive or naturally passive. Although some of these challenges to the social order and sexual system were more subtle than overt, they existed just the same, and they paved the way for the more drastic changes that subsequently took place during the Weimar Republic. As women occupied new social roles and spaces in the wake of war and amid the chaos of revolution and inflation, Weimar-era thinkers, artists, and writers frequently discussed and depicted the blurred boundaries between career prostitutes, occasional prostitutes, and nonprostitutes. My book has

---

5. Pappritz, "Die Sittlichkeitsfrage in der 'schönen' Literatur," 99.
6. Pappritz, "Die Sittlichkeitsfrage in der 'schönen' Literatur," 101.
7. Stöcker, "Neue Ethik in der Kunst." For a more extensive discussion of Stöcker's review, see chapter 2.

shown, however, that merely drawing attention to these blurred boundaries is not enough. It is only by critically examining how, when, by whom, and to what end this blurring takes place that readers contemplate both the emancipatory potential and the possible pitfalls of such deliberate confusion. After all, in the same era and the same city, images of prostitutes were used by some writers to decry women's increased agency and by others to celebrate women's public visibility and sexual freedom. As the contours of polite society and sexual propriety became increasingly difficult to define in Weimar Berlin, the novelist Vicki Baum played with this very notion by referring to *Grand Hotel*'s Flämmchen, the cool and sexy stenotypist who also moonlights as a nude model and escort, as upstanding or respectable (*anständig*). Irmgard Keun's novel *The Artificial Silk Girl* presents readers not only with a protagonist, Doris, who takes on a variety of roles throughout the book—secretary, aspiring actress, rationalized homemaker, hustler—but also with a humane, yet tragic, portrait of a street prostitute, Hulla. Both Baum and Keun portray their protagonists' matter-of-fact attitudes toward sex as refreshingly honest and present their altruism and goodness as evidence that women who use their bodies as commodities can also maintain a sense of community, compassion, and dignity. By deliberately conflating prostitutes with New Women, these authors draw attention to their protagonists' struggles to remain autonomous, desiring women, and they also invite readers to contemplate the complex combination of need and choice that caused some Weimar-era women to turn to prostitution or other forms of commodified sex.

Cultural texts such as Baum's and Keun's were neither created nor consumed in a vacuum; their production and reception were deeply embedded in the sociohistorical context of Weimar Berlin. As a serialized novel, Baum's *Grand Hotel* provoked "enormous interest" from readers of the *Berliner Illustrirte Zeitung,* while Berlin booksellers exclaimed that they could hardly keep Keun's *Artificial Silk Girl* on the shelves.[8] Böhme's *Diary of a Lost Girl* continued to sell throughout the first three decades of the twentieth century, its popularity invigorated by both Richard Oswald's and G. W. Pabst's Weimar-era film adaptations. And readers of the popular illustrated magazine *Uhu* could open its pages every month to find essays and short prose by Baum and Kurt Tucholsky sandwiched between images of cabaret stars like Blandine Ebinger and Valeska Gert, as well as illustrations by Jeanne Mammen.[9] This cultural production and consumption took place within

---

8. *"Menschen im Hotel auf der Bühne," Berliner Illustrirte Zeitung,* January 26, 1930, 159. The Berlin booksellers' comments appeared in a survey conducted in 1932; see Barndt, *Sentiment und Sachlichkeit,* 167.

9. The illustrated magazine *Uhu* was launched in 1924 by the powerful and successful Ullstein publishing house and catered to a middle-class, mixed-gender readership. It became one of the publisher's most popular periodicals after the *BIZ,* boasting subscription numbers of over 200,000 by 1929. On *Uhu*'s audience and publication figures, see King, *Best-Sellers by Design,* 51, 84–88; Petro, *Joyless Streets,* 86; and Mila Ganeva, *Women in Weimar Fashion: Discourses and Displays in German Culture, 1918–1933* (Rochester, NY: Camden House, 2008), 55 and 79 n. 21.

the German capital at a time of great socioeconomic upheaval, but also at a time when municipal politicians and citizens alike fiercely debated yet eventually embraced the Law to Combat Venereal Diseases (RGBG) and its decriminalization of prostitution. Indeed just as Germany was unique among western industrial nations for passing the RGBG, Berlin was unique among German cities in its enthusiastic support for the new legislation.[10]

A social climate that supports prostitution's decriminalization, the feminist philosopher Laurie Schrage argues, is one that also allows "a robust pluralism with regard to sexual customs and practices" to thrive.[11] In no other German city did such a robust pluralism surrounding prostitution and sexuality thrive as it did in late Wilhelmine and Weimar Berlin. Despite a seemingly narrow focus on a particular western urban environment, on the works of individuals who are, with few exceptions, white, left-liberal, bourgeois, secular Jews or Christians, and on images of prostitutes that defy clear categorization as victims or femmes fatales, my book presents a diverse range of perspectives to its readers. This robust pluralism is evident in Bebel's plea for free love and Simmel's musings on the art of flirtation and on lesbian intimacy among prostitutes. An openness to alternative sexual customs and practices is clearly articulated in the works of sex reformers like Magnus Hirschfeld and Helene Stöcker, both of whom supported prostitution's decriminalization and deregulation and were ardent advocates for homosexual rights, comprehensive sexual education programs for German youth, and a broader acceptance of nonmarital sexual relations between consenting adults. An embrace of pluralism can be found in the saucy and irreverent cabaret texts written by Kurt Tucholsky and in Curt Moreck's vivid descriptions of urban nightlife, and it can be seen in Jeanne Mammen's portraits of Berlin women, some of whom are androgynous *garçonnes* who exemplify the blending of prostitutes and New Women, like the subject of her watercolor *Prostitute on a Green Couch* (Dirne auf grüner Couch; fig. 14).[12] In it, a slim young woman with bobbed hair is splayed across a humble sofa, a limp newspaper in one hand and a cigarette in the other. Her functional, boyish haircut and minimal makeup masculinize her appearance, while her red lipstick, high-heeled shoes, stockings, and short, sheer negligee serve to eroticize her femininity. Her cool expression is softened only slightly by the coy shrug of her shoulder, a characteristic of Mammen's work that is almost as common as the trademark narrow, squinted eyes of her subjects. The suggestive shape of the

---

10. Roos, *Weimar through the Lens of Gender,* 3, 199. As Roos documents, Berlin was one of only three cities whose citizens reacted positively to the new law; the other two cities were Hamburg and Stettin.

11. Laurie Schrage, "Prostitution and the Case for Decriminalization," in *Prostitution and Pornography: Philosophical Debate about the Sex Industry,* ed. Jessica Spector (Stanford, CA: Stanford University Press, 2006), 241.

12. Mammen's watercolor was first published in Hirschfeld's *Sittengeschichte der Nachkriegszeit* (Moral History of the Post-War Period) with the title *Garçonne,* but the work is catalogued by the Jeanne-Mammen-Stiftung as *Dirne auf grüner Couch,* presumably the title given to the watercolor by the artist herself. On this particular work, see also Meskimmon, *We Weren't Modern Enough,* 199–201, 227 n. 1.

Figure 14. Jeanne Mammen, *Garçonne* or *Dirne auf grüner Couch* (Prostitute on a Green Couch), 1930–31. Courtesy of Jeanne-Mammen-Stiftung. Copyright 2012 Artists Rights Society (ARS), New York / VG Bild-Kunst, Bonn.

tabletop lamp adds an erotic element to the dimly lit apartment, and the discarded suspenders draped over the chair to the right of the sofa inspire speculation about who the owner of the suspenders might be—a paying client, a casual lover (man or woman), or the boyish young woman herself. Mammen's work remains open to multiple readings, but it certainly can be read, Marsha Meskimmon argues, as an example of "the visualization of female sexuality beyond the framework of masculine, heterosexual desire."[13]

It was the very "robust pluralism" in the cultural discussion of prostitution, gender roles, and sexuality analyzed in the pages of this book that met an abrupt end in 1933 when the National Socialists seized power. The Nazis had always viewed the German capital as an unruly place, and they relished their chance to tame it.

---

13. Meskimmon, *We Weren't Modern Enough*, 208.

As Austrian and German Jews, Vicki Baum, Friedrich Hollaender, and Richard Oswald went into exile in the United States, as did the leftist intellectuals Helene Stöcker and Bertolt Brecht. Magnus Hirschfeld, a Jew, a socialist, a homosexual, and a sexologist, watched the news footage of young Nazi students plundering his Institute for Sexual Science and burning its contents from the safety of a Paris cinema; he died in southern France in 1935. Kurt Tucholsky took his own life in Swedish exile. Anna Pappritz resigned her leadership position in the League for Protection of Women and Youth after its forced "Aryanization" in 1933, only to see the organization disband that same year. Irmgard Keun and Curt Moreck saw their works blacklisted and destroyed by the new regime, and like Jeanne Mammen, they retreated into internal exile and would never again produce works of art that were as clever or as socially engaged as their Weimar-era works. Prostitutes' voices were silenced, some of them permanently. Classified as "asocials," many were arrested and eventually interned at the Ravensbrück concentration camp just north of Berlin. Some were forced to work in the brothels of men's camps like Sachsenhausen, a brothel system that followed a rigid racial and political hierarchy. In stark contrast to the multifaceted discourse on female sexuality that flourished in the Weimar era, blurred boundaries between prostitutes and New Women were redrawn and codified under the Nazis, often with fatal consequences. Pluralism was driven underground by a new racist, misogynist order.[14]

To end with doom, however, does an injustice to the vibrancy of the social debates and cultural images of prostitution in Berlin from 1890 to 1933, for these are not mere narratives of desperation and impending doom. The documents and social phenomena analyzed in this book illustrate Gayle Rubin's assertion that urban turmoil and contentious discussions of sex often open up spaces for "ferment and new possibility," creating room for alternative sexualities.[15] This idea of "ferment and new possibility" is one that is often associated with the image of Berlin in the so-called Golden Twenties, and yet, as my examination of prostitution in Berlin shows, even that which was considered "golden" had many shades of gray. The defining image of Berlin that this book puts forth is one that contains more gray than gold, for it is a fuzzy composite created by a pervasive sense of erotic confusion and the blurring of lines between respectable women and prostitutes. It is within these blurred lines, however, that the intricacies of women's financial and sexual autonomy were so provocatively explored by Wilhelmine and Weimar artists, activists,

---

14. On "asocials," see Wolfgang Ayaß, *"Asoziale" im Nationalsozialismus* (Stuttgart: Klett-Cotta, 1995); on the racialized hierarchy of the brothel system and the swift changes made to prostitution policy at the onset of National Socialism, see Roos, "Backlash against Prostitutes' Rights"; and Roos, *Weimar through the Lens of Gender*, 212–27, as well as Timm, *The Politics of Fertility*, 176–86. Files on prostitutes who were sent to Ravensbrück and Sachsenhausen can be read at the Landesarchiv Berlin; see also Christa Schikorra, "Prostitution weiblicher KZ-Häftlinge in Frauen-KZ Ravensbrück," *Dachauer Hefte* 16, no. 16 (2000): 112–24.

15. Rubin, "Thinking Sex," 310.

and writers. The works examined in *Berlin Coquette* do not feed into the image of Berlin as the Whore of Babylon, a sinful metropolis teetering on the brink of destruction. Rather, true to Berlin form, they acknowledge the mythic image that has been cast on them, and, in some cases, they poke a bit of fun at it. Two decades before Moreck scoffed at the idea of "Berlin, Babylon of Sin" and exposed it as a mere performance put on for foreign tourists in his *Guide to "Naughty" Berlin,* the social historian Robert Hessen, who wrote an extensive study of German prostitution, expressed his confidence in the Berliners' no-nonsense practicality (*Vernunft*) and their ability to laugh off externally imposed images like that of the Whore of Babylon. His advice for the citizens of the *Weltstadt?*—they should react to such allegations "with a cheerful smile" and "a shrug of the shoulder."[16] Hessen's advice to turn-of-the-century Berliners cannily anticipates what Jeanne Mammen's images of Berlin women would later convey: a distinctive air of irreverence, a lack of moralizing, an intense fascination with the urban milieu, and a mixture of earnestness and playfulness that is very Berlin and very coquette.

---

16. Hessen, *Die Prostitution in Deutschland*, 107.

Bibliography

Primary Sources

Archives

Bundesarchiv-Filmarchiv (BArch-Film). Berlin.
Geheimes Staatsarchiv Preussischer Kulturbesitz Berlin (GStA-PK).
    Rep. 76: Kulturministerium.
    Rep. 77: Ministerium des Innern.
Landesarchiv Berlin (LAB).
    A. Pr. Br. Rep. 030–05: Theaterzensur.
    B. Rep. 235: Helene-Lange-Archiv (HLA).
    HLA, B. Rep. 235–13: Nachlaß Anna Pappritz.
Stiftung Deutsche Kinemathek (SDK). Berlin.
    Filmarchiv.
    Schriftgutarchiv.
Swarthmore College Peace Collection (SCPC).
    Helene Stöcker Papers.

Books and Printed Material

Andreas-Salomé, Lou. "Hartlebens 'Erziehung zur Ehe.'" *Die neue Rundschau* 4 (1893): 1165–67.
"Aus der Tiefe der Weltstadt." Review of *Die Prostitution. Bühne und Film* 3 (1919).
Bab, Julius. *Berliner Bohême.* Vol. 2 of *Großstadt-Dokumente,* edited by Hans Ostwald. Berlin: Seeman, 1905.
——. *Das Theater der Gegenwart: Geschichte der dramatischen Bühne seit 1870.* Leipzig: Weber, 1928.
Baedeker, Karl. *Berlin und Umgebung: Handbuch für Reisende.* Leipzig: Verlag von Karl Baedeker, 1910.
Baum, Vicki. *Es war alles ganz anders.* Berlin: Ullstein, 1962.
——. *Menschen im Hotel: Ein Kolportageroman mit Hintergründen.* 1929. Reprint, Cologne: Kiepenheuer & Witsch, 2002. Translated by Basil Creighton as *Grand Hotel* (Garden City, NY: Doubleday, Doran & Company, 1931).
Bebel, August. *Die Frau und der Sozialismus.* 9th ed. Stuttgart: Dietz, 1891. Translated by Hope Adams Walther as *Women in the Past, Present, and Future* (Edited repr., Oxford: Zwan, 1988).
Benjamin, Walter. "Berliner Chronik." In *Gesammelte Schriften,* vol. 6, edited by Rolf Tiedemann and Hermann Schweppenhäuser, 465–519. Frankfurt am Main: Suhrkamp, 1985.
Bieber-Böhm, Hanna. *Die Sittlichkeitsfrage, eine Gesundheits-Frage, 2 Referate, gehalten beim Internationalen Frauen-Congress in Berlin, 1896.* Berlin: Reinke, 1896.

———. *Vorschläge zur Bekämpfung der Prostitution: Petition des Bundes deutscher Frauenvereine an den Reichstag betreffend Aufhebung der gewerblichen Prostitution.* Berlin: Osterheld, 1895.

Blass, Ernst. "Tagebuch einer Verlorenen." *Berliner Tageblatt,* October 20, 1929.

Böhme, Margarete. "Tagebuch einer Verlorenen: Eine Entgegnung." *Die Welt am Montag* 11, no. 36 (1905).

———. *Tagebuch einer Verlorenen: Von einer Toten.* 1905. Reprint, Witzwort: Kronacher, 1988.

Braun, Lily. "Die Entthronung der Liebe." 1905. Translated by Alfred G. Meyer as "The Dethroning of Love," in Lily Braun, *Selected Writings on Feminism and Socialism,* ed. Alfred G. Meyer (Bloomington: Indiana University Press, 1987), 117–23.

Brecht, Bertolt. *Aufstieg und Fall der Stadt Mahagonny.* 1927–29. Translated by Ralph Manheim and John Willet as *Rise and Fall of the City of Mahagonny,* in *Brecht: Collected Plays,* ed. Manheim and Willet (New York: Vintage, 1977), 2:85–143.

———. "Aus dem Theaterleben." In *Werke: Große, kommentierte Berliner und Frankfurter Ausgabe,* edited by Werner Hecht, Jan Knopf, Werner Mittenzwei, and Klaus-Detlef Müller, 21:40–42. Berlin and Frankfurt am Main: Aufbau & Suhrkamp, 1989–97.

———. *Die Dreigroschenoper.* In *Werke: Große, kommentierte Berliner und Frankfurter Ausgabe,* edited by Werner Hecht, Jan Knopf, Werner Mittenzwei, and Klaus-Detlef Müller, 2:230–322. Berlin and Frankfurt am Main: Aufbau & Suhrkamp, 1989–97. Translated by Ralph Manheim and John Willet as *The Threepenny Opera,* in *Brecht: Collected Plays* (New York: Vintage, 1977), 2:145–226.

Brück, Christa Anita. *Schicksale hinter Schreibmaschinen.* Berlin: Sieben-Stäbe, 1930.

"Das soziale Filmwerk *Die Prostitution.*" Promotional advertisement. *Der Film* 50 (1919).

"Die Films der Woche." Review of *Die Prostitution. Berliner Tageblatt,* May 4, 1919.

"Die Privatsekretärin." Special promotional issue, *Illustrierter Film-Kurier* 171 (1931).

Döblin, Alfred. *Berlin Alexanderplatz: Die Geschichte vom Franz Biberkopf.* 1929. Reprint, Munich: dtv, 2001.

———. "Das Theater der kleinen Leute." *Das Theater* 1 (1909): 191–92. Reprinted and translated in Hansen, "Early Silent Cinema," 147–84.

———. "Jungfräulichkeit und Prostitution" and "Über Jungfräulichkeit." In *Kleine Schriften,* edited by Anthony W. Riley, 1:117–28. Freiburg im Breisgau: Walter, 1985.

"Ein neuer deutscher Auslandsfilm." Review of *Die Prostitution. BZ am Mittag,* April 29, 1919.

Engels, Friedrich. *Der Ursprung der Familie, des Privateigentums und des Staats.* 1884. Reprinted in Karl Marx and Friedrich Engels, *Gesamtausgabe,* vol. 29 (Berlin: Dietz, 1990). Translated by Alec West as *The Origin of the Family, Private Property, and the State* (1942; rev. repr., New York: International, 1972).

Gert, Valeska. *Ich bin eine Hexe.* Reinbek bei Hamburg: Rowohlt, 1978.

Grelling, Richard. "Censur-Prozeß betreffend 'Hanna Jagert' von Otto Erich Hartleben." In *Streifzüge: Gesammelte Aufsätze,* edited by Richard Grelling, 227–52. Berlin: Verlag des Bibliographischen Bureaus, 1894.

Guillaume-Schack, Gertrud. "Über unsere sittlichen Verhältnisse und die Bestrebungen und Arbeiten des Britisch-Continentalen und Allgemeinen Bundes." In *Frauen und Sexualmoral,* edited by Marielouise Janssen-Jurreit, 61–70. Frankfurt am Main: Fischer, 1986.

Haas, Willy. *"Halbseide." Film-Kurier,* November 27, 1925.

Hammer, Wilhelm. *Zehn Lebensläufe Berliner Kontrollmädchen (und zehn Beiträge zur Behandlung der Geschlechtskrankheiten).* Vol. 23 of *Großstadt-Dokumente,* edited by Hans Ostwald. Berlin: Seemann, 1905.\

Hartleben, Otto Erich. *Ausgewählte Werke*. 3 vols. Berlin: Fischer, 1909–13.

——. *Briefe an seine Frau: 1887–1905*. Berlin: Fischer, 1908.

——. *Tagebuch: Fragment eines Lebens*. Munich: Albert Langen, 1906.

Hirschfeld, Magnus. *Berlins Drittes Geschlecht*. Vol. 3 of *Großstadt-Dokumente*, edited by Hans Ostwald. Berlin: Seeman, 1905.

——. *Geschlechtskunde*. Vol. 3. Stuttgart: Julius Püttmann, 1930.

——. *Sittengeschichte der Nachkriegszeit*. 2 vols. Leipzig: Verlag für Sexualwissenschaft Schneider & Co., 1931.

——. *Sittengeschichte des Weltkrieges*. 2 vols. Leipzig: Verlag für Sexualwissenschaft Schneider & Co., 1930.

Hollaender, Friedrich. *Von Kopf bis Fuß: Revue meines Lebens*. Berlin: Aufbau, 2001.

Kästner, Erich. *Fabian: Die Geschichte eines Moralisten*. 1931. Reprint, Munich: dtv, 1989.

Kaul, Walter. Review of *Halbseide*. *Berliner Börsen-Courier,* November 29, 1925.

Keun, Irmgard. *Das kunstseidene Mädchen*. 1932. Reprint, Munich: List, 2000. Translated by Katharina von Ankum as *The Artificial Silk Girl* (New York: Other Press, 2002).

Kracauer, Siegfried. *Die Angestellten: Aus dem neuesten Deutschland*. 1929. Reprint, Frankfurt am Main: Suhrkamp, 1971. Translated by Quintin Hoare as *The Salaried Masses: Duty and Distraction in Weimar Germany* (London: Verso, 1998).

——. "Die kleinen Ladenmädchen gehen ins Kino." In *Das Ornament der Masse: Essays,* 279–94. Frankfurt am Main: Suhrkamp, 1977. Translated by Thomas Y. Levin as "The Little Shopgirls Go to the Movies," in *The Mass Ornament: Weimar Essays* (Cambridge, MA: Harvard University Press, 1995), 291–304.

——. *From Caligari to Hitler: A Psychological History of the German Film*. Princeton, NJ: Princeton University Press, 1947.

Krafft-Ebing, Richard von. *Psychopathia sexualis*. 1886. Translated by Franklin S. Klaf. New York: Stein & Day, 1965.

Lombroso, Cesare, and Guglielmo Ferrero. *The Female Offender*. 1894. Translated by William Ferrero. New York: D. Appleton, 1899.

Mackay, John Henry. *Der Puppenjunge*. 1926. Translated by Hubert Kennedy as *The Hustler* (New York: Xlibris, 2002).

"*Menschen im Hotel* auf der Bühne." Pictorial report. *Berliner Illustrirter Zeitung,* January 26, 1930, 159.

Moreck, Curt [Konrad Haemmerling]. "Die Erotik des Hinterlandes." In Hirschfeld, *Sittengeschichte des Weltkrieges*, 2:1–42.

——. "Frauenideale der Nachkriegszeit." In Hirschfeld, *Sittengeschichte der Nachkriegszeit,* 1:391–423.

——. *Führer durch das "lasterhafte" Berlin*. Leipzig: Verlag moderner Stadtführer, 1931.

——. *Kultur- und Sittengeschichte der Neuesten Zeit: Geschlechtsleben und Erotik in der Gesellschaft der Gegenwart*. Dresden: Paul Aretz Verlag, 1928.

——. *Sittengeschichte des Kinos*. Dresden: Paul Aretz Verlag, 1926.

Ostwald, Hans. *Berliner Kultur- und Sittengeschichte*. 1926. Reprint, Paderborn: Voltmedia, 2006.

——. *Das Berliner Dirnentum*. 10 vols. Leipzig: Fiedler, 1905–7.

——. *Die Berlinerin: Kultur- und Sittengeschichte Berlins*. Berlin: Verlag für Kunstwissenschaft, 1921.

——. *Großstadt-Dokumente*. Vol. 1, *Dunkle Winkel in Berlin;* vol. 4, *Berliner Tanzlokale;* vol. 5, *Das Zuhältertum in Berlin*. Berlin: Seeman, 1905.

——. *Kultur- und Sittengeschichte Berlins*. 2nd ed. Berlin: Klemm, 1924.

———. *Sittengeschichte der Inflation: Ein Kulturdokument aus den Jahren des Marktsturzes.* Berlin: Neufeld & Henius, 1931.

———. *Vagabunden.* 1900. Edited by Klaus Bergmann. Reprint, Frankfurt am Main: Campus, 1980.

Oswald, Richard. "Der Film als Kulturfaktor." In *Das Kulturfilmbuch,* edited by Edgar Beyfuss and I. Kossowsky, 103–6. Berlin: Cryselius & Schulz, 1924.

Pappritz, Anna. "Die Sittlichkeitsfrage in der 'schönen' Literatur." *Der Abolitionist* 4, no. 9 (1905): 99–101.

———. *Die Welt, von der man nicht spricht!* Leipzig: Felix Dietrich, 1907.

———, ed. *Einführung in das Studium der Prostitutionsfrage.* Leipzig: Johann Ambrosius Barth, 1919.

———. "Frauenarbeit und Volkssittlichkeit: Volksgesundung durch Erziehung." *Monatshefte für Lebenserziehung im Haus, Gesellschaft, Staat, Schule und Kirche* 7 (1911): 1–28.

———. "Herrenmoral." 1903. Reprinted in *Frauen und Sexualmoral,* edited by Marielouise Janssen-Jurreit (Frankfurt am Main: Fischer, 1986), 83–94.

———. *Prostitution und Abolitionismus.* Flugschriften der Deutschen Gesellschaft zur Bekämpfung der Geschlechtskrankheiten, vol. 21. Leipzig: Barth, n.d. [1917?].

———. "Welchen Schutz können Bordellstrassen gewähren?" *Zeitschrift für Bekämpfung der Geschlechtskrankheiten* 3, no. 11 (1904/5): 417–24.

Pappritz, Anna, and Katharina Scheven. "Die positiven Aufgaben und strafrechtlichen Forderungen der Föderation." *Abolitionistische Flugschriften* 5 (1913): 3–12.

Prostituierten-Projekt Hydra (Hydra), ed. *Beruf: Hure.* Hamburg: Galgenberg, 1988.

Reichsfilmblatt. Unsigned review of *Halbseide.* November 1925, no. 48.

Rossi, Sonia. *Fucking Berlin.* Berlin: Ullstein, 2008.

Schweisheimer, Waldemar. *Die Bedeutung des Films für soziale Hygiene und Medizin.* Munich: Georg Müller, 1920.

Simmel, Georg. "Der Frauenkongreß und die Sozialdemokratie." 1896. In Dahme and Köhnke, *Schriften zur Philosophie und Soziologie der Geschlechter,* 133–38.

———. "Die Großstädte und das Geistesleben." 1903. Reprint, Frankfurt am Main: Suhrkamp, 2006. Translated by Edward A. Shils as "The Metropolis and Mental Life" and reprinted in *Georg Simmel: On Individuality and Social Forms,* ed. Donald N. Levine (Chicago: University of Chicago Press, 1971), 324–39.

———. "Einiges über die Prostitution in Gegenwart und Zukunft." 1892. In *Schriften zur Philosophie und Soziologie der Geschlechter,* edited by Heinz-Jürgen Dahme and Klaus Christian Köhnke, 60–71. Frankfurt am Main: Suhrkamp, 1985.

———. *Philosophie des Geldes.* 1900, 1907. Reprint, Frankfurt am Main: Suhrkamp, 1989. Translated by Tom Bottomore and David Frisby as *The Philosophy of Money* (London: Routledge & Kegan Paul, 1978).

———. "Psychologie der Koketterie." 1909. In Dahme and Köhnke, *Schriften zur Philosophie und Soziologie der Geschlechter,* 187–99. Translated by Guy Oakes as "Flirtation," in *Georg Simmel: On Women, Sexuality, and Love,* ed. Guy Oakes (New Haven, CT: Yale University Press, 1984), 133–52.

———. "Weibliche Kultur." 1902. In Dahme and Köhnke, *Schriften zur Philosophie und Soziologie der Geschlechter,* 159–76. Translated by Guy Oakes as "Female Culture," in Oakes, *Georg Simmel* (New Haven, CT: Yale University Press, 1984), 65–101.

Stöcker, Helene. "Aufruf der Internationalen Vereinigung für Mutterschutz und Sexualreform." 1911. In Janssen-Jurreit, *Frauen und Sexualmoral,* 202–4.

———. "Das Werden der sexuellen Reform seit hundert Jahren." In *Ehe? Zur Reform der sexuellen Moral,* edited by Hedwig Dohm, 36–58. Berlin: Internationale Verlagsanstalt, 1911.

———. "Die beabsichtigte Ausdehnung des §175 auf die Frau." 1911. In Janssen-Jurreit, *Frauen und Sexualmoral,* 191–201.

———. *Die Liebe und die Frauen.* Minden: J. C. C. Brun, 1906.

———. "Die Neue Ethik und ihre Gegner." Helene Stöcker Papers, Swarthmore College Peace Collection (SCPC), Box 6.

———. "Lebensabrisse." Helene Stöcker Papers, Swarthmore College Peace Collection (SCPC), Box 1.

———. "Neue Ethik in der Kunst." *Mutterschutz* 1, no. 8 (1905): 301–6.

———. *Sexualpädagogik, Krieg und Mutterschutz.* Berlin: Osterheld, 1917. Helene Stöcker Papers, Swarthmore College Peace Collection (SCPC), Box 10.

———. "Von neuer Ethik." Helene Stöcker Papers, Swarthmore College Peace Collection (SCPC), Box 6.

———. "Zur Reform der sexuellen Ethik." *Mutterschutz* 1, no. 1 (1905): 3–12.

"Toshiwara im Zentrum Berlins." *Berliner Tageblatt,* August 29, 1923.

Tucholsky, Kurt [Peter Panther]. "Berlins Bester." In *Gesamtausgabe: Texte und Briefe,* edited by Antje Bonitz, Dirk Grathoff, Michael Hepp, and Gerhard Kraiker, vol. 7, *Texte 1925,* edited by Bärbel Boldt and Andrea Spingler, 42–43. Reinbek bei Hamburg: Rowohlt, 2002.

———. "Das Tauentzien-Girl." / "Das Tauentzienmädel." In Bonitz et. al., *Gesamtausgabe,* vol. 4, *Texte 1920,* edited by Bärbel Boldt, Gisela Enzmann-Kraiker, and Christian Jäger, 128–31.

———. "Die Dame mit 'n Avec." In Bonitz et. al., *Gesamtausgabe,* vol. 4, *Texte 1920,* edited by Boldt, Enzmann-Kraiker, and Jäger, 106–7. Reinbek bei Hamburg: Rowohlt, 1996.

———. "Die Prostitution mit der Maske." In *Gesammelte Werke,* vol. 1, edited by Mary Gerold-Tucholsky and Fritz J. Raddatz, 404–6. Reinbek bei Hamburg: Rowohlt, 1960.

———. "Massary." In Bonitz et. al., *Gesamtausgabe,* vol. 1, *Texte 1907–1913,* edited by Bärbel Boldt, Dirk Grathoff, and Michael Hepp, 347–51. Reinbek bei Hamburg: Rowohlt, 1997.

———. "Zieh dich aus, Petronella!" In Bonitz et. al., *Gesamtausgabe,* vol. 4, *Texte 1920,* edited by Boldt, Enzmann-Kraiker, and Jäger, 10–11.

Vogel, Bruno. "Geschichte der Prostitution seit dem Kriegsende." In Hirschfeld, *Sittengeschichte der Nachkriegszeit,* 2:89–152.

Wedekind, Frank. *Die Büchse der Pandora.* 1904. Reprint, Stuttgart, Reclam, 2001.

———. *Frühlings Erwachen.* 1891. Reprint, Stuttgart: Reclam, 1995.

Wehrling, Thomas. "Berlin Is Becoming a Whore." 1920. Translated and reprinted in Kaes, Jay, and Dimendberg, *The Weimar Republic Sourcebook,* 721–23.

Weininger, Otto. *Geschlecht und Charakter: Eine prinzipielle Untersuchung.* Vienna: Braumüller, 1903.

Zille, Heinrich. *Kinder der Strasse: 100 Berliner Bilder.* 1908. Reprint, Hannover: Fackelträger Verlag, 1997.

Films

Arm wie eine Kirchenmaus (Poor as a Church Mouse). Directed by Richard Oswald. Germany, 1930. SDK, Berlin.

Cabaret. Directed by Bob Fosse. USA, 1972. U.S. dist.: Facets Multimedia.

Das Tagebuch einer Verlorenen (Diary of a Lost Girl). Restored version, DVD. Directed by Georg Wilhelm Pabst. Germany, 1929. U.S. dist.: Kino International.

Der blaue Engel (The Blue Angel). DVD. Directed by Josef von Sternberg. Germany, 1930. U.S. dist.: Kino International.

Die Büchse der Pandora (Pandora's Box). Restored Version. Directed by Georg Wilhelm Pabst. Germany, 1928/9. U.S. dist.: Facets Multimedia.

Die Dreigroschenoper. Directed by Georg Wilhelm Pabst. Germany, 1931.

Die freudlose Gasse (The Joyless Street). Directed by Georg Wilhelm Pabst. Germany, 1925. SDK, Berlin.

Die Privatsekretärin (The Private Secretary). Fragment. Directed by Wihelm Thiele. Germany, 1931. BArch-Film.

Die Straße (The Street). Directed by Karl Grune. Germany, 1923. SDK, Berlin.

Dirnentragödie (Tragedy of a Prostitute). Directed by Bruno Rahn. Germany, 1927. SDK, Berlin.

Grand Hotel. Directed by Edmund Goulding. USA, 1932.

Irma la Douce. Directed by Billy Wilder. USA, 1963.

Mutter Krausens Fahrt ins Glück (Mother Krause's Journey to Happiness). Directed by Piel Jutzi. Germany, 1929. SDK, Berlin.

Secondary Sources

Abrams, Lynn. "Companionship and Conflict: The Negotiation of Marriage Relations in the Nineteenth Century." In *Gender Relations in German History: Power, Agency, and Experience from the Sixteenth to the Twentieth Century,* edited by Lynn Abrams and Elizabeth Harvey, 101–20. Durham, NC: Duke University Press, 1997.

——. "Prostitutes in Imperial Germany, 1870–1918: Working Girls or Social Outcasts?" In *The German Underworld: Deviants and Outcasts in German History,* edited by Richard J. Evans, 189–209. London: Routledge, 1988.

Adams, Carol Elizabeth. *Women Clerks in Wilhelmine Germany.* Cambridge: Cambridge University Press, 1988.

Adorno, Theodor W., and Max Horkheimer. *Dialectic of Enlightenment.* Translated by John Cumming. New York: Continuum, 1999.

Allen, Ann Taylor. *Feminism and Motherhood in Germany, 1800–1914.* New Brunswick, NJ: Rutgers University Press, 1991.

——. "Feminism, Venereal Diseases, and the State in Germany, 1890–1918." *Journal of the History of Sexuality* 4 (1993): 27–50.

——. "Patriarchy and Its Discontents: The Debate on the Origins of the Family in the German-Speaking World, 1860–1930." In Marchand and Lindenfeld, *Germany at the Fin de Siècle,* 81–101.

Ankum, Katharina von. "Gendered Urban Spaces in Irmgard Keun's *Das kunstseidene Mädchen.*" In *Women in the Metropolis,* 162–84.

——. "'Ich liebe Berlin mit einer Angst in den Knien': Weibliche Stadterfahrung in Irmgard Keuns *Das kunstseidene Mädchen.*" *German Quarterly* 67, no. 3 (Summer 1994): 369–88.

——. Introduction to *Women in the Metropolis,* 1–11.

——. "Material Girls: Consumer Culture and the 'New Woman' in Anita Loos' *Gentlemen Prefer Blondes* and Irmgard Keun's *Das kunstseidene Mädchen.*" *Colloquia Germanica* 27, no. 2 (1994): 159–72.

———. "Motherhood and the New Woman: Vicki Baum's *stud. chem. Helene Willfüer* and Irmgard Keun's *Gilgi—eine von uns.*" *Women in German Yearbook* 11 (1995): 171–88.

———, ed. *Women in the Metropolis.* Berkeley: University of California Press, 1997.

Aschheim, Steven E. *The Nietzsche Legacy in Germany, 1890–1990.* Berkeley: University of California Press, 1992.

Ayaß, Wolfgang. *"Asoziale" im Nationalsozialismus.* Stuttgart: Klett-Cotta, 1995.

Bammé, Arno, ed. *Margarete Böhme: Die Erfolgsschriftstellerin aus Husum.* Munich: Profil, 1994.

Barndt, Kerstin. *Sentiment und Sachlichkeit: Der Roman der Neuen Frau in der Weimarer Republik.* Cologne: Böhlau, 2003.

Bauschinger, Sigrid. "The Berlin Moderns: Else Lasker-Schüler and Café Culture." In *Berlin Metropolis: Jews and the New Culture, 1890–1918,* edited by Emily D. Bilski, 58–83. Berkeley: University of California Press, 2000.

Becker, Sabina. "Großstädtische Metamorphosen: Vicki Baums Roman *Menschen im Hotel.*" In *Jahrbuch zur Literatur der Weimarer Republik: Frauen in der Literatur der Weimarer Republik,* edited by Sabina Becker, 167–94. St. Ingbert: Röhrig, 2000.

———. *Neue Sachlichkeit.* Cologne: Böhlau, 2000.

Behrend, F. J. *Die Prostitution in Berlin.* Erlangen: Palm & Enke, 1850.

Behrmann, Nicola. "Sucht: Abgründiger Körper; Die Prostituierte als Medium der literarischen Moderne." In Grenz and Lücke, *Verhandlungen im Zwielicht,* 223–35.

Beiträge zur feministischen Theorie und Praxis 58 (2001). Special issue on prostitution.

Belach, Helga, and Wolfgang Jacobsen, eds. *Richard Oswald: Regisseur und Produzent.* Munich: Text + Kritik, 1990.

Bell, Shannon. *Reading, Writing, and Rewriting the Prostitute Body.* Bloomington: Indiana University Press, 1994.

Berger, Michael. "Richard Oswald: Kitschkönig und Volksaufklärer." In *Pioniere in Celluloid: Juden in der frühen Filmwelt,* edited by Irene Stratenwerth and Hermann Simon, 201–5. Berlin: Henschel, 2004.

Bergius, Hanne. "Berlin als Hure Babylon." In *Die Metropole: Industriekultur in Berlin im 20. Jahrhundert,* edited by Jochen Boberg, Tilman Fichter, and Eckhart Gillen, 102–19. Berlin: Beck, 1986.

Bernheimer, Charles. *Figures of Ill Repute: Representing Prostitution in Nineteenth-Century France.* Cambridge, MA: Harvard University Press, 1989.

Bernstein, Elizabeth. *Temporarily Yours: Intimacy, Authenticity, and the Commerce of Sex.* Chicago: University of Chicago Press, 2007.

Bessel, Richard. *Germany after the First World War.* Oxford: Clarendon Press, 1993.

Biermann, Pieke. *"Wir sind Frauen wie andere auch!": Prostituierte und ihre Kämpfe.* Reinbek bei Hamburg: Rowohlt, 1980.

Birett, Herbert, ed. *Verzeichnis in Deutschland gelaufener Filme: Entscheidungen der Filmzensur, 1911–1920; Berlin, Hamburg, München, Stuttgart.* Munich: K. G. Saur, 1980.

Blackbourn, David, and Geoff Eley, eds. *The Peculiarities of German History: Bourgeois Society and Politics in Nineteenth-Century Germany.* Oxford: Oxford University Press, 1984.

Blackbourn, David, and Richard J. Evans, eds. *The German Bourgeoisie.* London: Routledge, 1990.

Blaschko, Alfred. *Die Prostitution im 19. Jahrhundert.* Berlin: Aufklärung, 1902.

Bloch, Iwan. *Die Prostitution.* Vol. 1 of *Handbuch der gesamten Sexualwissenschaft in Einzeldarstellungen.* Berlin: Marcus, 1912.

Bock, Gisela. "'Keine Arbeitskräfte in diesem Sinne': Prostituierte im Nazi-Staat." In Biermann, *Wir sind Frauen,* 70–106.

Bock, Hans-Michael. "Biographie." In Belach and Jacobsen, *Richard Oswald,* 119–32.

——. "Filmographie." In Belach and Jacobsen, *Richard Oswald,* 136–80.

——. "Filmographie." In Kasten und Loacker, *Richard Oswald,* 542–61.

Böllinger, Lorenz, and Gaby Temme. "Prostitution and Strafrecht—Bewegt sich doch etwas?" *Zeitschrift für Sexualforschung* 14, no. 4 (December 2001): 336–48.

Borst, Eva. *Über jede Scham erhaben: Das Problem der Prostitution im literarischen Werk von Else Jerusalem, Margarete Böhme und Ilse Frapan.* Frankfurt am Main: Lang, 1993.

Breithaupt, Fritz. *Der Ich-Effekt des Geldes: Zur Geschichte einer Legitimationsfigur.* Frankfurt am Main: Fischer, 2008.

——. "Urszenen der Ökonomie: Von *Peter Schlemihl* zur *Philosophie des Geldes.*" In *Singularitäten: Literatur—Wissenschaft—Verantwortung,* edited by Marianne Schuller and Elisabeth Strowick, 185–205. Freiburg im Breisgau: Rombach, 2001.

Bridenthal, Renate, Atina Grossmann, and Marion Kaplan, eds. *When Biology Became Destiny: Women in Weimar and Nazi Germany.* New York: Monthly Review Press, 1984.

Bristow, Edward. *Prostitution and Prejudice: The Jewish Fight against White Slavery, 1870–1939.* New York: Schocken, 1983.

Brockmann, Stephen. "Weimar Sexual Cynicism." In *Dancing on the Volcano: Essays on the Culture of the Weimar Republic,* edited by Thomas Kniesche and Stephen Brockmann, 165–80. Columbia, SC: Camden House, 1994.

Bruggemann, Julia. "Prostitution, Sexuality, and Gender Roles in Imperial Germany: Hamburg, A Case Study." In *Genealogies of Identity: Interdisciplinary Readings on Sex and Sexuality,* edited by Margaret Sönser Breen and Fiona Peters, 19–38. Amsterdam: Rodopi, 2005.

Buck-Morss, Susan. *The Dialectics of Seeing: Walter Benjamin and the Arcades Project.* Cambridge, MA: MIT Press, 1989.

——. "The Flaneur, the Sandwichman, and the Whore." *New German Critique* 39 (1986): 99–139.

Buruma, Ian. "Desire in Berlin." Review of *Kirchner and the Berlin Street,* by Deborah Wye. *New York Review of Books,* December 4, 2008, 19–20.

Canning, Kathleen. *Gender History in Practice: Historical Perspectives on Bodies, Class, and Citizenship.* Ithaca, NY: Cornell University Press, 2006.

——. *Languages of Labor and Gender: Female Factory Work in Germany, 1850–1914.* 1996. Reprint, Ann Arbor: University of Michigan Press, 2002.

Case, Sue-Ellen. *The Divided Home/Land: Contemporary German Women's Plays.* Ann Arbor: University of Michigan Press, 1998.

Certeau, Michel de, Luce Giard, and Pierre Mayol. *The Practice of Everyday Life.* Vol. 2, *Living and Cooking.* Revised and expanded edition. Translated by Timothy J. Tomasik. Minneapolis: University of Minnesota Press, 1998.

Chickering, Roger. *Imperial Germany and the Great War, 1914–1918.* Cambridge: Cambridge University Press, 1998.

Clark, T. J. *The Painting of Modern Life: Paris in the Art of Manet and His Followers.* Rev. ed. Princeton, NJ: Princeton University Press, 1999.

Corbin, Alain. *Women for Hire: Prostitution and Sexuality in France after 1850.* Translated by Alan Sheridan. Cambridge, MA: Harvard University Press, 1990.

Coser, Lewis A. "Georg Simmels vernachlässigter Beitrag zur Soziologie der Frau." In Dahme and Rammstedt, *Georg Simmel und die Moderne,* 80–90.

Dahme, Heinz-Jürgen, and Otthein Rammstedt, eds. *Georg Simmel und die Moderne: Neue Interpretationen und Materialien.* Frankfurt am Main: Suhrkamp, 1984.

Davis, Belinda. *Home Fires Burning: Food, Politics, and Everyday Life in World War I Berlin.* Chapel Hill: University of North Carolina Press, 2000.

——. "Homefront: Food, Politics, and Women's Everyday Life during the First World War." In Hagemann and Schüler-Springorum, *Home/Front,* 115–37.

Delacoste, Frédérique, and Priscilla Alexander, eds. *Sex Work: Writings by Women in the Sex Industry.* Pittsburgh: Cleis, 1987.

Ditmore, Melissa. "Trafficking in Lives: How Ideology Shapes Policy." In *Trafficking and Prostitution Reconsidered,* edited by Kamala Kempadoo, 107–26. Boulder, CO: Paradigm, 2005.

Doane, Mary Ann. *Femmes Fatales: Feminism, Film Theory, Psychoanalysis.* New York: Routledge, 1991.

Dodillet, Susanne. "Cultural Clash on Prostitution: Debates on Prostitution in Germany and Sweden in the 1990s." In Sönser Breen and Peters, *Genealogies of Identity,* 39–56. Amsterdam: Rodopi, 2005.

Doezema, Jo. "Forced to Choose: Beyond the Voluntary v. Forced Prostitution Dichotomy." In Kempadoo and Doezema, *Global Sex Workers,* 34–50.

Dollard, Catherine L. *The Surplus Woman: Unmarried in Imperial Germany, 1871–1918.* New York: Berghahn, 2009.

Domansky, Elisabeth. "Militarization and Reproduction in World War I Germany." In Eley, *Society, Culture, and the State,* 427–63.

Eckardt, Wolf von, and Sander L. Gilman, eds. *Bertolt Brecht's Berlin: A Scrapbook of the Twenties.* Lincoln: University of Nebraska Press, 1993.

Eley, Geoff. "Is There a History of the *Kaiserreich?*" In Eley, *Society, Culture, and the State,* 1–42.

——, ed. *Society, Culture, and the State in Germany, 1870–1930.* Ann Arbor: University of Michigan Press, 1996.

Evans, Jennifer V. "Bahnhof Boys: Policing Male Prostitution in Post-Nazi Berlin." *Journal of the History of Sexuality* 12 (October 2003): 605–36.

——. *Life among the Ruins: Cityscape and Sexuality in Cold War Berlin.* Basingstoke, UK: Palgrave Macmillan, 2011.

Evans, Richard J. *Comrades and Sisters: Feminism, Socialism, and Pacifism in Europe, 1870–1945.* Sussex: Wheatsheaf, 1987.

——. *The Feminist Movement in Germany, 1894–1933.* London: Sage, 1976.

——, ed. *The German Underworld: Deviants and Outcasts in German History.* London: Routledge, 1988.

——. *Proletarians and Politics: Socialism, Protest, and the Working Class in Germany before the First World War.* New York: St. Martin's Press, 1990.

——. "Prostitution, State, and Society in Imperial Germany." *Past and Present* 70 (February 1976): 106–29.

——. *Tales from the German Underworld.* New Haven, CT: Yale University Press, 1998.

Falck, Uta. *VEB Bordell: Geschichte der Prostitution in der DDR.* Berlin: Ch. Links, 1998.

Federle, Courtney. "Picture Postcard: Kracauer Writes from Berlin." In *Peripheral Visions: The Hidden Stages of Weimar Cinema,* edited by Kenneth S. Calhoon, 39–54. Detroit: Wayne State University Press, 2001.

Figura, Starr, ed. *German Expressionism: The Graphic Impulse.* New York: Museum of Modern Art, 2011.

Filter, Cornelia, and Ellen Petry. "Prostitution: Echt geil oder hart drauf?" *Emma* 2 (March/April 1993): 36–43.

Fischer, Lothar. *Tanz zwischen Rausch und Tod: Anita Berber 1918–1929 in Berlin.* Berlin: Haude & Spener, 1996.

Flexner, Abraham. *Prostitution in Europe.* New York: Century, 1914.

Flügge, Matthias. *H. Zille, Berliner Leben: Zeichnungen, Photographien und Druckgraphiken 1890–1914.* Berlin: Akademie der Künste; Munich: Schirmer/Mosel, 2008.

Föllmer, Moritz, and Rüdiger Graf, eds. *Die "Krise" der Weimarer Republik: Zur Kritik eines Deutungsmusters.* Frankfurt am Main: Campus, 2005.

Foucault, Michel. *The History of Sexuality.* Translated by Robert Hurley. 3 vols. New York: Vintage, 1978–90.

Fout, John C., ed. *German Women in the Nineteenth Century: A Social History.* New York: Holmes & Meier, 1984.

——. "Sexual Politics in Wilhelmine Germany: The Male Gender Crisis, Moral Purity, and Homophobia." In *Forbidden History: The State, Society, and the Regulation of Sexuality in Modern Europe,* edited by John Fout, 259–92. Chicago: University of Chicago Press, 1992.

Frevert, Ute. *Women in German History: From Bourgeois Emancipation to Sexual Liberation.* Translated by Stuart McKinnon-Evans. Oxford: Berg, 1989.

Friedman, Susan S. *Mappings: Feminism and the Geographies of Encounter.* Princeton, NJ: Princeton University Press, 1998.

Frisby, David. *Cityscapes of Modernity: Critical Explorations.* Cambridge: Polity, 2001.

——. "Deciphering the Hieroglyphics of Weimar Berlin: Siegfried Kracauer." In Haxthausen and Suhr, *Berlin: Culture and Metropolis,* 152–65.

——. *Fragments of Modernity: Theories of Modernity in the Work of Simmel, Kracauer, and Benjamin.* Cambridge, MA: MIT Press, 1986.

——. *Georg Simmel.* London: Tavistock, 1984.

——. "Georg Simmels Theorie der Moderne." In Dahme and Rammstedt, *Georg Simmel und die Moderne,* 9–79.

Fritzsche, Peter. *Reading Berlin 1900.* Cambridge, MA: Harvard University Press, 1996.

——. "Vagabond in the Fugitive City: Hans Ostwald, Imperial Berlin, and the *Großstadtdokumente.*" *Journal of Contemporary History* 29 (1994): 385–402.

Führich, Angelika. "Woman and Typewriter: Gender, Technology, and Work in Late Weimar Film." *Women in German Yearbook* 16 (2000): 151–66.

Ganeva, Mila. *Women in Weimar Fashion: Discourses and Displays in German Culture, 1918–1933.* Rochester, NY: Camden House, 2008.

Gardiner, Judith Kegan. *Provoking Agents: Gender and Agency in Theory and Practice.* Urbana: University of Illinois Press, 1995.

Gay, Peter. *Weimar Culture: The Outsider as Insider.* New York: Harper & Row, 1968.

Gerhard, Ute. *Unerhört: Die Geschichte der deutschen Frauenbewegung.* Reinbek bei Hamburg: Rowohlt, 1992.

——. *Verhältnisse und Verhinderungen: Frauenarbeit, Familie und Rechte der Frauen im 19. Jahrhundert.* Frankfurt am Main: Suhrkamp, 1978.

Gilfoyle, Timothy J. *City of Eros: New York City, Prostitution, and the Commercialization of Sex, 1790–1920.* New York: W. W. Norton, 1992.

——. "Prostitutes in History: From Parables of Pornography to Metaphors of Modernity." *American Historical Review* 104 (February 1999): 117–41.

Gilman, Sander. *Difference and Pathology: Stereotypes of Sexuality, Race, and Madness.* Ithaca, NY: Cornell University Press, 1985.

Gleber, Anke. *The Art of Taking a Walk: Flanerie, Literature, and Film in Weimar Culture.* Princeton, NJ: Princeton University Press, 1999.

——. "Female Flanerie and the *Symphony of the City.*" In Ankum, *Women in the Metropolis,* 67–88.

Goergen, Jeanpaul. Introductory essay on Richard Oswald. *Filmblatt* 12, no. 34 (Summer 2007): 3–4.

Gordon, Mel. *Voluptuous Panic: The Erotic World of Weimar Berlin.* Venice, CA: Feral House, 2000.

Grenz, Sabine, and Martin Lücke, eds. *Verhandlungen im Zwielicht: Momente der Prostitution in Geschichte und Gegenwart.* Bielefeld: Transcript, 2006.

Greven-Aschoff, Barbara. *Die bürgerliche Frauenbewegung in Deutschland 1894–1933.* Göttingen: Vandenhoeck & Ruprecht, 1981.

Grossmann, Atina. "*Girlkultur* or Thoroughly Rationalized Female: A New Woman in Weimar Germany?" In *Women in Culture and Politics: A Century of Change,* edited by Judith Friedlander, Blanche Wiesen Cook, Alice Kessler-Harris, and Carroll Smith-Rosenberg, 62–80. Bloomington: Indiana University Press, 1986.

——. "The New Woman and the Rationalization of Sexuality in Weimar Germany." In Snitow, Stansell, and Thompson, *Powers of Desire,* 190–208.

——. *Reforming Sex: The German Movement for Birth Control and Abortion Reform, 1920–1950.* New York: Oxford University Press, 1995.

Günther, Stephanie. *Weiblichkeitsentwürfe des Fin de Siècle: Berliner Autorinnen; Alice Behrend, Margarete Böhme, Clara Viebig.* Bonn: Bouvier, 2007.

Guy, Donna J. *Sex and Danger in Buenos Aires: Prostitution, Family, and Nation in Argentina.* Lincoln: University of Nebraska Press, 1991.

Hackett, Amy. "Helene Stöcker: Left-Wing Intellectual and Sex Reformer." In Bridenthal, Grossmann, and Kaplan, *When Biology Became Destiny,* 109–30.

Hagemann, Karen, and Stefanie Schüler-Springorum, eds. *Home/Front: The Military, War, and Gender in Twentieth-Century Germany.* Oxford: Berg, 2002.

Hagener, Malte, ed. *Geschlecht in Fesseln: Sexualität zwischen Aufklärung und Ausbeutung im Weimarer Kino 1918–1933.* Munich: Text + Kritik, 2000.

Hagener, Malte, and Jan Hans. "Von Wilhelm zu Weimar: Der Aufklärungs- und Sittenfilm zwischen Zensur und Markt." In Hagener, *Geschlecht in Fesseln,* 7–22.

Hake, Sabine. "In the Mirror of Fashion." In Ankum, *Women in the Metropolis,* 185–201.

——. *Topographies of Class: Modern Architecture and Mass Society in Weimar Berlin.* Ann Arbor: University of Michigan Press, 2008.

Hales, Barbara. "Blond Satan: Weimar Constructions of the Criminal *Femme Fatale.*" In Schönfeld, *Commodities of Desire,* 131–52.

——. "Woman as Sexual Criminal: Weimar Constructions of the Criminal Femme Fatale." *Women in German Yearbook* 12 (1996): 100–121.

Hansen, Miriam. "Early Silent Cinema: Whose Public Sphere?" *New German Critique* 29 (Spring-Summer 1983): 147–84.

Hanssen, Paula. "Women of the Street: Prostitution in Bertolt Brecht's Works." In Schönfeld, *Commodities of Desire,* 153–64.

Häntzschel, Hiltrud. *Irmgard Keun.* Reinbek bei Hamburg: Rowohlt, 2001.

Harris, Victoria. *Selling Sex in the Reich: Prostitutes in German Society, 1914–1945.* Oxford: Oxford University Press, 2010.

Haustedt, Birgit. *Die wilden Jahre in Berlin: Eine Klatsch- und Kulturgeschichte der Frauen.* Berlin: Edition Ebersbach, 2002.

Haxthausen, Charles W. "'A New Beauty': Ernst Ludwig Kirchner's Images of Berlin." In Haxthausen and Suhr, *Berlin: Culture and Metropolis,* 58–94.

Haxthausen, Charles W., and Heidrun Suhr, eds. *Berlin: Culture and Metropolis.* Minneapolis: University of Minnesota Press, 1990.

Hebdige, Dick. *Subculture: The Meaning of Style.* London: Routledge, 1979.

Heller, Reinhold, ed. *Brücke: The Birth of Expressionism in Dresden and Berlin, 1905–1913.* Ostfildern: Hatje Cantz, 2009.

Herzog, Dagmar. *Sex after Fascism: Memory and Morality in Twentieth-Century Germany.* Princeton, NJ: Princeton University Press, 2005.

Hessen, Robert. *Die Prostitution in Deutschland.* Munich: Albert Langen, 1910.

Hett, Benjamin Carter. *Death in the Tiergarten: Murder and Criminal Justice in the Kaiser's Berlin.* Cambridge, MA: Harvard University Press, 2004.

Hoppe, Ralf. "Die bürgerlichen Huren." *Der Spiegel,* August 27, 2001, 84–90.

Horney, Karen. "The Flight from Womanhood: The Masculinity Complex in Women, as Viewed by Men and Women." *International Journal of Psychoanalysis* 7 (1926): 324–39.

Hügel, Franz Seraph. *Zur Geschichte, Statistik und Regelung der Prostitution.* Vienna: Typographisch-literarisch-artistische Anstalt, 1865.

Hull, Isabel V. *Sexuality, State, and Civil Society in Germany, 1700–1815.* Ithaca, NY: Cornell University Press, 1996.

Hütt, Wolfgang. *Hintergrund: Mit den Unzüchtigkeits- und Gotteslästerungsparagraphen des Strafgesetzbuches gegen Kunst und Künstler 1900–1933.* Berlin: Henschel, 1990.

Huyssen, Andreas. "Mass Culture as Woman: Modernism's Other." In *After the Great Divide: Modernism, Mass Culture, Postmodernism,* 44–64. Bloomington: Indiana University Press, 1986.

———. "Modernist Miniatures: Literary Snapshots of Urban Spaces." *PMLA* 122, no. 1 (2007): 27–42.

Janssen-Jurreit, Marielouise, ed. *Frauen und Sexualmoral.* Frankfurt am Main: Fischer, 1986.

Jazbinsek, Dietmar. "Lebensgeschichte und Eigensinn: Über die Biographie und die Biographieforschung des Dirnenarztes Wilhelm Hammer." *Mitteilungen der Magnus-Hirschfeld-Gesellschaft* 37/38 (June 2007): 32–61.

Jeanne Mammen 1890–1976: Gemälde, Aquarelle, Zeichnungen. Cologne: Wienand, 1997.

Jeffries, Matthew. *Imperial Culture in Germany, 1871–1918.* Basingstoke, UK: Palgrave, 2003.

Jelavich, Peter. "'Am I Allowed to Amuse Myself Here?': The German Bourgeoisie Confronts Early Film." In Marchand and Lindenfeld, *Germany at the Fin de Siècle,* 227–49.

———. *Berlin Cabaret.* Cambridge, MA: Harvard University Press, 1993.

Jensen, Erik N. *Body by Weimar: Athletes, Gender, and German Modernity.* Oxford: Oxford University Press, 2010.

Kaes, Anton, ed. *Kino-Debatte: Texte zum Verhältnis von Literatur und Film, 1909–1929.* Tübingen: Niemeyer, 1978.

Kaes, Anton, Martin Jay, and Edward Dimendberg, eds. *The Weimar Republic Sourcebook.* Berkeley: University of California Press, 1994.

Kaplan, Marion A. *The Jewish Feminist Movement in Germany: The Campaigns of the Jüdischer Frauenbund, 1904–1938.* Westport: Greenwood, 1979.

Kasten, Jürgen, and Armin Loacker, eds. *Richard Oswald: Kino zwischen Spektakel, Aufklärung und Unterhaltung.* Vienna: Verlag Filmarchiv Austria, 2005.

Keitz, Ursula von. *Der Schatten des Gesetzes: Schwangerschaftskonflikt und Reproduktion im deutschsprachigen Film 1918–1933.* Marburg: Schüren, 2005.

Kempadoo, Kamala. "Introduction: Globalizing Sex Workers' Rights." In Kempadoo and Doezema, *Global Sex Workers,* 1–28.

——. "Women of Color and the Global Sex Trade: Transnational Feminist Perspectives." *Meridians: Feminism, Race, Transnationalism* 1, no. 2 (2001): 28–51.

Kempadoo, Kamala, and Jo Doezema, eds. *Global Sex Workers: Rights, Resistance, and Redefinition.* New York: Routledge, 1998.

King, Lynda J. *Best-Sellers by Design: Vicki Baum and the House of Ullstein.* Detroit: Wayne State University Press, 1988.

——. "*Grand Hotel:* The Sexual Politics of a Popular Culture Classic." *Women in German Yearbook* 15 (2000): 185–200.

——. "*Menschen im Hotel/Grand Hotel:* Seventy Years of a Popular Culture Classic." *Journal of American and Comparative Cultures* 23, no. 2 (Summer 2000): 17–23.

Kittler, Friedrich A. *Gramophone, Film, Typewriter.* Translated by Geoffrey Winthrop-Young and Michael Wutz. Stanford, CA: Stanford University Press, 1999.

Klement, Alfred von. *Die Bücher von Otto Erich Hartleben: Eine Bibliographie.* Salò: Halkyonischen Akademie für unangewandte Wissenschaften, 1951.

Kniesche, Thomas, and Stephen Brockmann, eds. *Dancing on the Volcano: Essays on the Culture of the Weimar Republic.* Columbia, SC: Camden House, 1994.

Knop, Matthias. "G. W. Pabsts *Tagebuch einer Verlorenen:* Zensur und Rekonstruktion." Unpublished essay. BArch-Film Sg. 1_16488.

Knopf, Jan. *Brecht Handbuch.* Vol. 1. Stuttgart: Metzler, 1980.

Koonz, Claudia. *Mothers in the Fatherland: Women, the Family, and Nazi Politics.* New York: St. Martin's Press, 1987.

Koshar, Rudi. *German Travel Cultures.* Oxford: Berg, 2000.

Kühl, Richard. "'Aber in unserem Buch, Herr Sanitätsrat': Fragen an Magnus Hirschfelds Publikationspraxis 1929/30." *Mitteilungen der Magnus-Hirschfeld-Gesellschaft* 41/42 (2009): 32–42.

——. "Zur Wirkung und Wahrnehmung von Magnus Hirschfelds *Sittengeschichte des Weltkrieges.*" *Mitteilungen der Magnus-Hirschfeld-Gesellschaft* 39/40 (2008): 23–35.

Kühn, Julius. *Die Prostitution im 19. Jahrhundert.* Leipzig: Barsdorf, 1871.

Kundrus, Birthe. "Gender Wars: The First World War and the Construction of Gender Relations in the Weimar Republic." In Hagemann and Schüler-Springorum, *Home/Front,* 159–79.

Kupschinsky, Elke. "Die vernünftige Nephertete." In *Die Metropole: Industriekultur in Berlin im 20. Jahrhundert,* edited by Jochen Boberg, Tilman Fichter, and Eckhart Gillen, 164–73. Berlin: Beck, 1986.

Lareau, Alan. "The Genesis of 'Jenny': Prostitute Songs, the Mythology of Pimps, and the *Threepenny Opera.*" In Schönfeld, *Commodities of Desire,* 167–90.

——. *The Wild Stage: Literary Cabarets of the Weimar Republic.* Columbia, SC: Camden House, 1995.

Large, David Clay. *Berlin.* New York: Basic Books, 2000.

Lees, Andrew. *Cities, Sin, and Social Reform in Imperial Germany.* Ann Arbor: University of Michigan Press, 2002.

Lefebvre, Henri. *The Urban Revolution.* Translated by Robert Bononno. Minneapolis: University of Minnesota Press, 2003.

Lenman, R. J. V. "Art, Society, and the Law in Wilhelmine Germany: The Lex Heinze." *Oxford German Studies* 8 (1973): 86–113.

Lensing, Leo. "Cinema, Society, and Literature in Irmgard Keun's *Das kunstseidene Mädchen.*" *Germanic Review* 60 (1985): 129–34.

Lethen, Helmut. *Cool Conduct: The Culture of Distance in Weimar Germany.* Translated by Don Reneau. Berkeley: University of California Press, 2002.

Lewis, Beth Irwin. "*Lustmord:* Inside the Windows of the Metropolis." In Ankum, *Women in the Metropolis,* 202–32.

Leydecker, Karl. "Prostitution, Free Love, and Marriage in German Drama in the 1890s." In Schönfeld, *Commodities of Desire,* 31–45.

Lopes, Anne, and Gary Roth. *Men's Feminism: August Bebel and the German Socialist Movement.* Amherst, NY: Humanity Books, 2000.

Lücke, Martin. "Beschmutzte Utopien: Subkulturelle Räume, begehrte Körper und sexuelle Identitäten in belletristischen Texten über männliche Prostitution 1900–1933." In Grenz and Lücke, *Verhandlungen im Zwielicht,* 301–18.

———. *Männlichkeit und Unordnung: Homosexualität und männliche Prostitution in Kaiserreich und Weimarer Republik.* Frankfurt am Main: Campus, 2008.

Lütgens, Annelie. "The Conspiracy of Women: Images of City Life in the Work of Jeanne Mammen." In Ankum, *Women in the Metropolis,* 89–105.

———. *"Nur ein paar Augen sein": Jeanne Mammen, eine Künstlerin in ihrer Zeit.* Berlin: Erich Reimer, 1991.

Marchand, Suzanne, and David Lindenfeld, eds. *Germany at the Fin de Siècle: Culture, Politics, and Ideas.* Baton Rouge: University of Louisiana Press, 2004.

Marhoefer, Laurie. "Degeneration, Sexual Freedom, and the Politics of the Weimar Republic, 1918–1933." *German Studies Review* 34, no. 3 (2011): 529–49.

Mast, Peter. *Künstlerische und wissenschaftliche Freiheit im Deutschen Reich 1890–1901.* Munich: Schäuble, 1980.

Matlock, Jann. *Scenes of Seduction: Prostitution, Hysteria, and Reading Difference in Nineteenth-Century France.* New York: Columbia University Press, 1994.

Matthias, Bettina. *The Hotel as Setting in Early Twentieth-Century German and Austrian Literature: Checking In to Tell a Story.* Rochester, NY: Camden House, 2006.

McBride, Patrizia. "Learning to See in Irmgard Keun's *Das kunstseidene Mädchen.*" *German Quarterly* 84, no. 2 (Spring 2011): 220–38.

McCarthy, Margaret. "The Representation of Prostitutes in Literature and Film: Margarete Böhme and G. W. Pabst." In Schönfeld, *Commodities of Desire,* 77–97.

McCombs, Nancy. *Earth Spirit, Victim, or Whore? The Prostitute in Literature, 1880–1925.* New York: Lang, 1986.

McCormick, Richard W. *Gender and Sexuality in Weimar Modernity: Film, Literature, and "New Objectivity."* New York: Palgrave, 2001.

Mennel, Barbara. *The Representation of Masochism and Queer Desire in Film and Literature.* New York: Palgrave, 2007.

Meskimmon, Marsha. *We Weren't Modern Enough: Women Artists and the Limits of German Modernism.* Berkeley: University of California Press, 1999.

Meyer, Alfred G. *Lily Braun: Selected Writings on Feminism and Socialism.* Bloomington: Indiana University Press, 1987.

Miller, Christanne. *Cultures of Modernism: Marianne Moore, Mina Loy, and Else Lasker-Schüler.* Ann Arbor: University of Michigan Press, 2005.

Morris, Meaghan. "Things to Do with Shopping Centres." In *The Cultural Studies Reader,* edited by Simon During, 391–409. 2nd ed. London: Routledge, 1993.

Mosse, George L. *Nationalism and Sexuality: Respectability and Abnormal Sexuality in Modern Europe.* 1985. Reprint, New York: Fertig, 1997.

Mulvey, Laura. *Visual and Other Pleasures.* Bloomington: Indiana University Press, 1989.

Nenno, Nancy. "Femininity, the Primitive, and Modern Urban Space: Josephine Baker in Berlin." In Ankum, *Women in the Metropolis,* 145–61.

Nienhaus, Ursula. "Einsatz für die 'Sittlichkeit': Die Anfänge der weiblichen Polizei im Wilhelminischen Kaiserreich und in der Weimarer Republik." In *"Sicherheit" und "Wohlfahrt": Polizei, Gesellschaft und Herrschaft im 19. und 20. Jahrhundert*, edited by Alf Lüdtke. 243–66. Frankfurt am Main: Suhrkamp, 1992.

Nolan, Mary. *Visions of Modernity: American Business and the Modernization of Germany*. New York: Oxford University Press, 1994.

Nottelmann, Nicole. *Die Karrieren der Vicki Baum: Eine Biographie*. Cologne: Kiepenheuer & Witsch, 2007.

Oakes, Guy. "The Problem of Women in Georg Simmel's Theory of Culture." In *Georg Simmel: On Women, Sexuality, and Love*, edited by Guy Oakes, 3–62. New Haven, CT: Yale University Press, 1984.

O'Connell-Davidson, Julia. *Prostitution, Power, and Freedom*. Ann Arbor: University of Michigan Press, 1999.

Oosterhuis, Harry. *Stepchildren of Nature: Krafft-Ebing, Psychiatry, and the Making of Sexual Identity*. Chicago: University of Chicago Press, 2000.

Overall, Christine. "What's Wrong with Prostitution? Evaluating Sex Work." *Signs* 4 (1992): 705–24.

Parsons, Deborah L. *Streetwalking the Metropolis: Women, the City, and Modernity*. Oxford: Oxford University Press, 2000.

Paul, Christa. *Zwangsprostitution: Staatlich errichtete Bordelle im Nationalsozialismus*. Berlin: Hentrich, 1994.

Peter, Frank-Manuel. *Valeska Gert: Tänzerin, Schauspielerin, Kabarettistin*. Berlin: Frolich & Kaufmann, 1985.

Peters, Olaf, ed. *Otto Dix*. Munich: Prestel, 2010.

Petersen, Vibeke Rützou. *Women and Modernity in Weimar Germany: Reality and Representation in Popular Fiction*. New York: Berghahn, 2001.

Petro, Patrice. *Joyless Streets: Women and Melodramatic Representation in Weimar Germany*. Princeton, NJ: Princeton University Press, 1989.

———. "Perceptions of Difference: Woman as Spectator and Spectacle." In Ankum, *Women in the Metropolis*, 41–66.

Peukert, Detlev. *Die Weimarer Republik: Krisenjahre der klassischen Moderne*. Frankfurt am Main: Suhrkamp, 1987.

Pivar, David J. *Purity Crusade: Sexual Morality and Social Control, 1868–1900*. Westport, CT: Greenwood, 1973.

Poggi, Gianfranco. *Money and the Modern Mind: Georg Simmel's "Philosophy of Money."* Berkeley: University of California Press, 1993.

Prickett, David James. "Defining Identity via Homosexual Spaces: Locating the Male Homosexual in Weimar Berlin." *Women in German Yearbook* 21 (2005): 143–61.

Quataert, Jean H. "Introduction 2: Writing the History of Women and Gender in Imperial Germany." In Eley, *Society, Culture, and the State*, 43–66.

Rauch, Angelika. "The 'Trauerspiel' of the Prostituted Body, or Woman as Allegory of Modernity." *Cultural Critique* 10 (1988): 77–88.

Rentschler, Eric, ed. *The Films of G. W. Pabst: An Extraterritorial Cinema*. New Brunswick, NJ: Rutgers University Press, 1990.

Repp, Kevin. "'More Corporeal, More Concrete': Liberal Humanism, Eugenics, and German Progressives at the Last Fin de Siècle." *Journal of Modern History* 72, no. 3 (September 2000): 683–730.

———. *Reformers, Critics, and the Paths of German Modernity: Anti-Politics and the Search for Alternatives, 1890–1914*. Cambridge, MA: Harvard University Press, 2000.

——. "'*Sexualkrise und Rasse*': Feminist Eugenics at the Fin de Siècle." In Marchand and Lindenfeld, *Germany at the Fin de Siècle,* 102–26.

Rewald, Sabine, ed. *Glitter and Doom: German Portraits from the 1920s.* New Haven, CT: Yale University Press, 2006.

Richards, Anna. "Sense and Sentimentality? Margarete Böhme's *Tagebuch einer Verlorenen* in Context." In Schönfeld, *Commodities of Desire,* 98–109.

Richards, Donald Ray. *The German Bestseller in the Twentieth Century: A Complete Bibliography and Analysis.* Bern: Herbert Lang, 1968.

Richie, Alexandra. *Faust's Metropolis: A History of Berlin.* New York: Carroll & Graf, 1998.

Riviere, Joan. "Womanliness as a Masquerade." 1929. In *Formations of Fantasy,* edited by Victor Burgin, James Donald, and Cora Kaplan, 35–44. London: Routledge, 1986.

Rogowski, Christian, ed. *The Many Faces of Weimar Cinema: Rediscovering Germany's Filmic Legacy.* Rochester, NY: Camden House, 2010.

——. "Schattenboxen: Zum Warencharakter von Geschlecht und 'Rasse' in *Aufstieg und Fall der Stadt Mahagonny.*" *The Brecht Yearbook* 29 (2004): 325–40.

Roos, Julia. "Backlash against Prostitutes' Rights: Origins and Dynamics of Nazi Prostitution Policies." *Journal of the History of Sexuality* 11 (January/April 2002): 67–94.

——. *Weimar through the Lens of Gender: Prostitution Reform, Women's Emancipation, and German Democracy, 1919–33.* Ann Arbor: University of Michigan Press, 2010.

Rosenstein, Doris. "'Mit der Wirklichkeit auf du und du?' Zu Irmgard Keuns Romanen *Gilgi, eine von uns* und *Das kunstseidene Mädchen.*" In *Neue Sachlichkeit im Roman: Neue Interpretationen zum Roman der Weimarer Republik,* edited by Sabina Becker and Christoph Weiß, 273–90. Stuttgart: Metzler, 1995.

Rowe, Dorothy. *Representing Berlin: Sexuality and the City in Imperial and Weimar Germany.* Aldershot, UK: Ashgate, 2003.

Royal, Suzanne. "Fashion and Conflict: Kirchner's Representations of the Fashionably Dressed Woman in Berlin." In *Fashion and Transgression,* edited by Nancy J. Troy, 32–37. Los Angeles: USC Fisher Gallery, 2003.

——. "Graphic Art in Weimar Berlin: The Case of Jeanne Mammen." PhD diss., University of Southern California, 2007.

Rubin, Gayle. "Thinking Sex: Notes for a Radical Theory of the Politics of Sexuality." In Vance, *Pleasure and Danger,* 267–319.

Saße, Günther. *Die Ordnung der Gefühle: Das Drama der Liebesheirat im 18. Jahrhundert.* Darmstadt: Wissenschaftliche Buchgesellschaft, 1996.

Schebera, Jürgen. *Damals im Romanischen Café: Künstler und ihre Lokale im Berlin der zwanziger Jahre.* Berlin: Das neue Berlin, 2005.

Scheub, Ute. "Das Leben ist ein Kabarett: Die Kabarett-Gründerinnen Rosa Valetti, Trude Hesterberg, Dinah Nelken und Valeska Gert." In Täuber, *Femme Flaneur,* 85–91.

Schikorra, Christa. "Prostitution weiblicher KZ-Häftlinge im Frauen-KZ Ravensbrück." *Dachauer Hefte* 16, no. 16 (2000): 112–24.

Schlüpmann, Heide. "The Brothel as Arcadian Space? *Diary of a Lost Girl.*" In Rentschler, *The Films of G. W. Pabst,* 80–90.

——. "Radikalisierung der Philosophie: Die Nietzsche-Rezeption und die sexualpolitische Publizistik Helene Stöckers." *Feministische Studien* 3 (1984): 10–34.

——. *Unheimlichkeit des Blicks: Das Drama des frühen deutschen Kinos.* Basel: Stroemfeld / Roter Stern, 1990.

Schmackpfeffer, Petra. *Frauenbewegung und Prostitution.* Oldenburg: Bibliotheks- und Informationssystem der Universität Oldenburg, 1989.

Schmidt, Dietmar, ed. *Gebuchte Lust: Texte zur Prostitution.* Leipzig: Reclam, 1996.

——. *Geschlecht unter Kontrolle: Prostitution und moderne Literatur.* Freiburg im Breisgau: Rombach, 1998.

Schmidt, Ulf. "'Der Blick auf den Körper': Sozialhygienische Filme, Sexualaufklärung und Propaganda in der Weimarer Republik." In Hagener, *Geschlecht in Fesseln,* 23–46.

Schneider, Karl Camillo. *Die Prostituierte und die Gesellschaft: Eine soziologisch-ethische Studie.* Leipzig: Barth, 1908.

Schönfeld, Christiane, ed. *Commodities of Desire: The Prostitute in Modern German Literature.* Columbia, SC: Camden House, 2000.

——. *Dialektik und Utopie: Die Prostituierte im deutschen Expressionismus.* Würzburg: Königshausen & Neumann, 1996.

——. "The Urbanization of the Body: Prostitutes, Dialectics, and Utopia in German Expressionism." *German Studies Review* 20, no. 1 (1997): 49–63.

Schrage, Laurie. "Prostitution and the Case for Decriminalization." In Spector, *Prostitution and Pornography,* 240–46.

Schulte, Regina. *Sperrbezirke: Tugendhaftigkeit und Prostitution in der bürgerlichen Welt.* Frankfurt am Main: Syndikat, 1984.

Schütz, Erhard. *Romane der Weimarer Republik.* Munich: Fink, 1986.

Sengoopta, Chandak. *Otto Weininger: Sex, Science, and Self in Imperial Vienna.* Chicago: University of Chicago Press, 2000.

Shafi, Monika. "'Aber das ist es ja eben, ich habe ja keine Meinesgleichen': Identitätsprozeß und Zeitgeschichte in dem Roman *Das kunstseidene Mädchen* von Irmgard Keun." *Colloquia Germanica* 21, no. 4 (1988): 314–25.

Sieg, Katrin. "Postcolonial Berlin? Pieke Biermann's Crime Novels as Globalization Critique." "Writing and Reading Berlin," edited by Stephen Brockmann. Special issue, *Studies in Twentieth- and Twenty-First-Century Literature* 28, no. 1 (Winter 2004): 152–82.

Siegmund, Judith. "Prostitution—Was macht hier die Kunst?" In *Sexwork: Kunst Mythos Realität,* edited by Stéphane Bauer, Boris von Brauchitsch, Katharina Kaiser, Maika Leffers, Jörg Leidig, Judith Siegmund, and Ulrika Sobrig, 10–11. Heidelberg: Kehrer, 2007.

Siemes, Isabelle. *Die Prostituierte in der literarischen Moderne 1890–1933.* Düsseldorf: Hagemann, 2000.

Smail, Deborah. *White Collar Workers, Mass Culture, and "Neue Sachlichkeit" in Weimar Berlin.* Frankfurt am Main: Lang, 1999.

Smith, Jill Suzanne. "Just How Naughty *Was* Berlin? The Geography of Prostitution and Female Sexuality in Curt Moreck's Erotic Travel Guide." In *Spatial Turns: Space, Place, and Mobility in German Literary and Visual Culture,* edited by Barbara Mennel and Jaimey Fisher, 53–77. Amsterdam: Rodopi, 2010.

——. "Prostitutes in Weimar Berlin: Moving beyond the Victim-Whore Dichotomy." In *Beyond Glitter and Doom: The Contingency of the Weimar Republic,* edited by Godela Weiss-Sussex, Jochen Hung, and Geoff Wilkes, 135–47. Munich: Iudicium, 2012.

——. "Richard Oswald and the Social Hygiene Film: Promoting Public Health or Promiscuity?" In Rogowski, *The Many Faces of Weimar Cinema,* 13–30.

——. "Working Girls: White-Collar Workers and Prostitutes in Late Weimar Fiction." *German Quarterly* 81, no. 4 (2008): 449–70.

Smith, Woodruff D. "Colonialism and the Culture of Respectability." In *Germany's Colonial Pasts,* edited by Eric Ames, Marcia Klotz, and Lora Wildenthal, 3–20. Lincoln: University of Nebraska Press, 2005.

———. *Consumption and the Making of Respectability, 1600–1800.* London: Routledge, 2002.

Snitow, Ann, Christine Stansell, and Sharon Thompson, eds. *Powers of Desire: The Politics of Sexuality.* New York: Monthly Review Press, 1983.

Soja, Edward W. *The Political Organization of Space.* Washington, DC: Association of American Geographers, 1971.

———. "The Socio-Spatial Dialectic." *Annals of the Association of American Geographers* 70, no. 2 (1980): 207–25.

Spain, Daphne. *Gendered Spaces.* Chapel Hill: University of North Carolina Press, 1992.

Spector, Jessica, ed. *Prostitution and Pornography: Philosophical Debate about the Sex Industry.* Stanford, CA: Stanford University Press, 2006.

Steakley, James D. "Cinema and Censorship in the Weimar Republic: The Case of *Anders als die Andern.*" *Film History* 11 (1999): 181–203.

Stein, Roger. *Das deutsche Dirnenlied: Literarisches Kabarett von Bruant bis Brecht.* Cologne: Böhlau, 2006.

Stratigakos, Despina. *A Women's Berlin: Building the Modern City.* Minneapolis: University of Minnesota Press, 2008.

Sturm, Eva. "Von der Zensurfreiheit zum Zensurgesetz: Das erste deutsche Lichtspielgesetz (1920)." In Hagener, *Geschlecht in Fesseln,* 63–79.

Tatar, Maria. *Lustmord: Sexual Murder in Weimar Germany.* Princeton, NJ: Princeton University Press, 1995.

Täuber, Rita. *Der häßliche Eros: Darstellungen zur Prostitution in der Malerei und Grafik 1855–1930.* Berlin: Mann, 1997.

———, ed. *Femme Flaneur: Erkundungen zwischen Boulevard und Sperrbezirk.* Bonn: August Macke Haus, 2004.

Teal, Laurie. "The Hollow Women: Modernism, the Prostitute, and Commodity Aesthetics." *Differences* 7, no. 3 (1995): 80–108.

Theweleit, Klaus. *Male Fantasies.* Translated by Stephen Conway. 2 vols. Minneapolis: University of Minnesota Press, 1985–89.

Thies, Ralf. *Ethnograph des dunklen Berlins: Hans Ostwald und die Großstadtdokumente 1904–1908.* Cologne: Böhlau, 2006.

Timm, Annette. "The Ambivalent Outsider: Prostitution, Promiscuity, and VD Control in Nazi Berlin." In *Social Outsiders in Nazi Germany,* edited by Robert Gellately and Nathan Stolzfuß, 192–211. Princeton, NJ: Princeton University Press, 2001.

———. *The Politics of Fertility in Twentieth-Century Berlin.* Cambridge: Cambridge University Press, 2010.

Timm, Annette, and Joshua A. Sanborn, eds. *Gender, Sex, and the Shaping of Modern Europe: A History from the French Revolution to the Present Day.* Oxford: Berg, 2007.

Usborne, Cornelie. *The Politics of the Body in Weimar Germany: Women's Reproductive Rights and Duties.* Ann Arbor: University of Michigan Press, 1992.

Vance, Carol S. "Pleasure and Danger: Towards a Politics of Sexuality." In *Pleasure and Danger: Exploring Female Sexuality,* edited by Carol S. Vance. 1–27. Boston: Routledge & Kegan Paul, 1984.

Van de Velde, Theodor Hendrik. *Die vollkommene Ehe: Eine Studie über ihre Physiologie und Technik.* Leipzig: Benno Konegen, 1926.

Vromen, Suzanne. "Georg Simmel and the Cultural Dilemma of Women." *History of European Ideas* 8, no. 4/5 (1987): 563–79.

Walkowitz, Judith. *City of Dreadful Delight: Narratives of Sexual Danger in Late-Victorian London.* Chicago: University of Chicago Press, 1992.

———. "Male Vice and Female Virtue: Feminism and the Politics of Prostitution in 19th-Century Britain." In Snitow, Stansell, and Thompson, *Powers of Desire,* 419–38.

———. *Prostitution and Victorian Society: Women, Class, and the State.* Cambridge: Cambridge University Press, 1980.

Ward, Janet. *Weimar Surfaces: Urban Visual Culture in 1920s Germany.* Berkeley: University of California Press, 2001.

Weindling, Paul. *Health, Race, and German Politics between National Unification and Nazism, 1870–1945.* Cambridge: Cambridge University Press, 1989.

Weitz, Eric D. *Weimar Germany: Promise and Tragedy.* Princeton, NJ: Princeton University Press, 2007.

Wickert, Christl. *Helene Stöcker 1869–1943: Frauenrechtlerin, Sexualreformerin und Pazifistin.* Berlin: Dietz, 1996.

Widdig, Bernd. *Culture and Inflation in Weimar Germany.* Berkeley: University of California Press, 2001.

Wigley, Mark. "Untitled: The Housing of Gender." In *Sexuality and Space,* edited by Beatriz Colomina, 327–89. Princeton, NJ: Princeton Architectural Press, 1992.

Wilson, Elizabeth. *The Sphinx in the City: Urban Life, the Control of Disorder, and Women.* Berkeley: University of California Press, 1991.

Wolff, Janet. "The Invisible Flâneuse: Women and the Literature of Modernity." *Theory, Culture and Society* 2, no. 3 (1985): 37–46.

Wright, Barbara. "'New Man,' Eternal Woman: Expressionist Responses to German Feminism." *German Quarterly* 60 (1987): 582–99.

Wulffen, Erich. *Das Weib als Sexualverbrecherin: Ein Handbuch für Juristen, Polizei- und Strafvollzugsbeamten.* Berlin: Langenscheidt, 1925.

Wye, Deborah. *Kirchner and the Berlin Street.* New York: Museum of Modern Art, 2008.

Züchner, Eva. "Langweilige Puppen: Jeanne Mammens Großstadt-Frauen." In *Jeanne Mammen 1890–1976,* 51–56.

INDEX

Literary and dramatic works and works of visual art are listed under the names of authors and artists. Page numbers in *italics* refer to figures.

female viewers' response to, 128–30, *129;* as feminized and eroticized space, 115–16, 127; *Das Gift im Weibe* (The Poison in Woman, 1919), 120; *Grand Hotel* (1931), 163; *Halbseide* (Half-Silk, 1925), 150–51; *Hyänen der Lust* (Hyenas of Lust, 1919), 120; *Im Rausche der Sinne* (Intoxicated with Sensuality, 1920), 120; Keun's *Das kunstseidene Mädchen,* filmic nature of, 172; *Lehrfilme* (documentaries), 117; in Moreck's *"Naughty Berlin,"* 144; *Die Privatsekretärin* (The Personal Secretary, 1931), 159n16, 174–75, 181; prostitutes as characters in, 116; prostitutes as viewers of, 116, 127, 150–52; *Die Prostitution* (Prostitution, 1922), 118, 119, 120–25, *121, 123; Sündige Mütter (Strafgesetz, §218)* (Sinful Mothers [Penal Code §218], 1918), 118; *Das Tagebuch einer Verlorenen (Diary of a Lost Girl,* 1929), 96, 100–101, 104–7, *105, 106,* 116n28, 131n63; *The Threepenny Opera* (film, 1931), 138n86

Clark, T. J., 11, 13

class. *See* bourgeoisie; social class; working class

cocottes: in Berlin, 13–18, 114; Böhme's *Tagebuch* and, 97–98; in cabaret performances in Weimar Berlin, 133–36; etymology of term, 11, 13–14; in Paris, 11, 13; prostitutes viewed as, 2, 3; visual images of, 11–18, *12, 15, 17*

communists and Communist Party in Germany, 24n44, 156, 170

Contagious Diseases Acts in Britain, 77

cool persona, 16, 19, 50, 52, 60, 63, 101, 135, 146–49, 164, 188, 189

Corbin, Alain, 11, 13, 43, 169

DDP (German Democratic Party), 120

decriminalization of prostitution: in Berlin, 28, 119; October 2001 passage of petition removing Paragraph 138 of Civil Law Code, 27–28; Prost G (Prostitutes' Law) of 2002, 28–29; RGBG (1927 Law to Combat Venereal Diseases) and, 24, 78, 119, 153–57, 158, 189; sexual pluralism and, 189–90

Degas, Edgar, 18

DGBG (German Society for Combating Venereal Diseases), 72, 76, 78, 79, 82, 84, 88, 89, 117

dichotomized victim/villain stereotypes of prostitutes, 1–3, 22, 113, 152, 176–77

Dirnenlieder (prostitutes' songs), cabaret performances of, 24, 130–39

division of labor, gendered, 39, 44, 48, 62, 63, 64, 70, 87, 108–10, 177

Dix, Otto, 8–9, 14, 18, 113

Döblin, Alfred: *Berlin Alexanderplatz* (1929), 2; on cinema, 115–16, 120, 125, 127–28; on equation of women with their sex organs, 45

Dohm, Hedwig, 85, 90

double standard: alternative moralities defying, 21; bourgeois conjugality, critiques of, 39–40, 55, 64; feminist social reformers and, 64, 67–69, 70, 78–79, 88, 94, 95, 98; increased demand for prostitutes and, 11; RGBG and, 154

Dumas, Alexandre, 102

Ebinger, Blandine, 131, 132, 139, 188

Ellis, Havelock, 90n72, 91

Engels, Friedrich, 36–37, 39n26, 42

entertainment venues: cabarets, *Dirnenlieder* (prostitutes' songs) performed in, 24, 130–39; as prostitution sites, 7; in visual arts, 18. *See also* cinema; street life and nightlife in Berlin; theater

eugenics, 32n9, 84, 89–91, 110

Evans, Richard J., 69, 80, 93, 98, 100

extramarital sex: consequences for wives of men indulging in, 40; defined, 22n37; double standard tolerating male indulgence in, 31 (*see also* double standard); feminist social reformers and, 67, 86–87; German discourse on, 2; "prosex feminism" and, 22. *See also* free love

female gaze, 144, 146

feminism: alternative moralities or countercultures, prostitution as means of talking about, 3; "prosex," 21–22. *See also* gender issues

feminist social reformers, 25, 65–107; activist prostitutes confronting, 24, 25, 82–83; antagonism toward prostitution attributed to, 22; biographies of prostitutes and, 65–69; Böhme's *Tagebuch* and, 68–69, 92, 93, 98, 99–101, 102–3, 107, 186–87 (*see also* Böhme, Margarete, *Tagebuch einer Verlorenen*); compared to male writers, 66–68, 86–88; on illegitimate children and single mothers, 67–68, 69, 80, 86, 89; on marriage and sexuality, 67, 74, 76, 79, 85–92; maternal feminism or social motherhood, 72, 77; moral and social issues addressed by, 5, 69–74; on New Morality, 64, 68, 73, 85–92, 93, 99,